TOMARE!

止まれ

[STOP!]

You're going the wrong way!

Manga is a completely different type of reading experience.

To start at the *beginning*, go to the *end*!

That's right! Authentic manga is read the traditional Japanese way—from right to left, exactly the *opposite* of how American books are read. It's easy to follow: Just go to the other end of the book, and read each page—and each panel—from right side to left side, starting at the top right. Now you're experiencing manga as it was meant to be!

Papillon

Miwa Ueda

Translated and adapted by Elina Ishikawa
Lettered by North Market Street Graphics

Ballantine Books · New York

Papillon volume 1 is a work of fiction. Names, characters, places, and incidents are the products of the author's imagination or are used fictitiously. Any resemblance to actual events, locales, or persons, living or dead, is entirely coincidental.

A Del Rey Manga/Kodansha Trade Paperback Original

Published in the United States by Del Rey Books, an imprint of The Random House Publishing Group, a division of Random House, Inc., New York.

Publication rights arranged through Kodansha Ltd.

First published in Japan in 2007 by Kodansha Ltd., Tokyo

ISBN 978-0-345-50519-4

Printed in the United States of America

www.delreymanga.com

2 4 6 8 9 7 5 3 1

Translator/Adapter:Elina Ishikawa
Lettering:North Market Street Graphics

CONTENTS

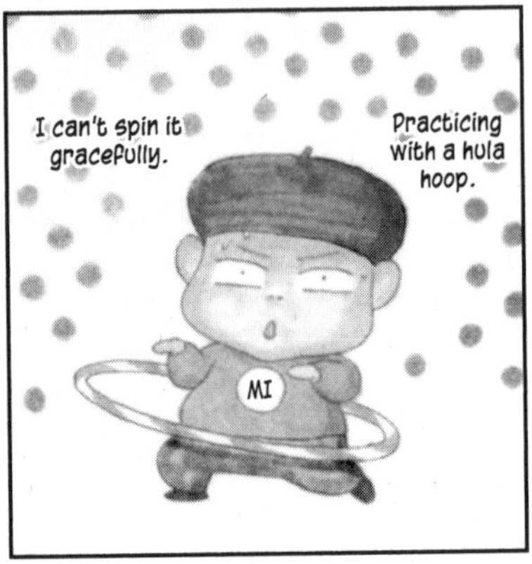
Practicing with a hula hoop.
I can't spin it gracefully.
MI

I spoke to several people about school guidance counselors when I researched this manga. It seems like the counseling procedure varies by school. How encouraging it must be to have someone like a guidance counselor—someone to be your friend, no matter what! I created this manga with my own idea of the perfect guidance counselor in mind.

—Miwa Ueda

Honorifics Explained

Throughout the Del Rey Manga books, you will find Japanese honorifics left intact in the translations. For those not familiar with how the Japanese use honorifics and, more important, how they differ from American honorifics, we present this brief overview.

Politeness has always been a critical facet of Japanese culture. Ever since the feudal era, when Japan was a highly stratified society, use of honorifics—which can be defined as polite speech that indicates relationship or status—has played an essential role in the Japanese language. When you address someone in Japanese, an honorific usually takes the form of a suffix attached to one's name (example: "Asuna-san"), is used as a title at the end of one's name, or appears in place of the name itself (example: "Negi-sensei," or simply "Sensei!").

Honorifics can be expressions of respect or endearment. In the context of manga and anime, honorifics give insight into the nature of the relationship between characters. Many English translations leave out these important honorifics and therefore distort the feel of the original Japanese. Because Japanese honorifics contain nuances that English honorifics lack, it is our policy at Del Rey not to translate them. Here, instead, is a guide to some of the honorifics you may encounter in Del Rey Manga.

-*san*: This is the most common honorific and is equivalent to Mr., Miss, Ms., or Mrs. It is the all-purpose honorific and can be used in any situation where politeness is required.

-*sama*: This is one level higher than "-san" and is used to confer great respect.

-*dono*: This comes from the word "tono," which means "lord." It is an even higher level than "-sama" and confers utmost respect.

-kun: This suffix is used at the end of boys' names to express familiarity or endearment. It is also sometimes used by men among friends, or when addressing someone younger or of a lower station.

-chan: This is used to express endearment, mostly toward girls. It is also used for little boys, pets, and even among lovers. It gives a sense of childish cuteness.

Bozu: This is an informal way to refer to a boy, similar to the English terms "kid" and "squirt."

Sempai/
Senpai: This title suggests that the addressee is one's senior in a group or organization. It is most often used in a school setting, where underclassmen refer to their upperclassmen as "sempai." It can also be used in the workplace, such as when a newer employee addresses an employee who has seniority in the company.

Kohai: This is the opposite of "sempai" and is used toward underclassmen in school or newcomers in the workplace. It connotes that the addressee is of a lower station.

Sensei: Literally meaning "one who has come before," this title is used for teachers, doctors, or masters of any profession or art.

-[blank]: This is usually forgotten in these lists, but it is perhaps the most significant difference between Japanese and English. The lack of honorific, known as *yobisute*, means that the speaker has permission to address the person in a very intimate way. Usually, only family, spouses, or very close friends have this kind of permission. It can be gratifying when someone who has earned the intimacy starts to call one by one's name without an honorific. But when that intimacy hasn't been earned, it can be very insulting.

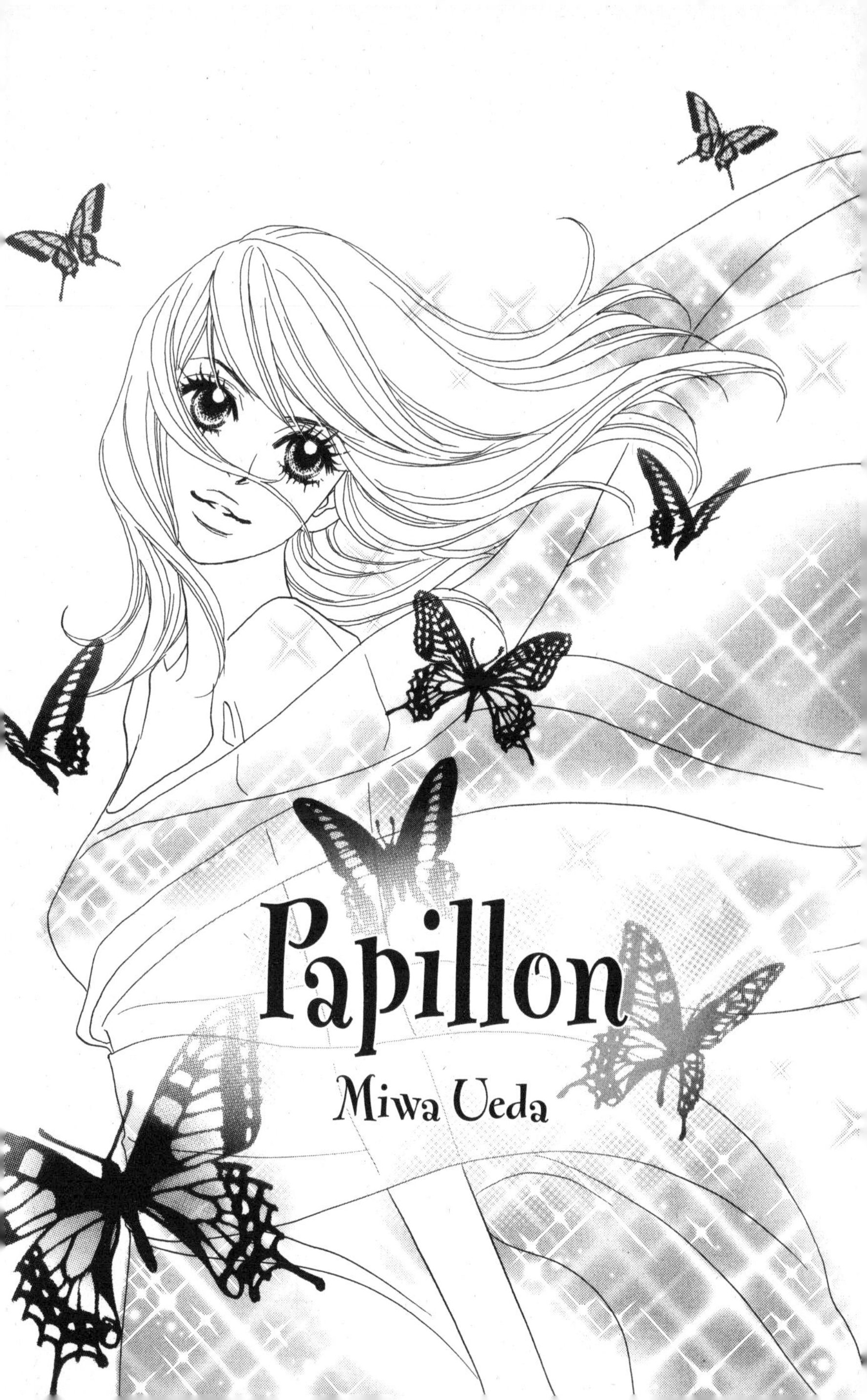
Papillon
Miwa Ueda

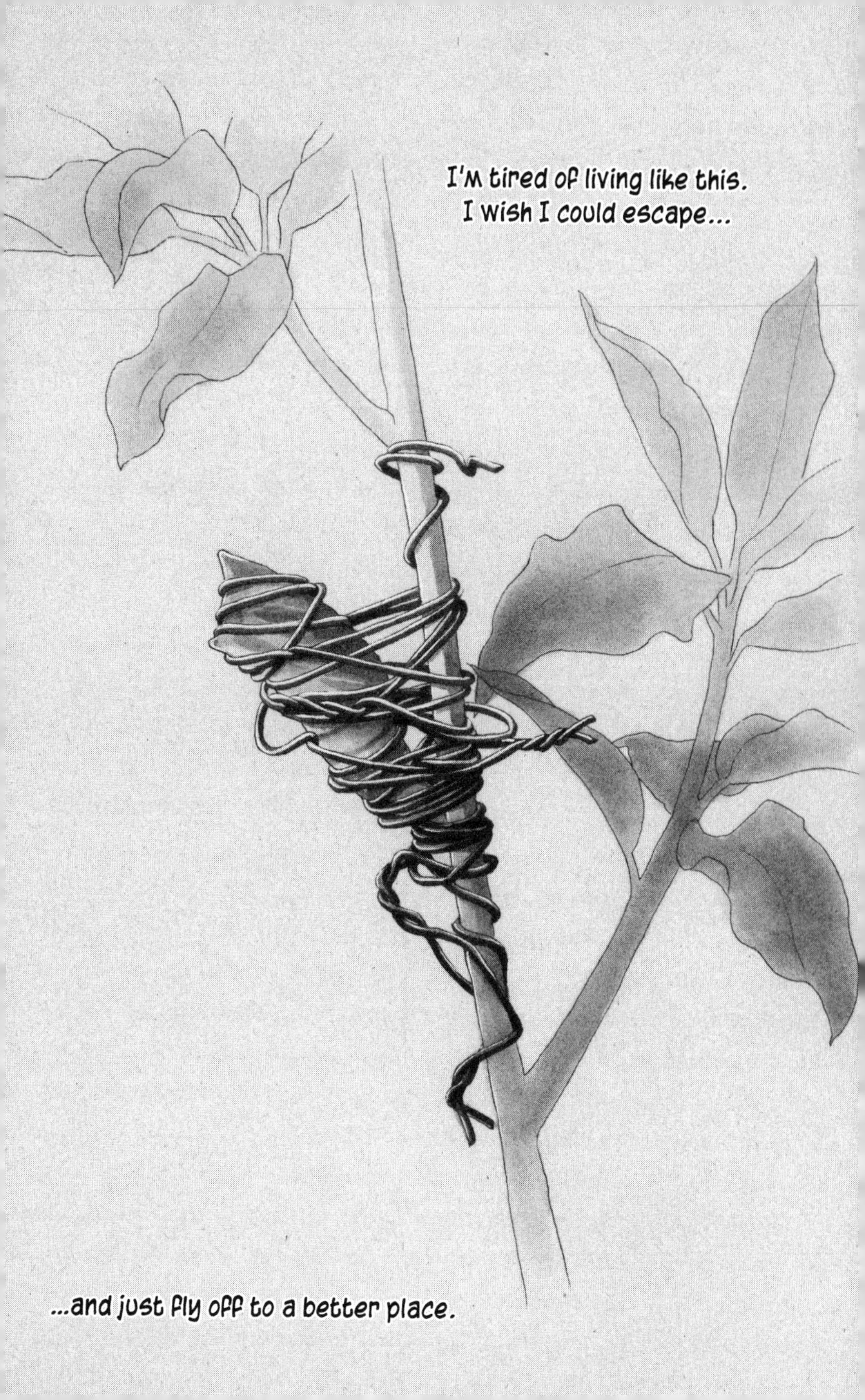
I'm tired of living like this.
I wish I could escape...
...and just fly off to a better place.

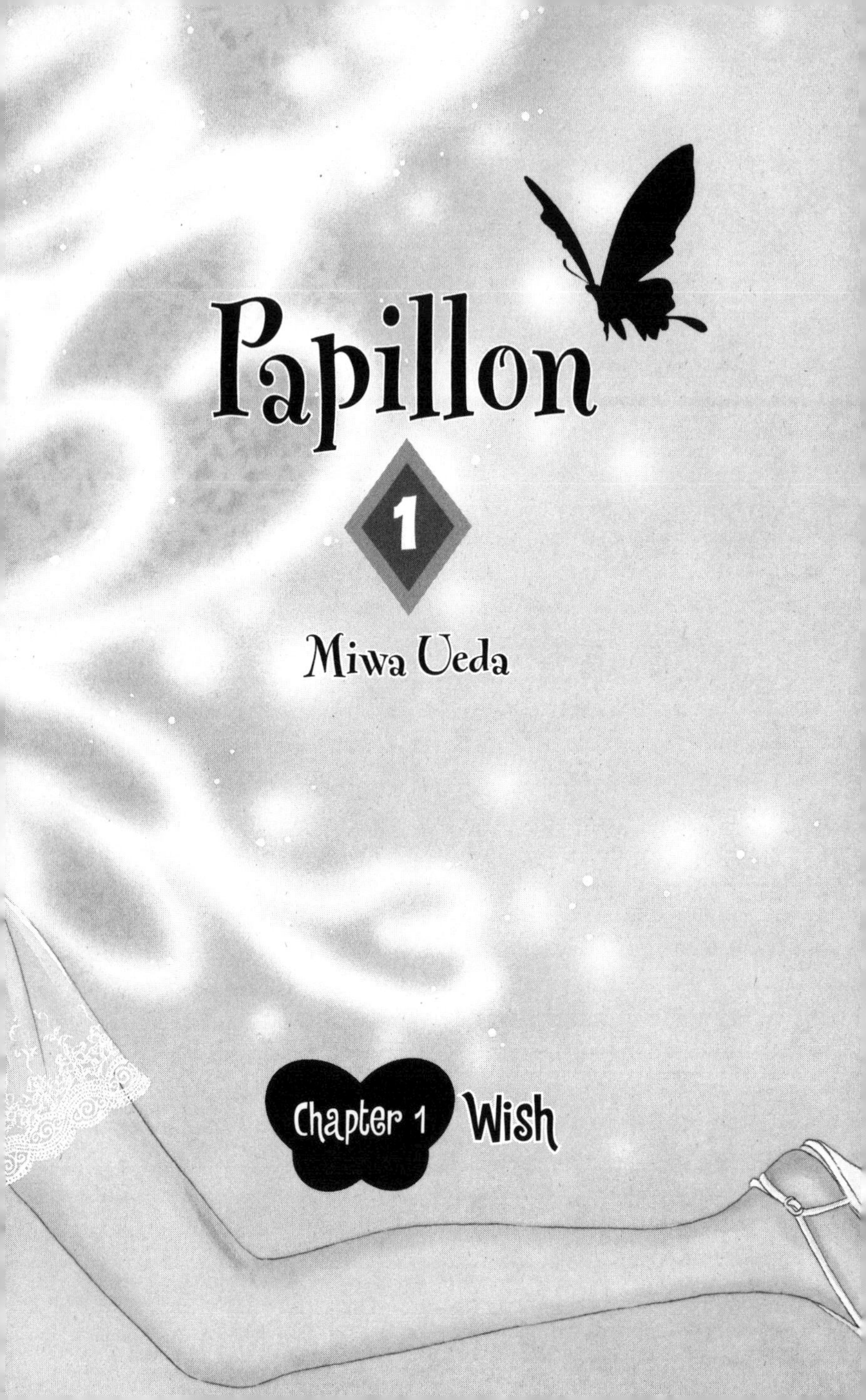
Papillon
1
Miwa Ueda
Chapter 1 Wish

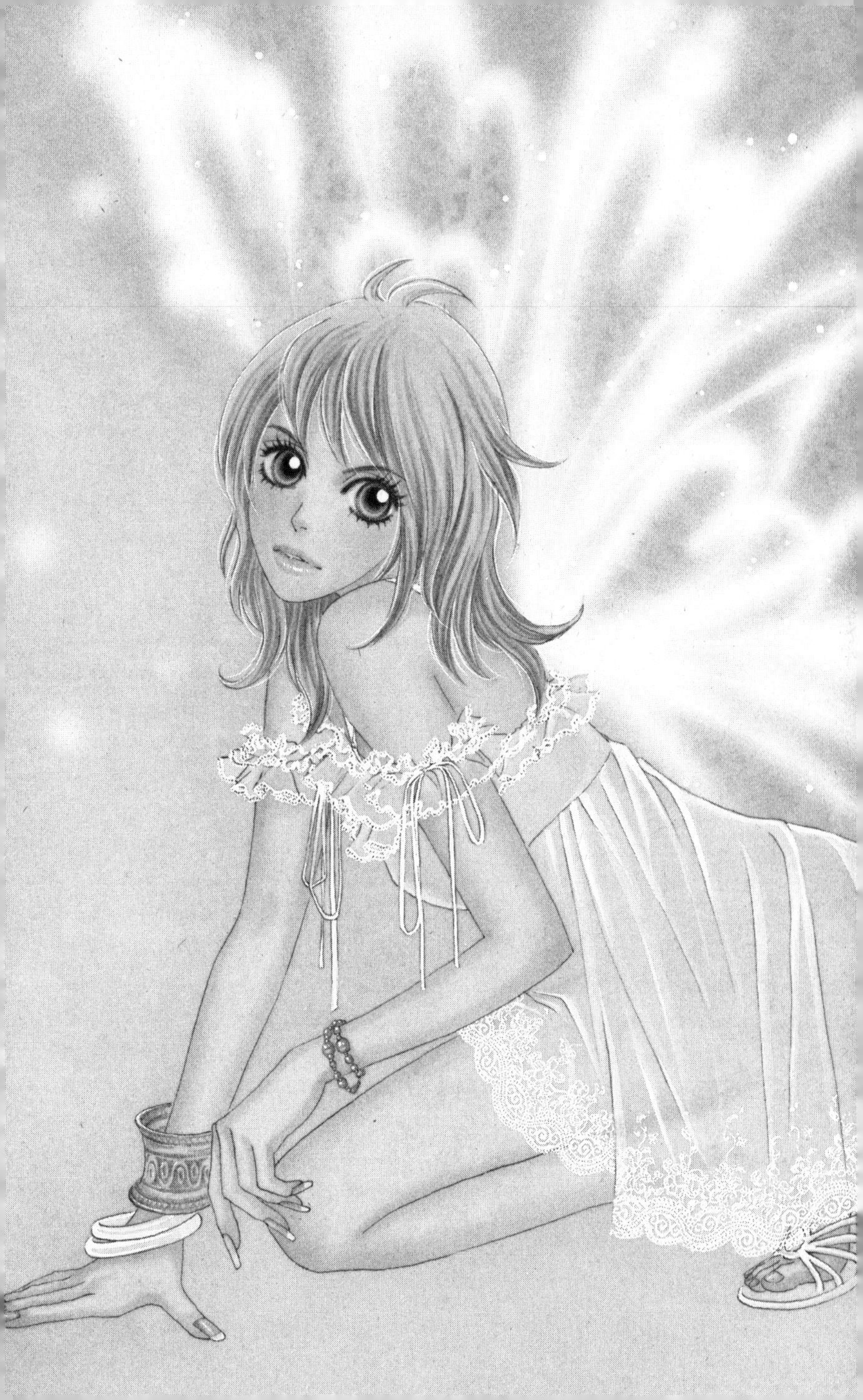

Papillon

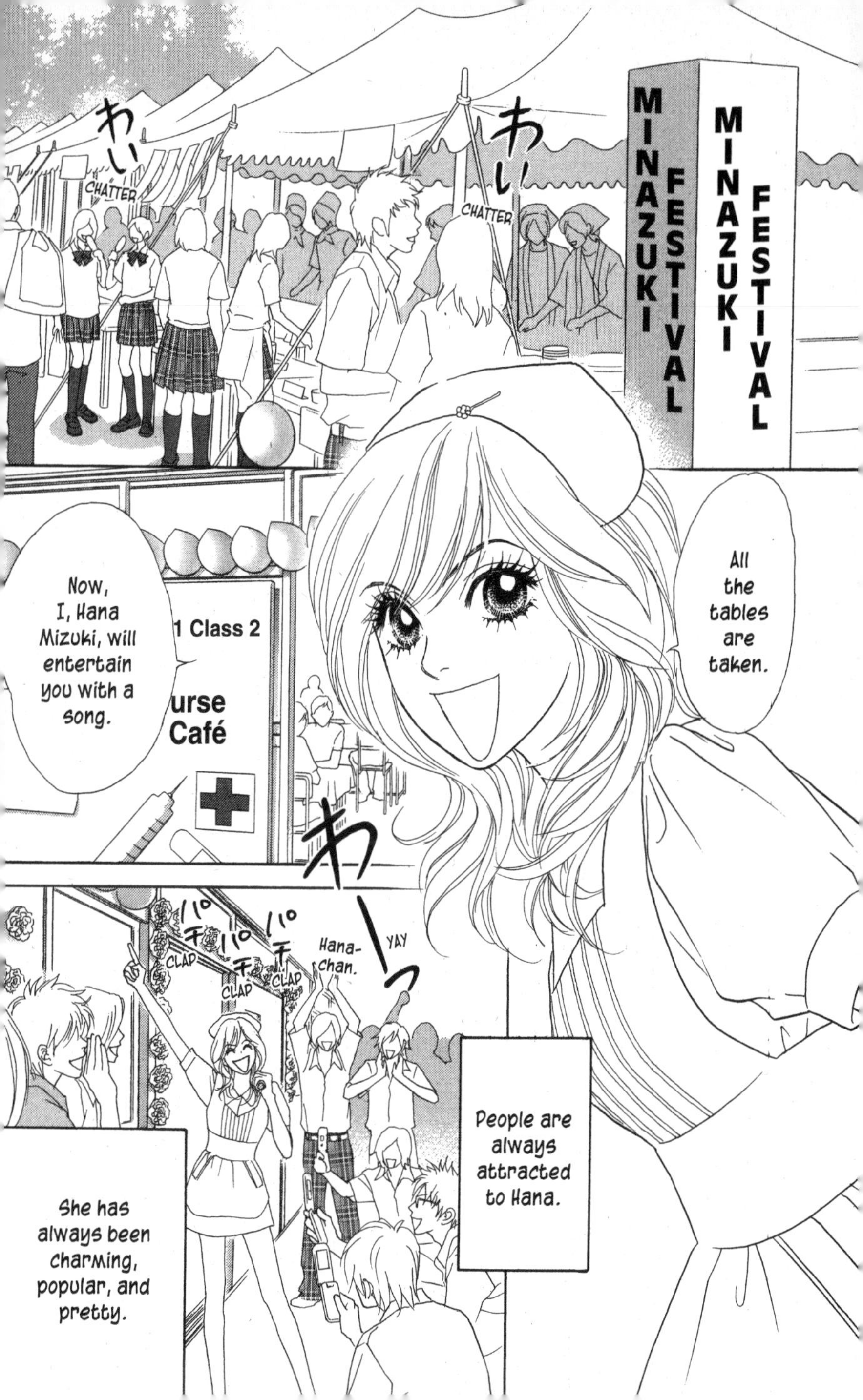
MINAZUKI FESTIVAL
MINAZUKI FESTIVAL
わい CHATTER
わい CHATTER
All the tables are taken.
1 Class 2
urse Café
Now, I, Hana Mizuki, will entertain you with a song.
わーっ YAY
People are always attracted to Hana.
Hana-chan.
パチ CLAP
パチ CLAP
パチ CLAP
She has always been charming, popular, and pretty.

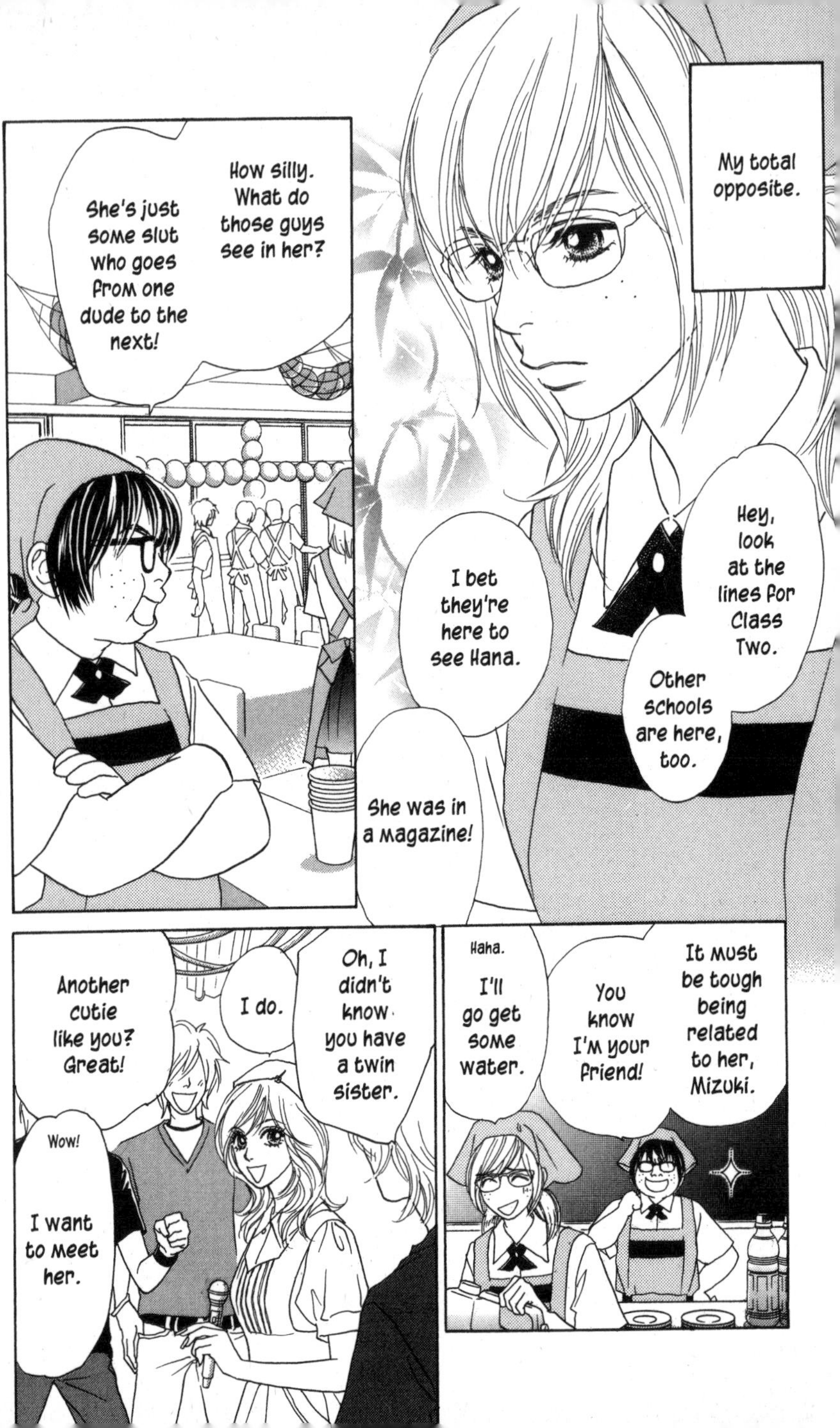
My total opposite.
Hey, look at the lines for Class Two.
Other schools are here, too.
I bet they're here to see Hana.
She was in a magazine!
How silly. What do those guys see in her?
She's just some slut who goes from one dude to the next!
It must be tough being related to her, Mizuki.
You know I'm your friend!
Haha.
I'll go get some water.
Oh, I didn't know you have a twin sister.
I do.
Another cutie like you? Great!
Wow!
I want to meet her.

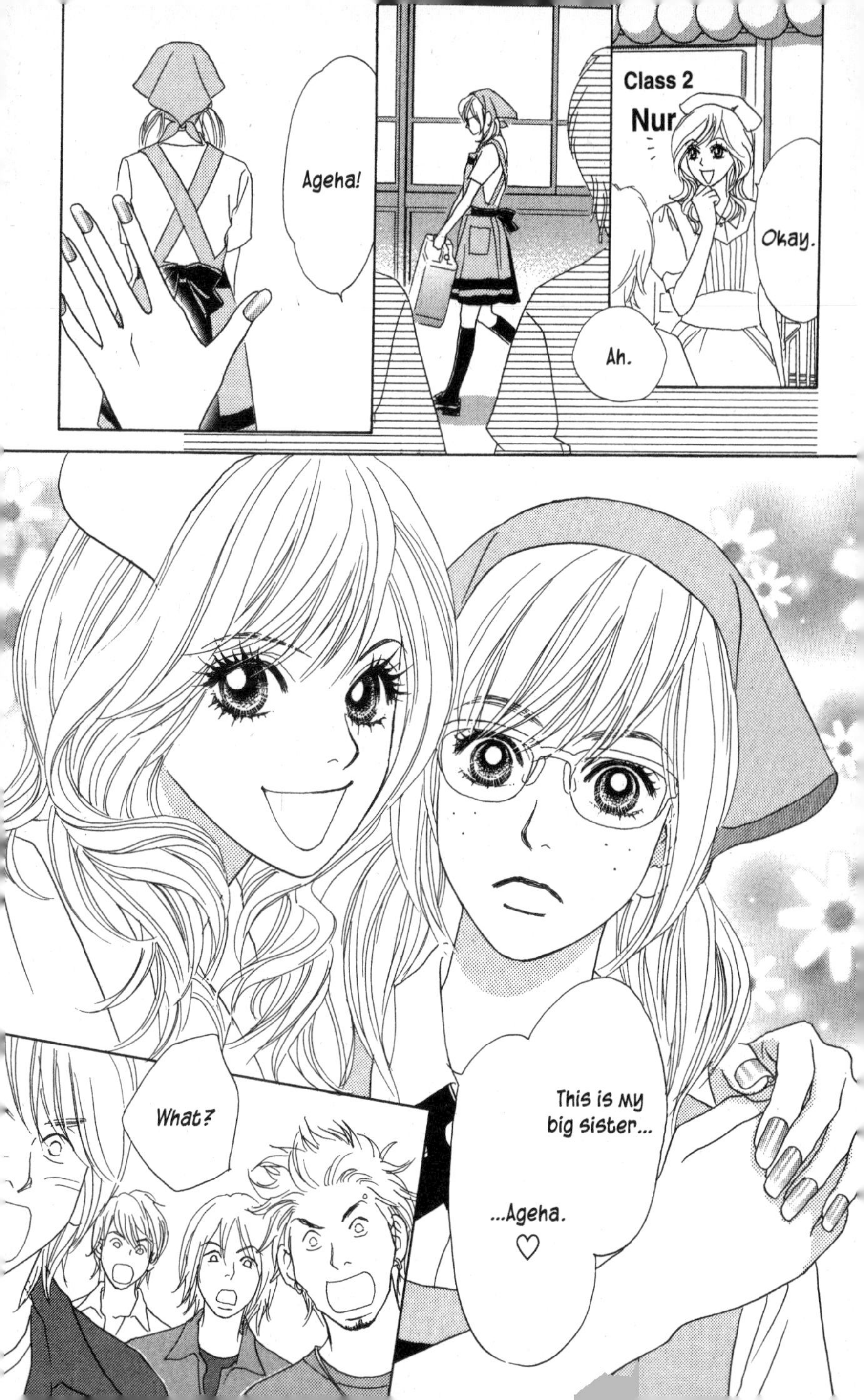
Class 2
Nur
Okay.
Ah.
Ageha!
This is my big sister...
...Ageha. ♡
What?

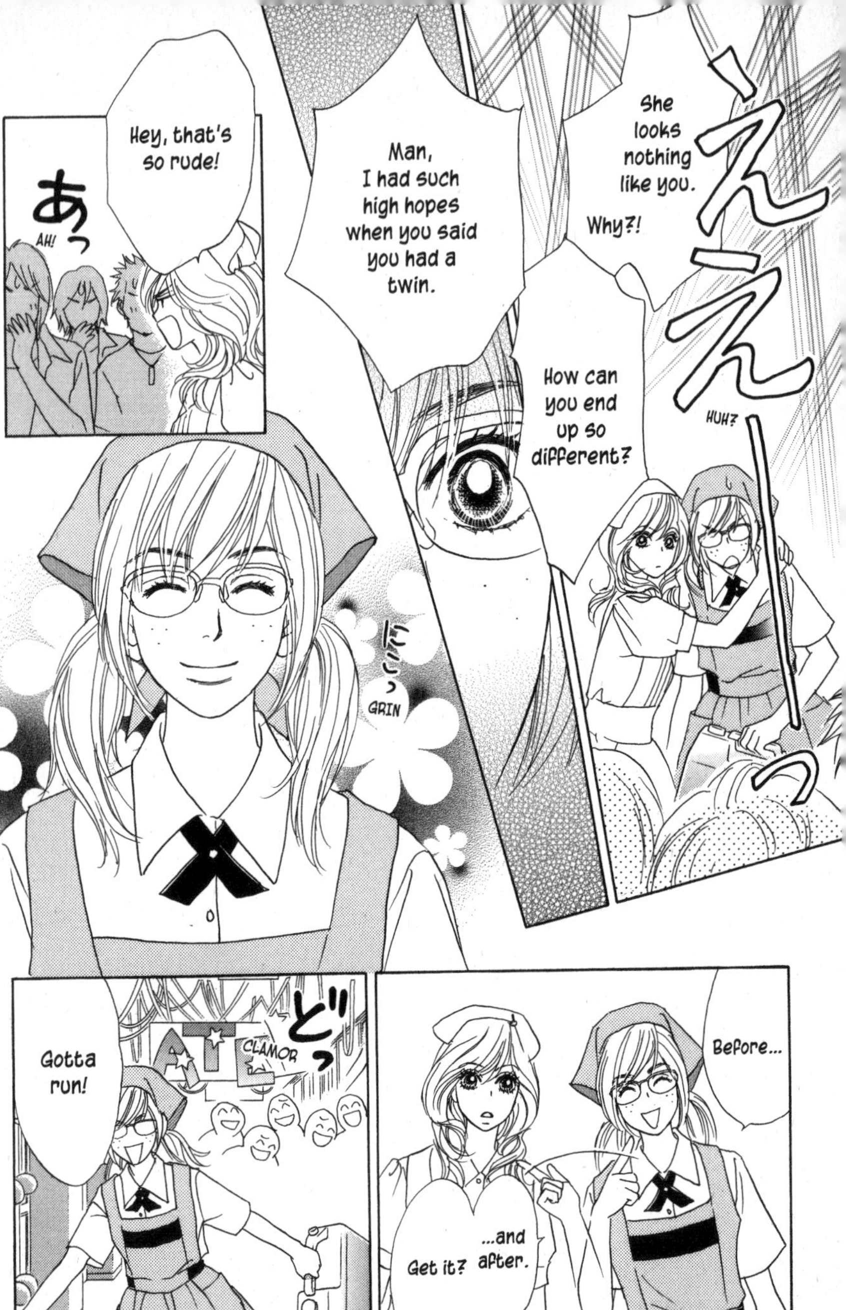

ええっ
HUH?
She looks nothing like you.
Why?!
How can you end up so different?
Man, I had such high hopes when you said you had a twin.
Hey, that's so rude!
あっ
AH!
にこっ
GRIN
Before...
...and after.
Get it?
Gotta run!
どっ
CLAMOR

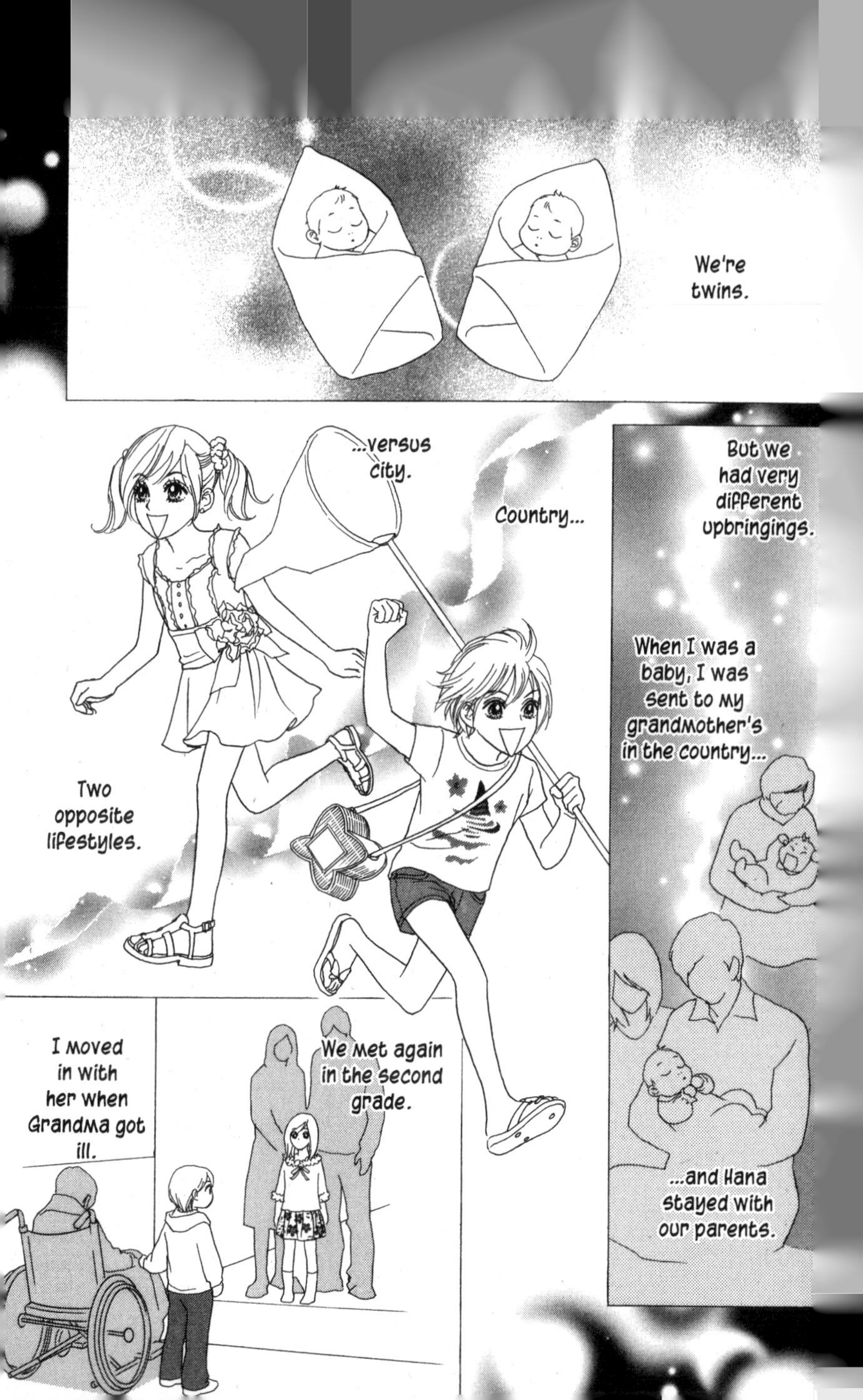
We're twins.
But we had very different upbringings.
When I was a baby, I was sent to my grandmother's in the country...
...and Hana stayed with our parents.
Country...
...versus city.
Two opposite lifestyles.
We met again in the second grade.
I moved in with her when Grandma got ill.

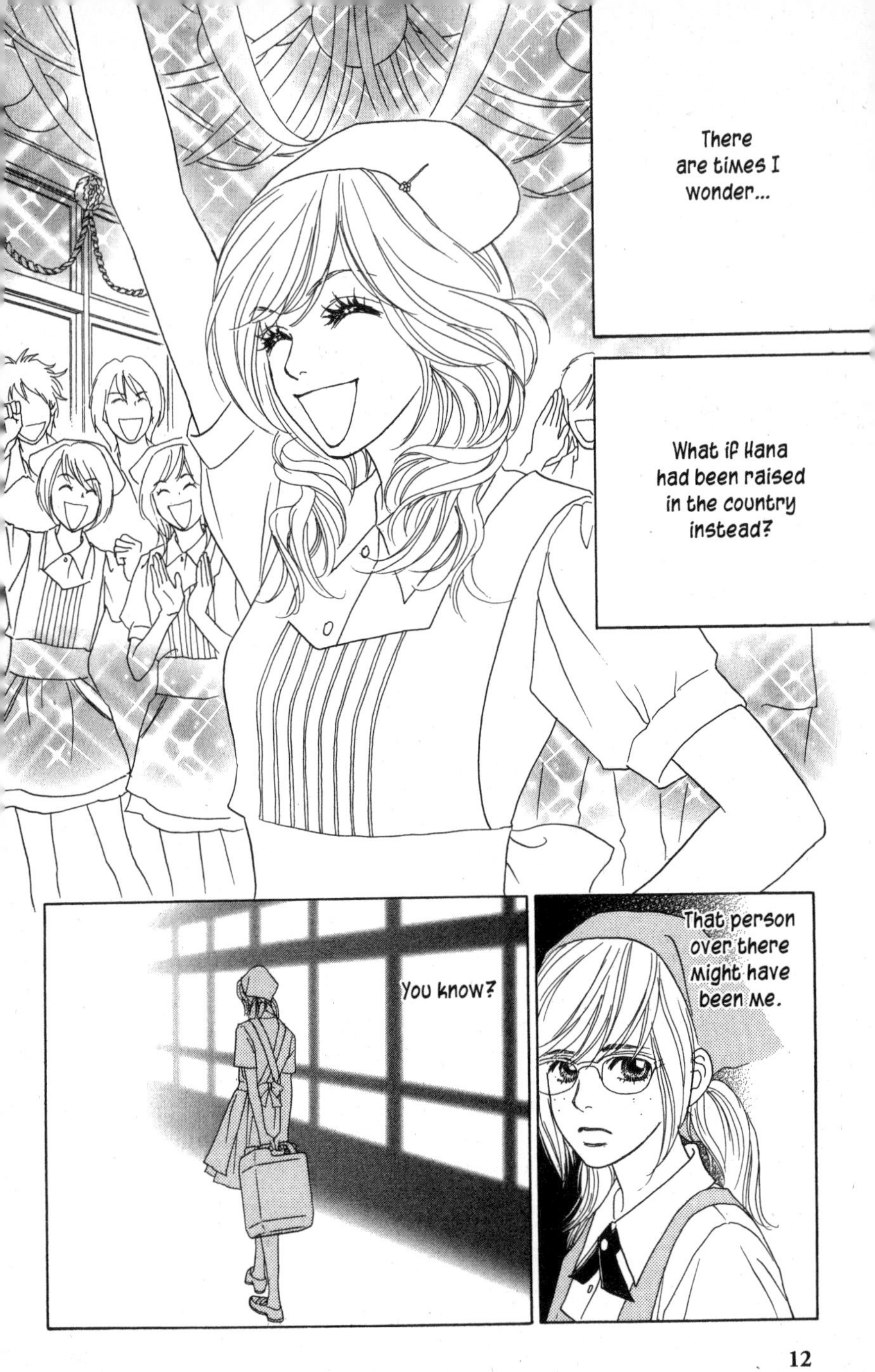
There are times I wonder...
What if Hana had been raised in the country instead?
That person over there might have been me.
You know?

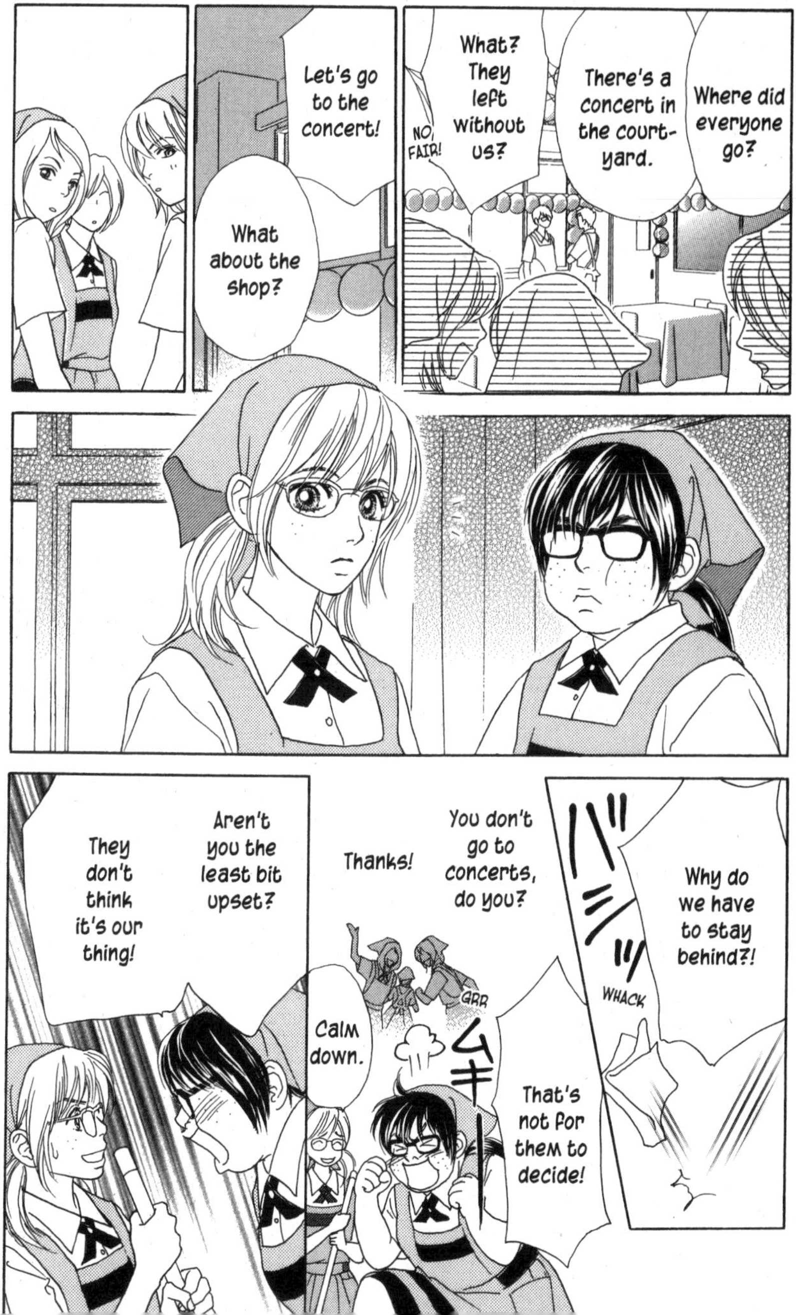
Where did everyone go?
There's a concert in the courtyard.
What? They left without us?
NO FAIR!
Let's go to the concert!
What about the shop?
Why do we have to stay behind?!
バシッ
WHACK
You don't go to concerts, do you?
Thanks!
GRR
ムキー
That's not for them to decide!
Calm down.
Aren't you the least bit upset?
They don't think it's our thing!

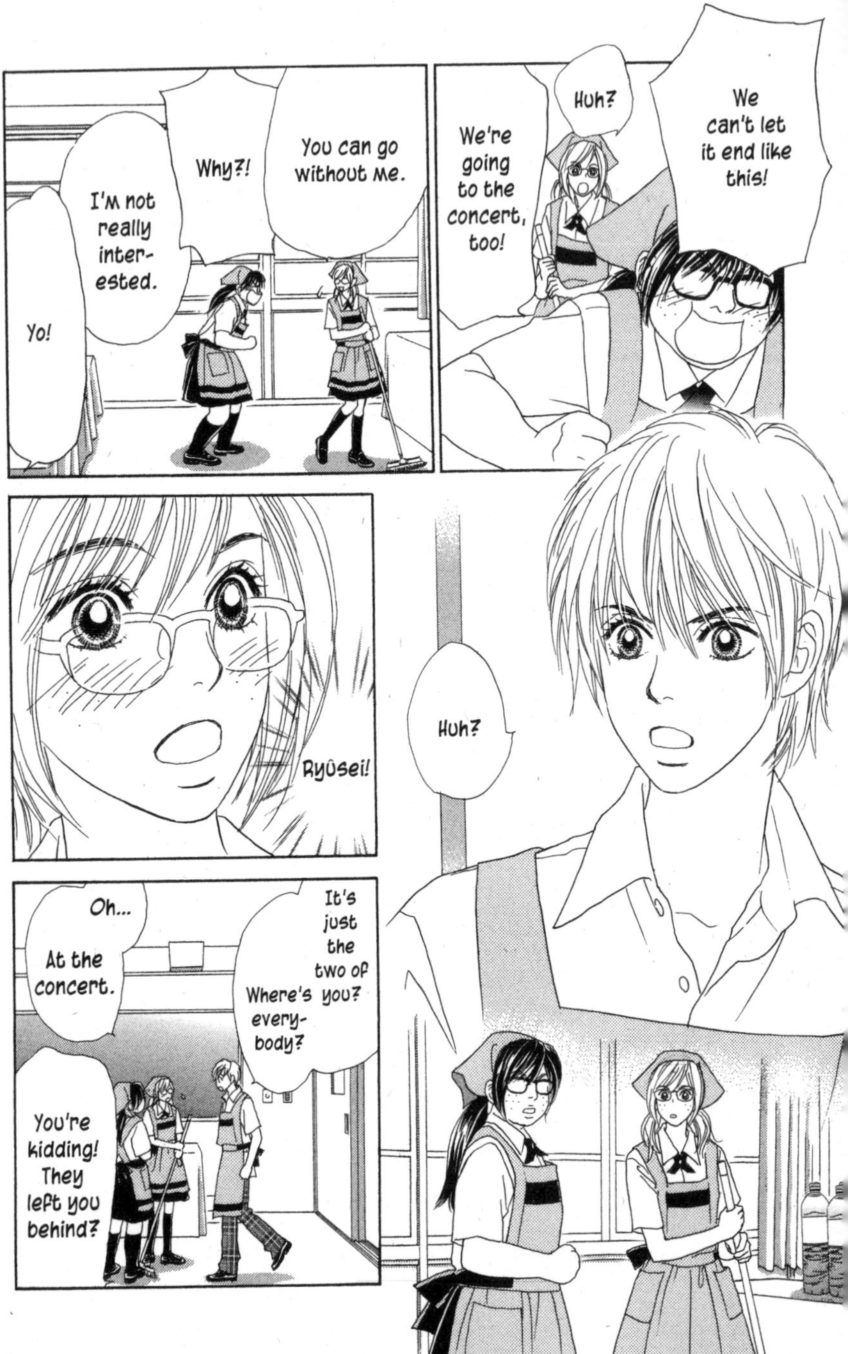
We can't let it end like this!
Huh?
We're going to the concert, too!
You can go without me.
Why?!
I'm not really interested.
Yo!
Huh?
Ryûsei!
It's just the two of you?
Where's everybody?
Oh...
At the concert.
You're kidding! They left you behind?

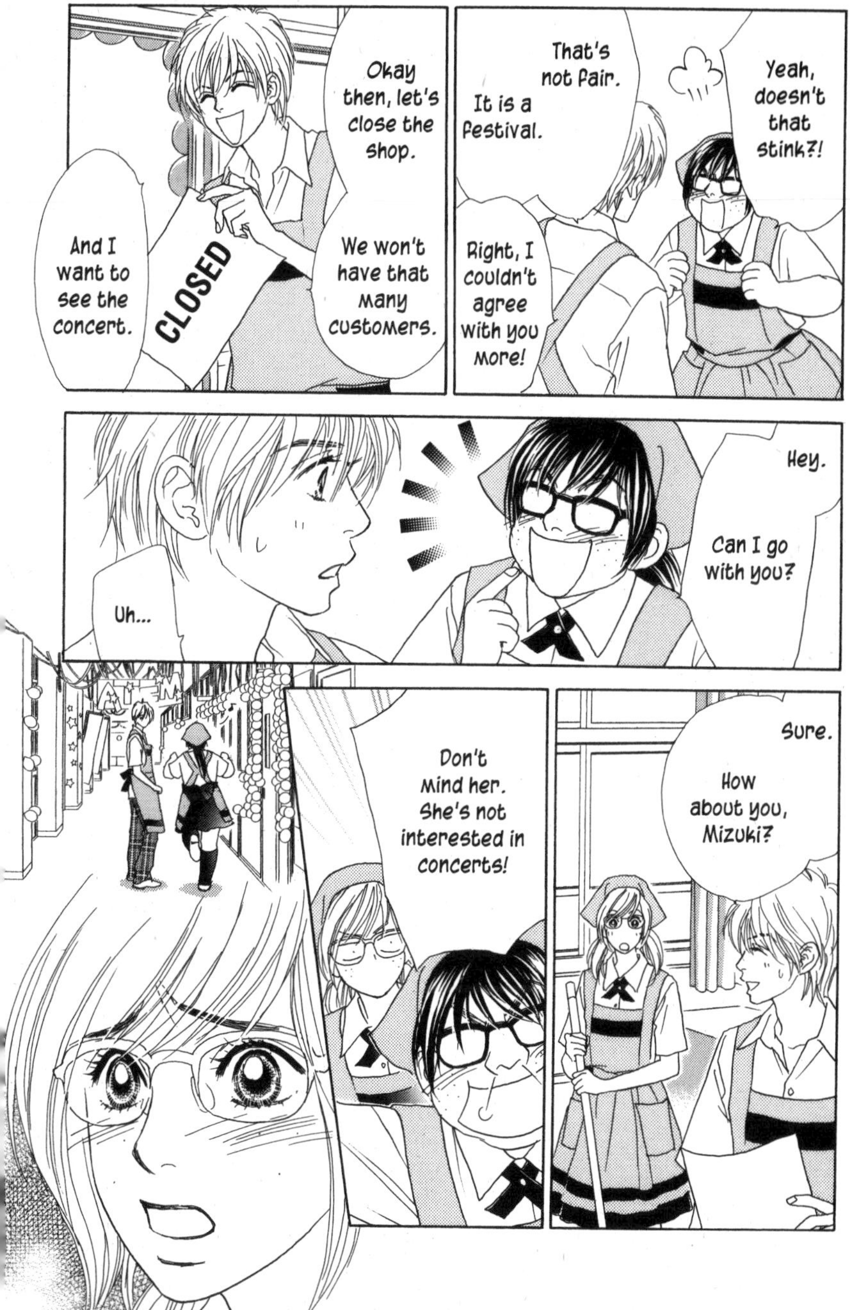
Yeah, doesn't that stink?!
That's not fair.
It is a festival.
Right, I couldn't agree with you more!
Okay then, let's close the shop.
We won't have that many customers.
CLOSED
And I want to see the concert.
Hey.
Can I go with you?
Uh...
Sure.
How about you, Mizuki?
Don't mind her. She's not interested in concerts!

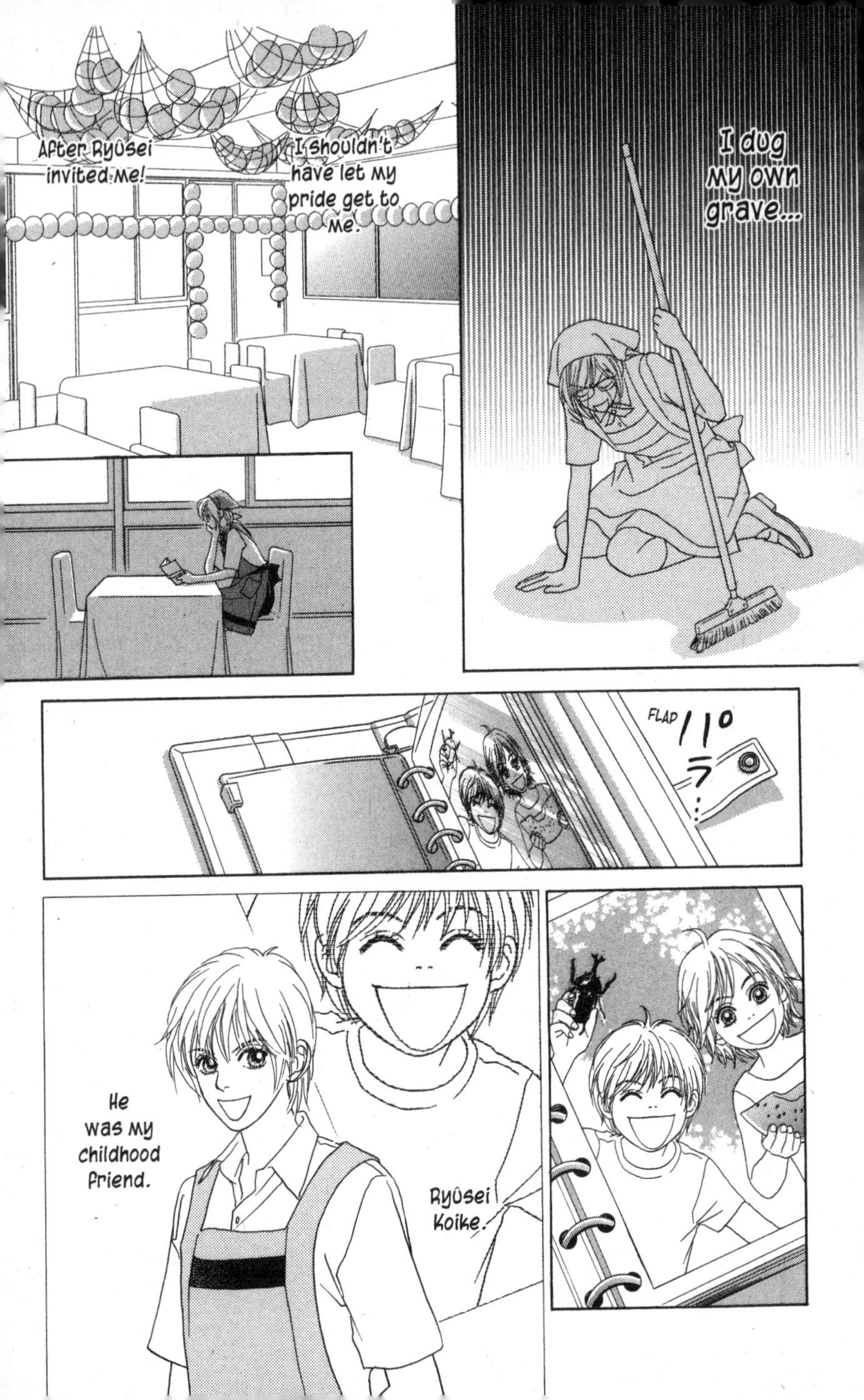
I dug my own grave...
I shouldn't have let my pride get to me.
After Ryûsei invited me!
FLAP
パラ
Ryûsei Koike.
He was my childhood friend.

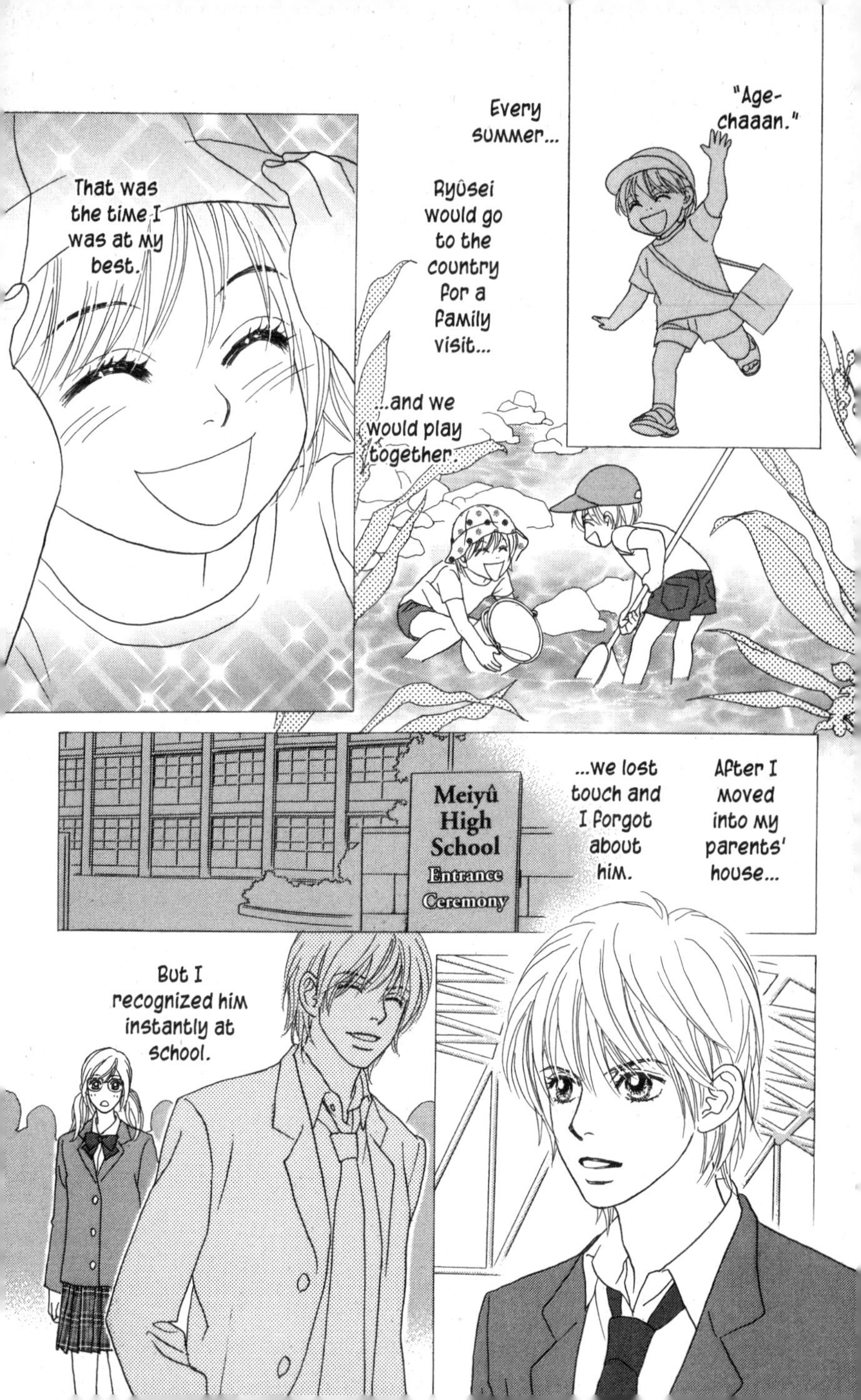
"Age-chaaan."
Every summer...
Ryûsei would go to the country for a family visit...
...and we would play together.
That was the time I was at my best.
After I moved into my parents' house...
...we lost touch and I forgot about him.
Meiyû High School
Entrance Ceremony
But I recognized him instantly at school.

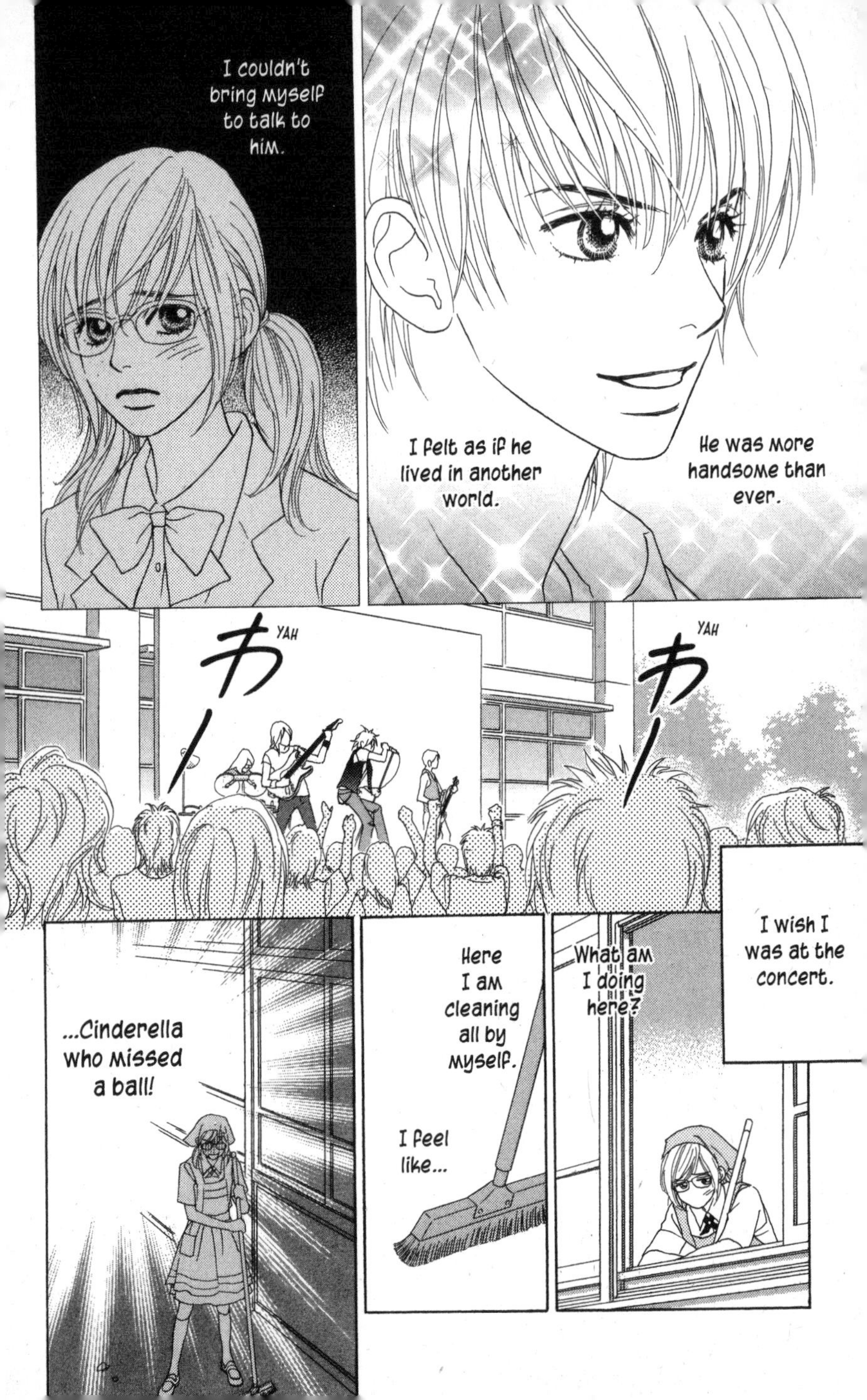
He was more handsome than ever.
I felt as if he lived in another world.
I couldn't bring myself to talk to him.
YAH
YAH
I wish I was at the concert.
What am I doing here?
Here I am cleaning all by myself.
I feel like...
...Cinderella who missed a ball!

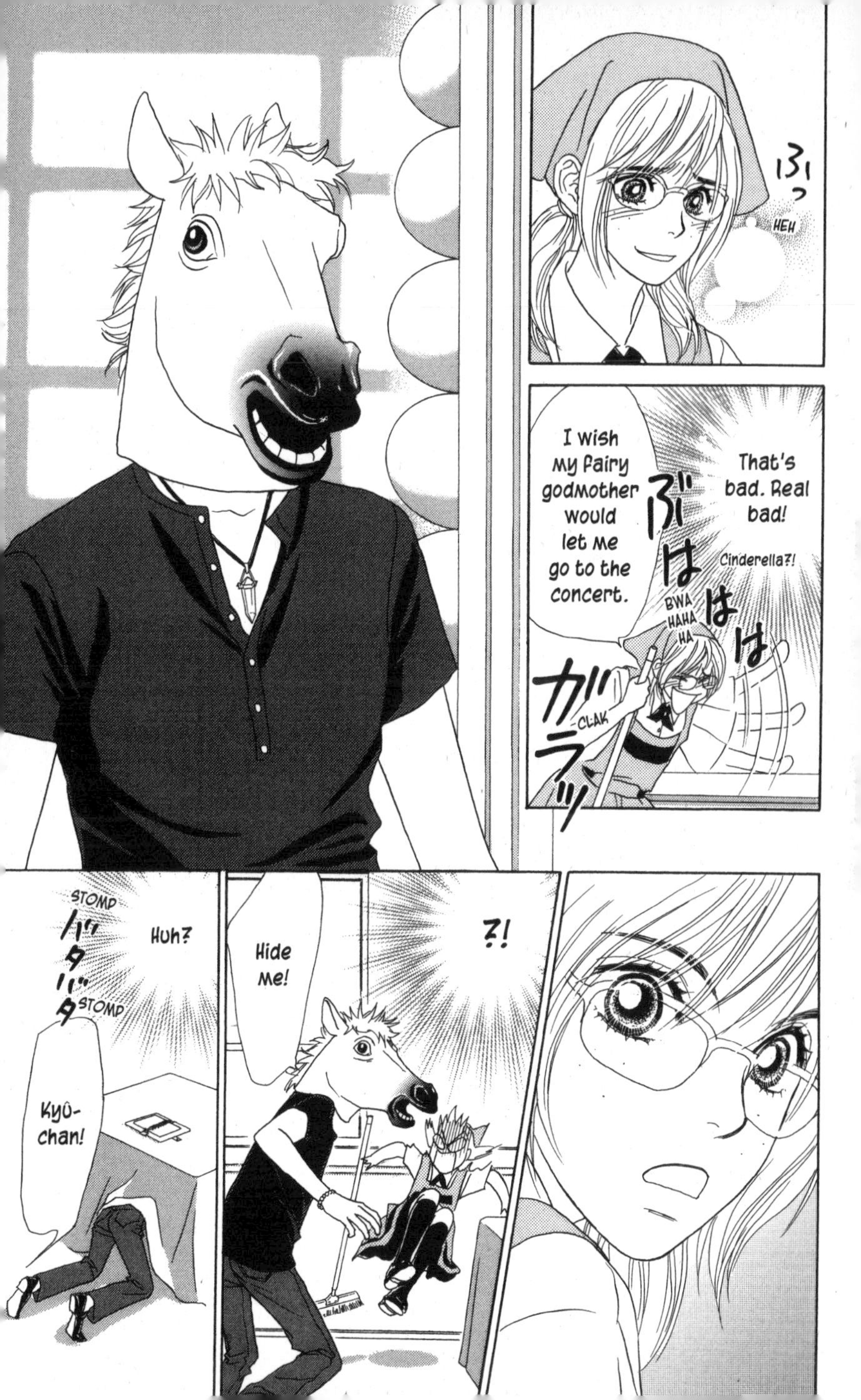
ふっ
HEH
That's bad. Real bad!
Cinderella?!
ぶははは
BWA HAHA HA
I wish my fairy godmother would let me go to the concert.
カラッ
CLAK
?!
Hide me!
Huh?
バタバタ
STOMP STOMP
Kyû-chan!

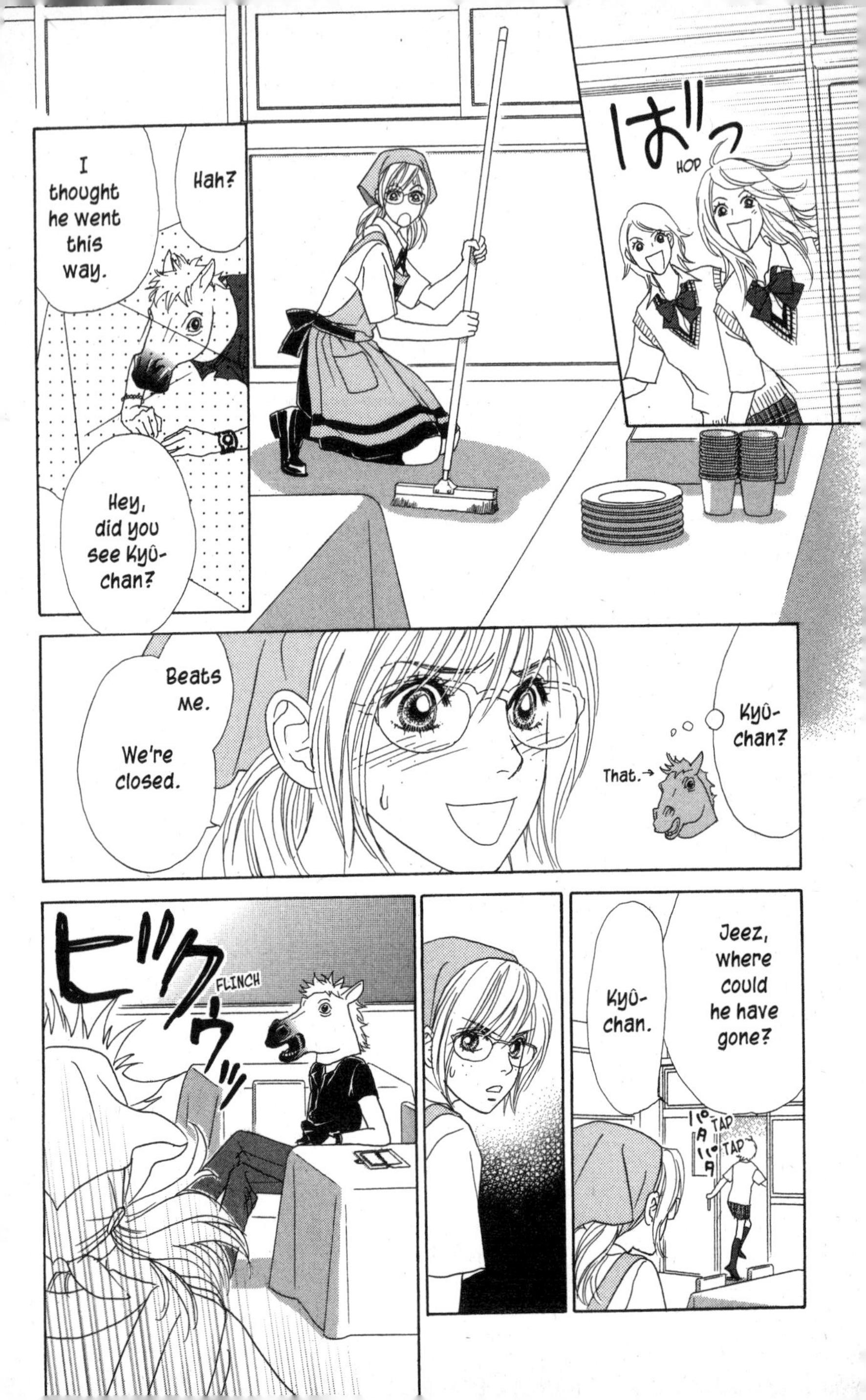
はっ
HOP
Hah?
I thought he went this way.
Hey, did you see Kyû-chan?
Kyû-chan?
That.→
Beats me.
We're closed.
Jeez, where could he have gone?
Kyû-chan.
パタパタ
TAP TAP
ビクゥッ
FLINCH

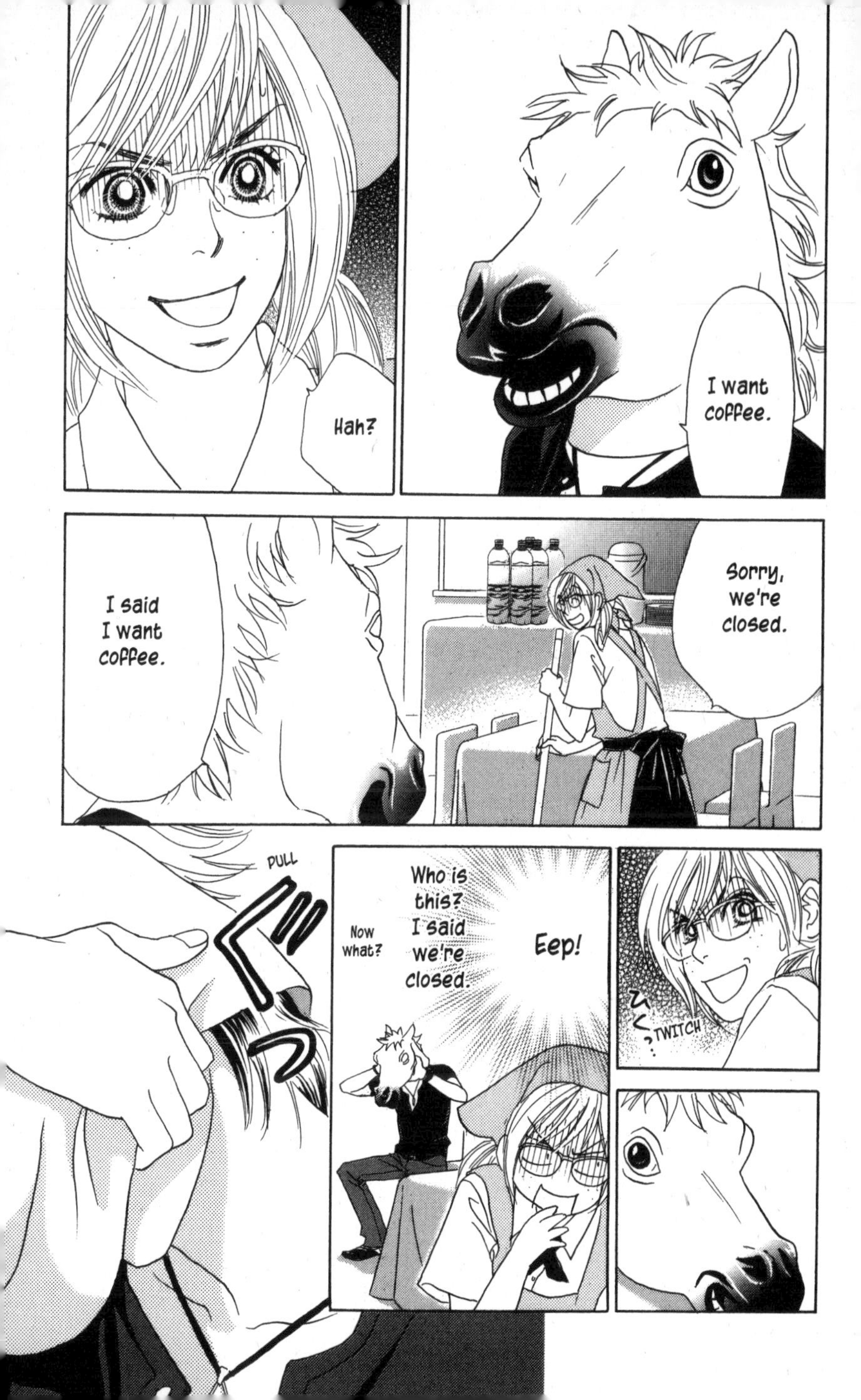
I want coffee.
Hah?
Sorry, we're closed.
I said I want coffee.
ひく…
TWITCH
Eep!
Who is this? I said we're closed.
Now what?
PULL

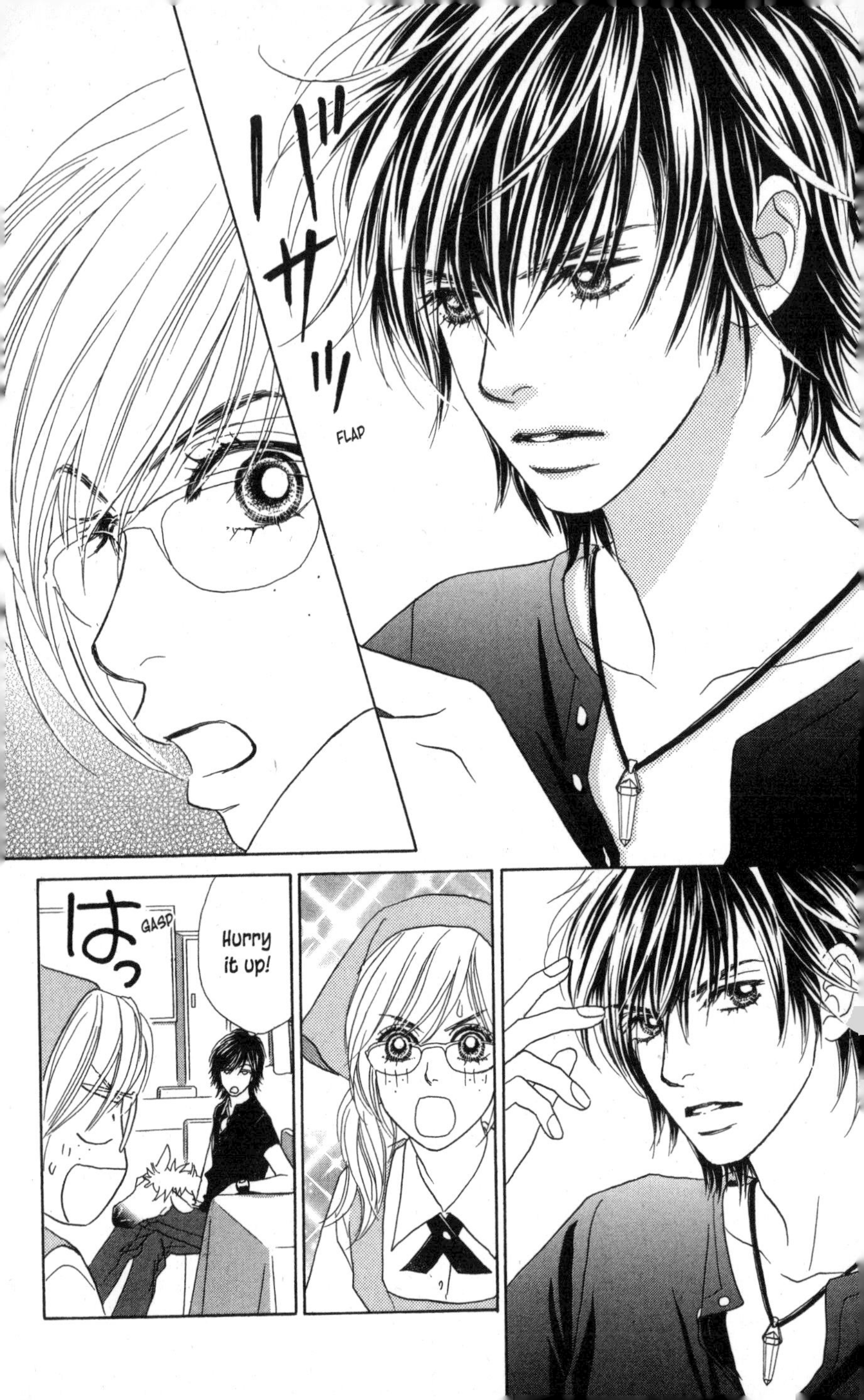
バサッ
FLAP
Hurry it up!
はっ
GASP

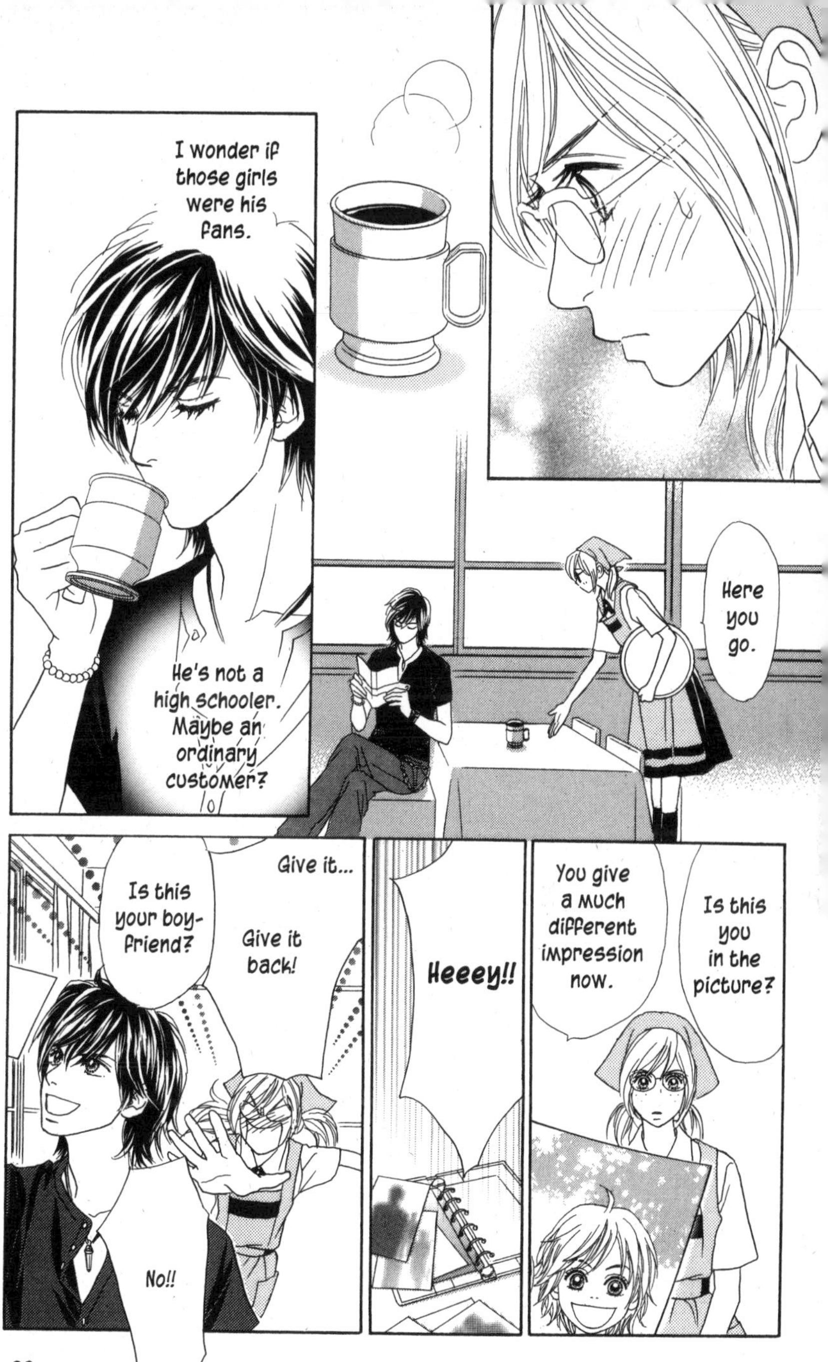
Here you go.
I wonder if those girls were his fans.
He's not a high schooler. Maybe an ordinary customer?
Is this you in the picture?
You give a much different impression now.
Heeey!!
Give it...
Is this your boy-friend?
Give it back!
No!!

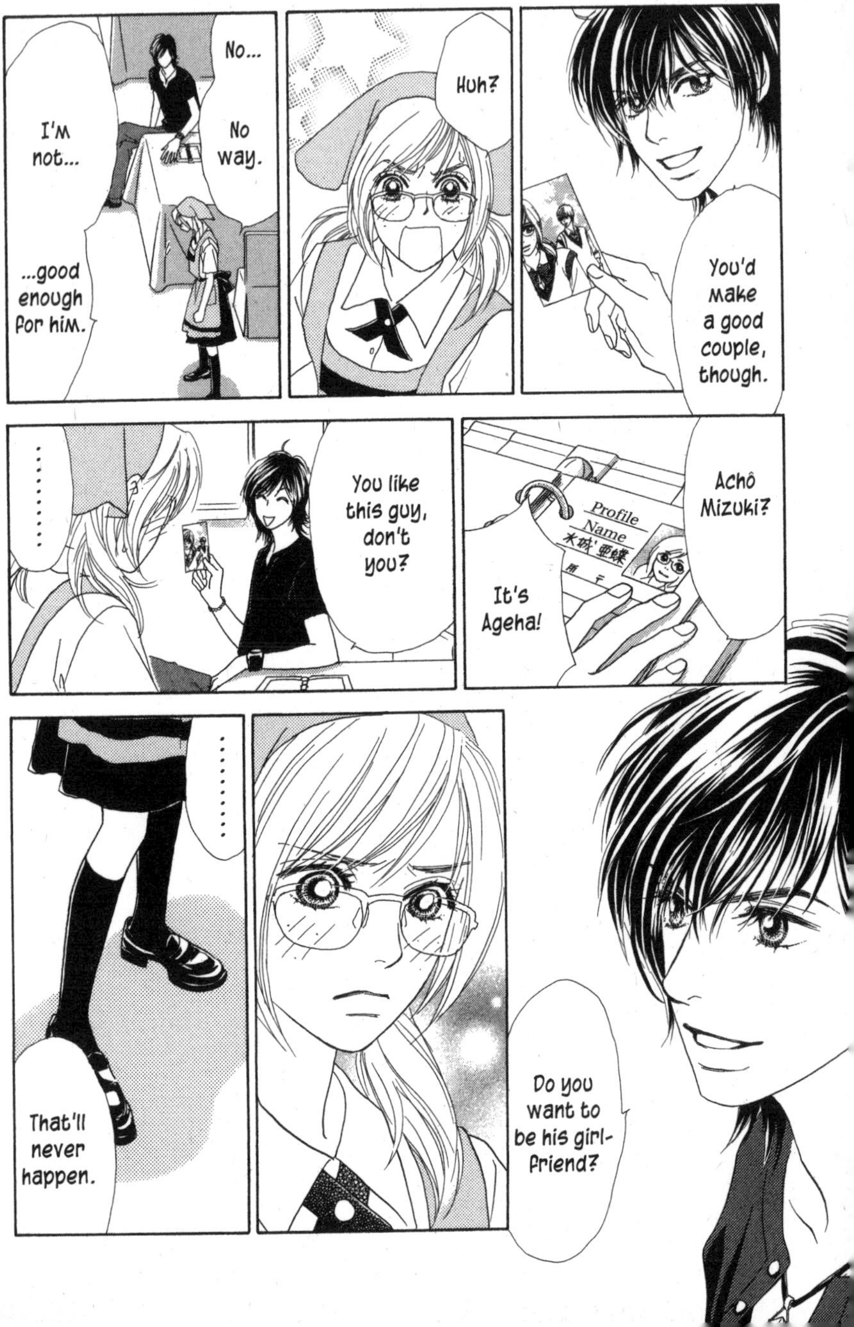
You'd make a good couple, though.
Huh?
No...
No way.
I'm not...
...good enough for him.
Achô Mizuki?
Profile
Name
水城 亜蝶
It's Ageha!
You like this guy, don't you?
....
Do you want to be his girl-friend?
....
That'll never happen.

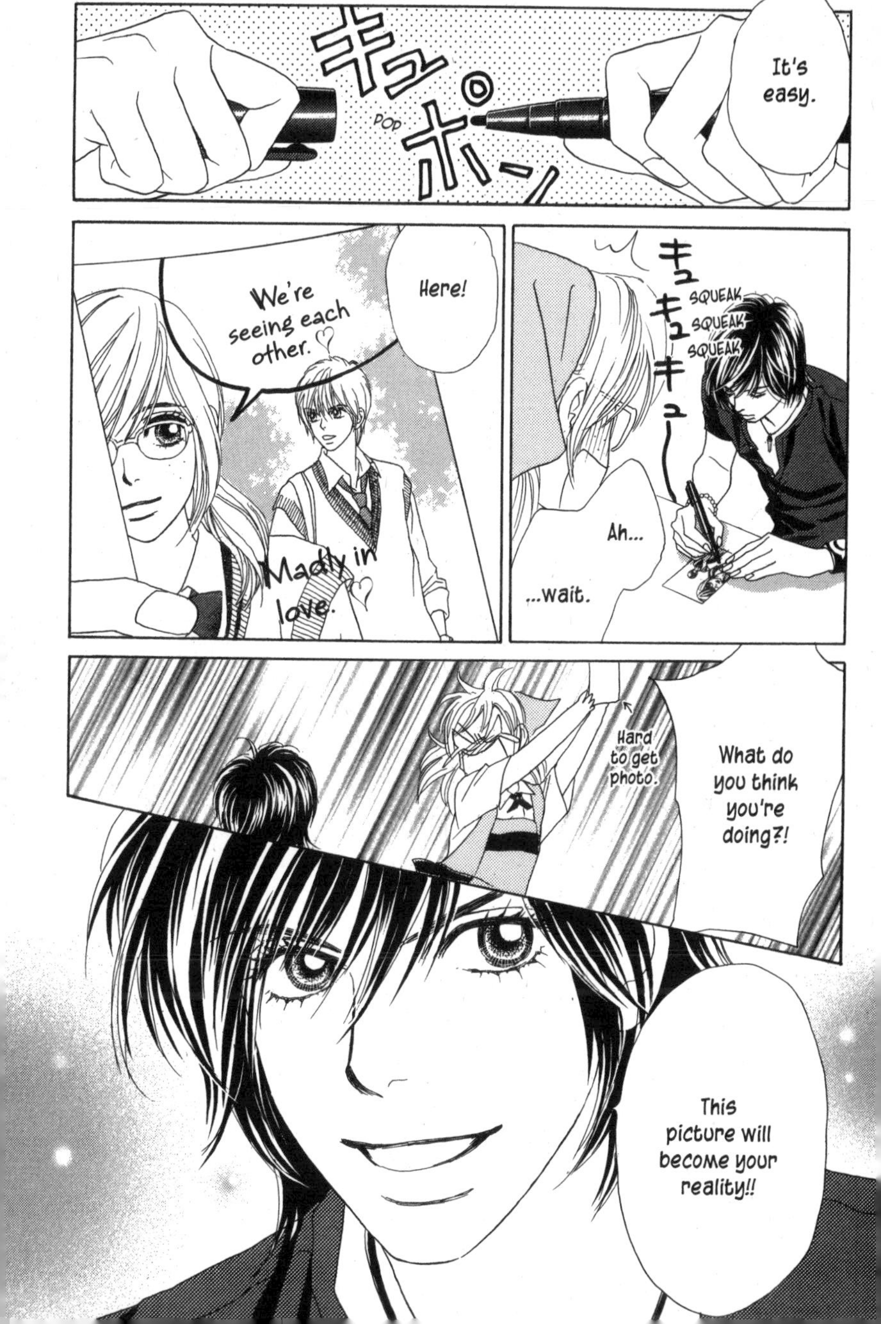
It's easy.
キュ
ポン
POP
キュキュキュー
SQUEAK
SQUEAK
SQUEAK
Ah...
...wait.
Here!
We're seeing each other.
Madly in love.
What do you think you're doing?!
Hard to get photo.
This picture will become your reality!!

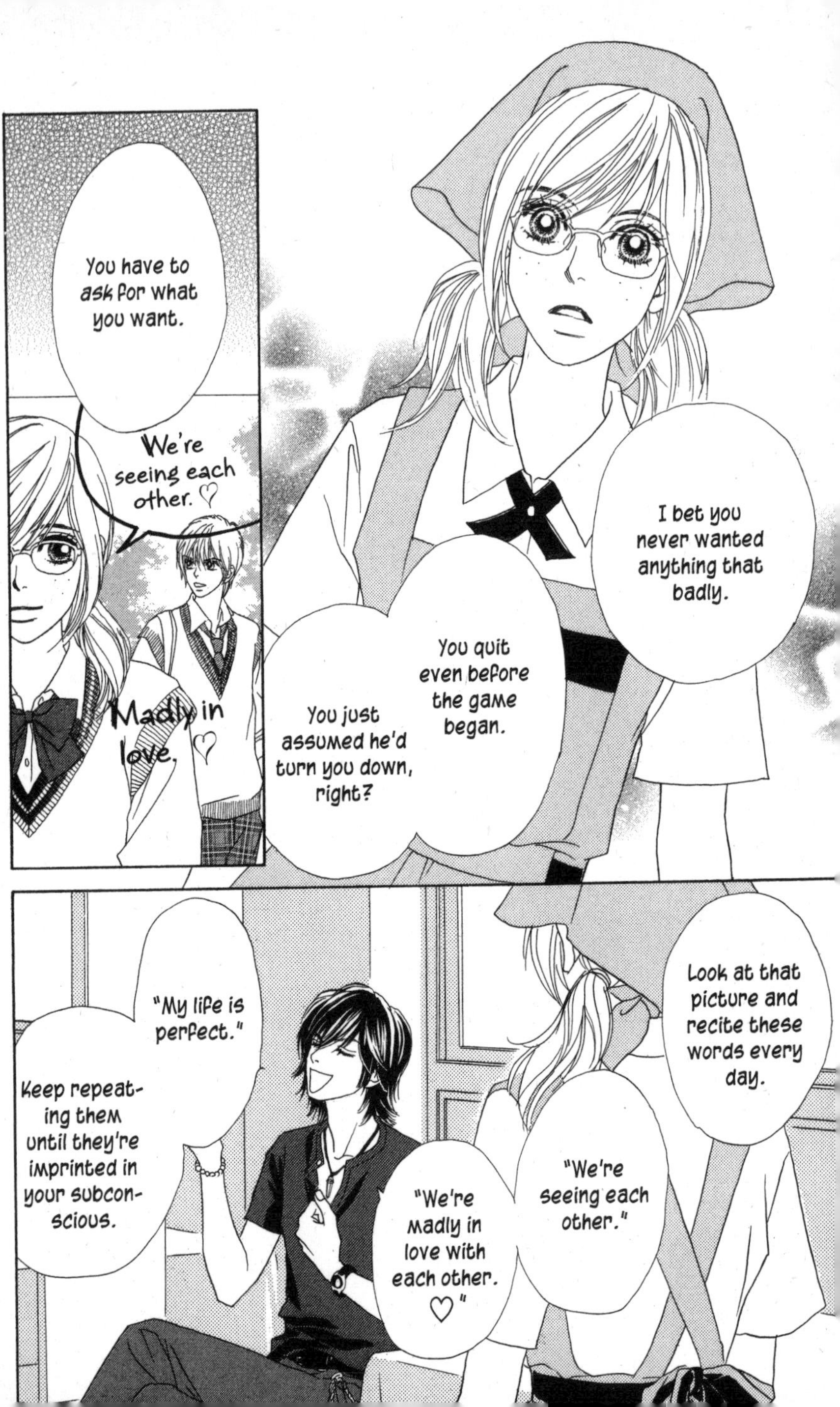
I bet you never wanted anything that badly.
You quit even before the game began.
You just assumed he'd turn you down, right?
You have to ask for what you want.
We're seeing each other. ♡
Madly in love. ♡
Look at that picture and recite these words every day.
"We're seeing each other."
"We're madly in love with each other. ♡"
"My life is perfect."
Keep repeating them until they're imprinted in your subconscious.

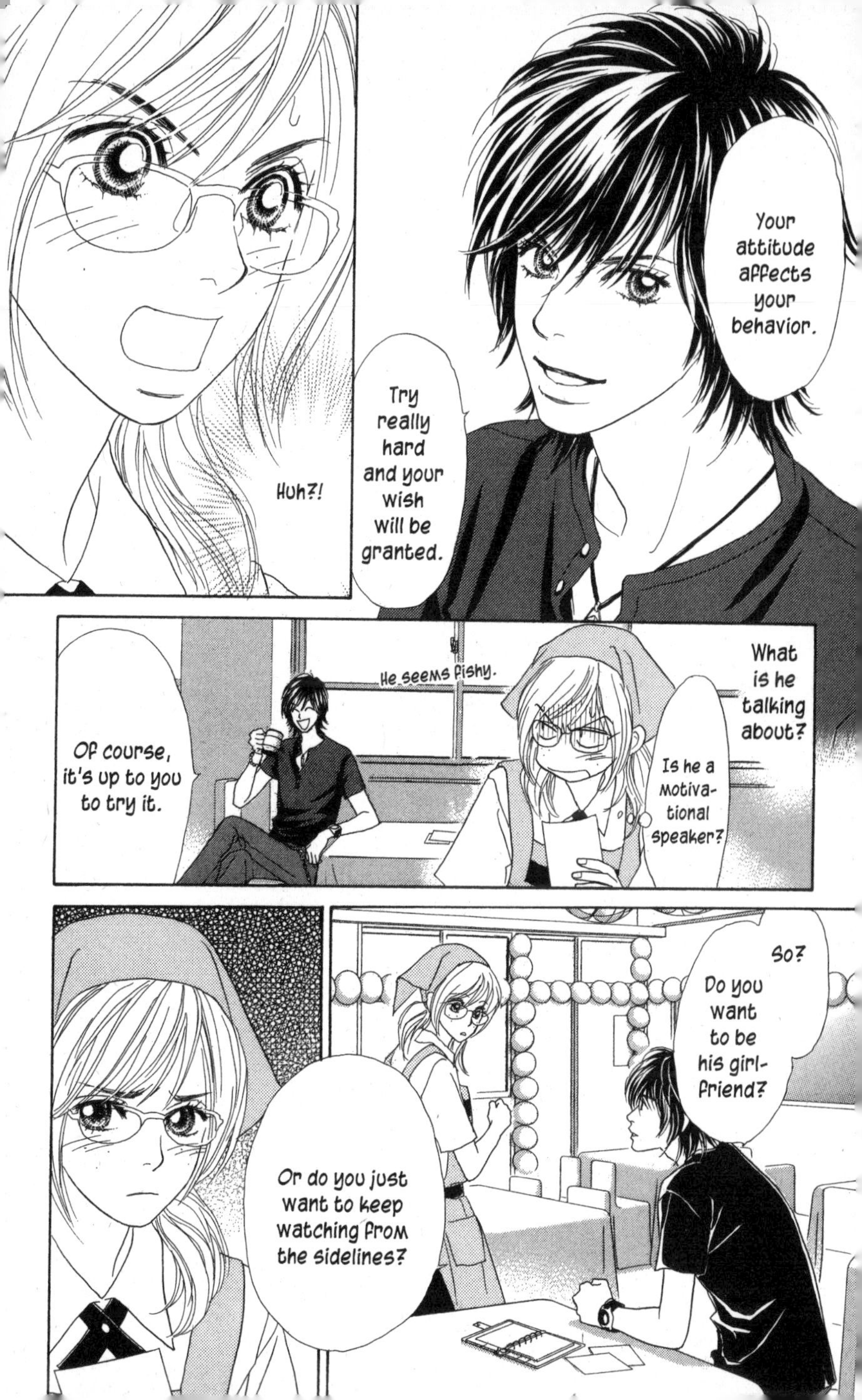
Your attitude affects your behavior.
Try really hard and your wish will be granted.
Huh?!
What is he talking about?
Is he a motiva-tional speaker?
He seems fishy.
Of course, it's up to you to try it.
So?
Do you want to be his girl-friend?
Or do you just want to keep watching from the sidelines?

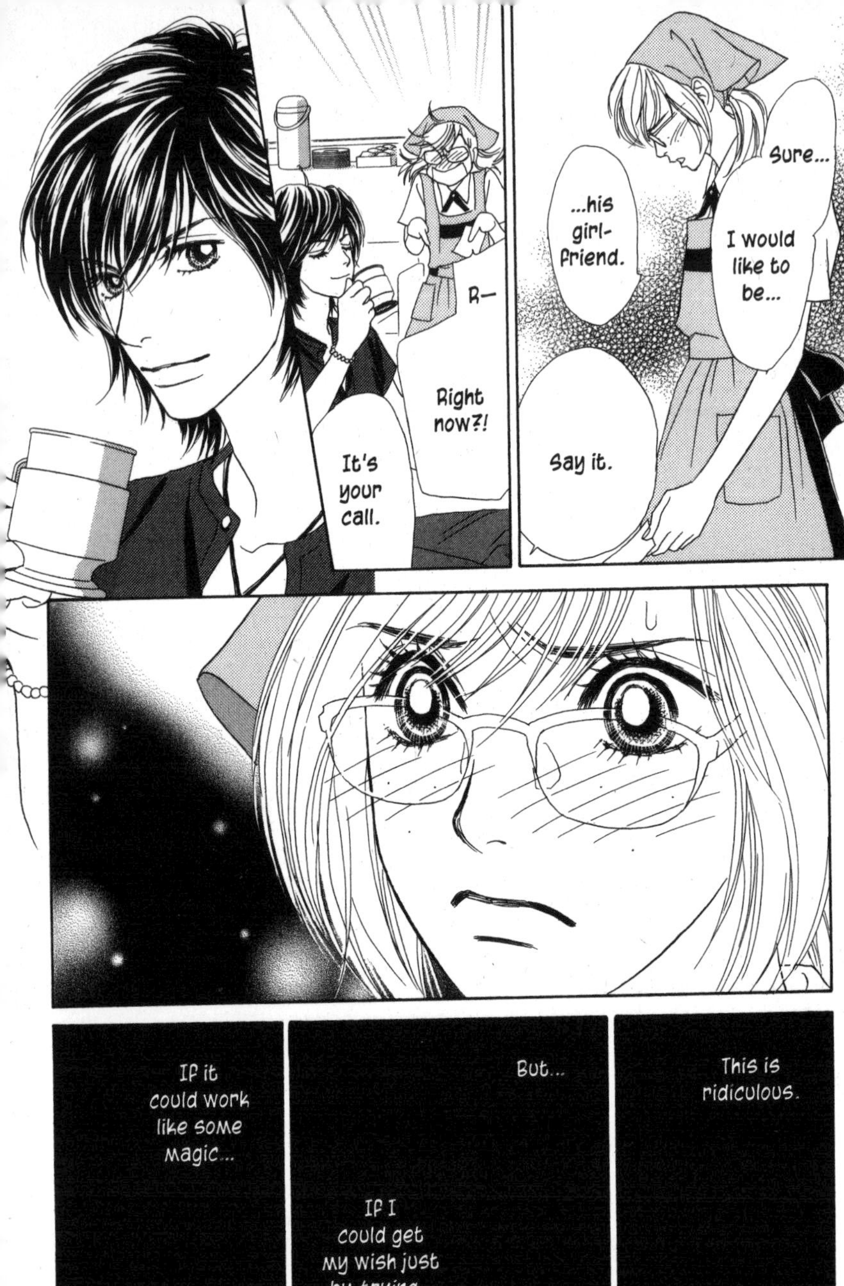
Sure...
I would like to be...
...his girl-friend.
Say it.
R—
Right now?!
It's your call.
This is ridiculous.
But...
If I could get my wish just by trying...
If it could work like some magic...

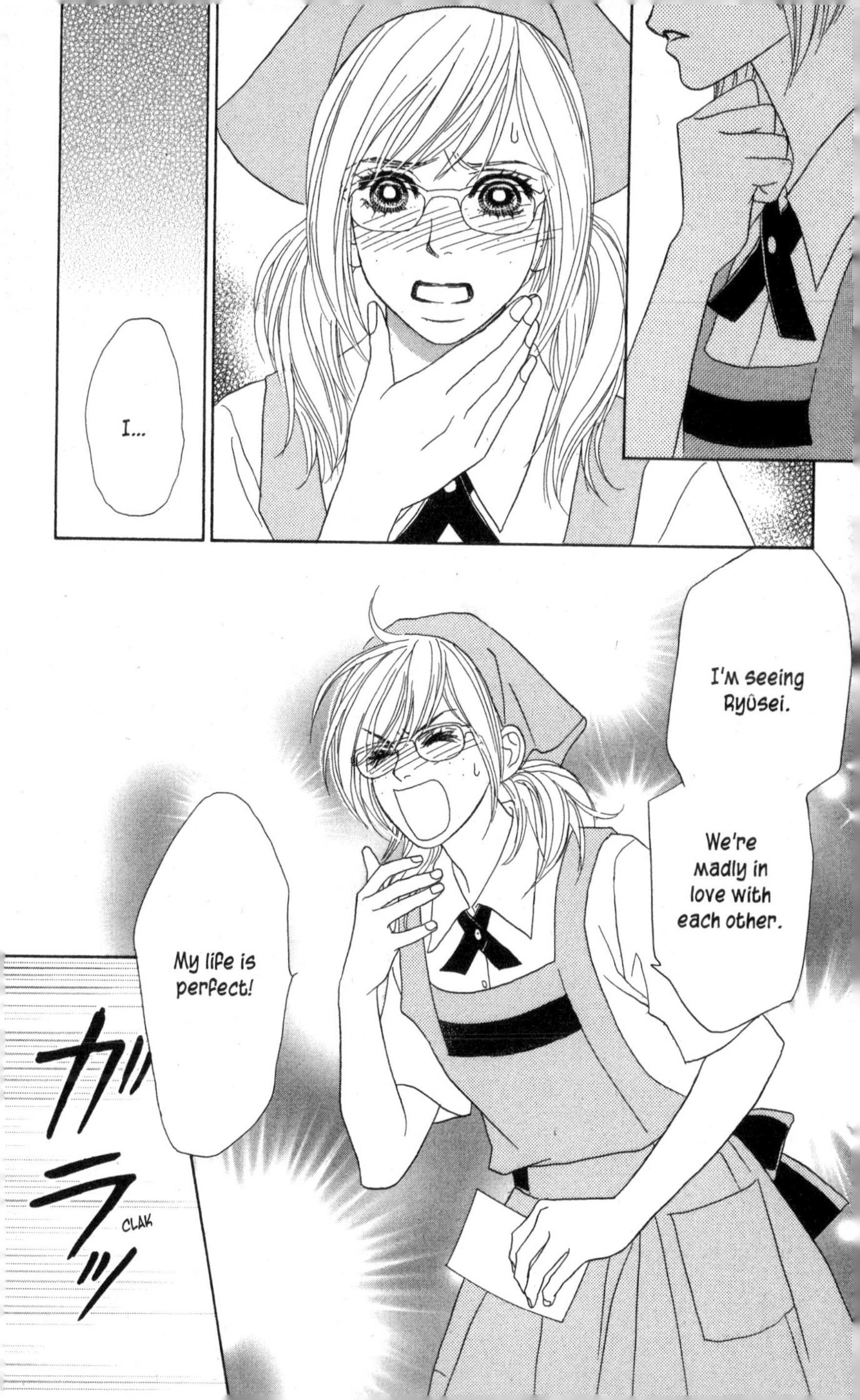
I...
I'm seeing Ryûsei.
We're madly in love with each other.
My life is perfect!
ガラッ
CLAK

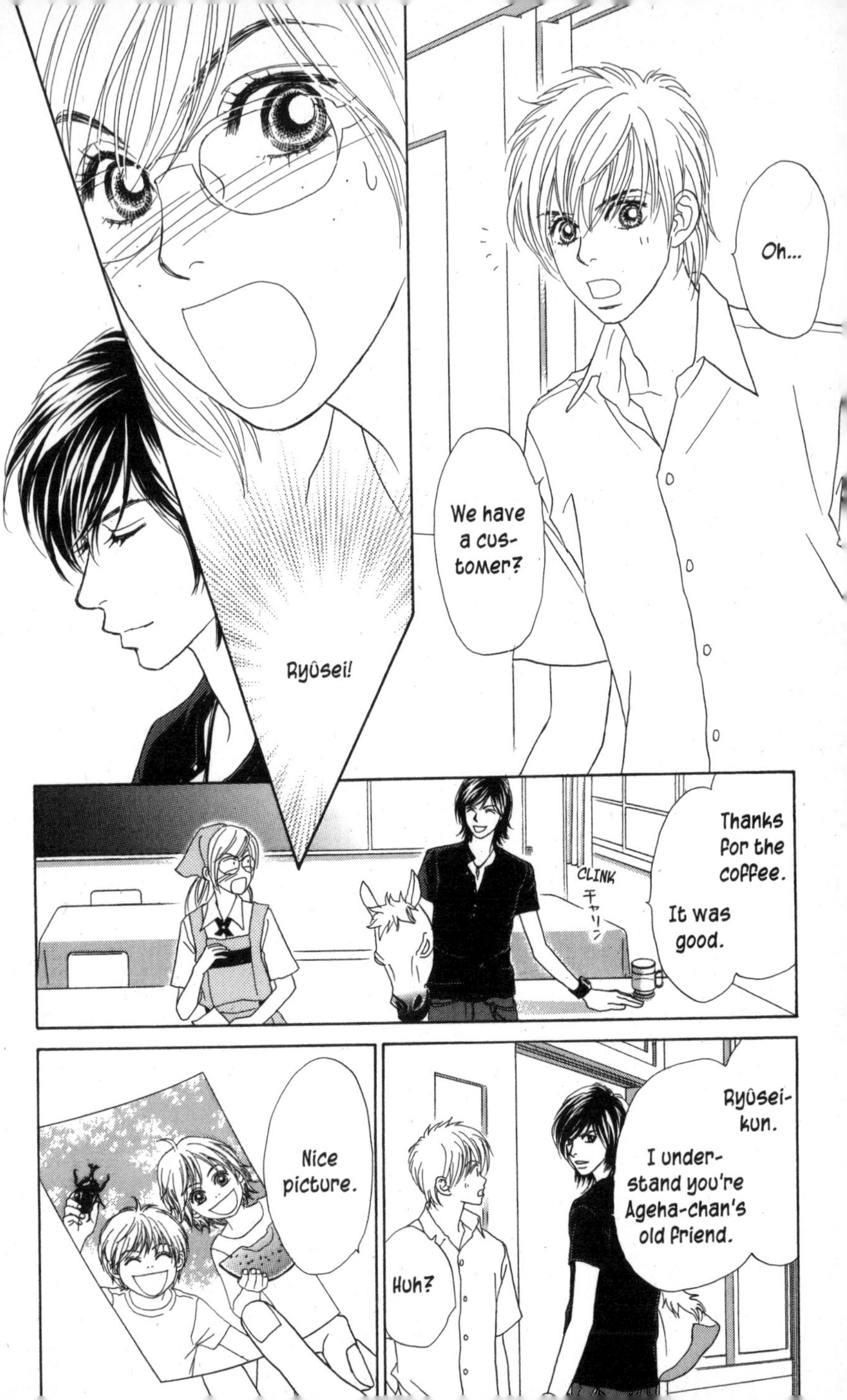
Oh...
We have a customer?
Ryûsei!
Thanks for the coffee.
It was good.
CLINK
チャリン
Ryûsei-kun.
I understand you're Ageha-chan's old friend.
Huh?
Nice picture.

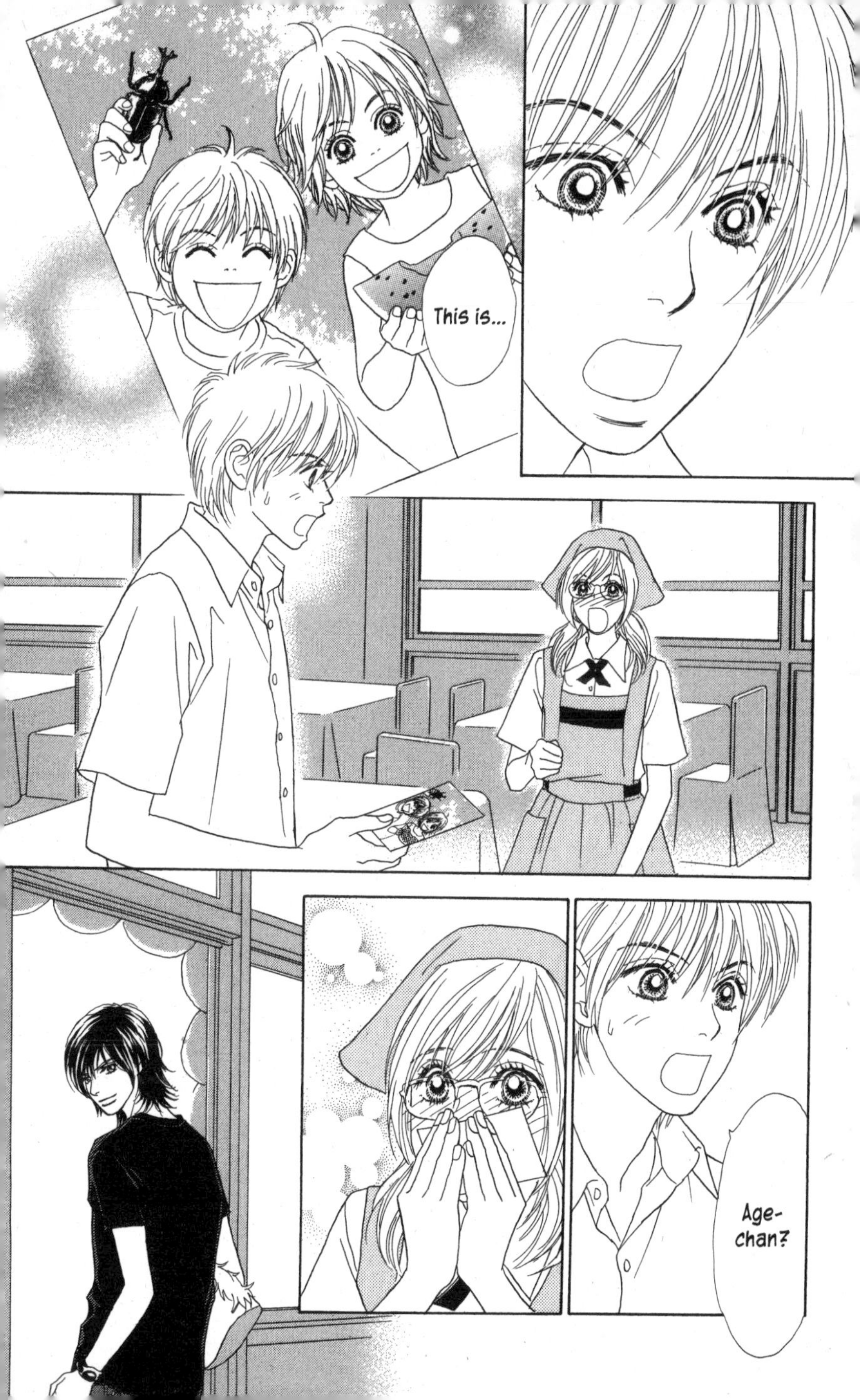
This is...
Age-chan?

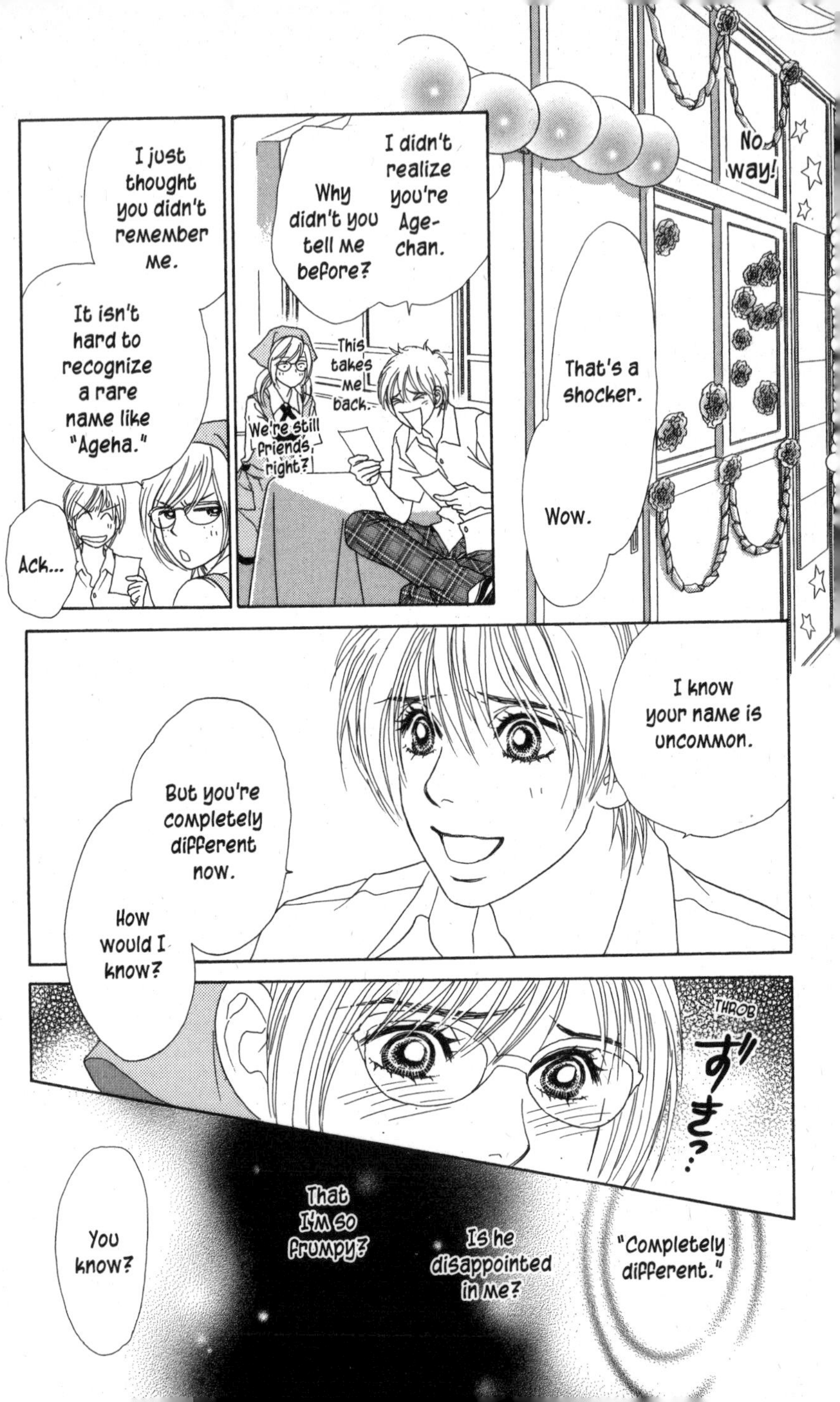
No way!
That's a shocker.
Wow.
I didn't realize you're Age-chan.
Why didn't you tell me before?
This takes me back.
We're still friends, right?
I just thought you didn't remember me.
It isn't hard to recognize a rare name like "Ageha."
Ack...
I know your name is uncommon.
But you're completely different now.
How would I know?
THROB
ずき…
"Completely different."
Is he disappointed in me?
That I'm so frumpy?
You know?

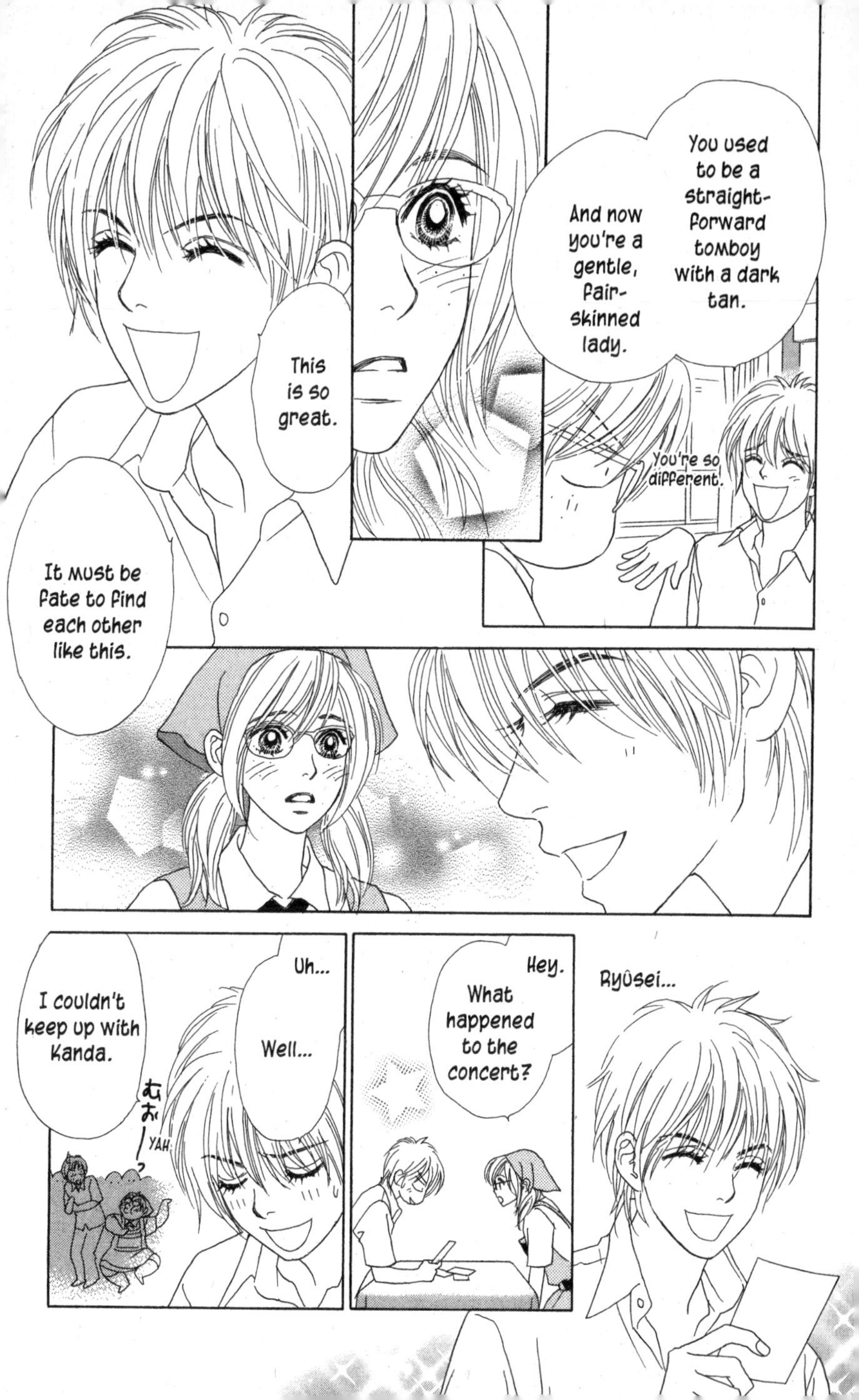
You used to be a straight-forward tomboy with a dark tan.
And now you're a gentle, fair-skinned lady.
You're so different.
This is so great.
It must be fate to find each other like this.
Ryûsei...
Hey.
What happened to the concert?
Uh...
Well...
I couldn't keep up with Kanda.
むお!
YAH

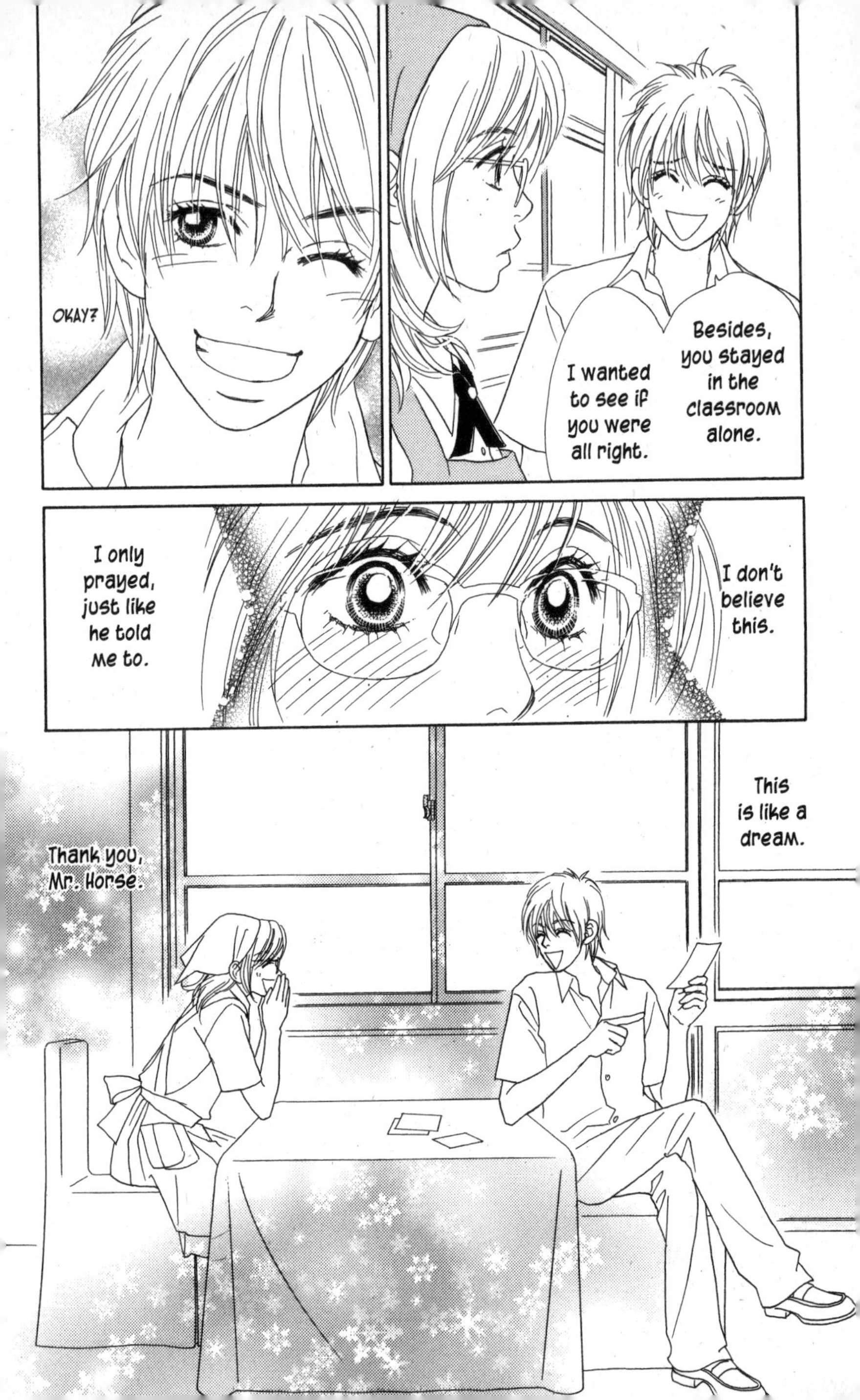
Besides, you stayed in the classroom alone.
I wanted to see if you were all right.
OKAY?
I don't believe this.
I only prayed, just like he told me to.
This is like a dream.
Thank you, Mr. Horse.

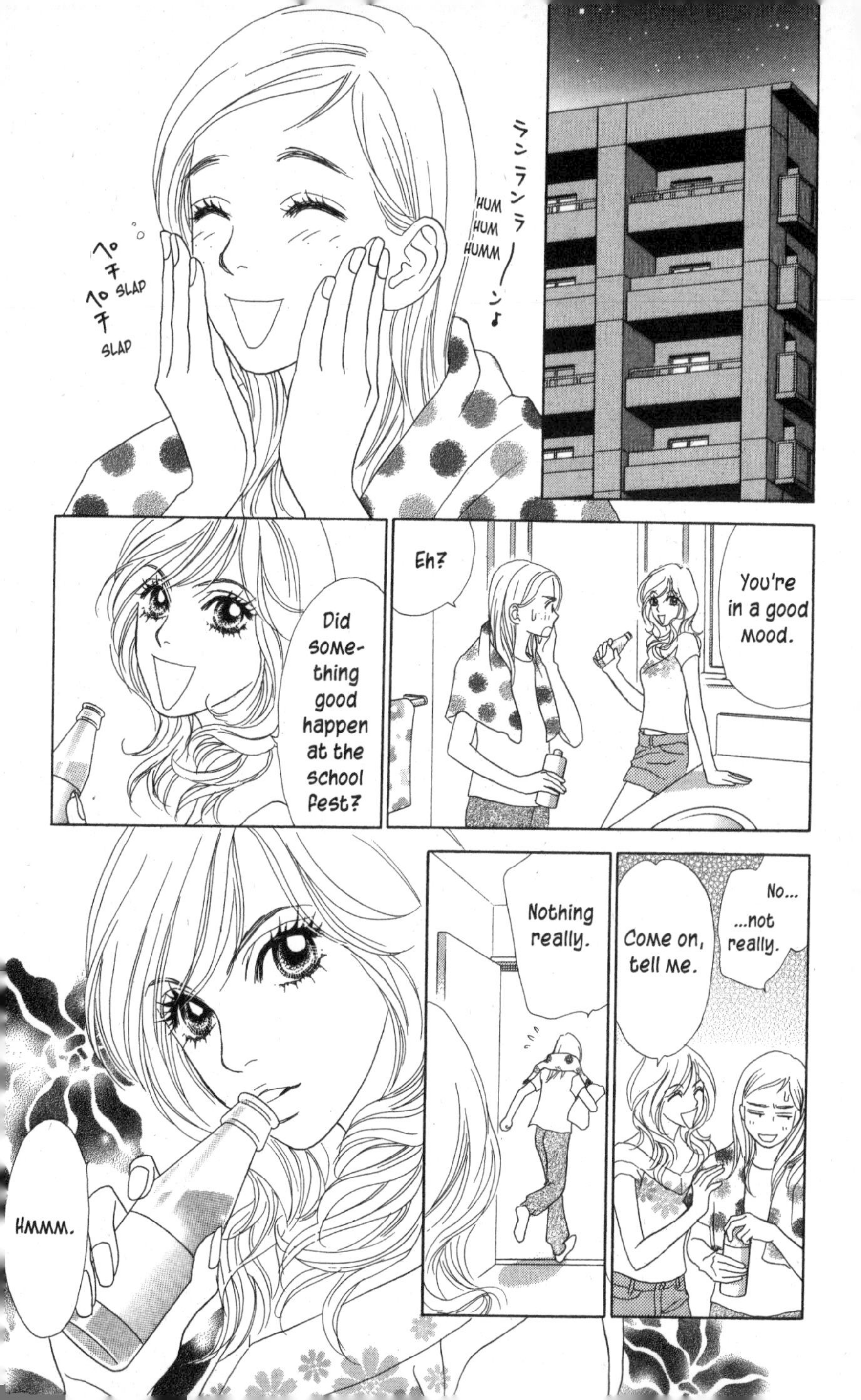
ランランラーン♪
HUM HUM HUMM
ペチ ペチ
SLAP SLAP
You're in a good mood.
Eh?
Did some-thing good happen at the school fest?
No... ...not really.
Come on, tell me.
Nothing really.
HMMM.

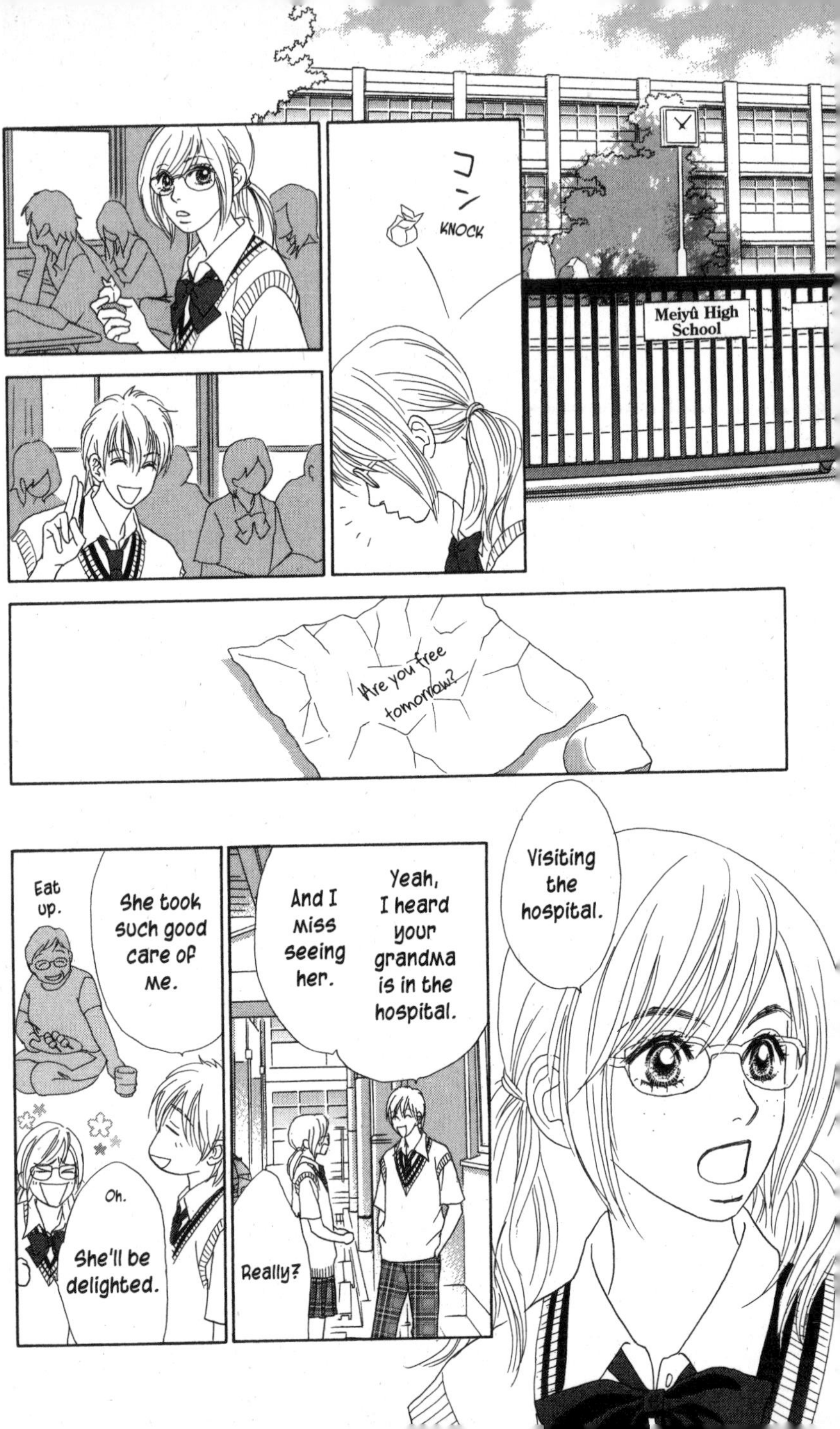

Meiyû High School
コン
KNOCK
Are you free tomorrow?
Visiting the hospital.
Yeah, I heard your grandma is in the hospital.
And I miss seeing her.
Really?
She took such good care of me.
Eat up.
Oh.
She'll be delighted.

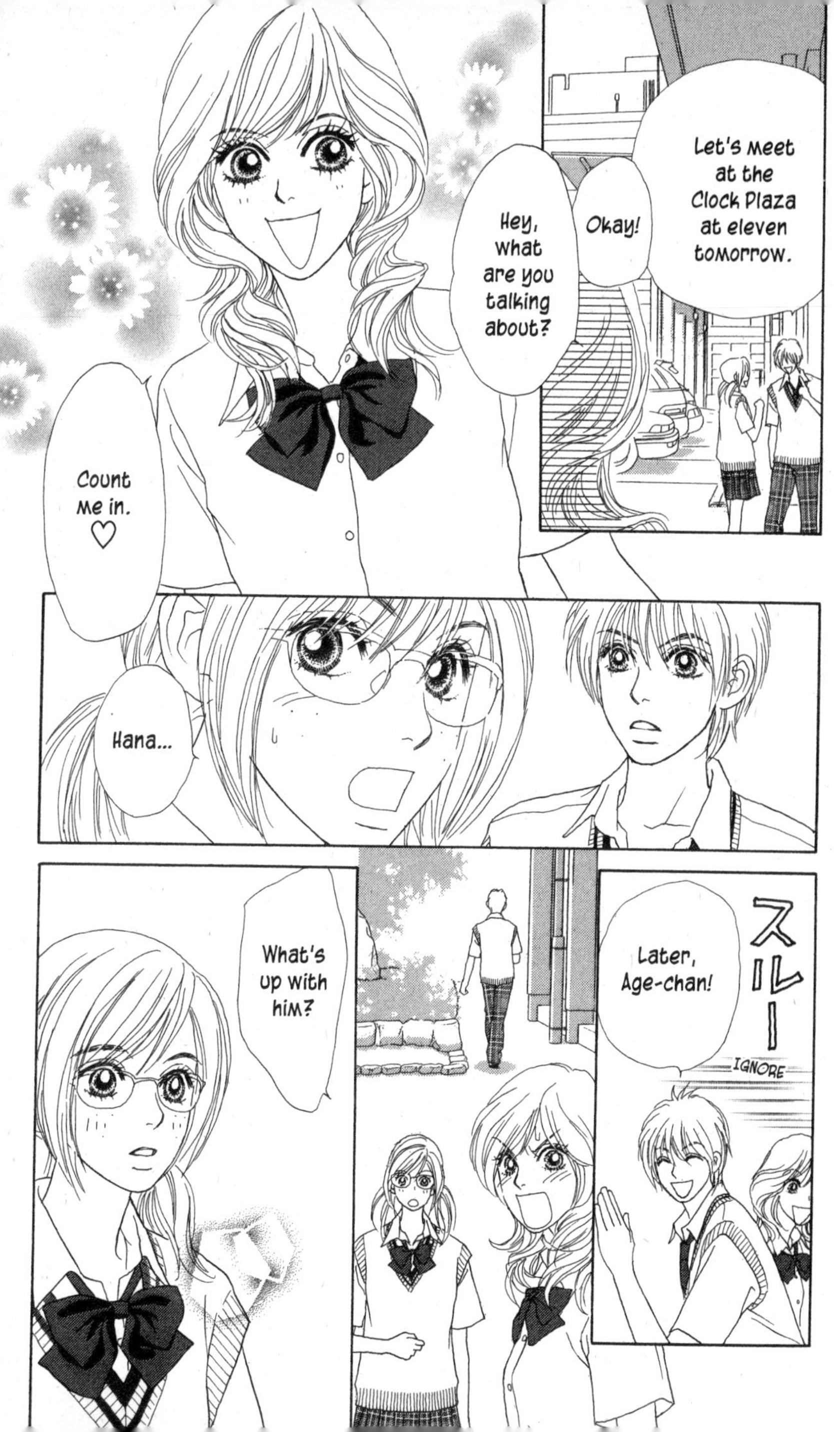
Let's meet at the Clock Plaza at eleven tomorrow.
Okay!
Hey, what are you talking about?
Count me in. ♡
Hana...
Later, Age-chan!
スルー
IGNORE
What's up with him?

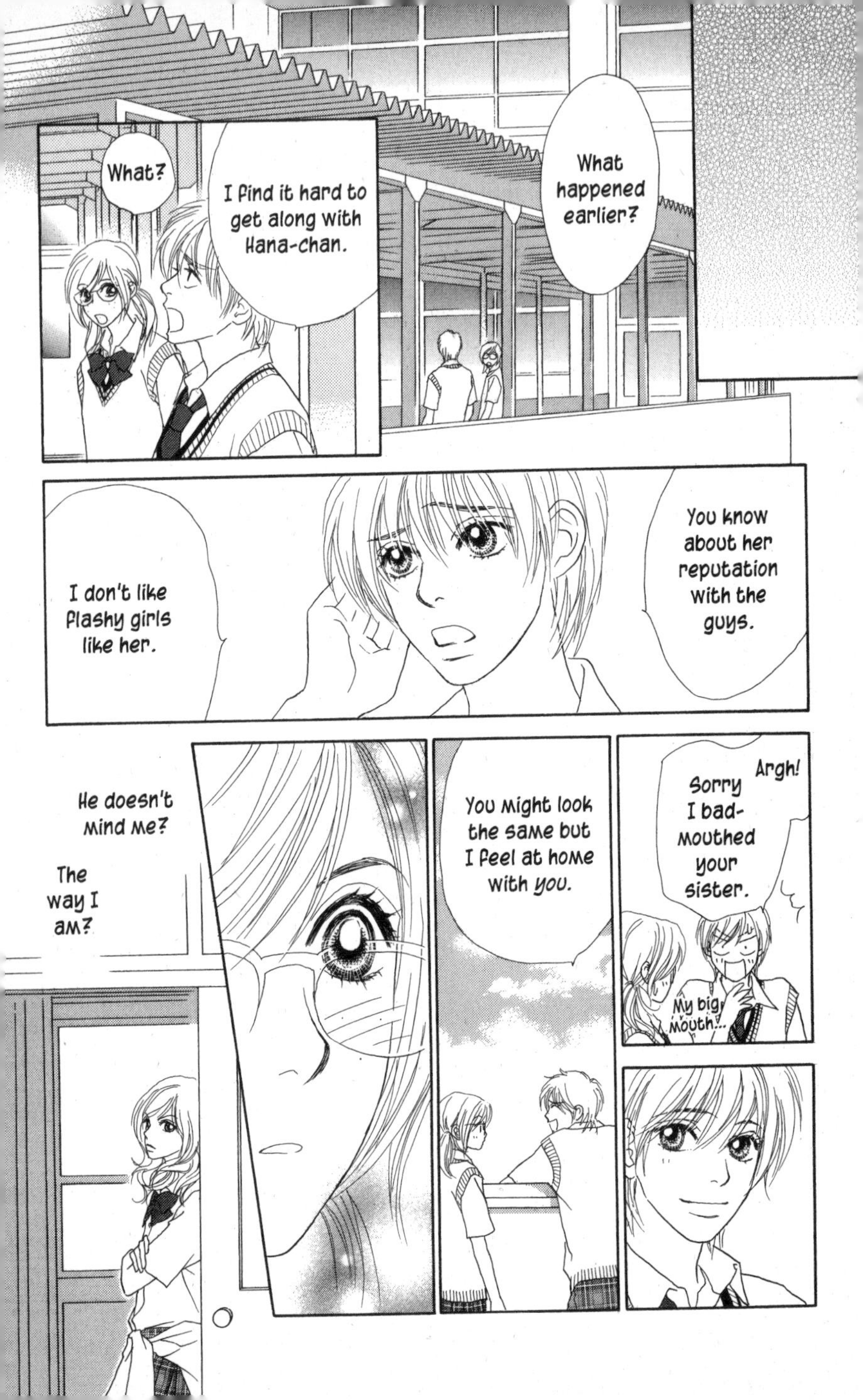
What happened earlier?
I find it hard to get along with Hana-chan.
What?
You know about her reputation with the guys.
I don't like flashy girls like her.
Argh!
Sorry I bad-mouthed your sister.
My big mouth...
You might look the same but I feel at home with *you*.
He doesn't mind me?
The way I am?

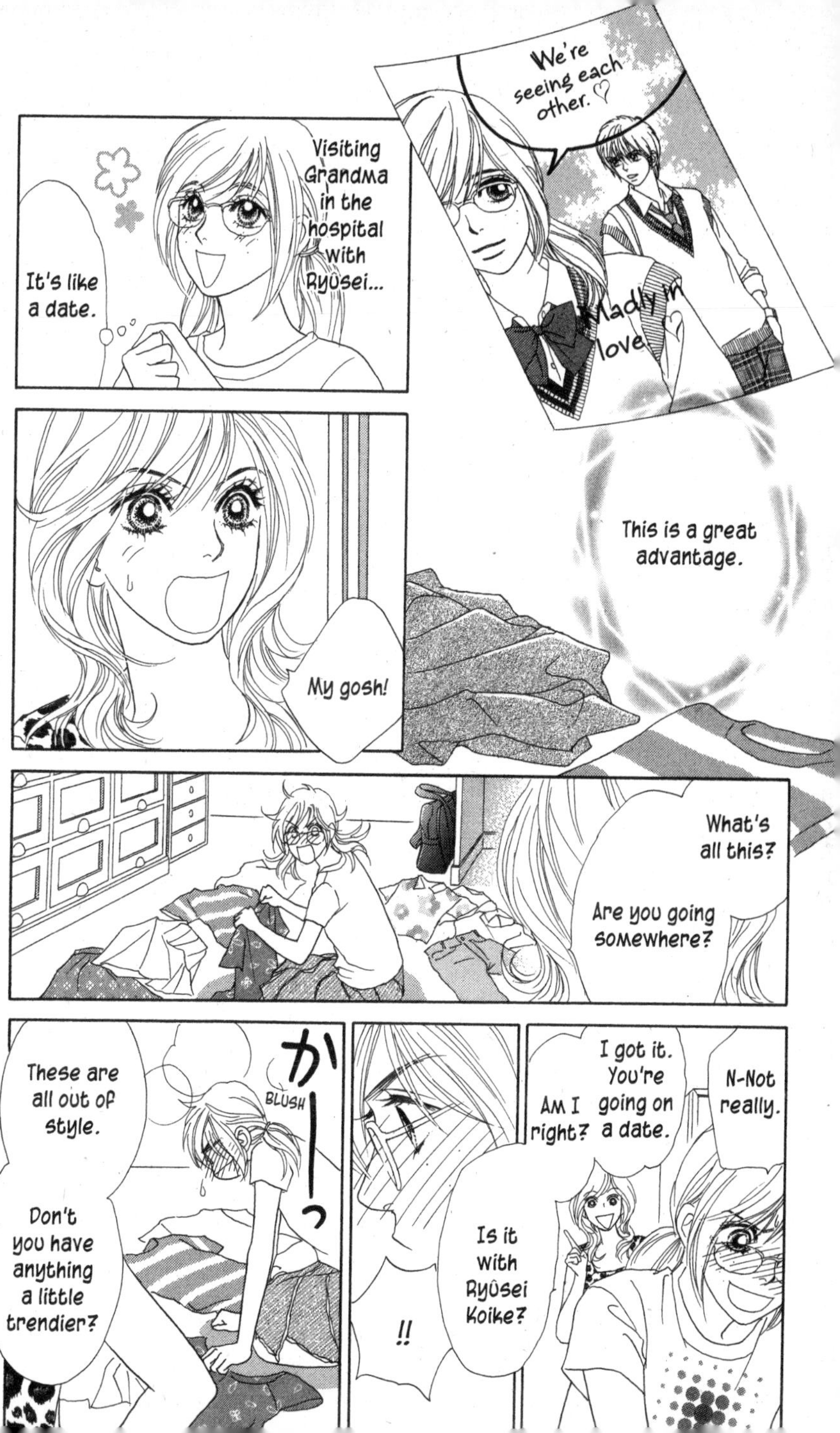
We're seeing each other. ♡
Madly in love ♡
Visiting Grandma in the hospital with Ryûsei...
It's like a date.
This is a great advantage.
My gosh!
What's all this?
Are you going somewhere?
N-Not really.
I got it. You're going on a date.
AM I right?
Is it with Ryûsei Koike?
!!
かーっ
BLUSH
These are all out of style.
Don't you have anything a little trendier?

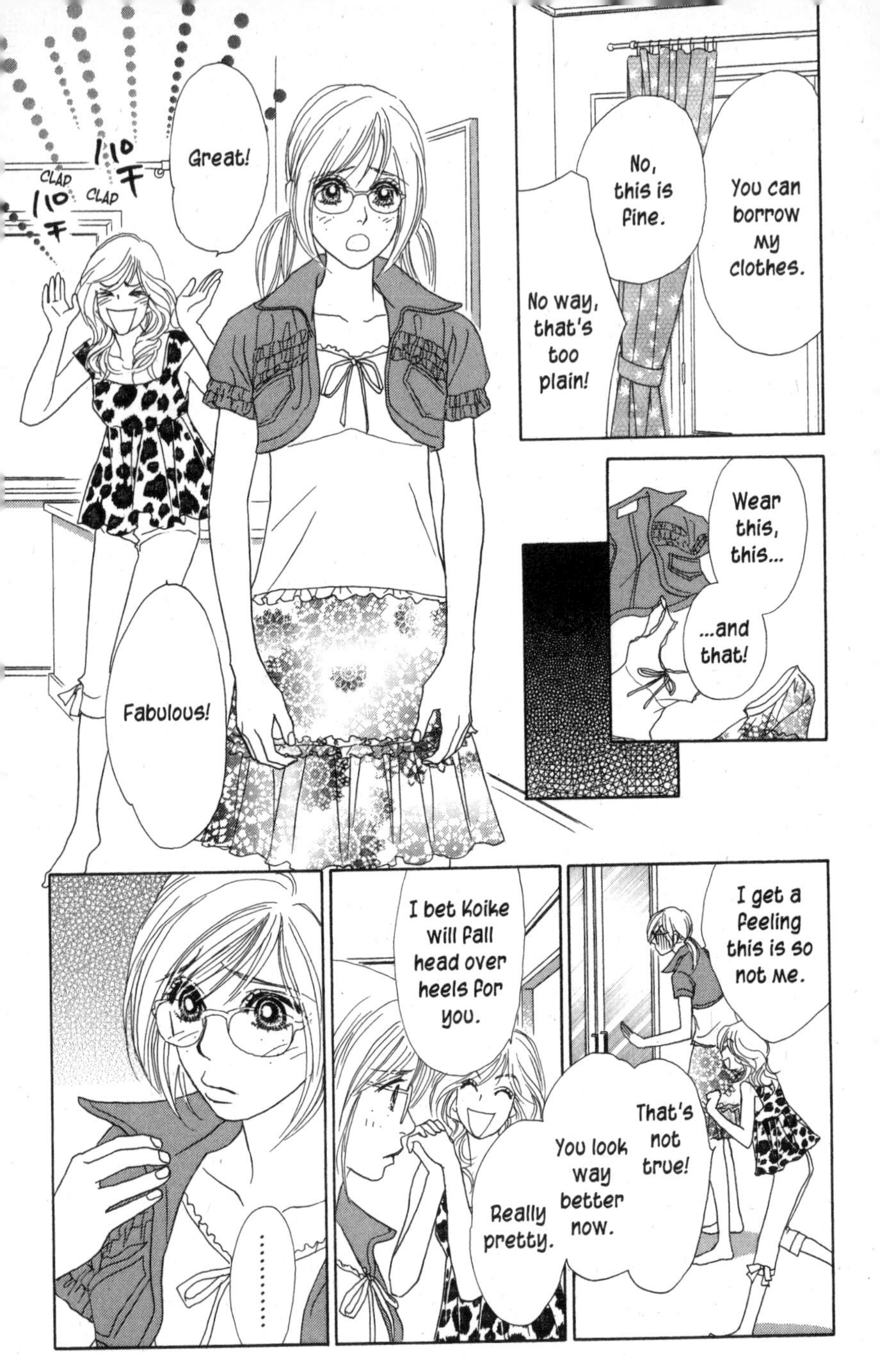
You can borrow my clothes.
No, this is fine.
No way, that's too plain!
Wear this, this...
...and that!
Great!
CLAP
CLAP
Fabulous!
I get a feeling this is so not me.
That's not true!
You look way better now.
I bet Koike will fall head over heels for you.
Really pretty.
....

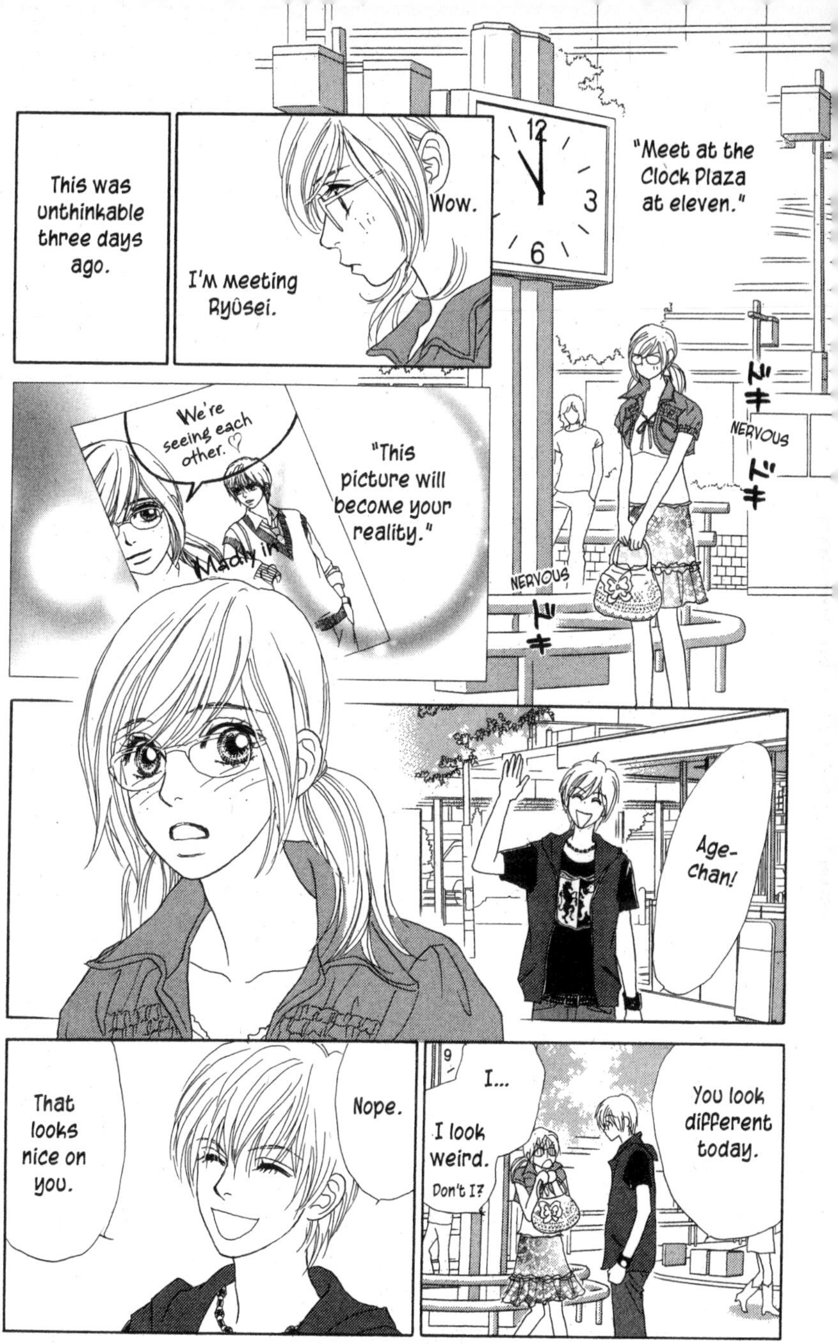
"Meet at the Clock Plaza at eleven."
ドキ
NERVOUS
ドキ
NERVOUS
ドキ
Wow.
I'm meeting Ryûsei.
This was unthinkable three days ago.
"This picture will become your reality."
We're seeing each other. ♡
Age-chan!
You look different today.
I...
I look weird.
Don't I?
Nope.
That looks nice on you.

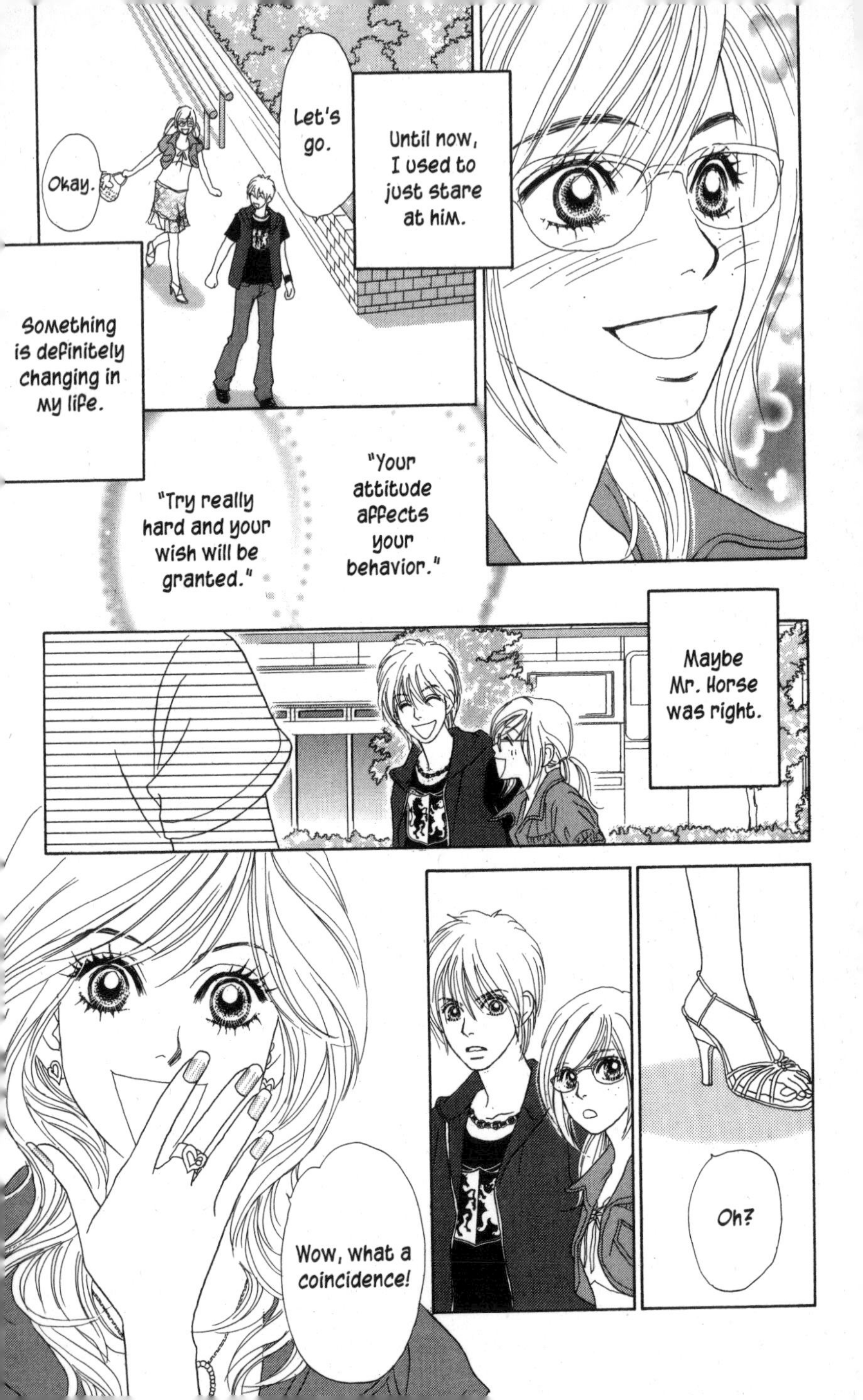
Until now, I used to just stare at him.
Let's go.
Okay.
Something is definitely changing in my life.
"Your attitude affects your behavior."
"Try really hard and your wish will be granted."
Maybe Mr. Horse was right.
Oh?
Wow, what a coincidence!

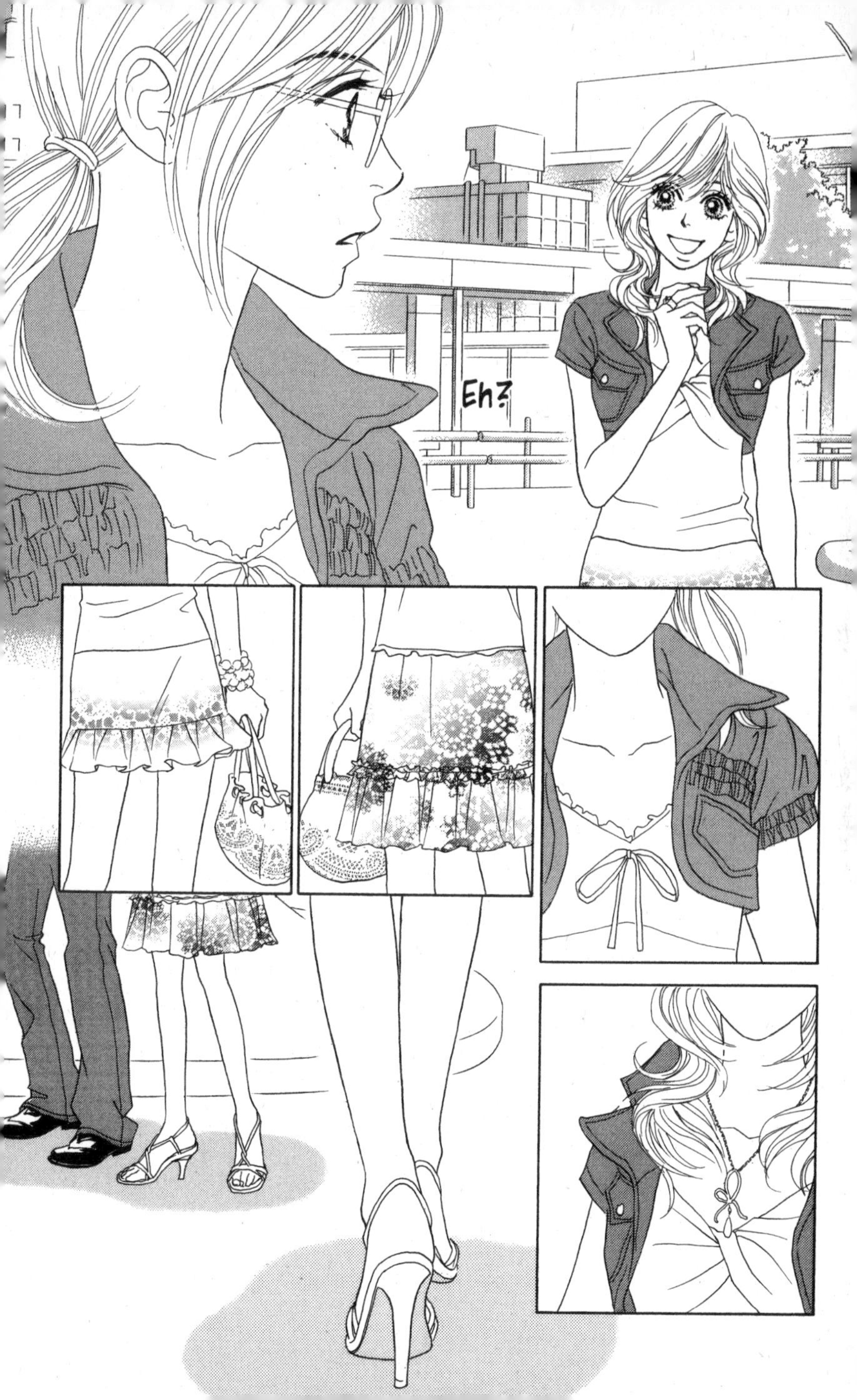
Eh?

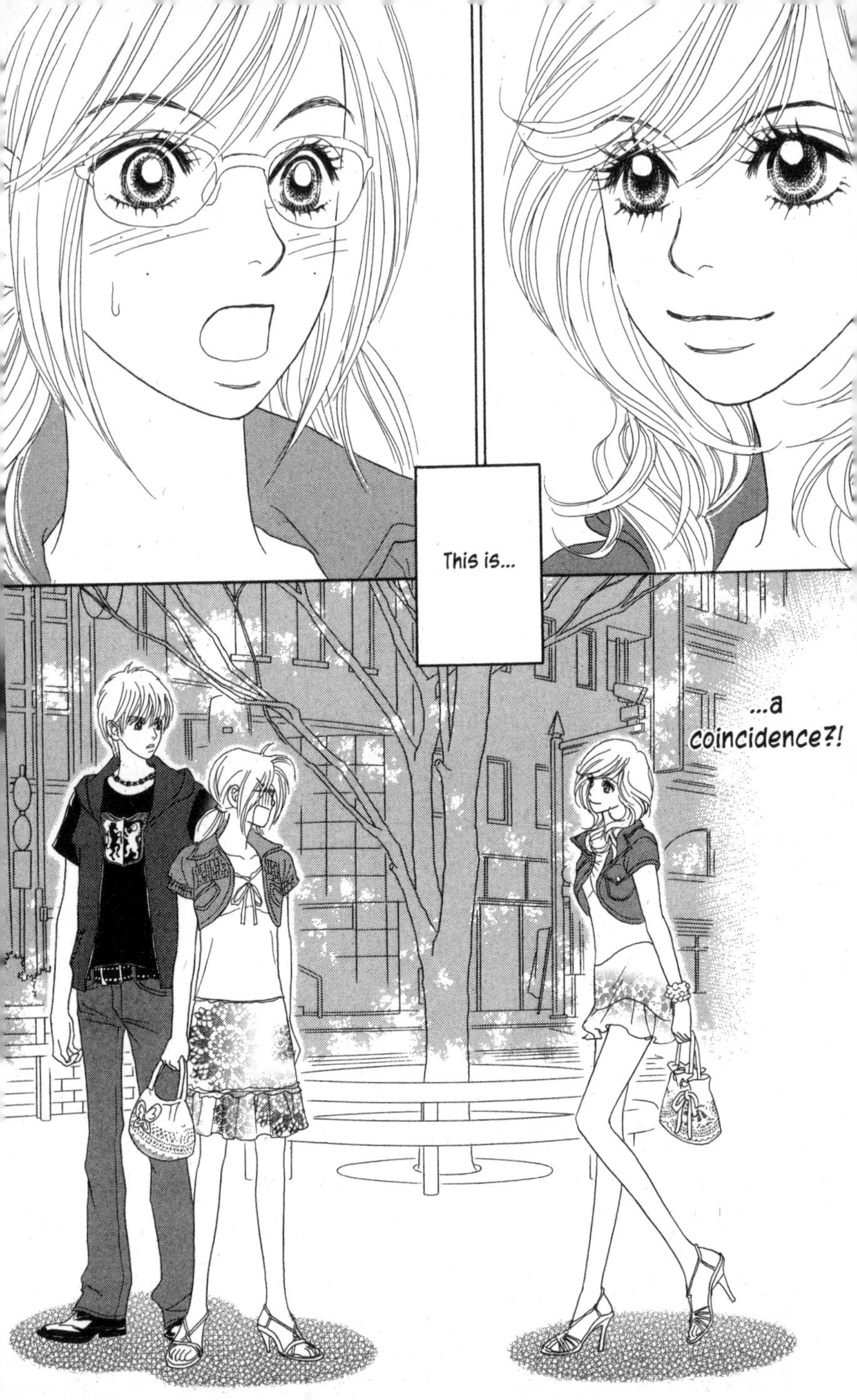

This is...
...a coincidence?!

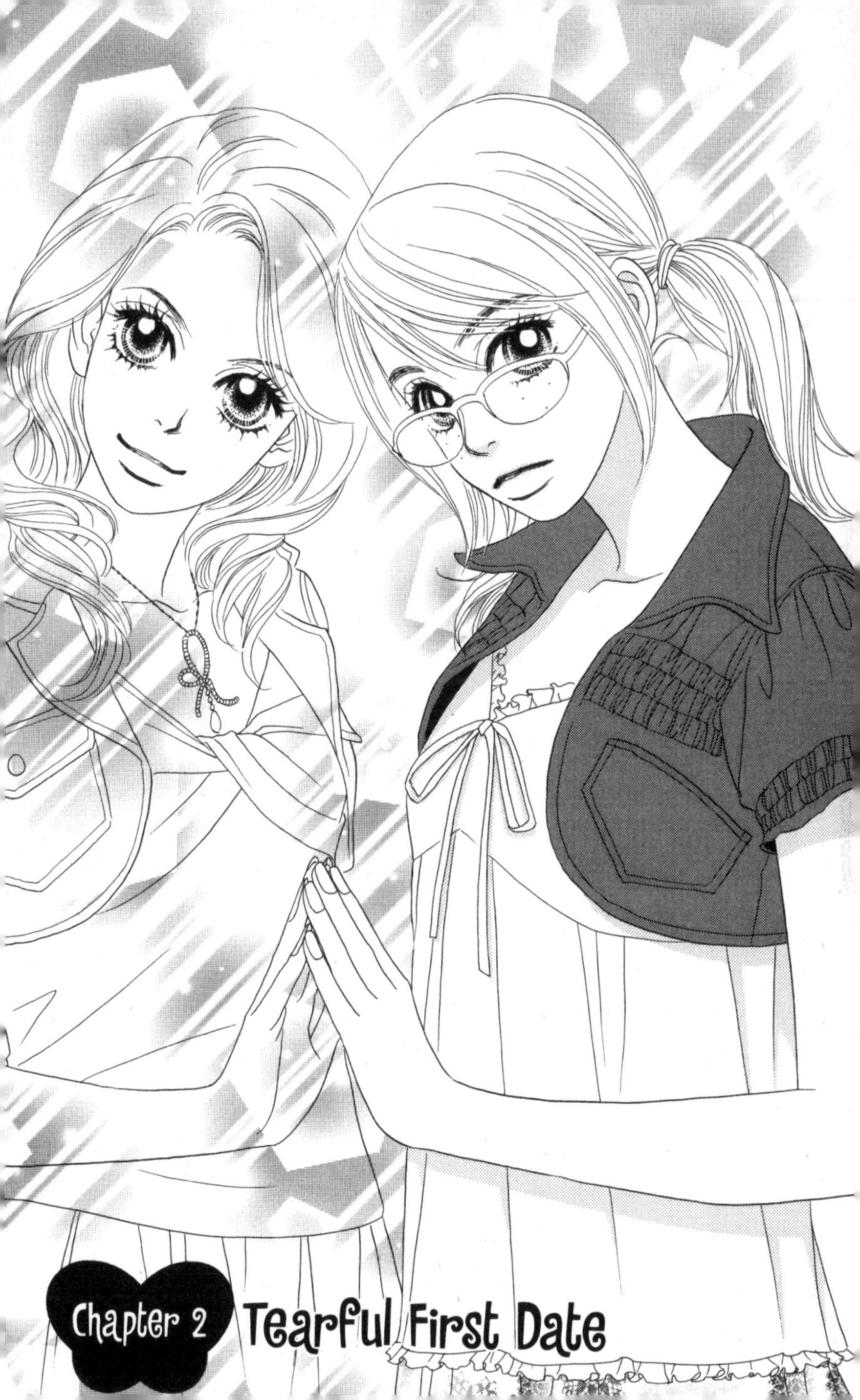
Chapter 2
Tearful First Date

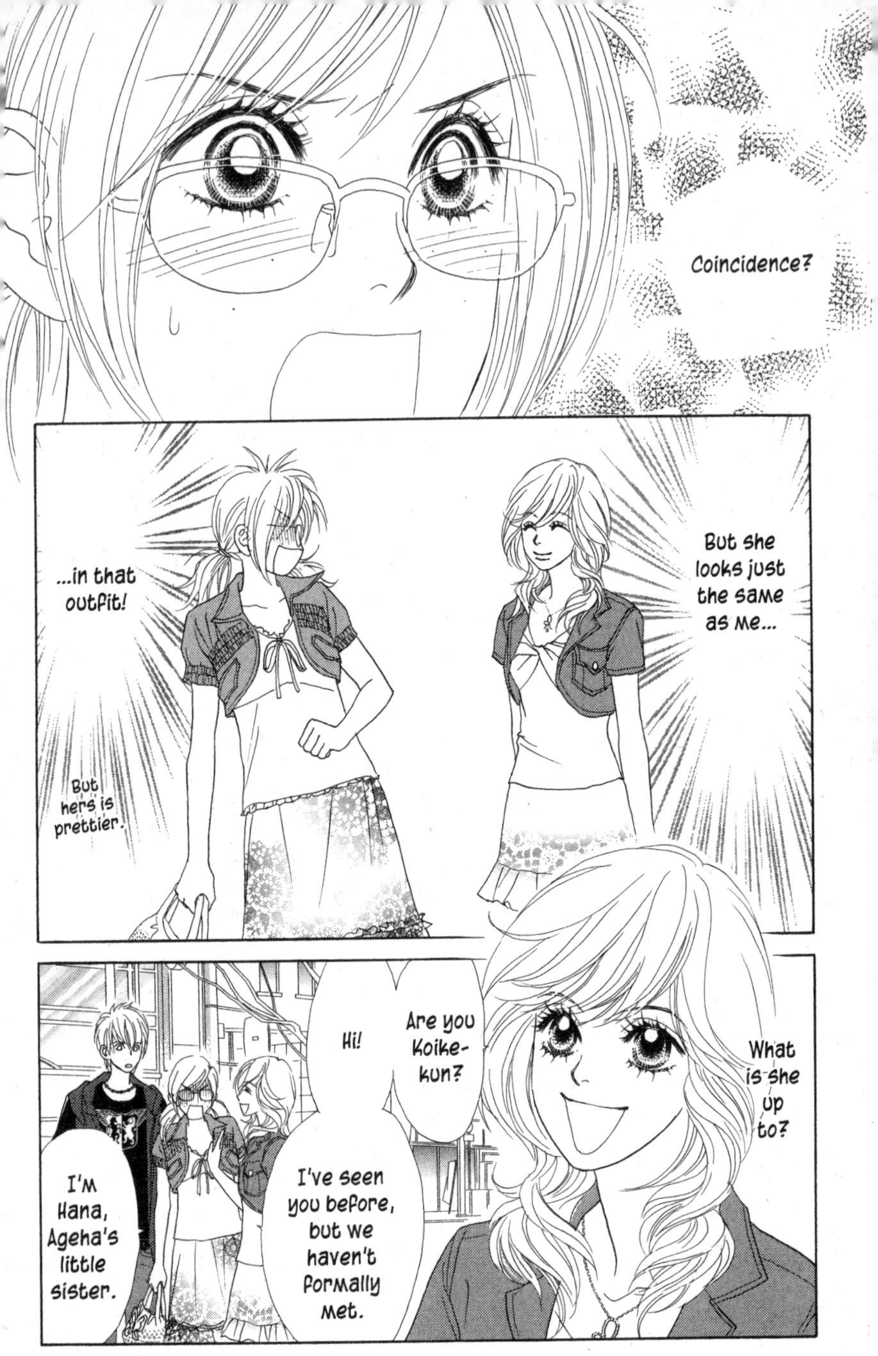
Coincidence?
But she looks just the same as me...
...in that outfit!
But hers is prettier.
What is she up to?
Are you Koike-kun?
Hi!
I've seen you before, but we haven't formally met.
I'm Hana, Ageha's little sister.

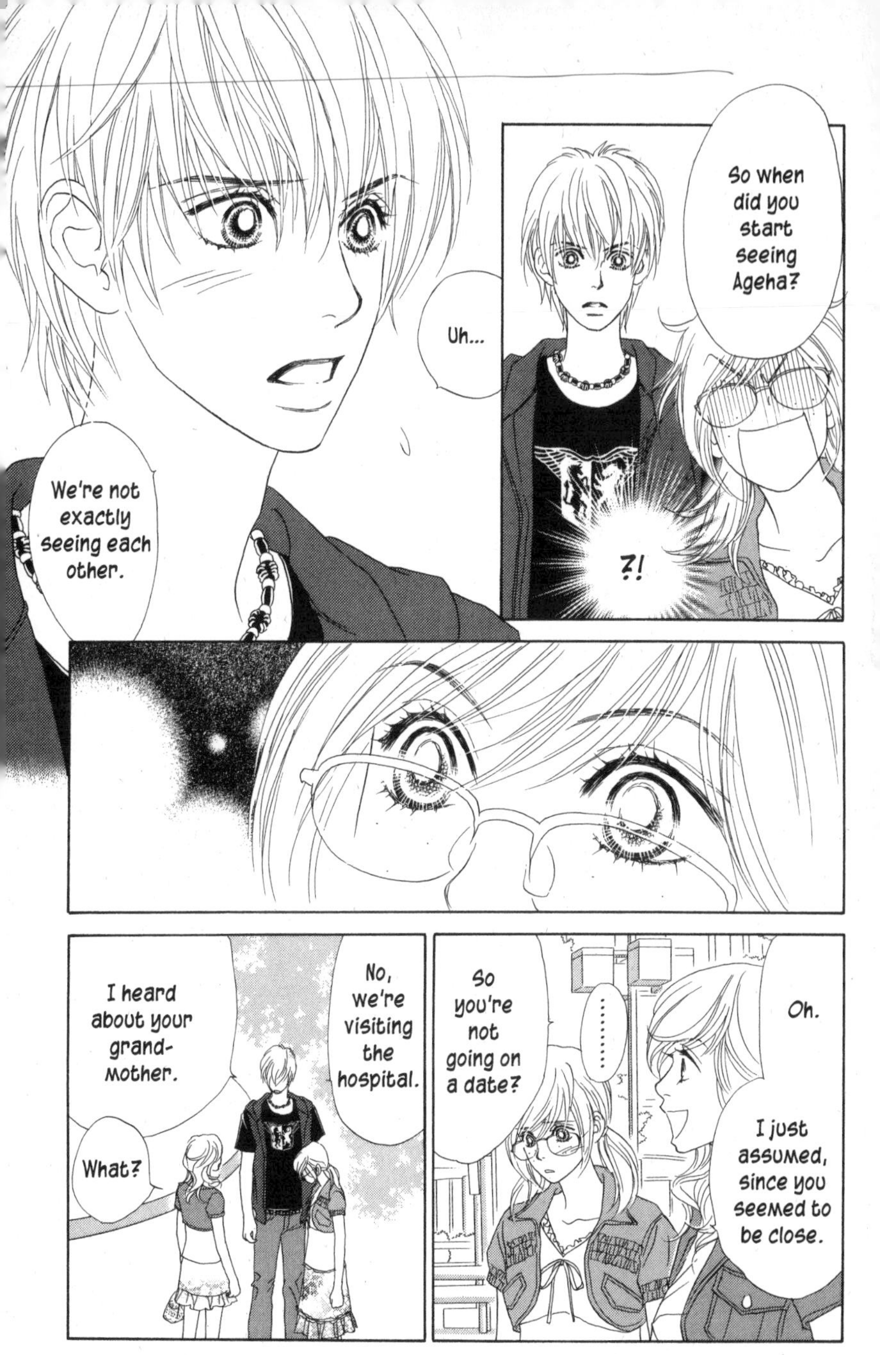
So when did you start seeing Ageha?
?!
Uh...
We're not exactly seeing each other.
Oh.
I just assumed, since you seemed to be close.
So you're not going on a date?
......
No, we're visiting the hospital.
I heard about your grand-mother.
What?

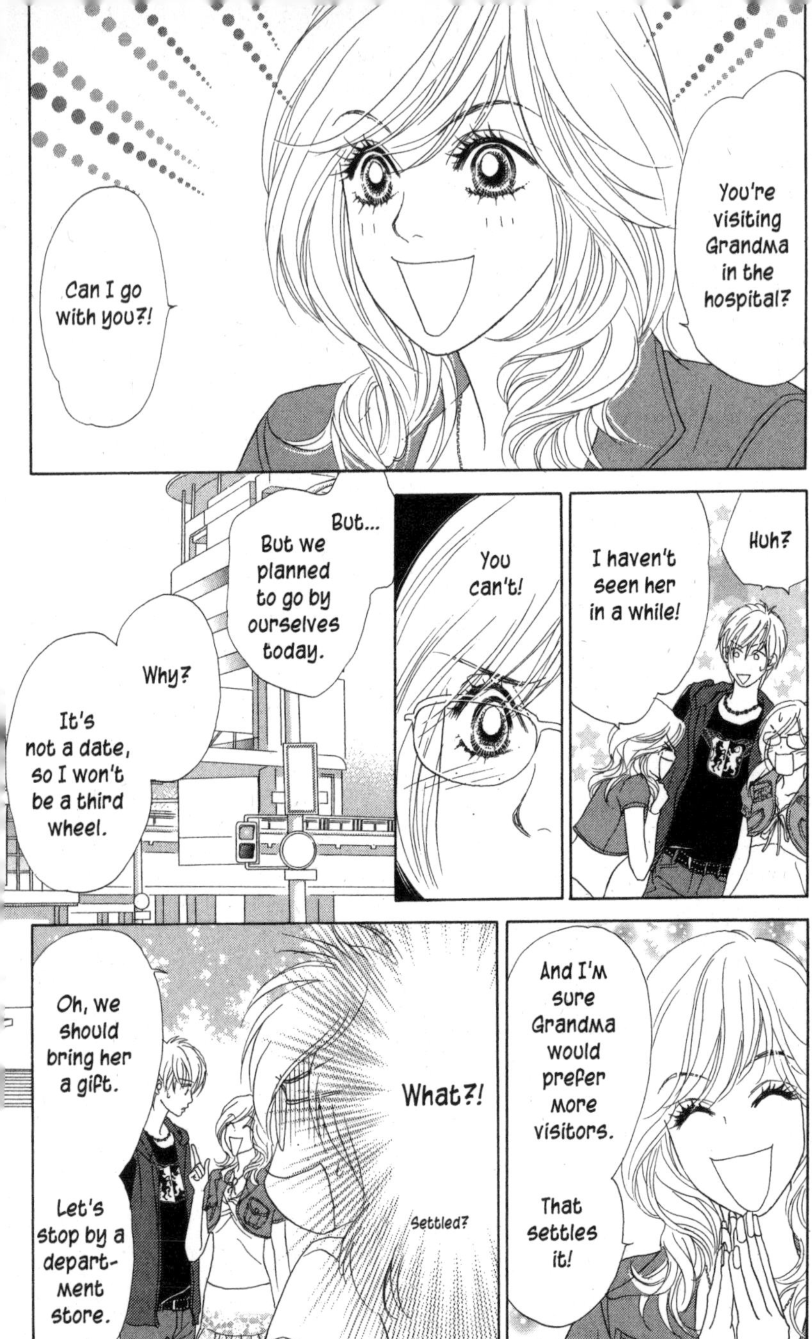
You're visiting Grandma in the hospital?
Can I go with you?!
Huh?
I haven't seen her in a while!
You can't!
But...
But we planned to go by ourselves today.
Why?
It's not a date, so I won't be a third wheel.
And I'm sure Grandma would prefer more visitors.
That settles it!
What?!
Settled?
Oh, we should bring her a gift.
Let's stop by a department store.

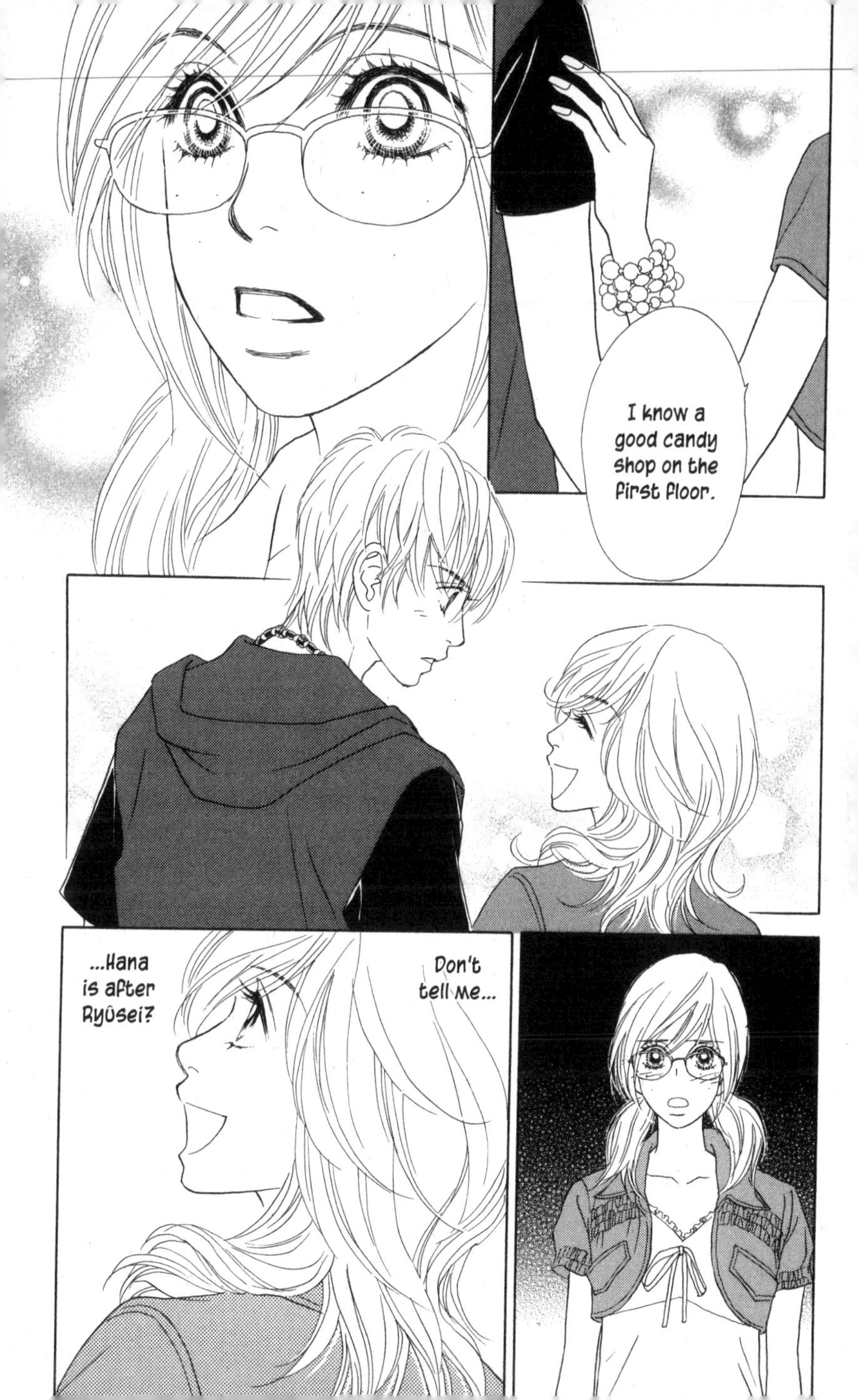
I know a good candy shop on the first floor.
Don't tell me...
...Hana is after Ryûsei?

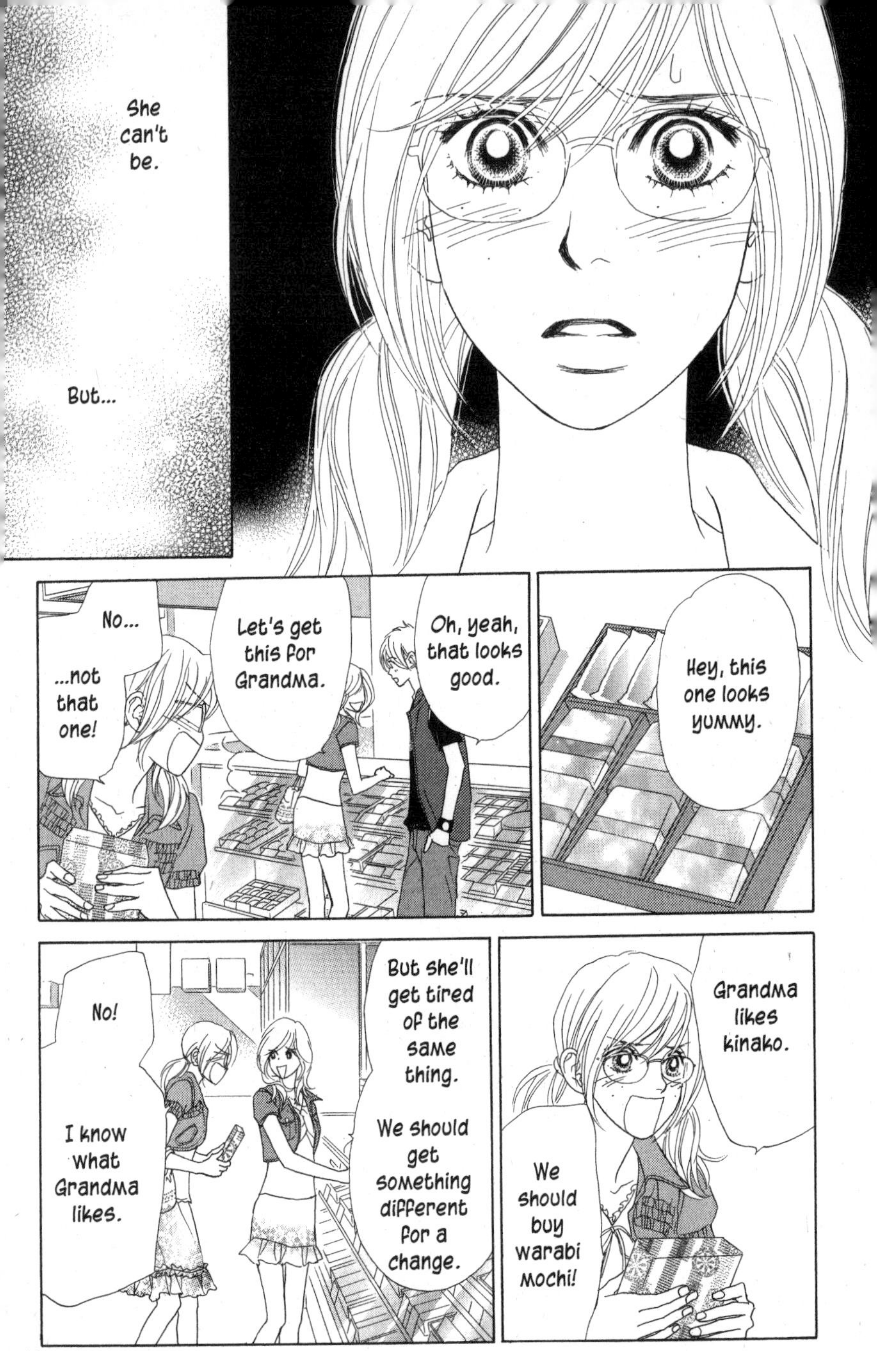
She can't be.
But...
Hey, this one looks yummy.
Oh, yeah, that looks good.
Let's get this for Grandma.
No...
...not that one!
Grandma likes kinako.
We should buy warabi mochi!
But she'll get tired of the same thing.
We should get something different for a change.
No!
I know what Grandma likes.

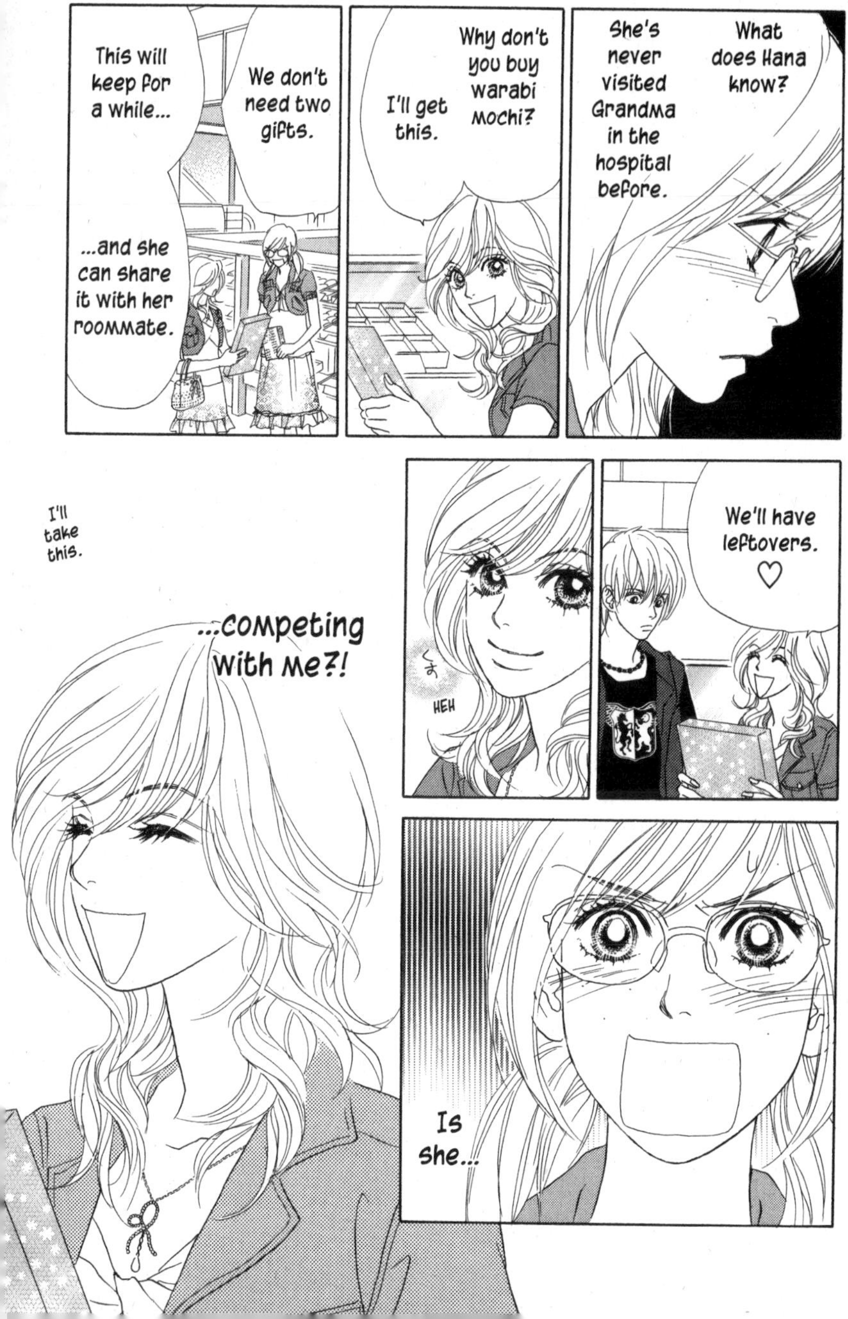
What does Hana know?
She's never visited Grandma in the hospital before.
Why don't you buy warabi mochi?
I'll get this.
We don't need two gifts.
This will keep for a while...
...and she can share it with her roommate.
We'll have leftovers. ♡
くす
HEH
Is she...
...competing with me?!
I'll take this.

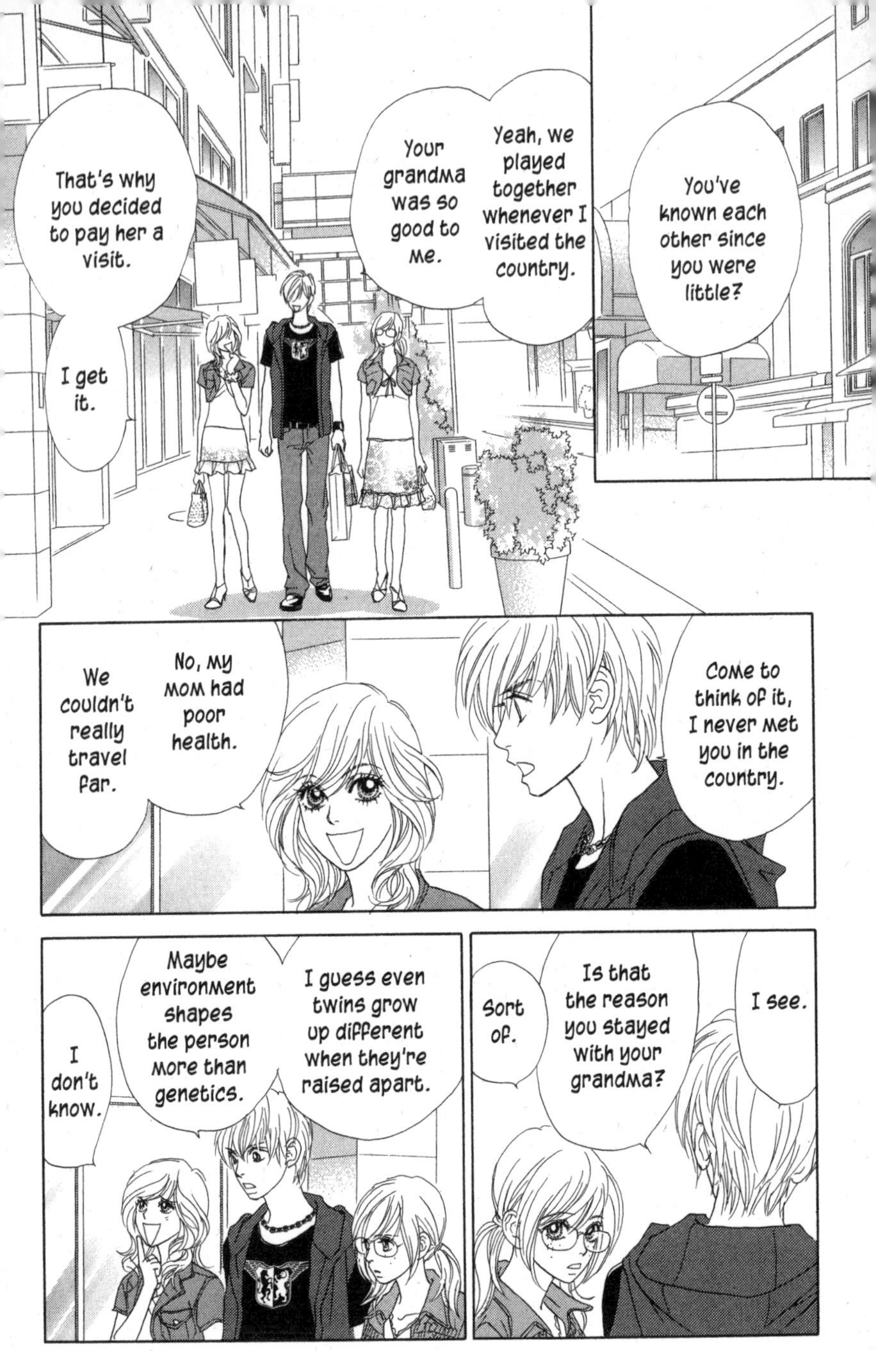
You've known each other since you were little?
Yeah, we played together whenever I visited the country.
Your grandma was so good to me.
That's why you decided to pay her a visit.
I get it.
Come to think of it, I never met you in the country.
No, my mom had poor health.
We couldn't really travel far.
I see.
Is that the reason you stayed with your grandma?
Sort of.
I guess even twins grow up different when they're raised apart.
Maybe environment shapes the person more than genetics.
I don't know.

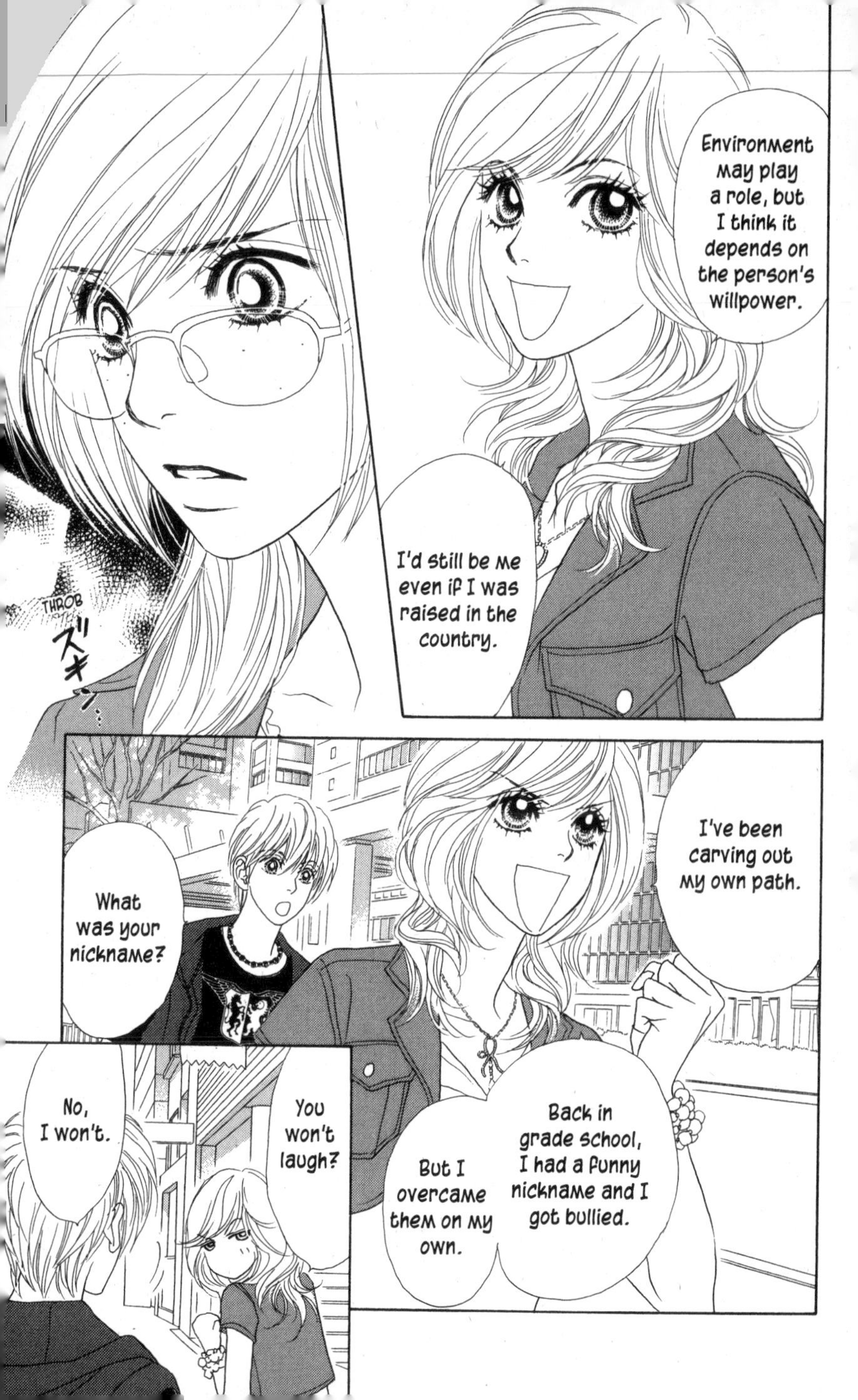
Environment may play a role, but I think it depends on the person's willpower.
I'd still be me even if I was raised in the country.
THROB
ズキ
I've been carving out my own path.
Back in grade school, I had a funny nickname and I got bullied.
But I overcame them on my own.
What was your nickname?
You won't laugh?
No, I won't.

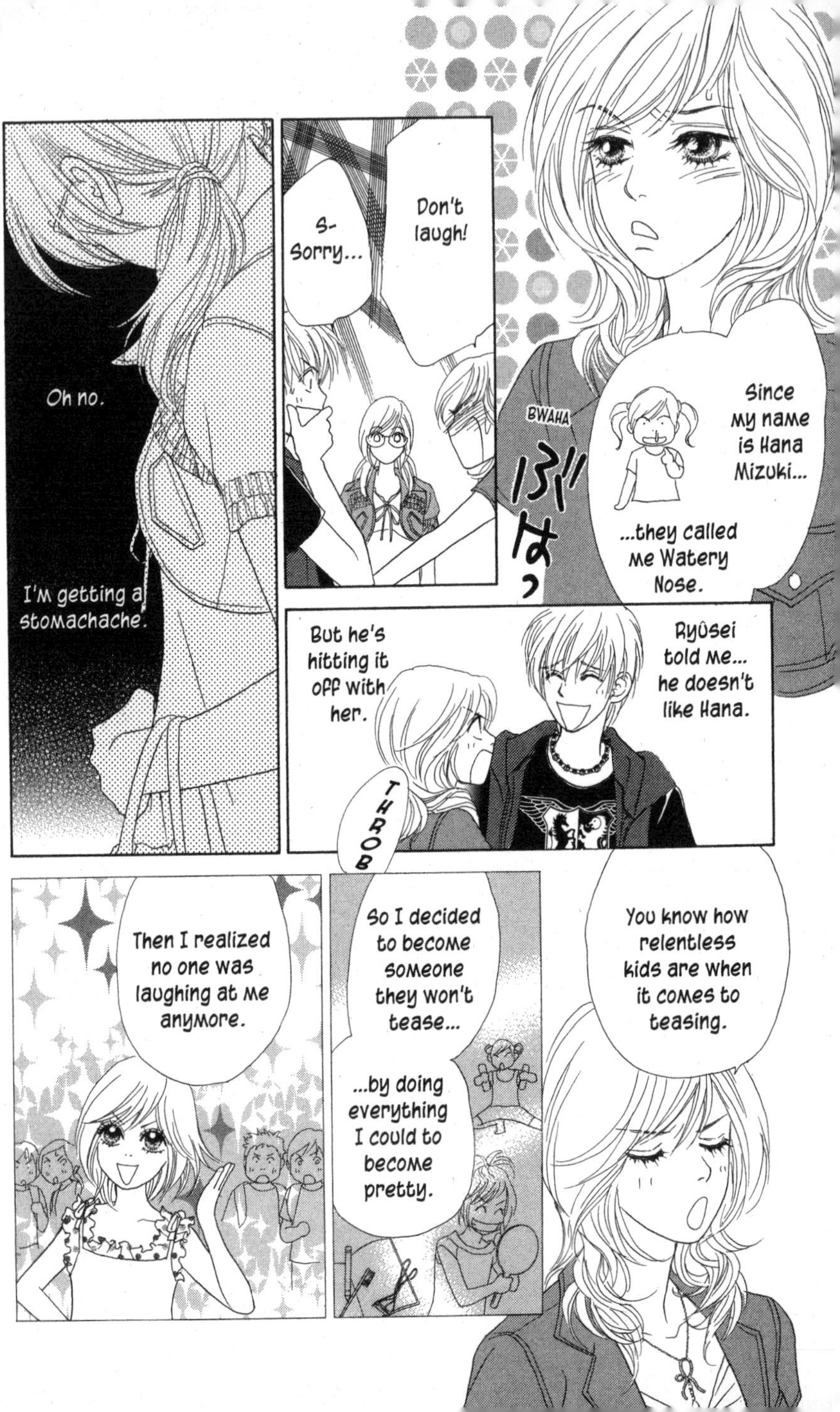
Since my name is Hana Mizuki...
BWAHA
ぶはっ
...they called me Watery Nose.
Don't laugh!
S- Sorry...
Ryûsei told me... he doesn't like Hana.
But he's hitting it off with her.
THROB
Oh no.
I'm getting a stomachache.
You know how relentless kids are when it comes to teasing.
So I decided to become someone they won't tease...
...by doing everything I could to become pretty.
Then I realized no one was laughing at me anymore.

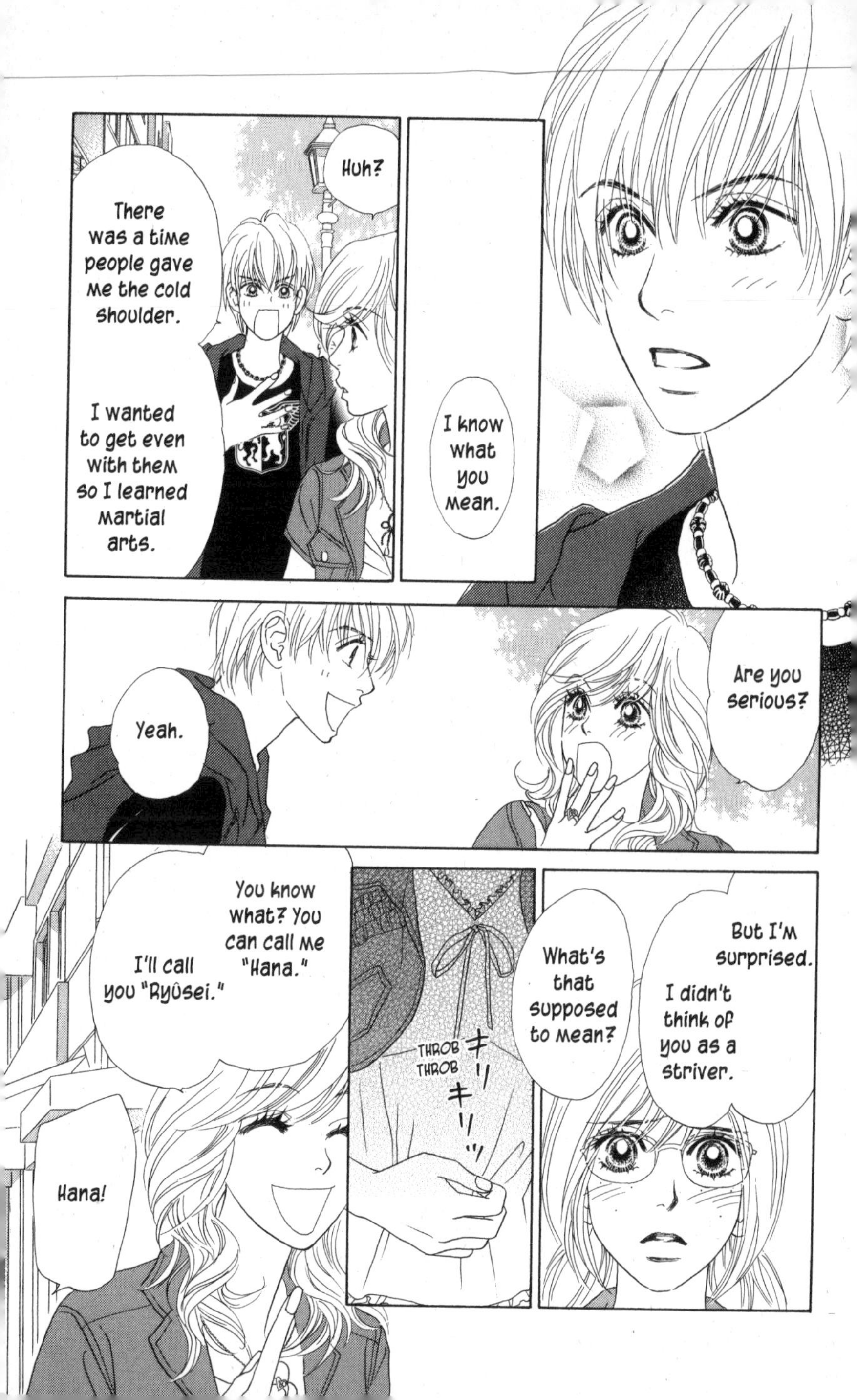
I know what you mean.
Huh?
There was a time people gave me the cold shoulder.
I wanted to get even with them so I learned martial arts.
Are you serious?
Yeah.
But I'm surprised.
I didn't think of you as a striver.
What's that supposed to mean?
THROB THROB
You know what? You can call me "Hana."
I'll call you "Ryûsei."
Hana!

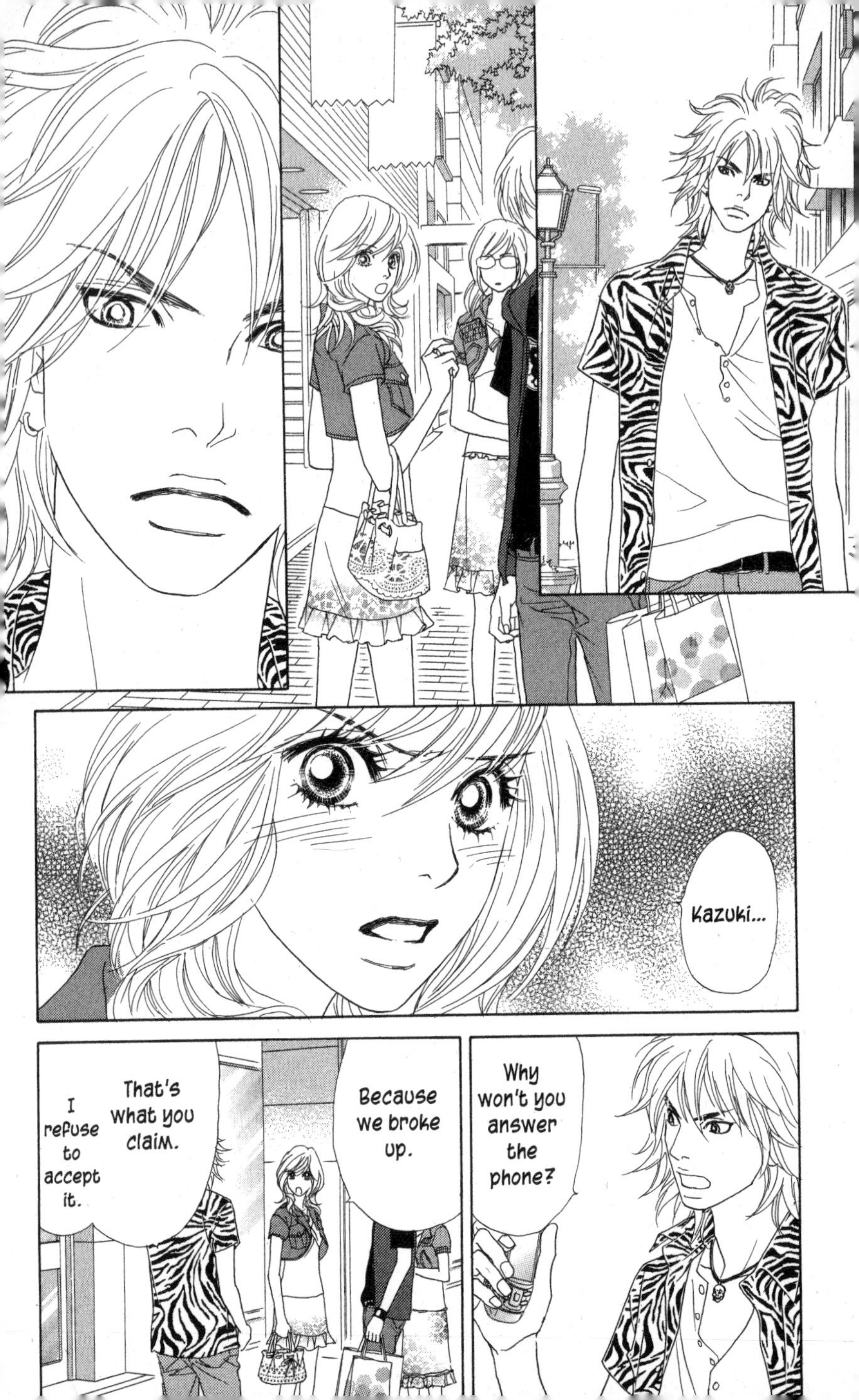
Kazuki...
Why won't you answer the phone?
Because we broke up.
That's what you claim.
I refuse to accept it.

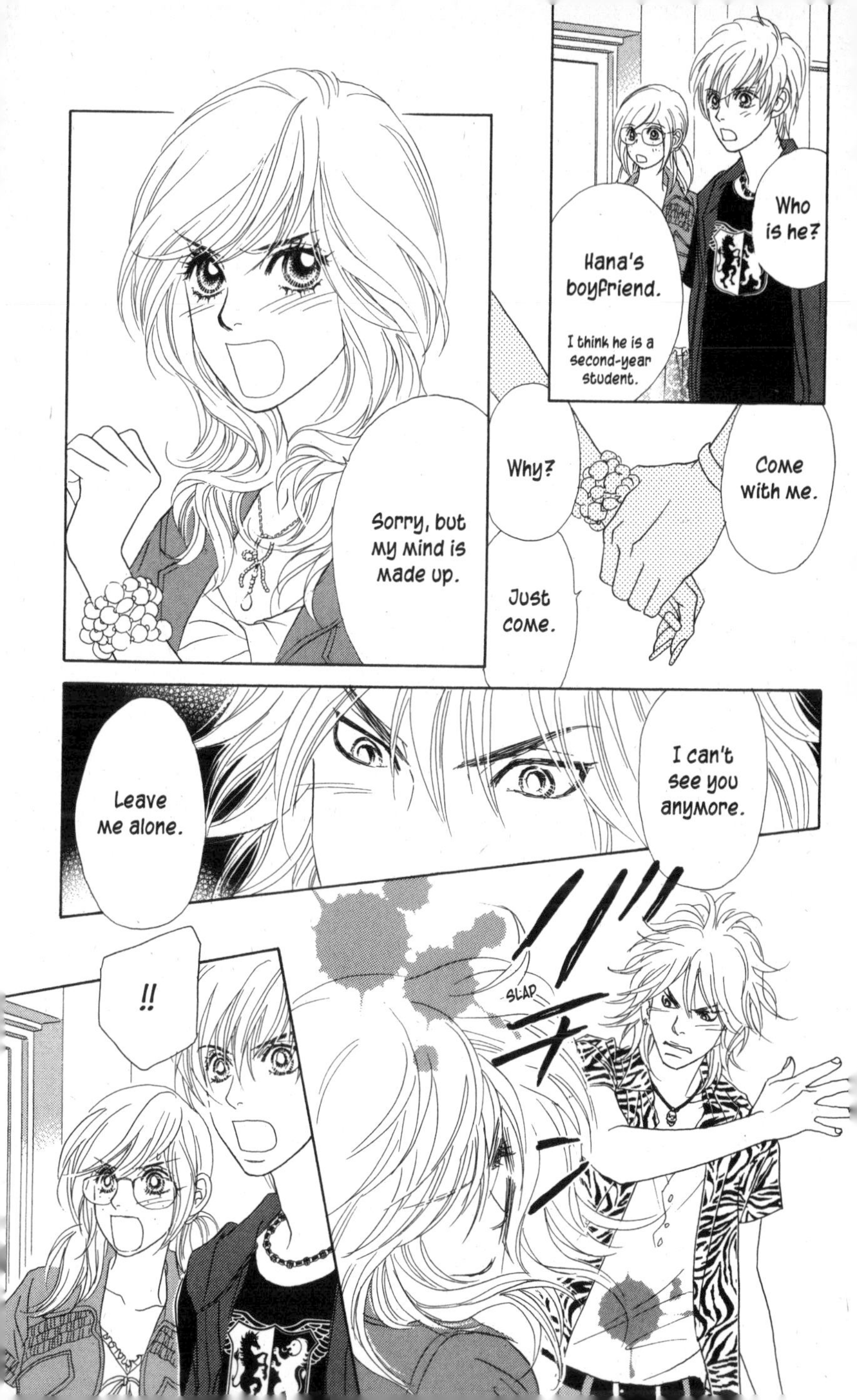
Who is he?
Hana's boyfriend.
I think he is a second-year student.
Come with me.
Why?
Just come.
Sorry, but my mind is made up.
I can't see you anymore.
Leave me alone.
SLAP
!!

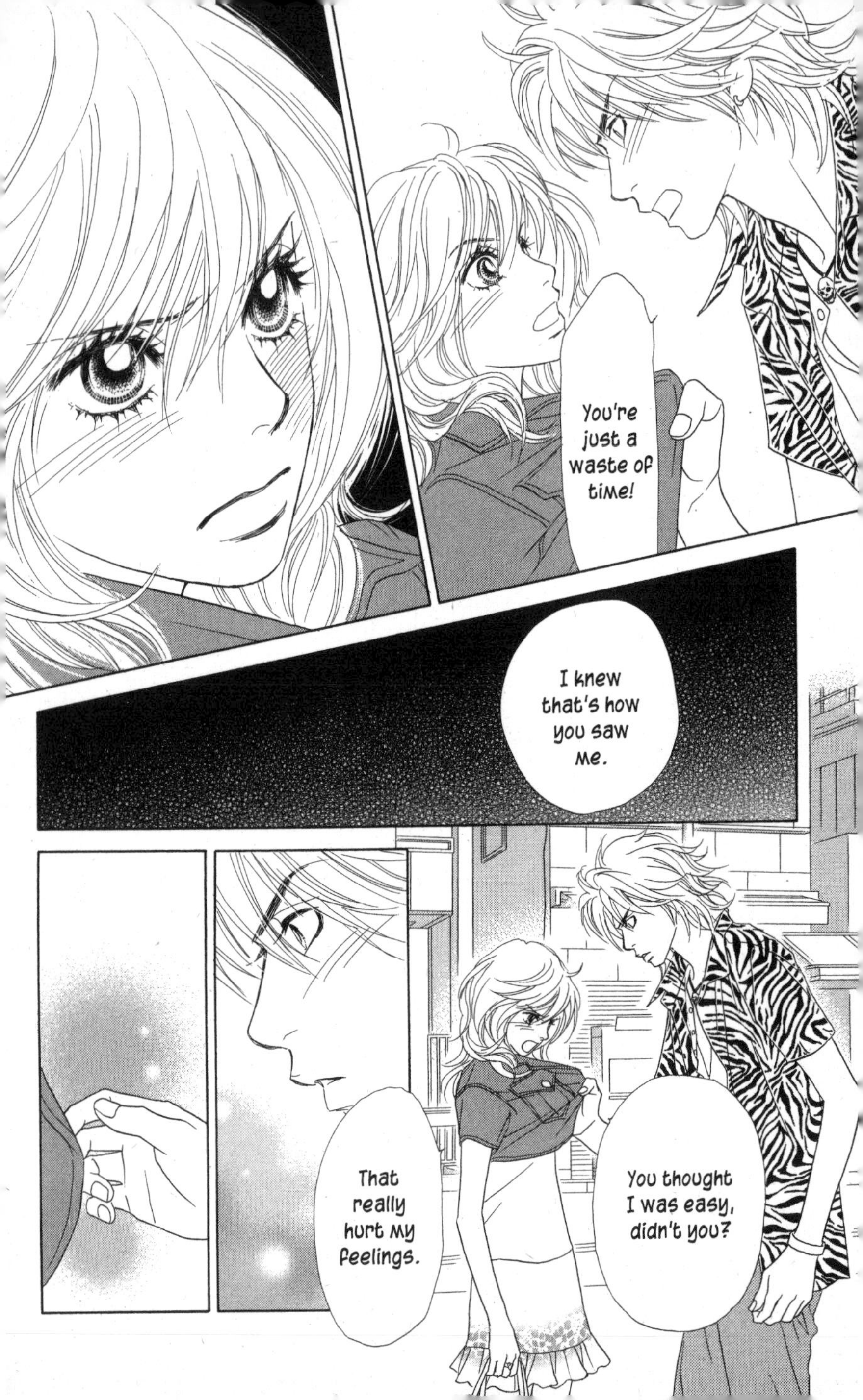
You're just a waste of time!
I knew that's how you saw me.
You thought I was easy, didn't you?
That really hurt my feelings.

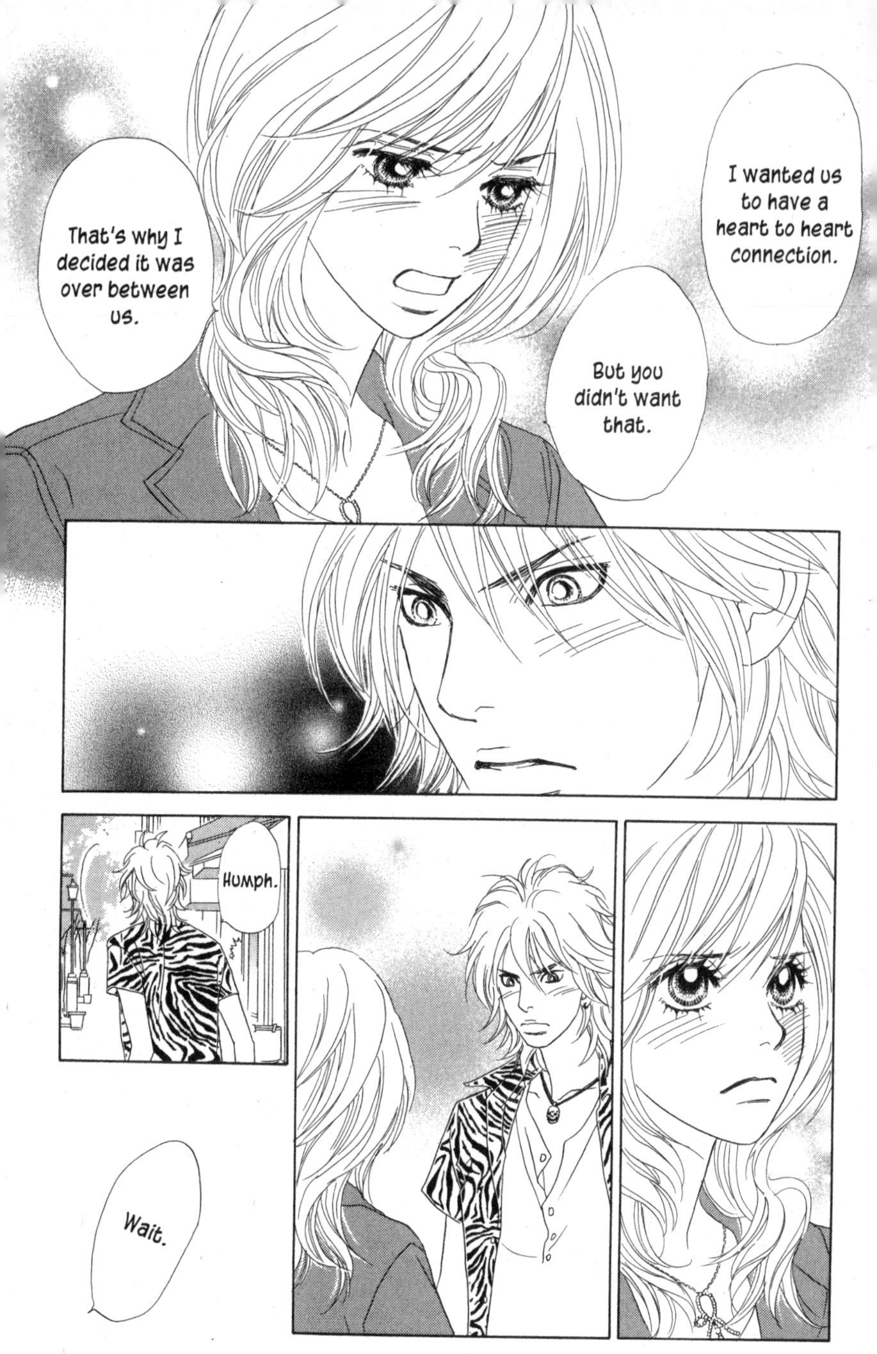
I wanted us to have a heart to heart connection.
But you didn't want that.
That's why I decided it was over between us.
Humph.
Wait.

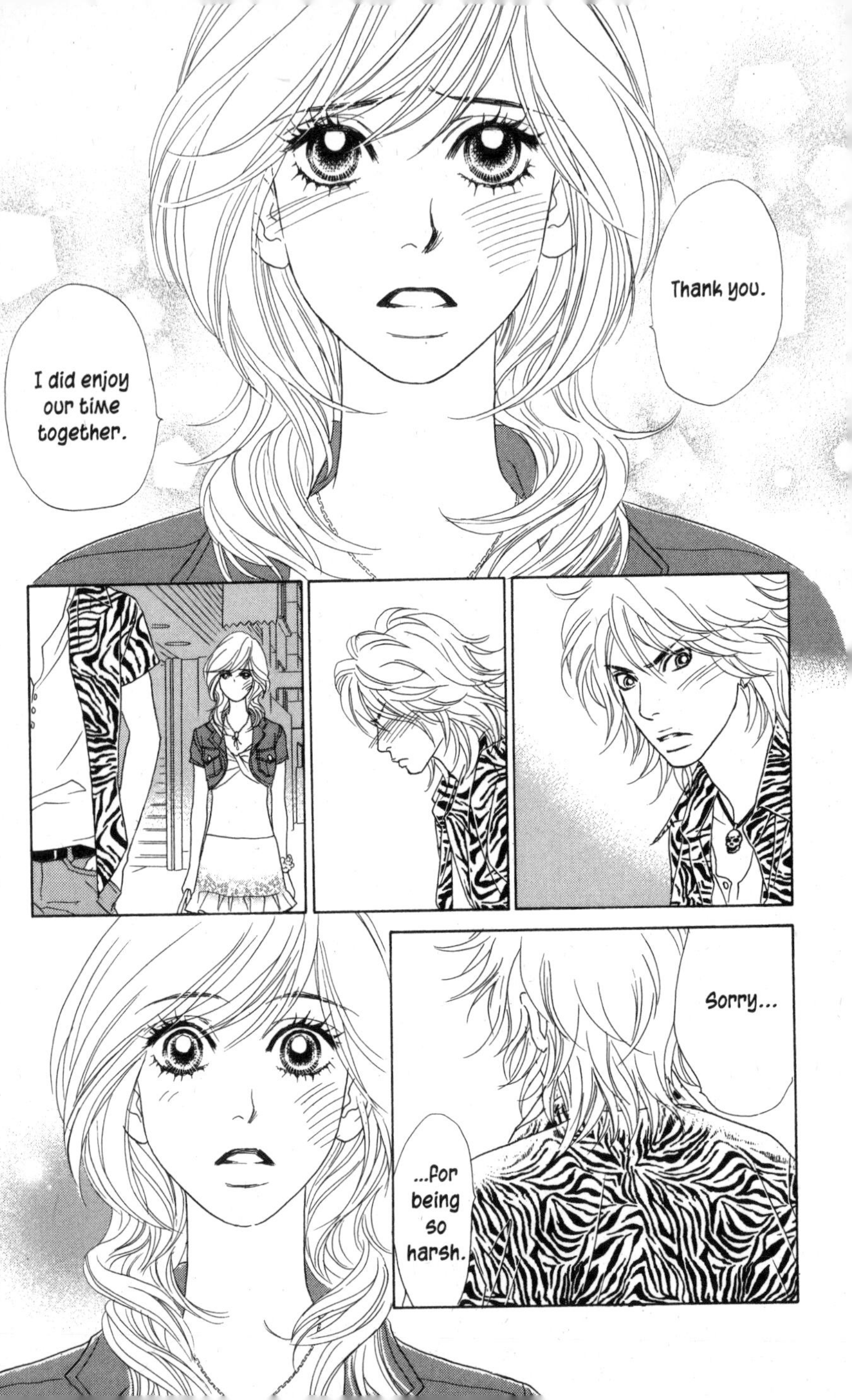
Thank you.
I did enjoy our time together.
Sorry...
...for being so harsh.

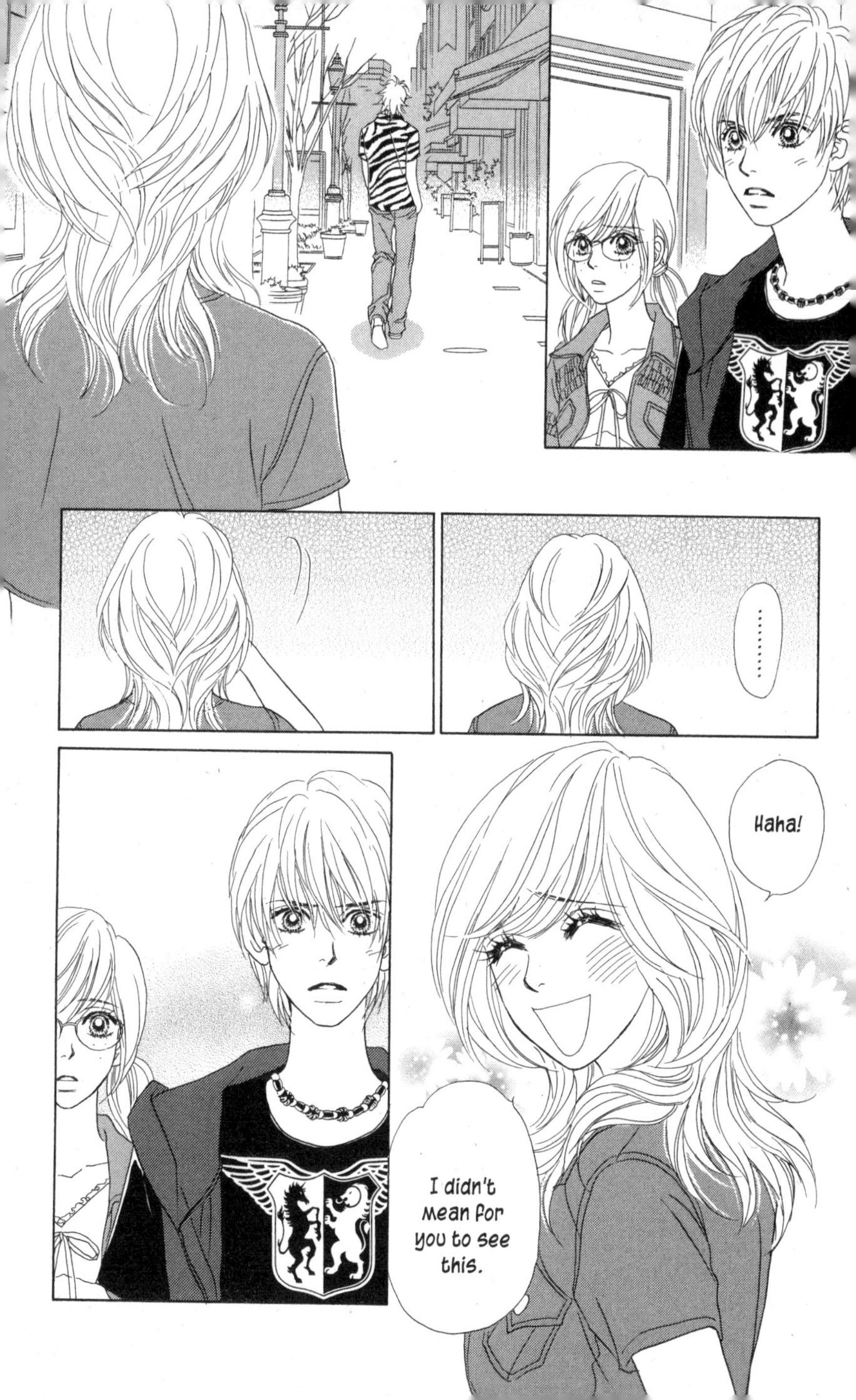
……
Haha!
I didn't mean for you to see this.

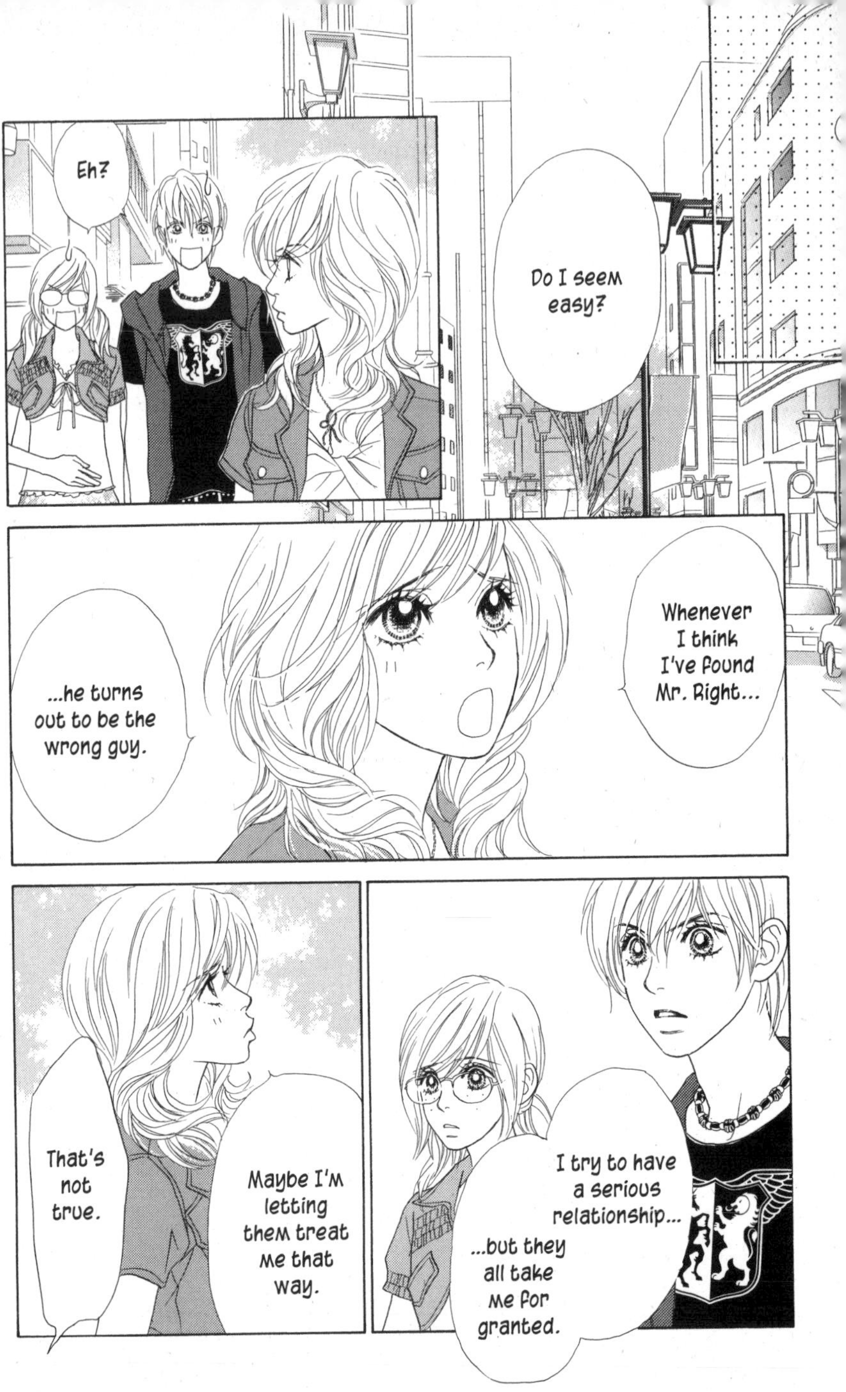
Do I seem easy?
Eh?
Whenever I think I've found Mr. Right...
...he turns out to be the wrong guy.
I try to have a serious relationship...
...but they all take me for granted.
Maybe I'm letting them treat me that way.
That's not true.

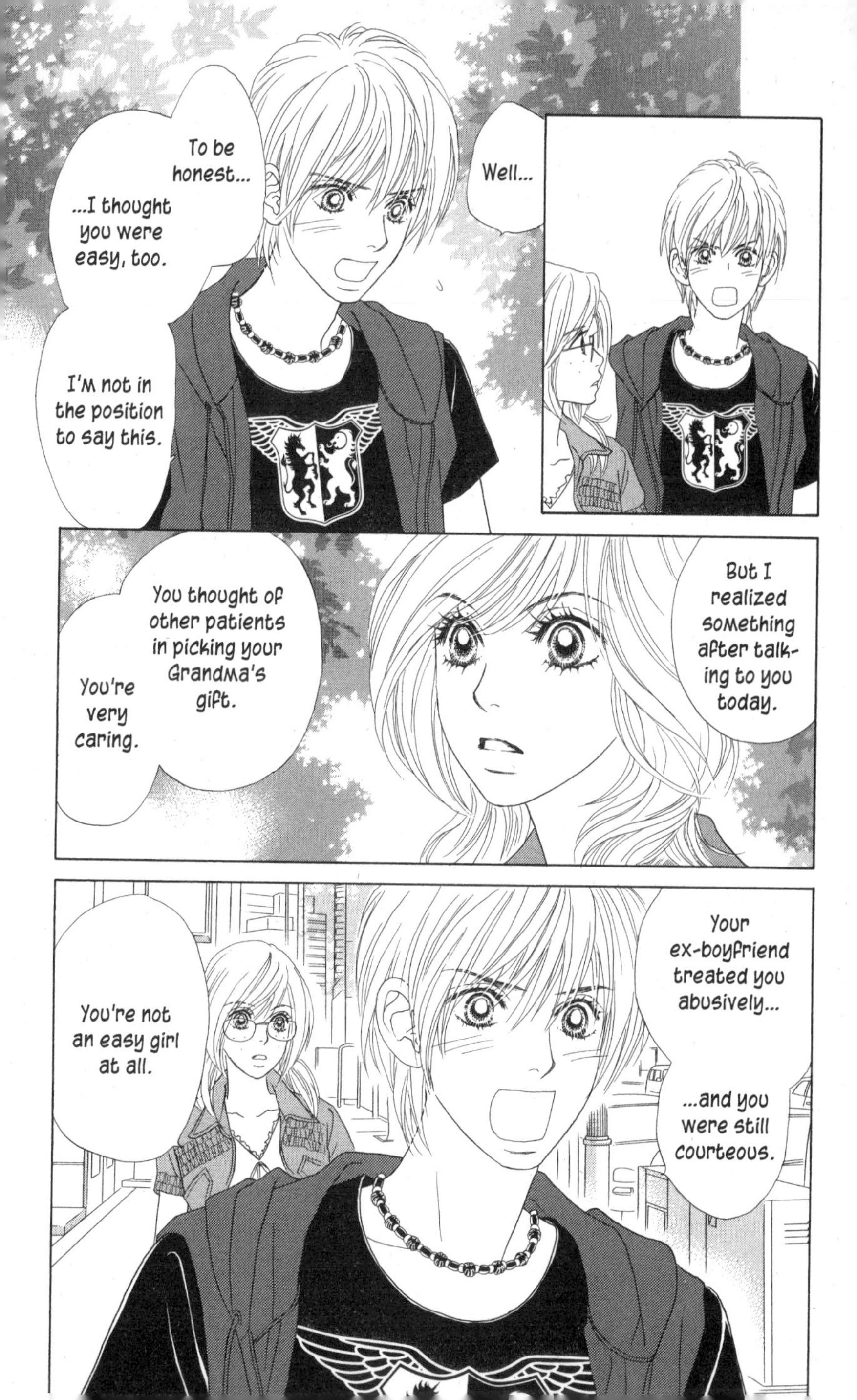
Well...
To be honest...
...I thought you were easy, too.
I'm not in the position to say this.
But I realized something after talk-ing to you today.
You thought of other patients in picking your Grandma's gift.
You're very caring.
Your ex-boyfriend treated you abusively...
...and you were still courteous.
You're not an easy girl at all.

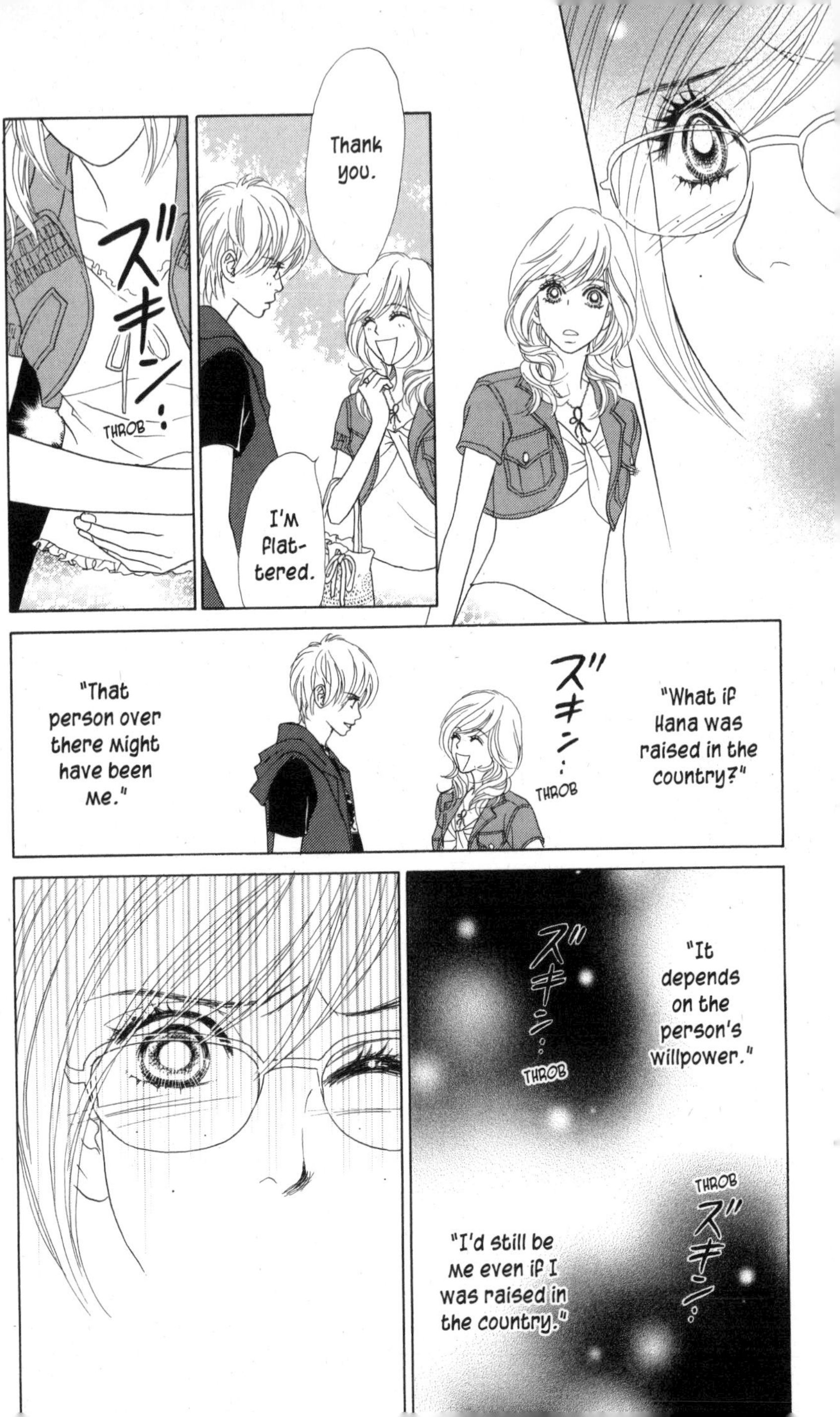
Thank you.
I'm flattered.
ズキン!
THROB
"What if Hana was raised in the country?"
ズキン…
THROB
"That person over there might have been me."
"It depends on the person's willpower."
ズキン。。
THROB
THROB
ズキン。。
"I'd still be me even if I was raised in the country."

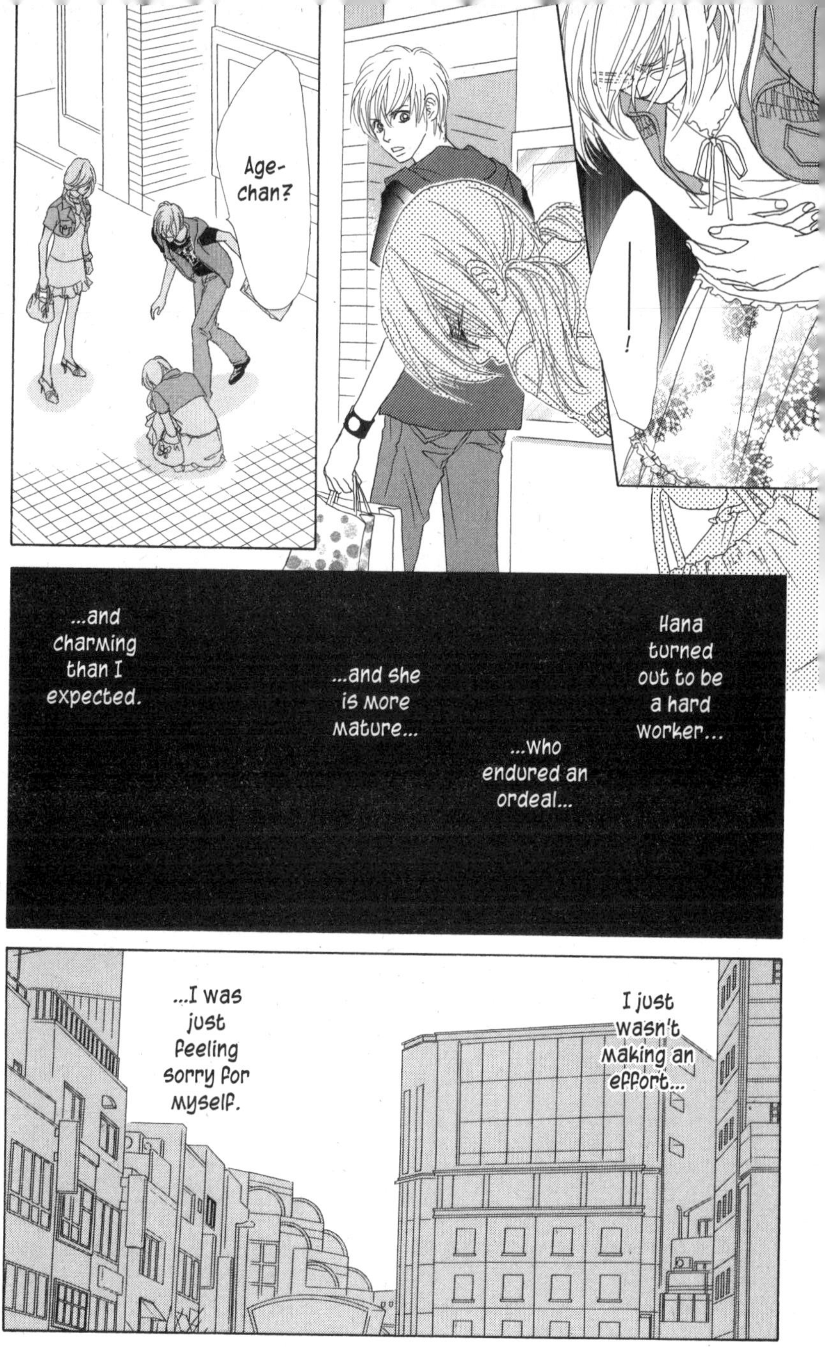
!
Age-chan?
Hana turned out to be a hard worker...
...who endured an ordeal...
...and she is more mature...
...and charming than I expected.
I just wasn't making an effort...
...I was just feeling sorry for myself.

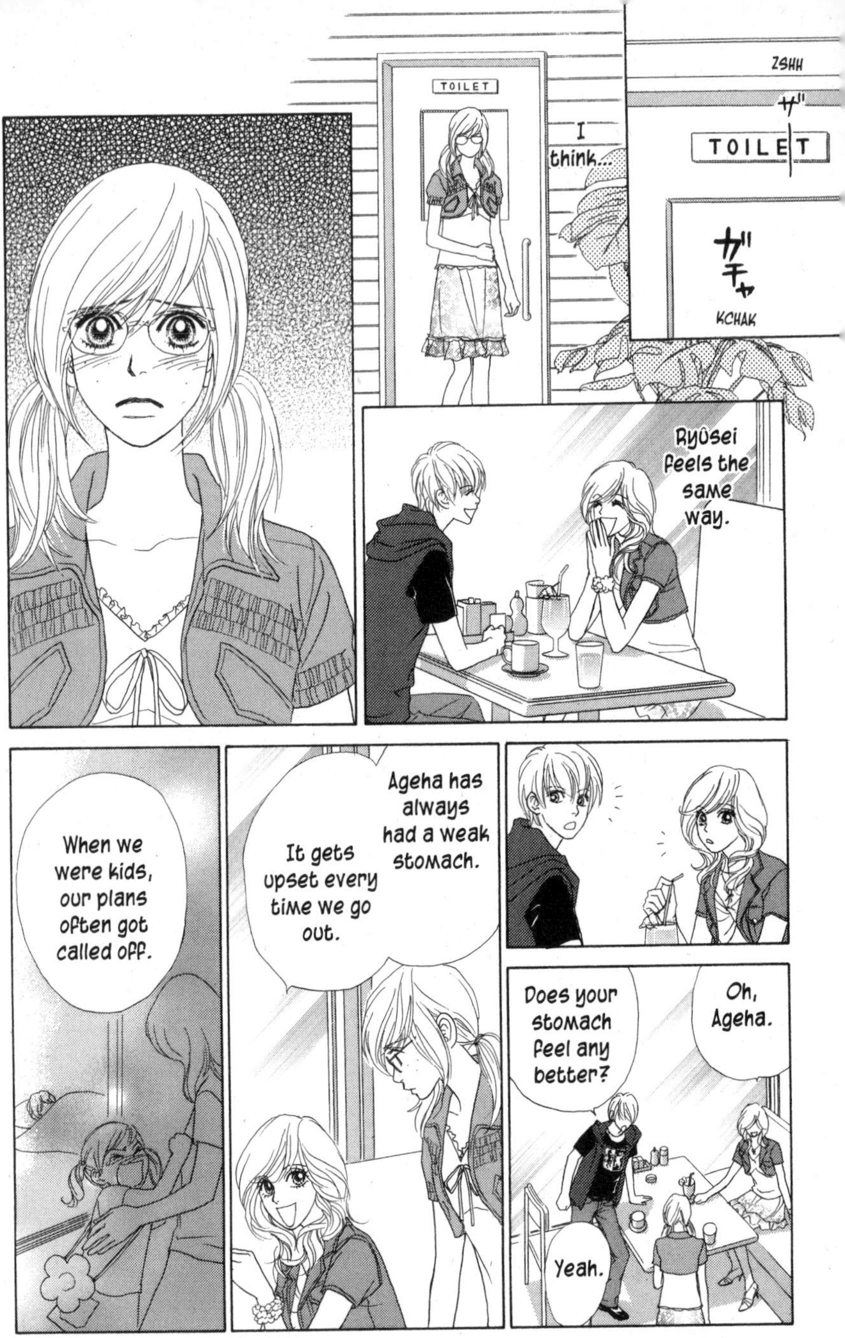
ZSHH
ザ
TOILET
ガチャ
KCHAK
TOILET
I think...
Ryûsei feels the same way.
Oh, Ageha.
Does your stomach feel any better?
Yeah.
Ageha has always had a weak stomach.
It gets upset every time we go out.
When we were kids, our plans often got called off.

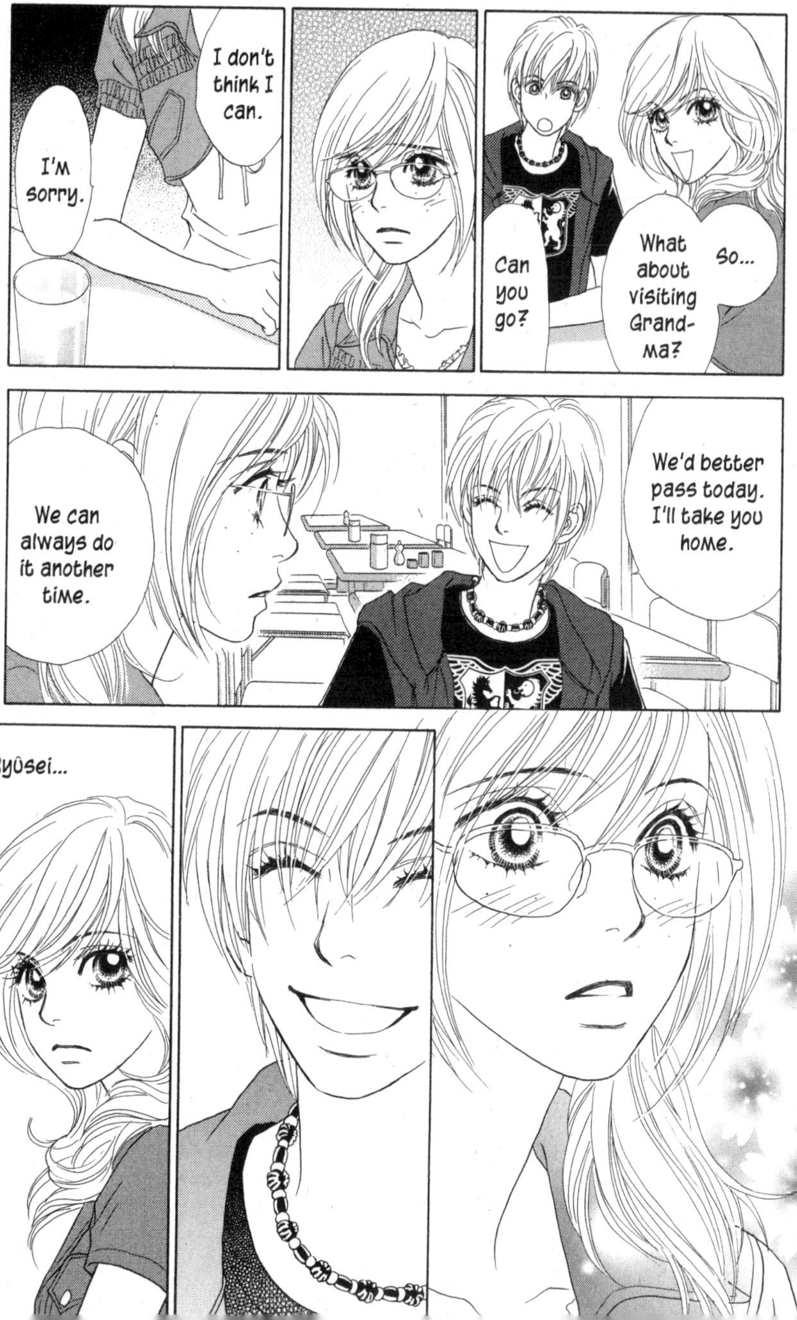
So...
What about visiting Grand-ma?
Can you go?
I don't think I can.
I'm sorry.
We'd better pass today. I'll take you home.
We can always do it another time.
Ryûsei...

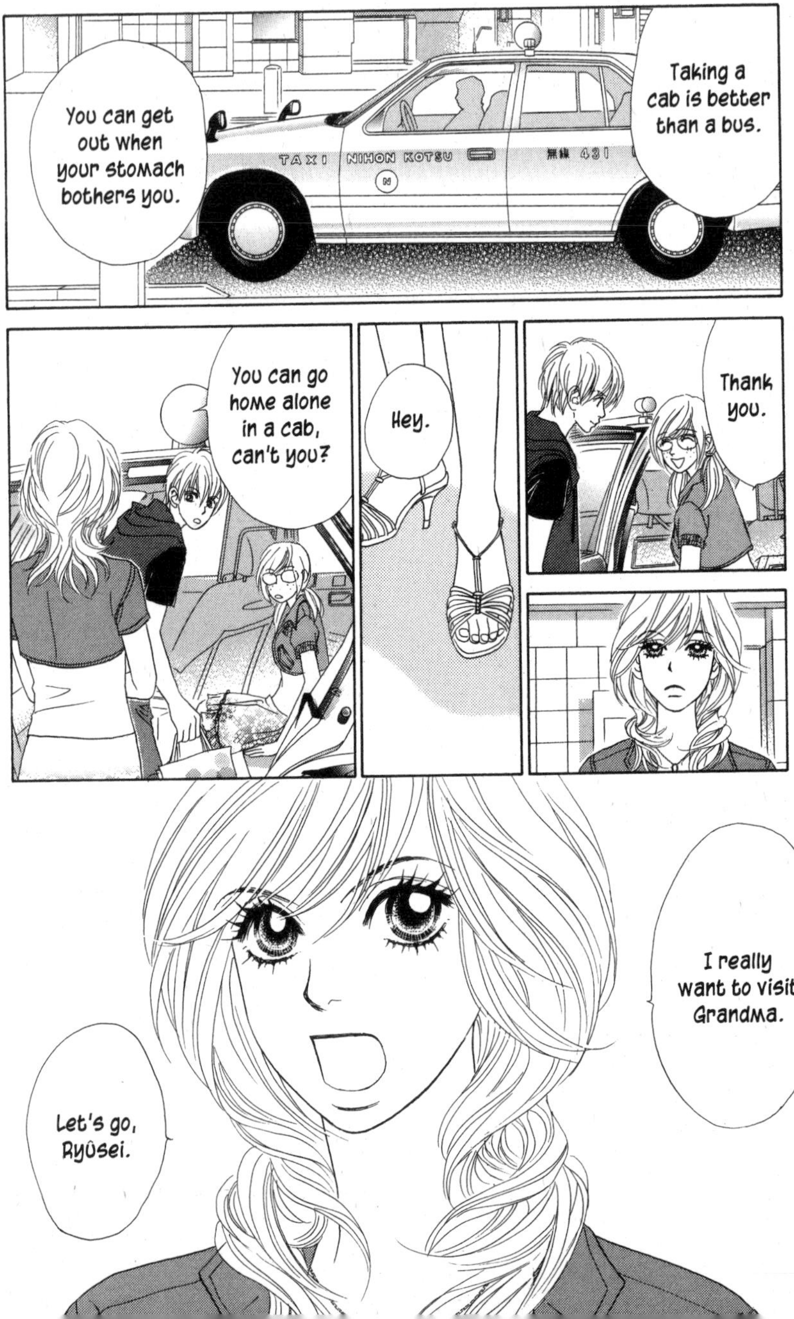
Taking a cab is better than a bus.
TAXI
NIHON KOTSU
無線 431
You can get out when your stomach bothers you.
Thank you.
Hey.
You can go home alone in a cab, can't you?
I really want to visit Grandma.
Let's go, Ryûsei.

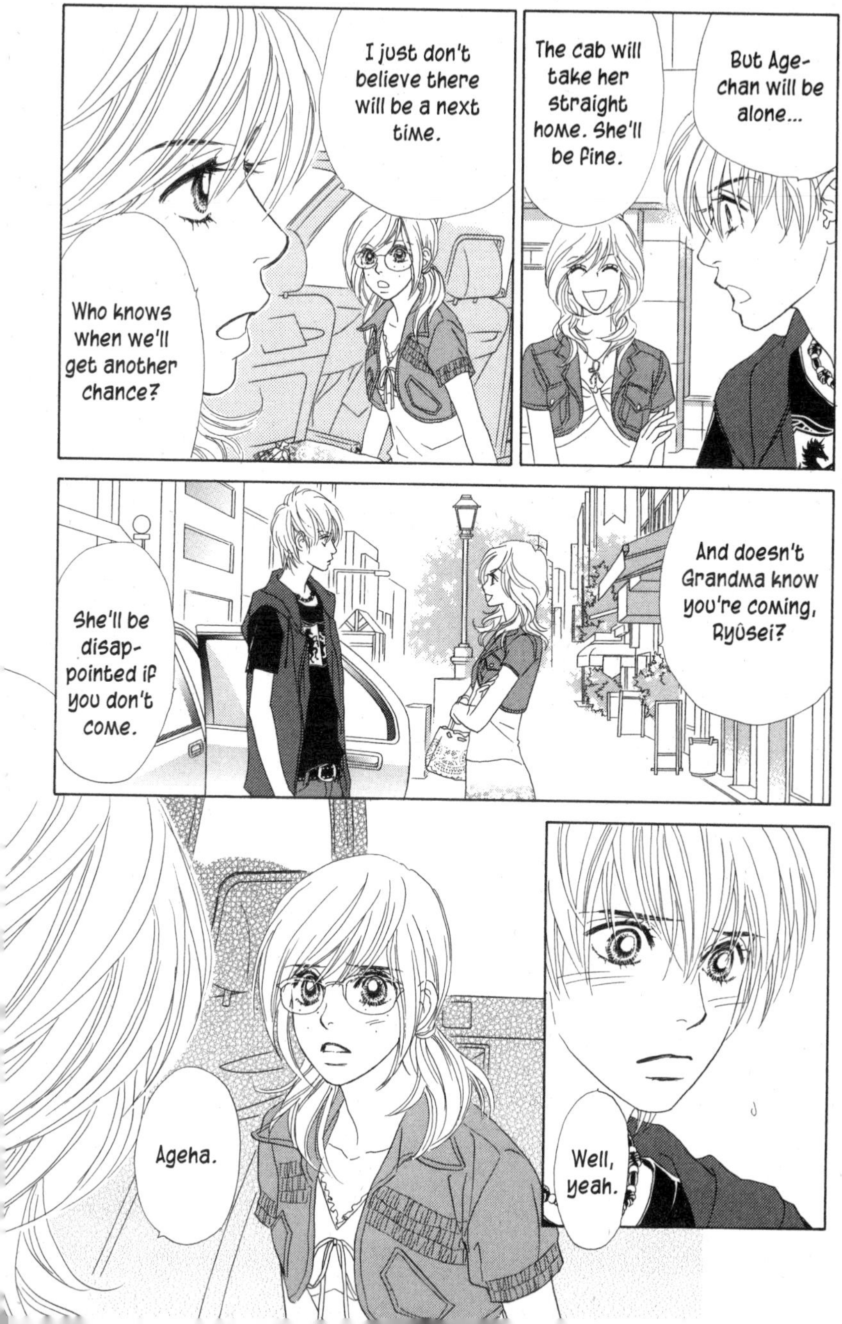
But Age-chan will be alone...
The cab will take her straight home. She'll be fine.
I just don't believe there will be a next time.
Who knows when we'll get another chance?
And doesn't Grandma know you're coming, Ryûsei?
She'll be disappointed if you don't come.
Well, yeah.
Ageha.

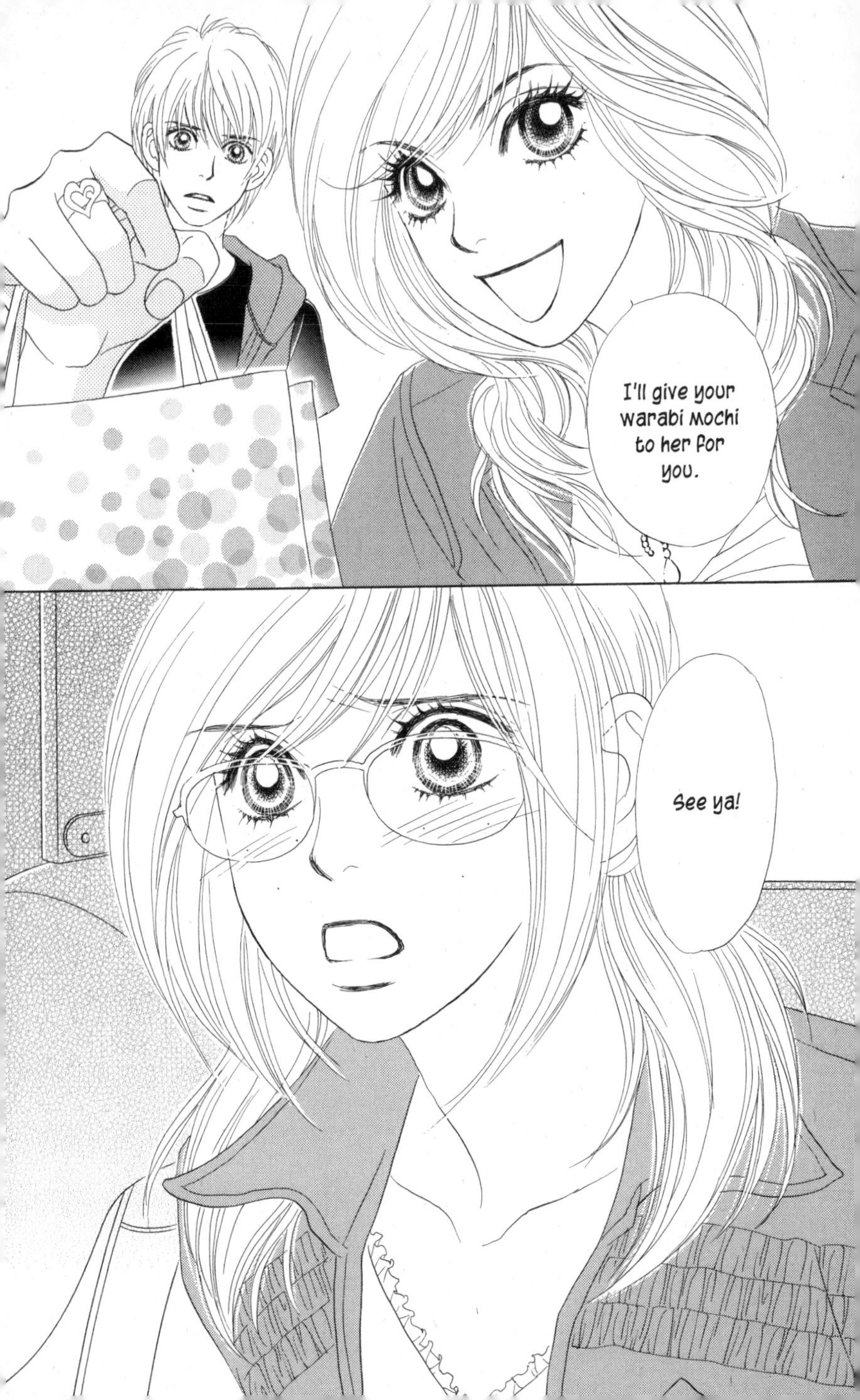
I'll give your warabi mochi to her for you.
See ya!

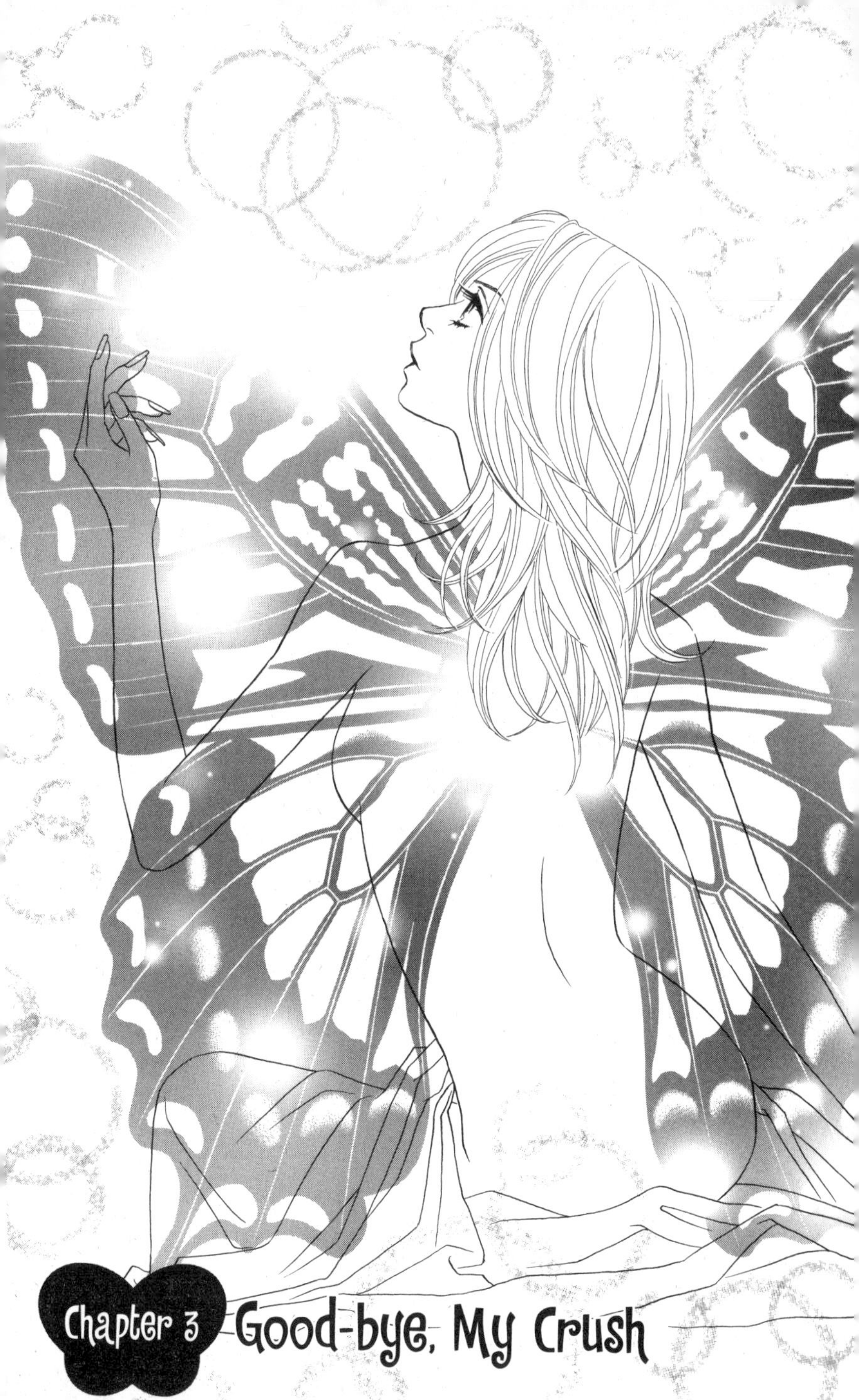

Chapter 3 Good-bye, My Crush

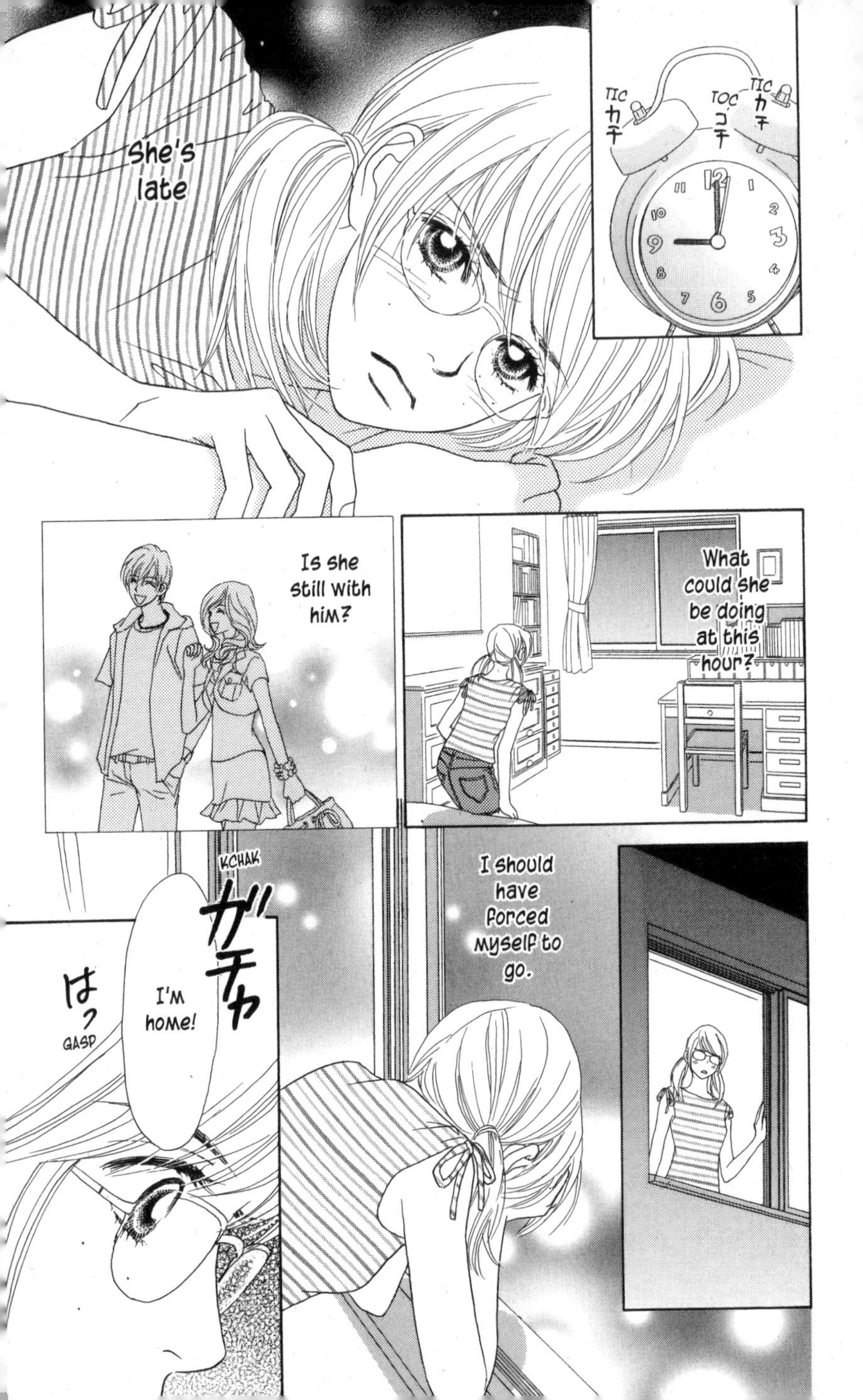
TIC カチ
TOC コチ
TIC カチ
She's late
What could she be doing at this hour?
Is she still with him?
I should have forced myself to go.
KCHAK ガチャ
I'm home!
はっ GASP

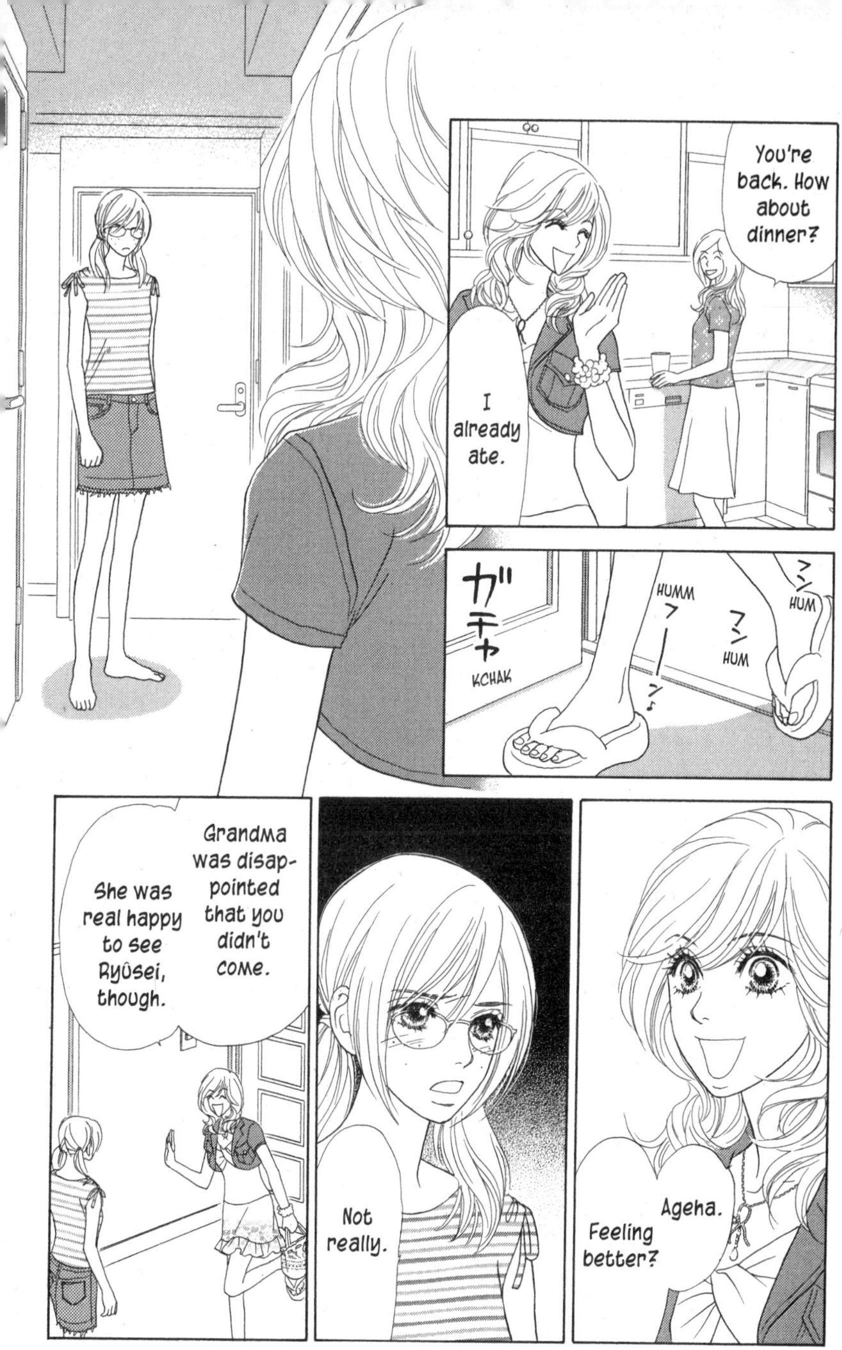
You're back. How about dinner?
I already ate.
フン
HUM
フ〜〜♪
HUMM
フン
HUM
ガチャ
KCHAK
Ageha. Feeling better?
Not really.
Grandma was disappointed that you didn't come.
She was real happy to see Ryûsei, though.

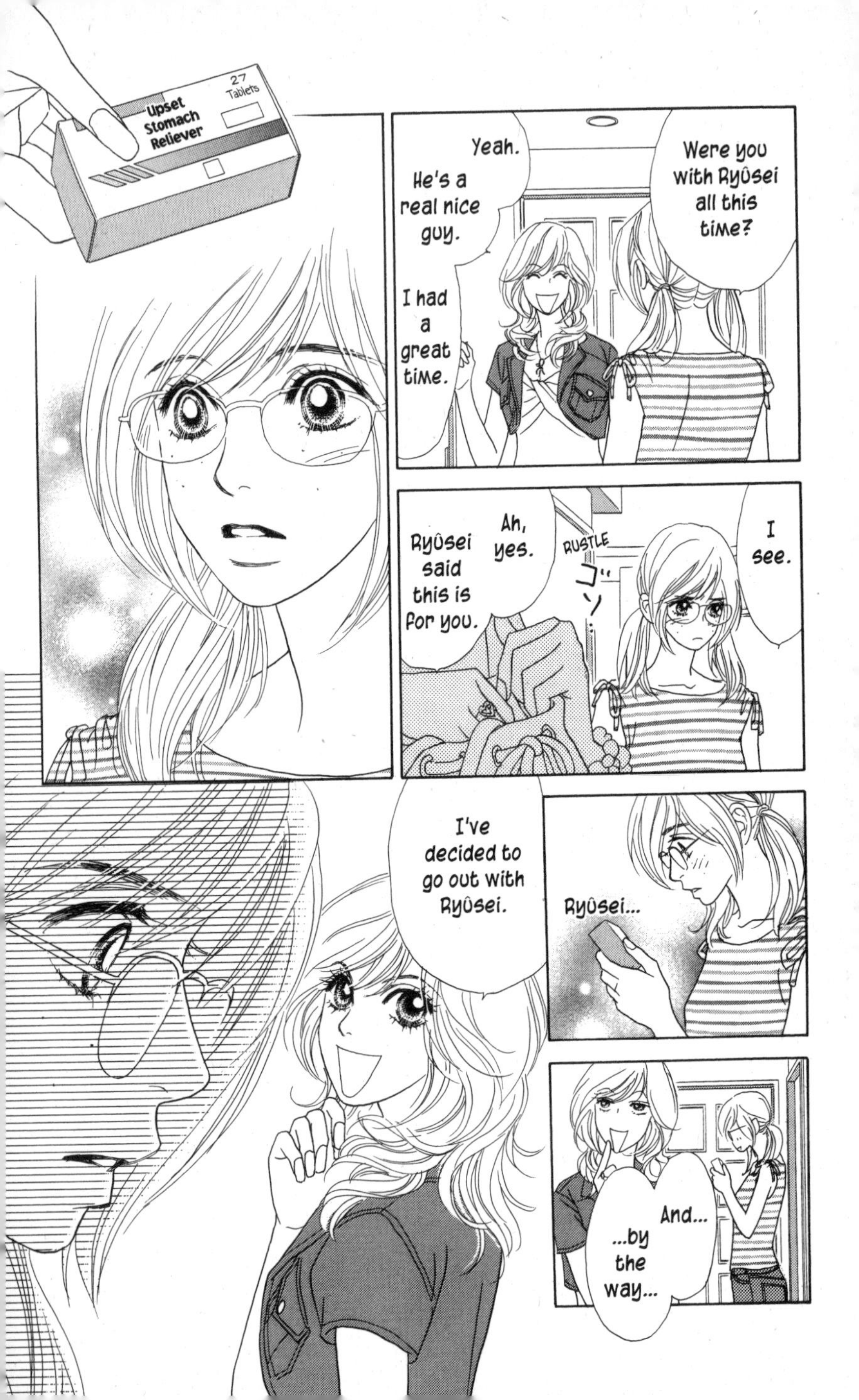

Were you with Ryûsei all this time?
Yeah.
He's a real nice guy.
I had a great time.
I see.
Ah, yes.
Ryûsei said this is for you.
RUSTLE
ゴソ
Upset Stomach Reliever
27 Tablets
Ryûsei...
And...
...by the way...
I've decided to go out with Ryûsei.

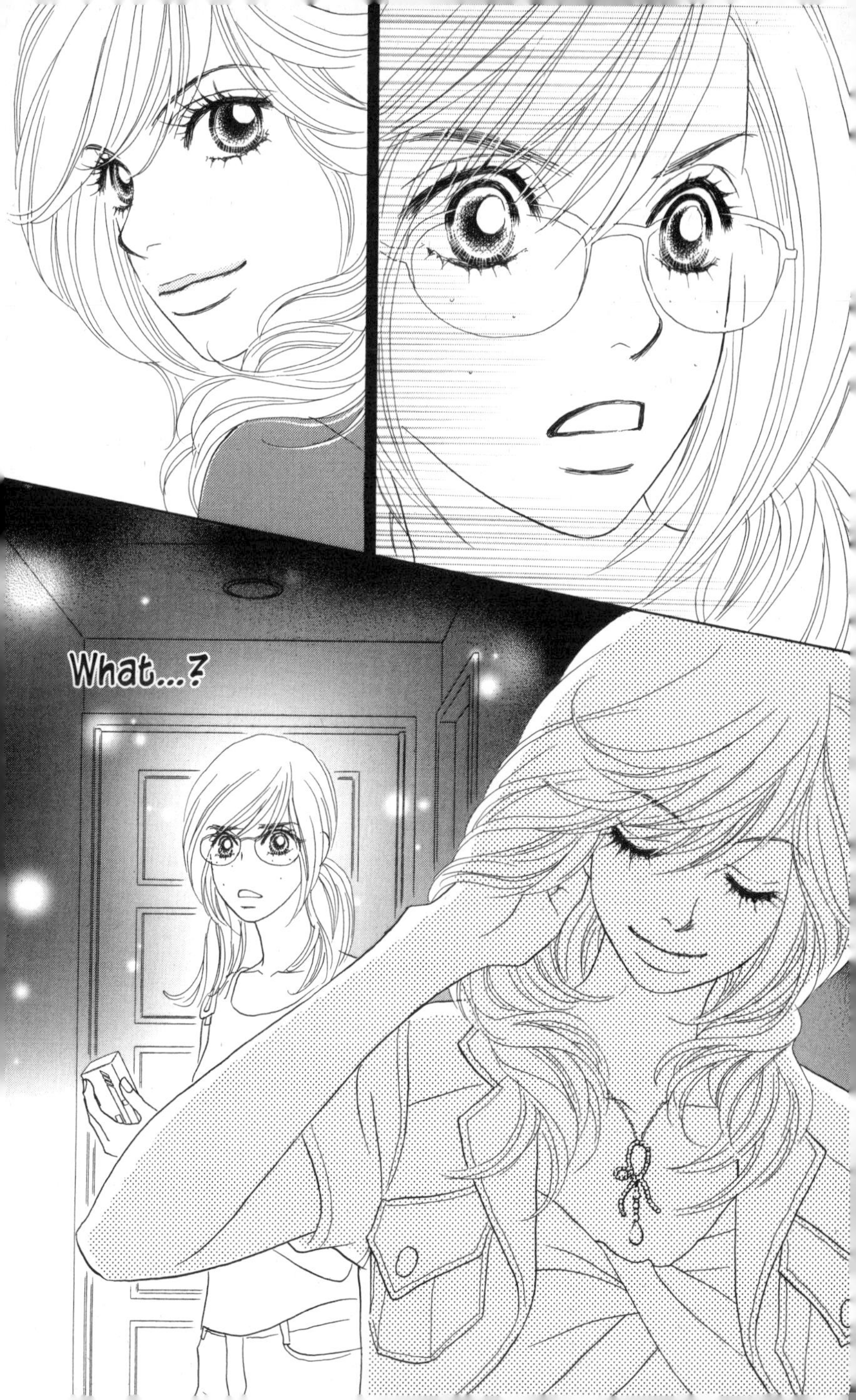
What...?

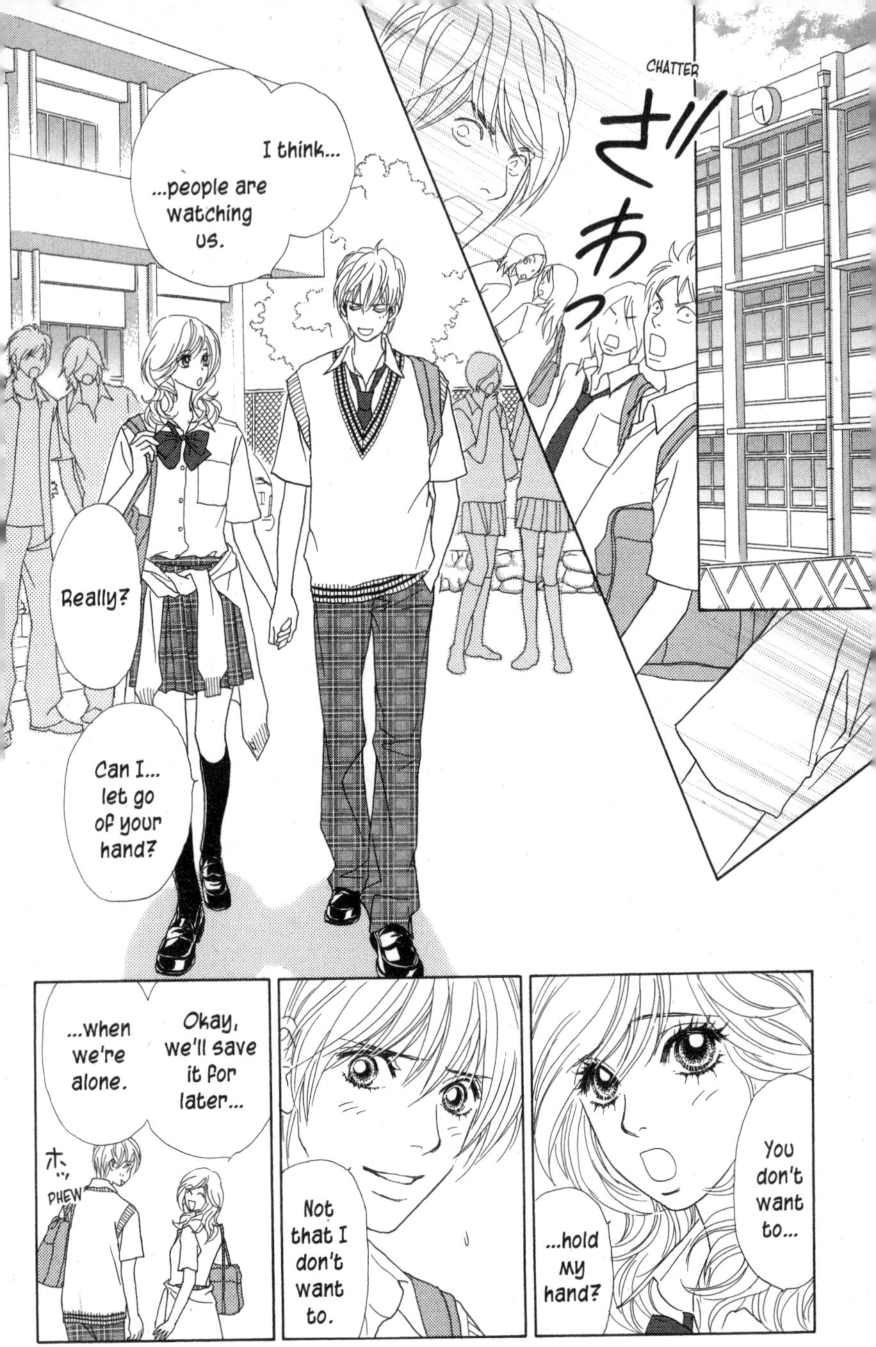
CHATTER
ざわっ
I think...
...people are watching us.
Really?
Can I... let go of your hand?
You don't want to...
...hold my hand?
Not that I don't want to.
Okay, we'll save it for later...
...when we're alone.
ホッ
PHEW

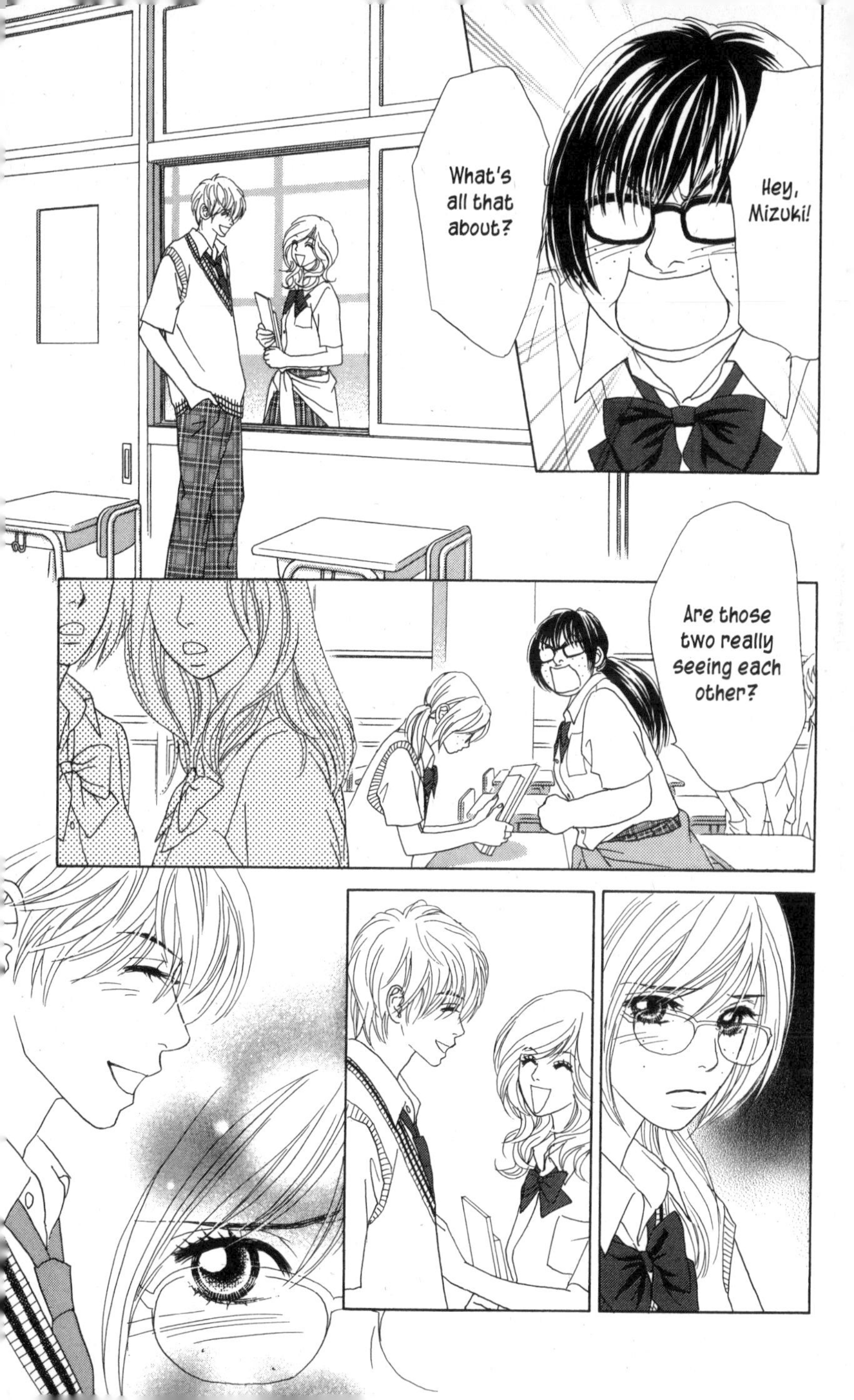
Hey, Mizuki!
What's all that about?
Are those two really seeing each other?

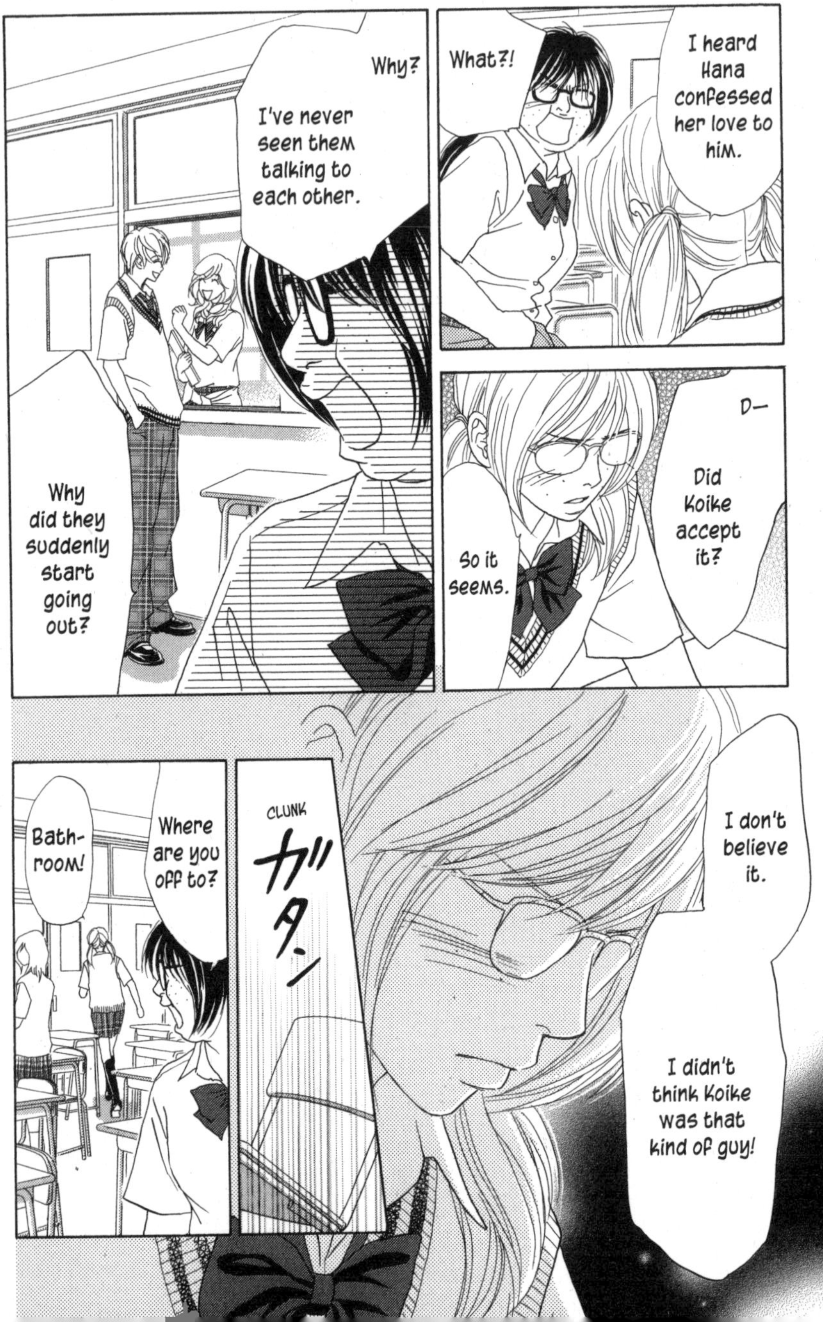
I heard Hana confessed her love to him.
What?!
D—
Did Koike accept it?
So it seems.
Why?
I've never seen them talking to each other.
Why did they suddenly start going out?
I don't believe it.
I didn't think Koike was that kind of guy!
CLUNK
ガタン
Where are you off to?
Bath-room!

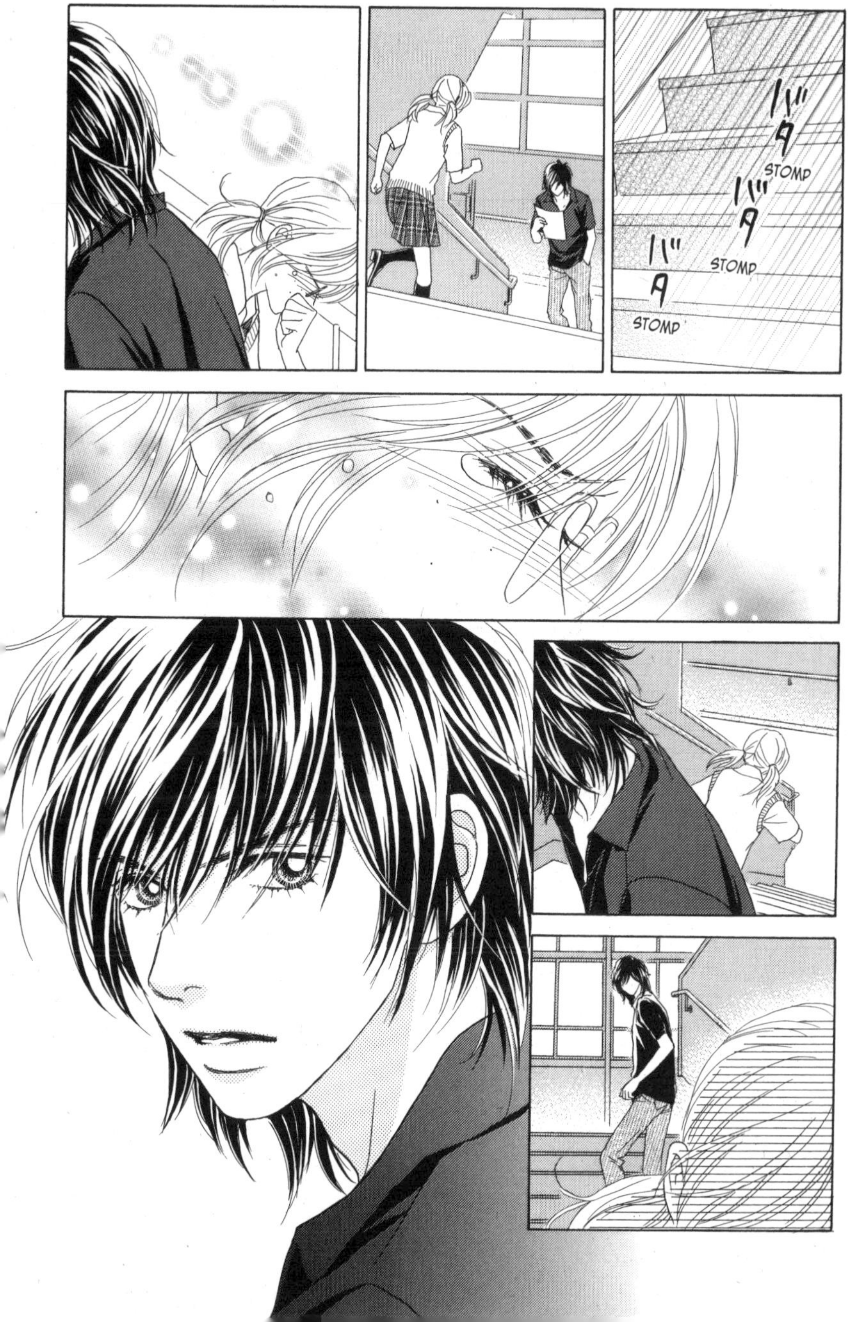
バタ
STOMP
バタ
STOMP
バタ
STOMP

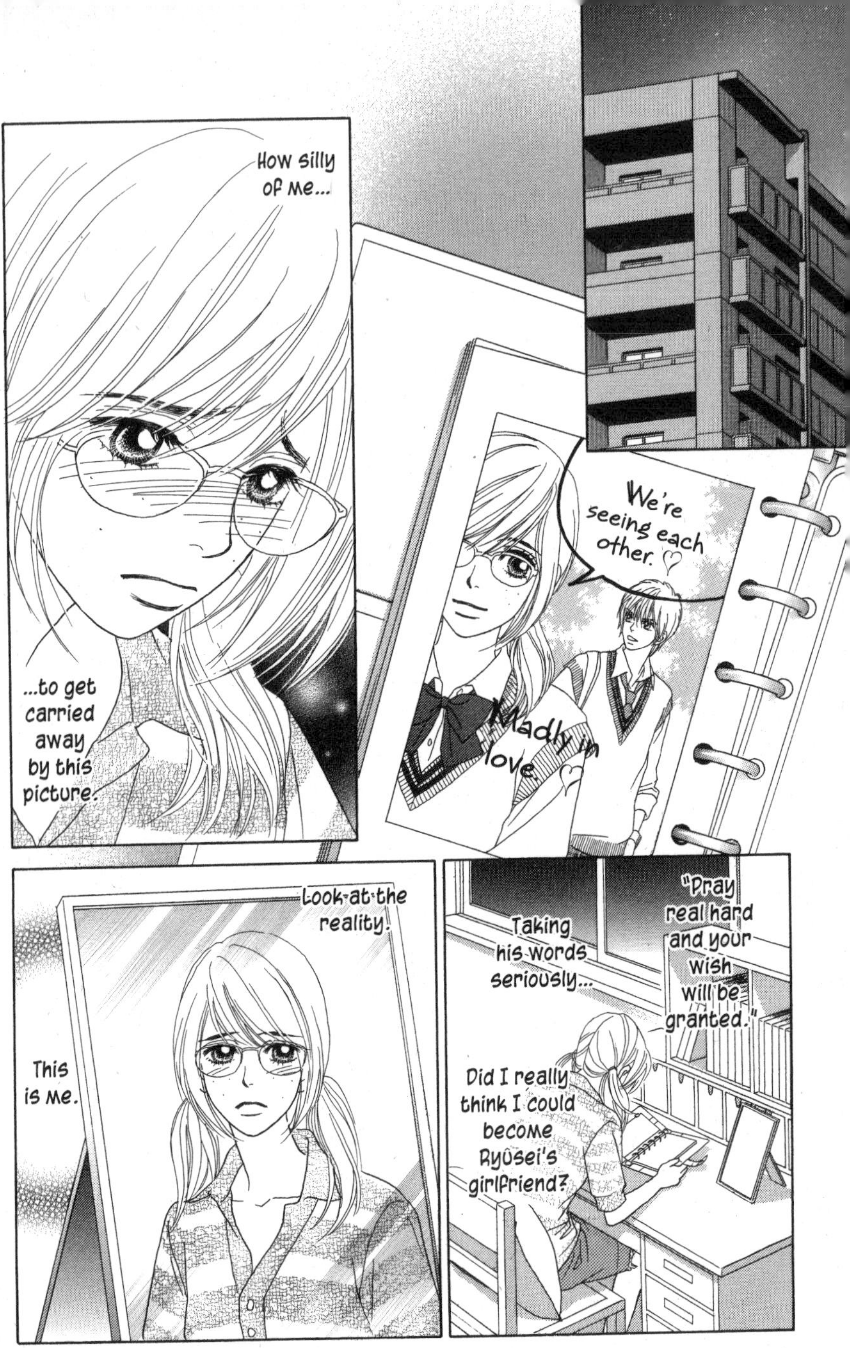
We're seeing each other. ♡
Madly in love. ♡
How silly of me...
...to get carried away by this picture.
"Pray real hard and your wish will be granted."
Taking his words seriously...
Did I really think I could become Ryusei's girlfriend?
Look at the reality.
This is me.

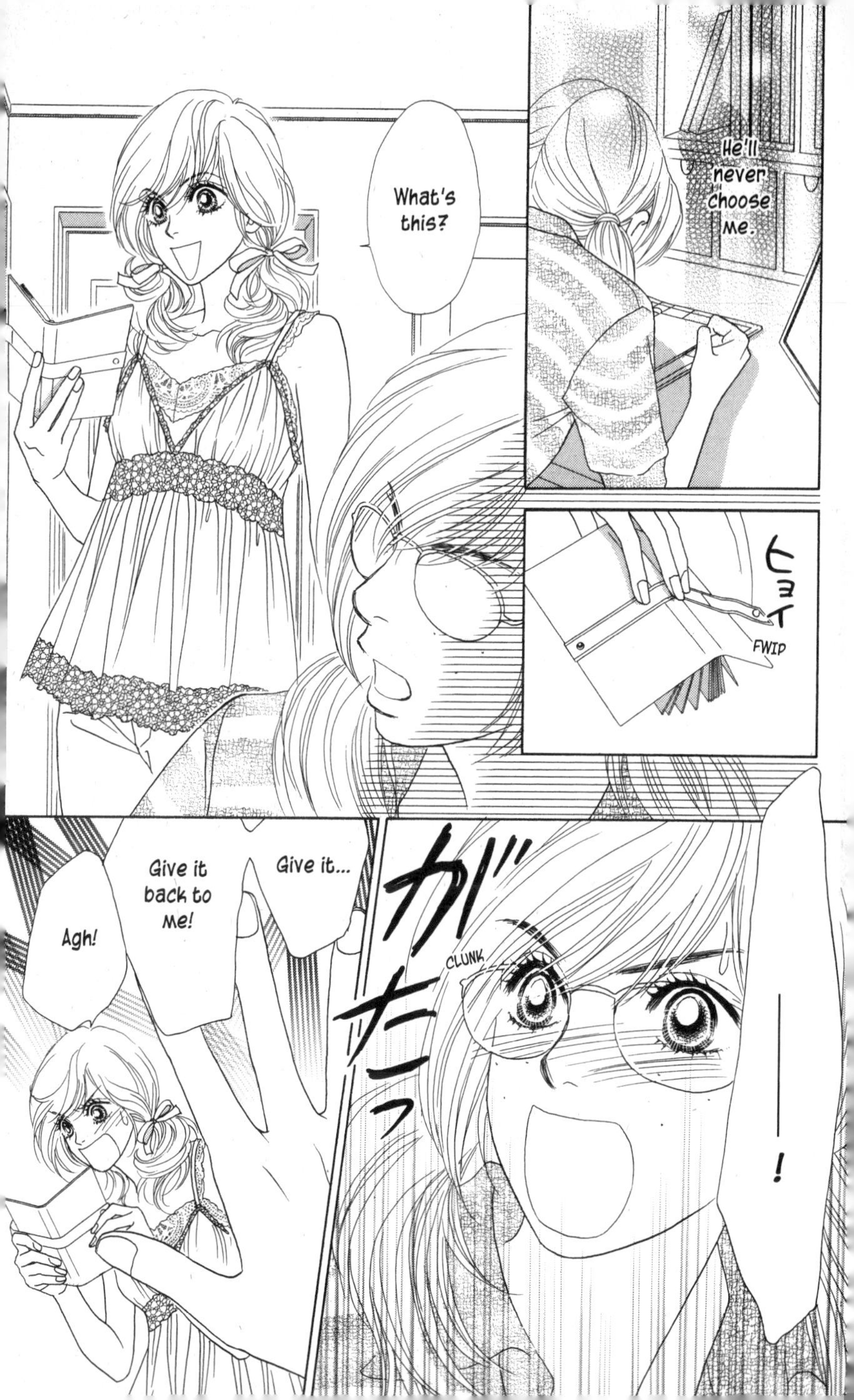
He'll never choose me.
ヒョイ
FWIP
What's this?
がたっ
CLUNK
—!
Give it...
Give it back to me!
Agh!

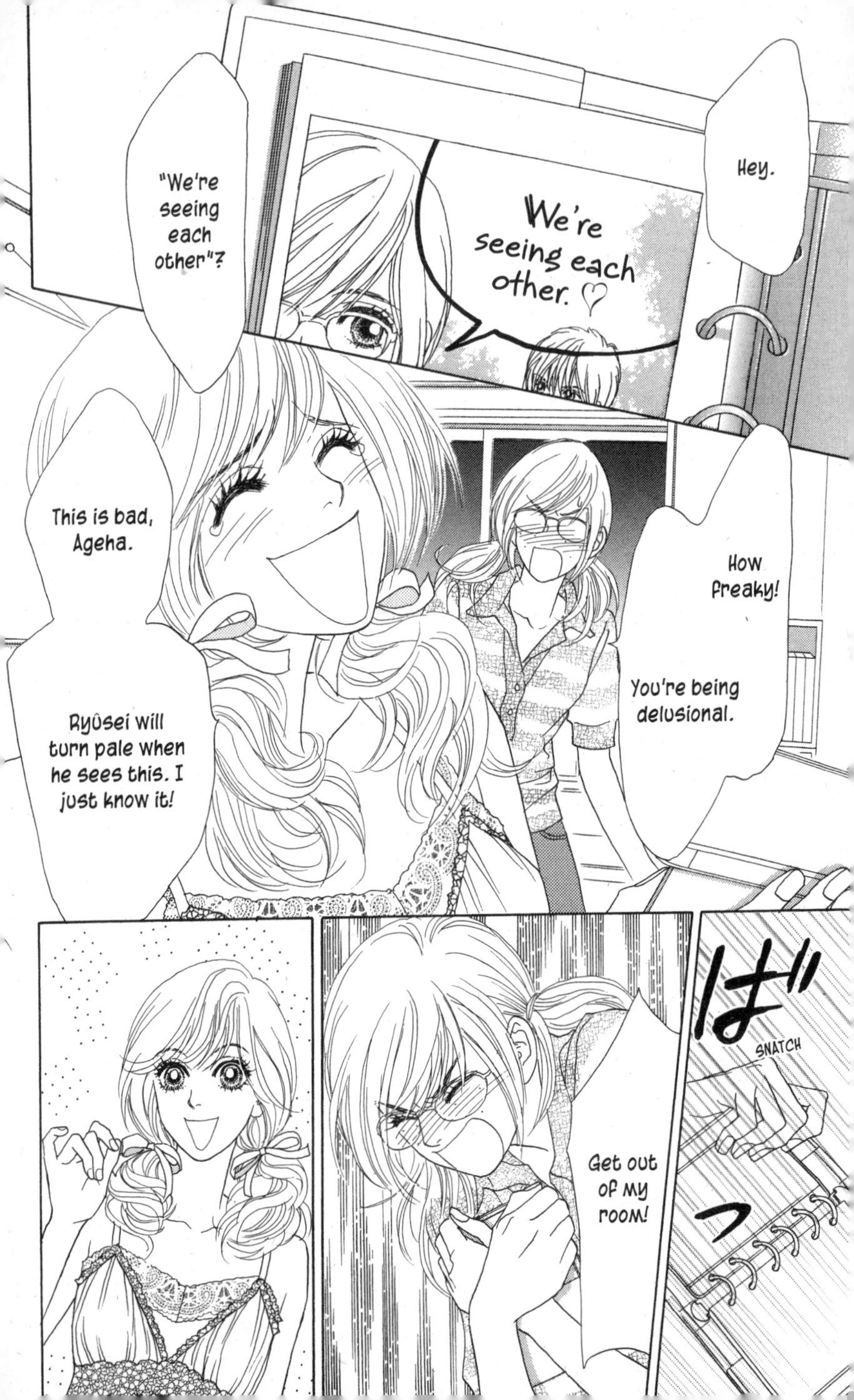
Hey.
We're seeing each other. ♡
"We're seeing each other"?
How freaky!
You're being delusional.
This is bad, Ageha.
Ryûsei will turn pale when he sees this. I just know it!
ばっ
SNATCH
Get out of my room!

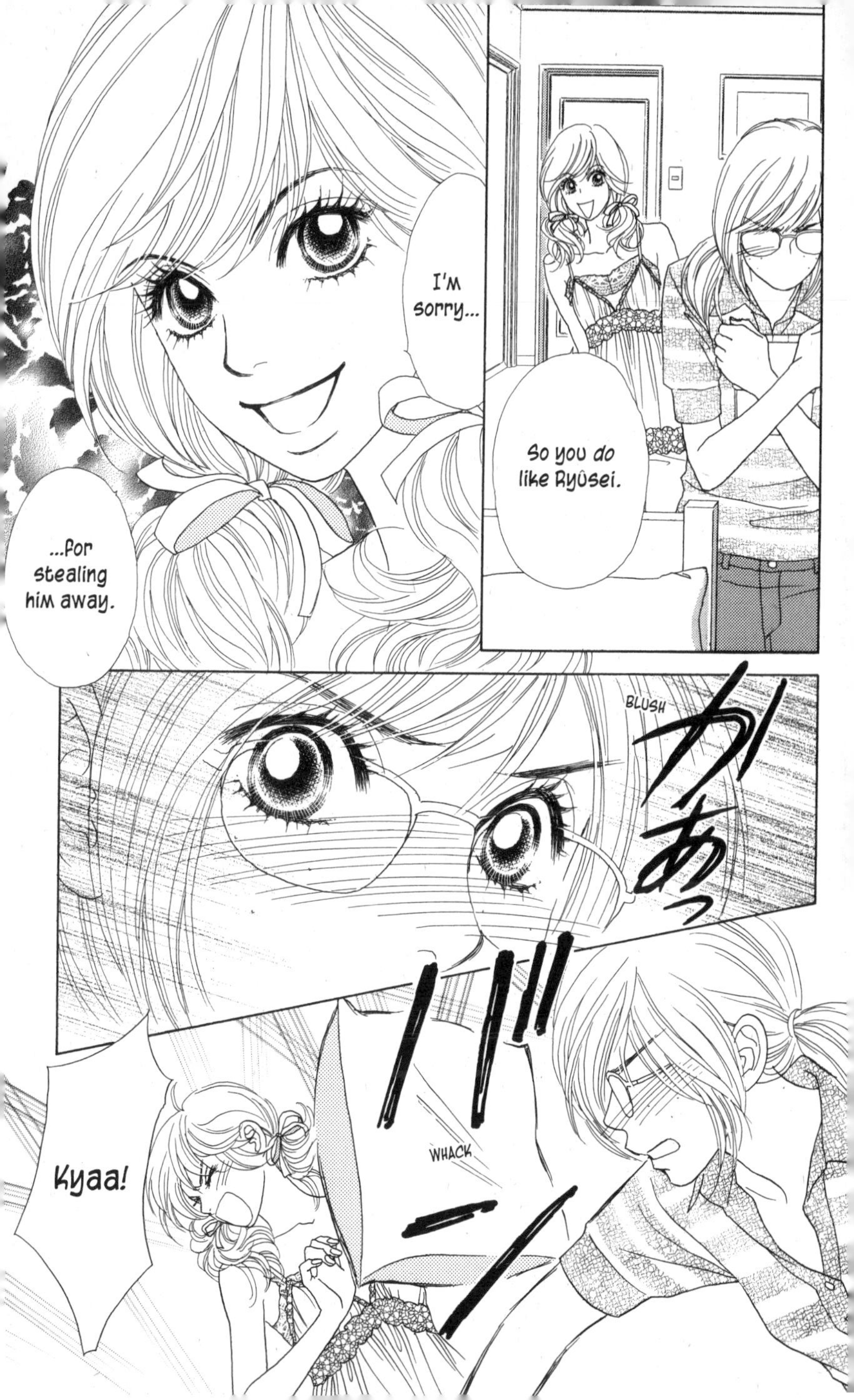
So you do like Ryûsei.
I'm sorry...
...for stealing him away.
BLUSH
かあっ
WHACK
Kyaa!

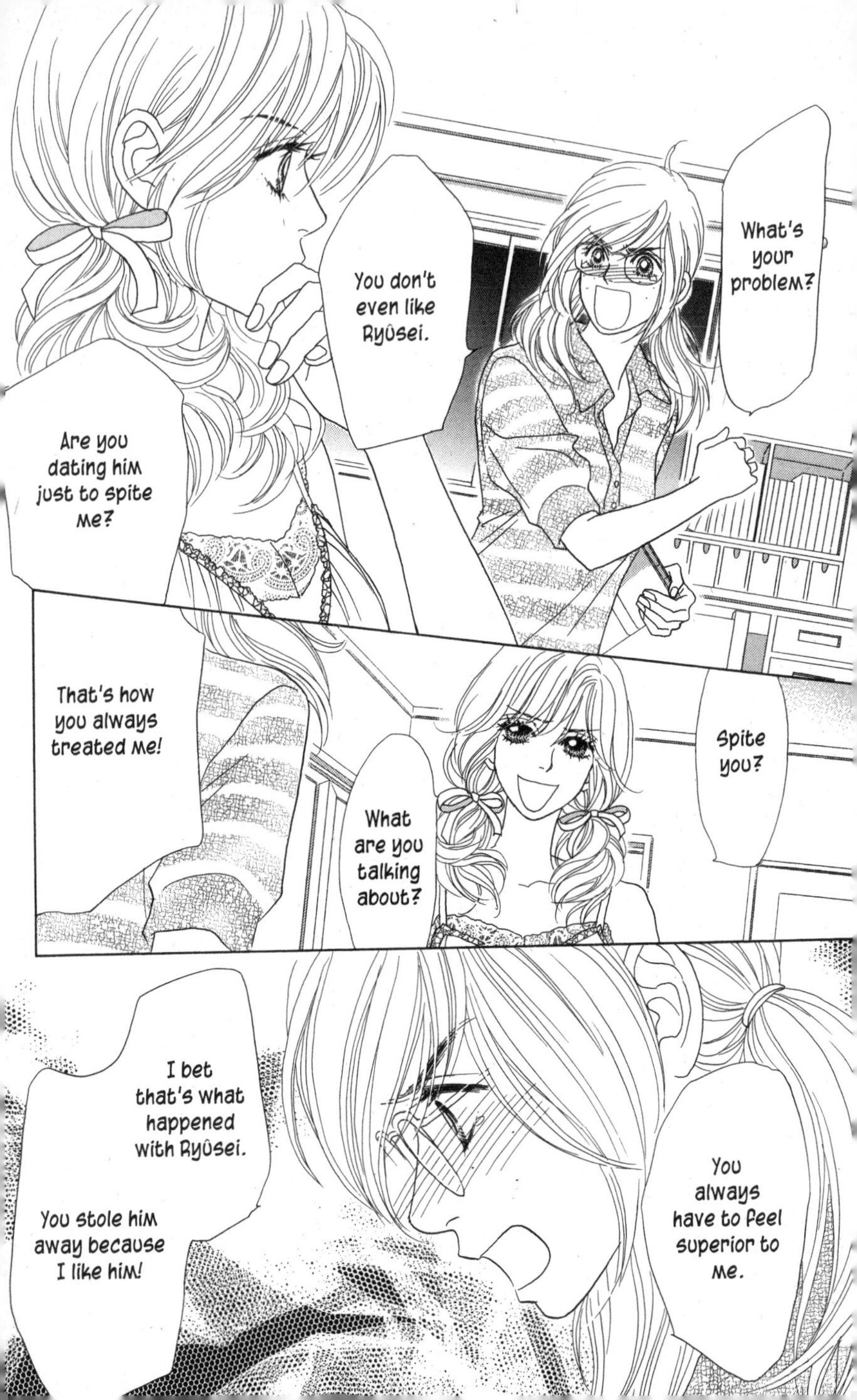
What's your problem?
You don't even like Ryûsei.
Are you dating him just to spite me?
Spite you?
What are you talking about?
That's how you always treated me!
You always have to feel superior to me.
I bet that's what happened with Ryûsei.
You stole him away because I like him!

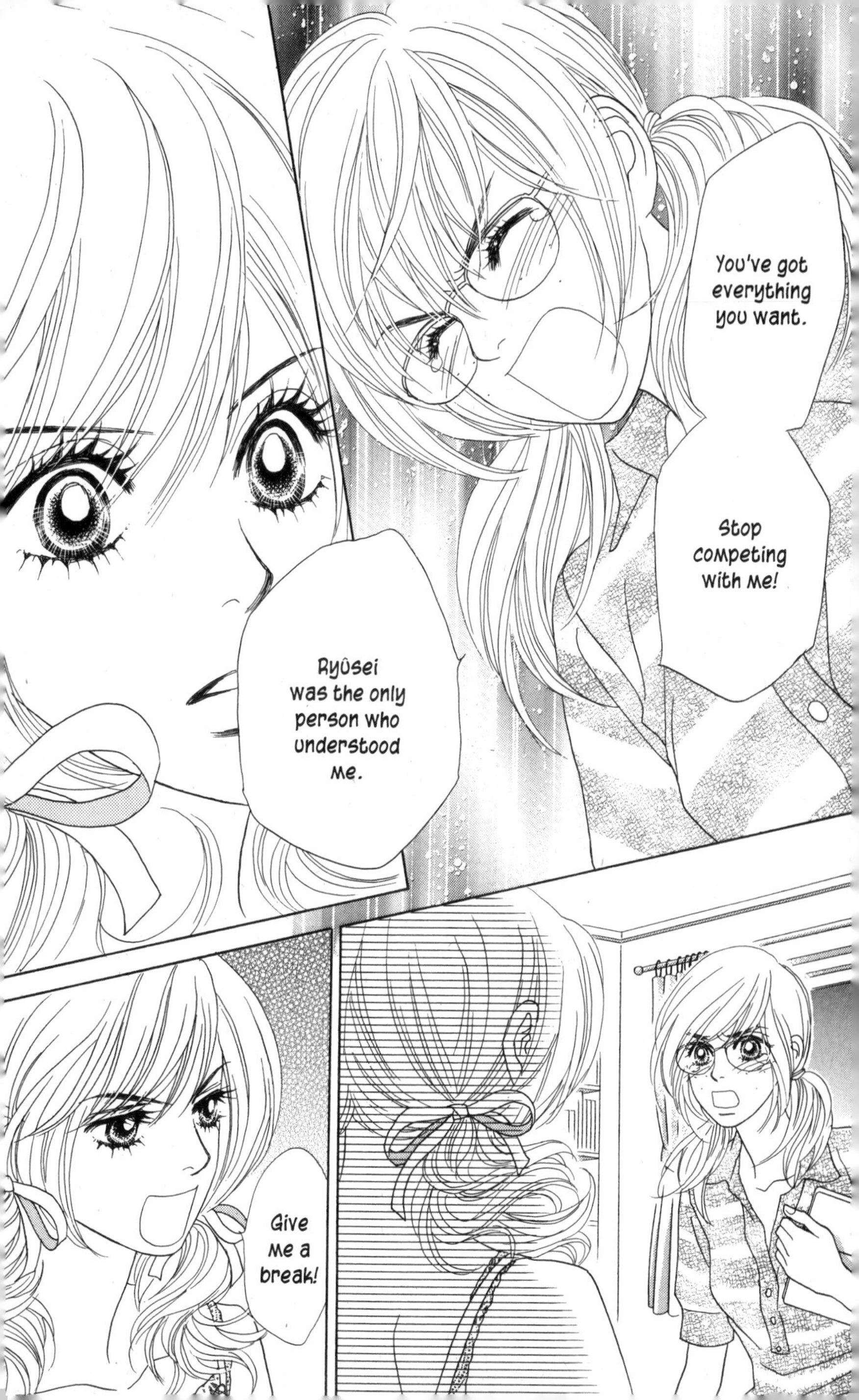
You've got everything you want.
Stop competing with me!
Ryûsei was the only person who understood me.
Give me a break!

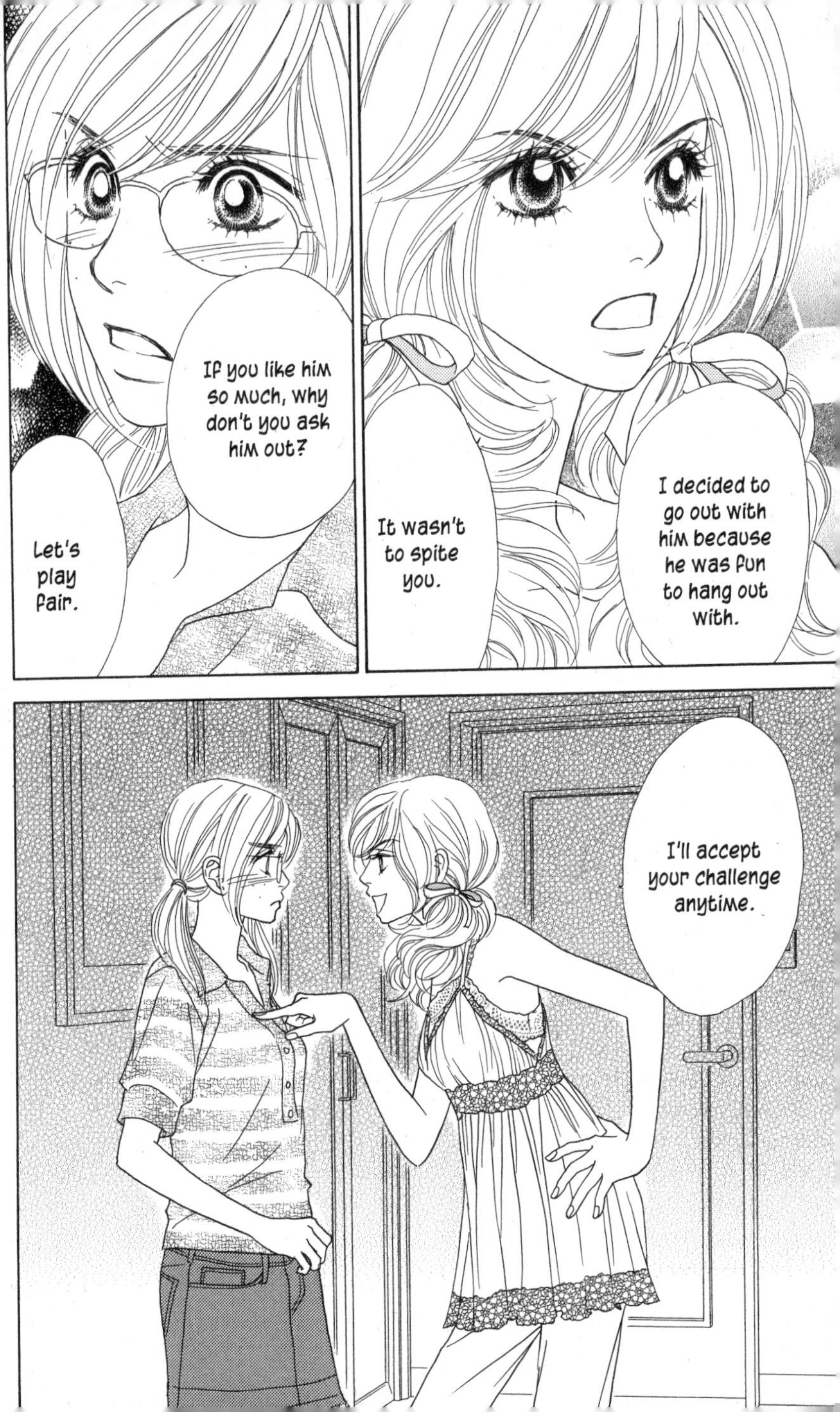
I decided to go out with him because he was fun to hang out with.
It wasn't to spite you.
If you like him so much, why don't you ask him out?
Let's play fair.
I'll accept your challenge anytime.

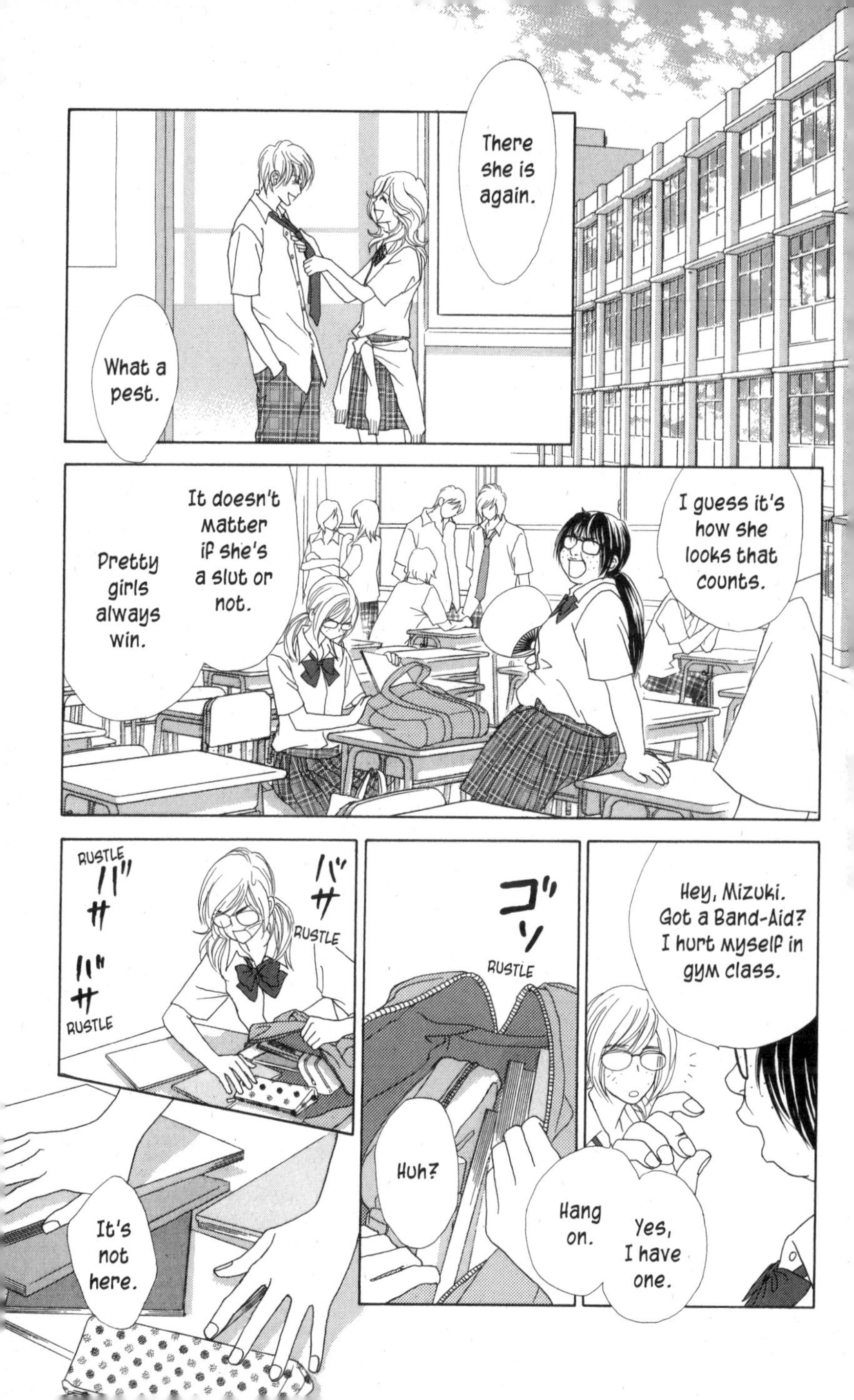
There she is again.
What a pest.
I guess it's how she looks that counts.
It doesn't matter if she's a slut or not.
Pretty girls always win.
Hey, Mizuki. Got a Band-Aid? I hurt myself in gym class.
Yes, I have one.
Hang on.
ゴソ
RUSTLE
Huh?
バサ
RUSTLE
RUSTLE
バサ
バサ
RUSTLE
It's not here.

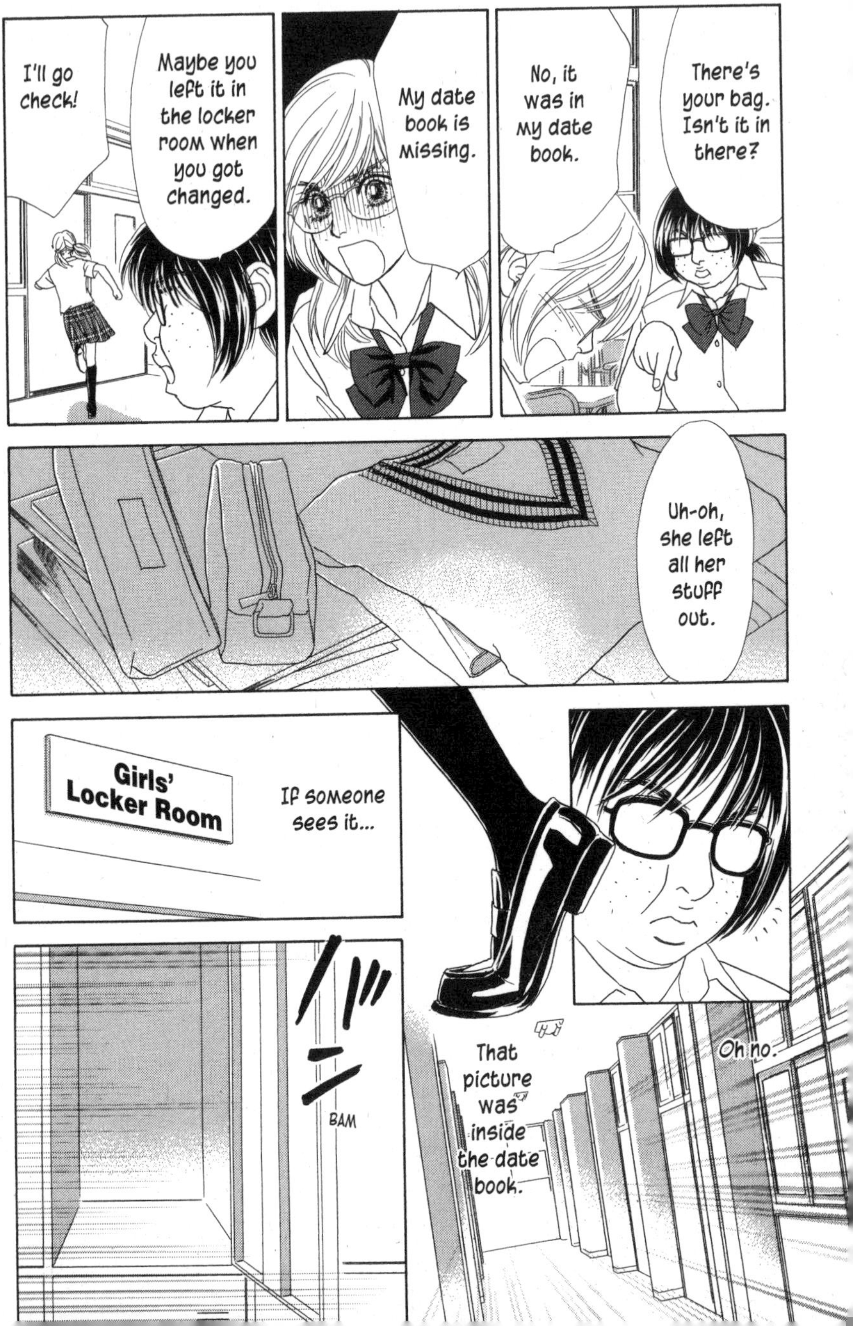
There's your bag. Isn't it in there?
No, it was in my date book.
My date book is missing.
Maybe you left it in the locker room when you got changed.
I'll go check!
Uh-oh, she left all her stuff out.
Girls' Locker Room
If someone sees it...
Oh no.
That picture was inside the date book.
BAM

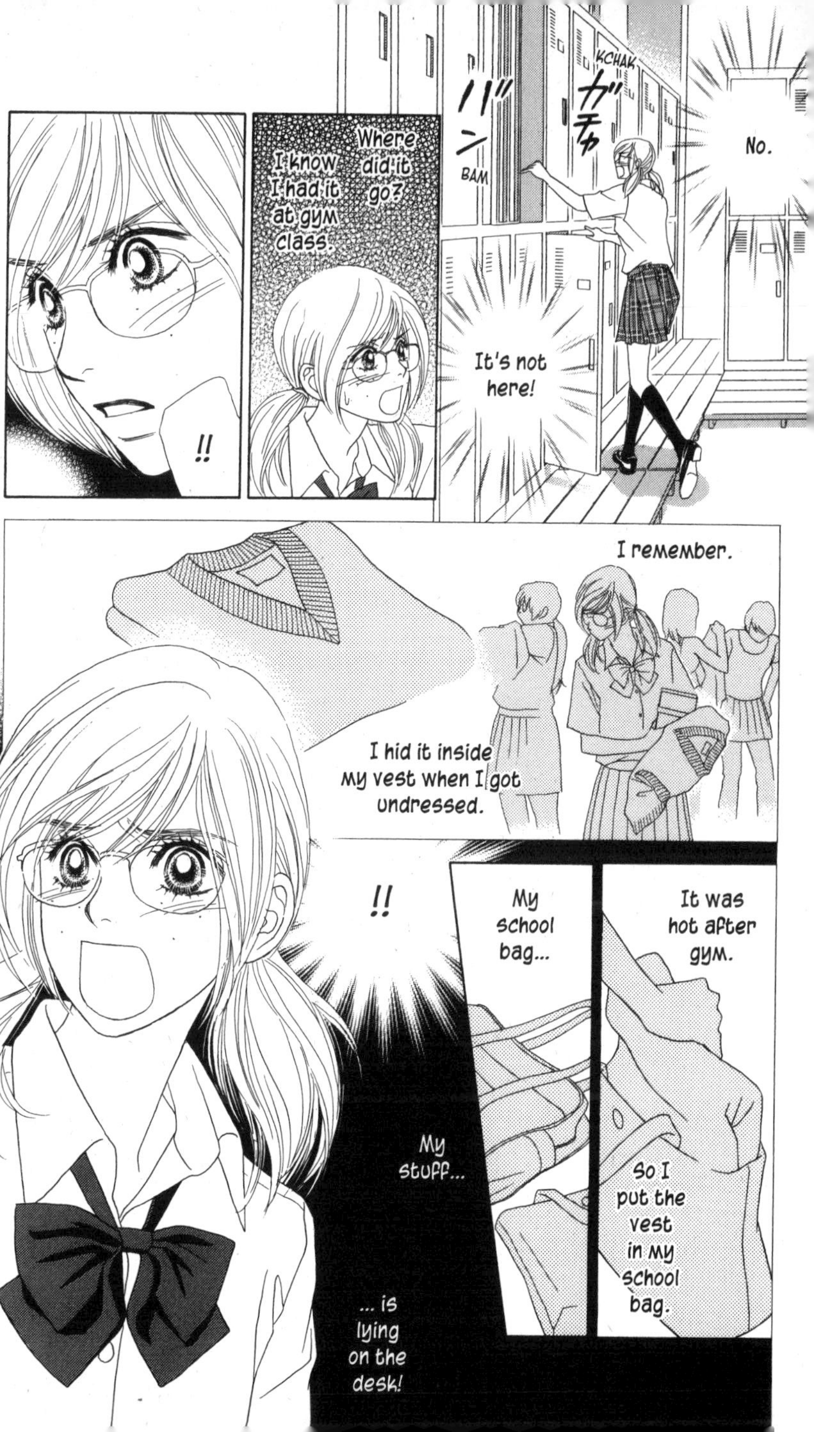
No.
KCHAK
ガチャ
バン
BAM
It's not here!
Where did it go?
I know I had it at gym class.
!!
I remember.
I hid it inside my vest when I got undressed.
It was hot after gym.
So I put the vest in my school bag.
My school bag...
!!
My stuff...
... is lying on the desk!

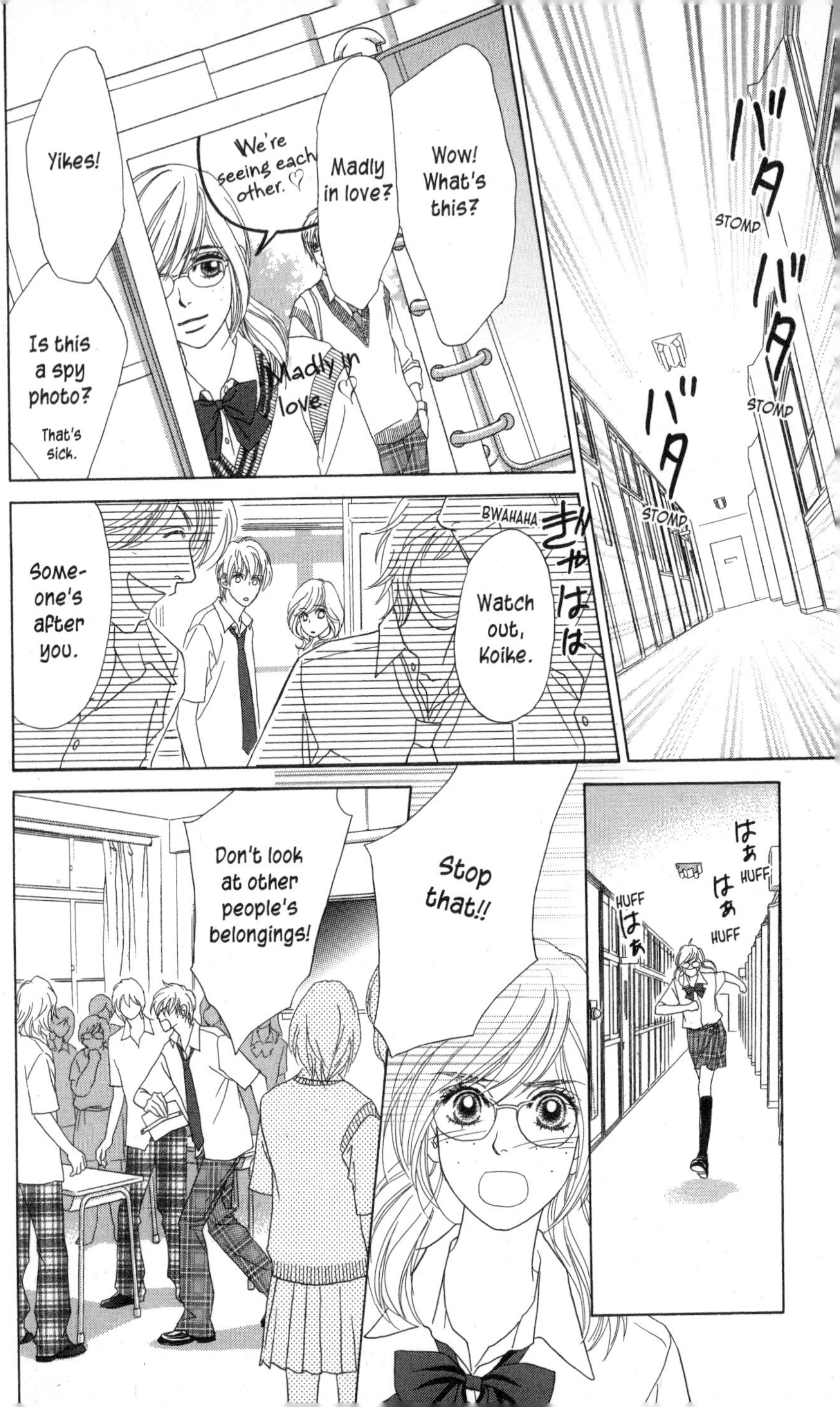
バタ
STOMP
バタ
STOMP
バタ
STOMP
Wow! What's this?
Madly in love?
We're seeing each other. ♡
Madly in love. ♡
Yikes!
Is this a spy photo?
That's sick.
きゃはは
BWAHAHA
Watch out, Koike.
Someone's after you.
はぁ
HUFF
はぁ
HUFF
はぁ
HUFF
Stop that!!
Don't look at other people's belongings!

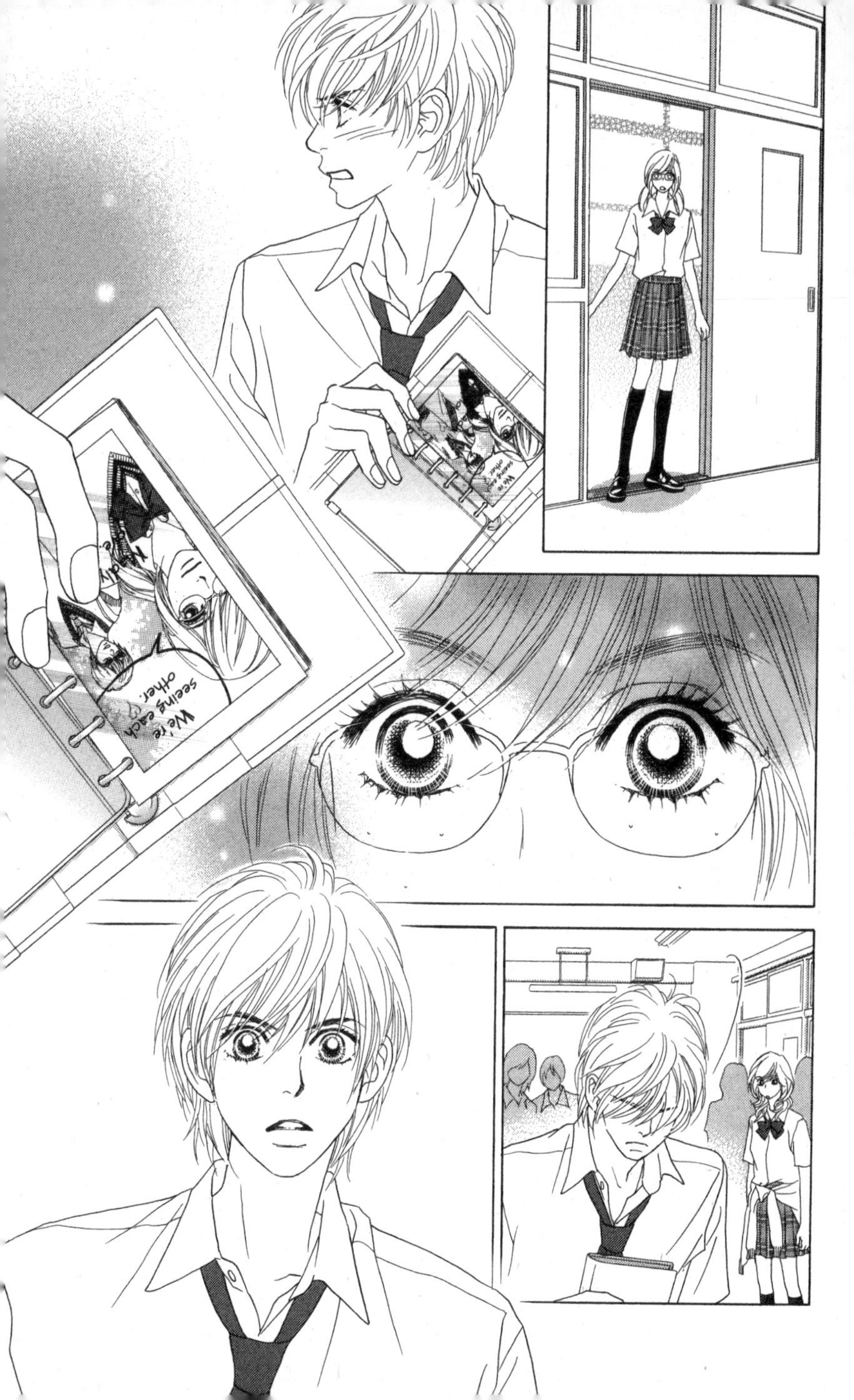

We're seeing each other.
We're seeing each other.

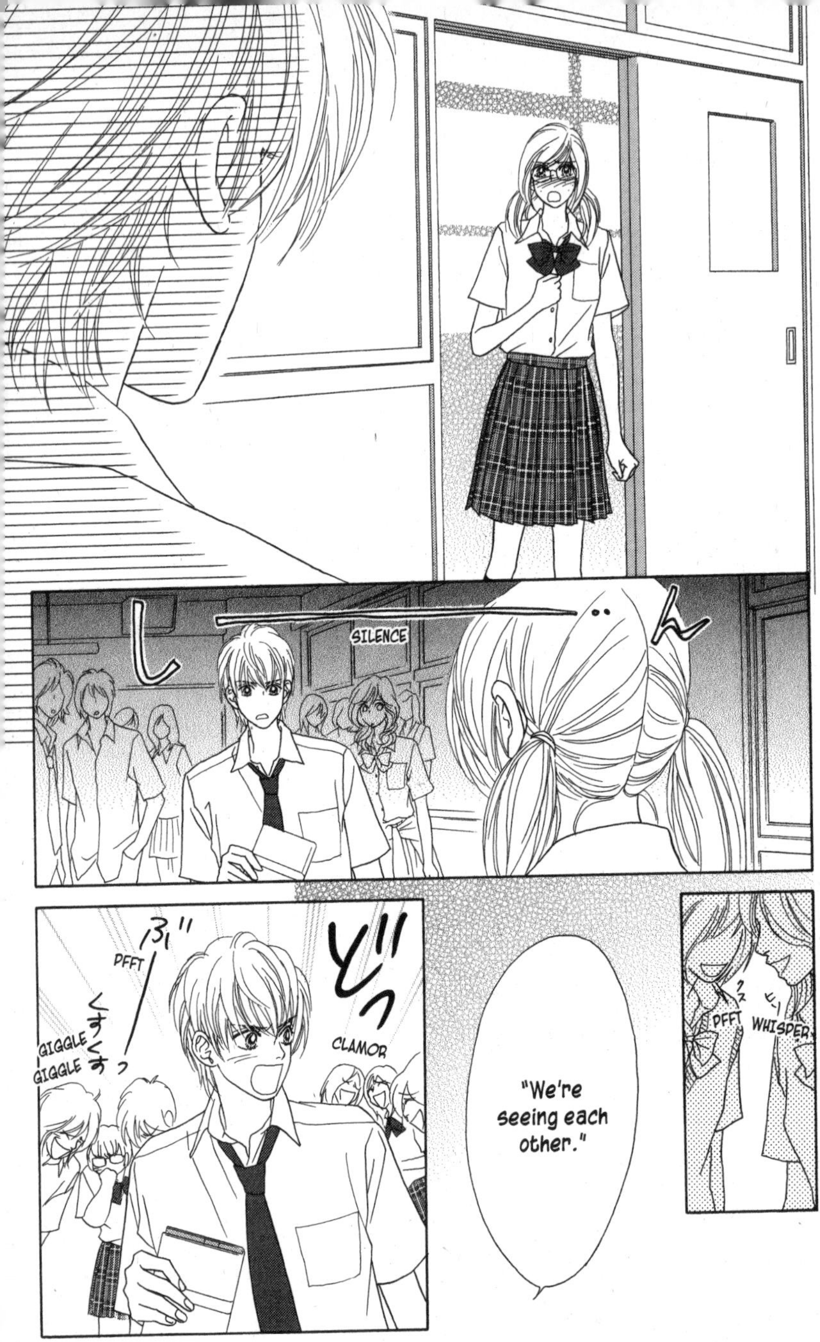
SILENCE
PFFT
WHISPER
"We're seeing each other."
CLAMOR
PFFT
GIGGLE GIGGLE

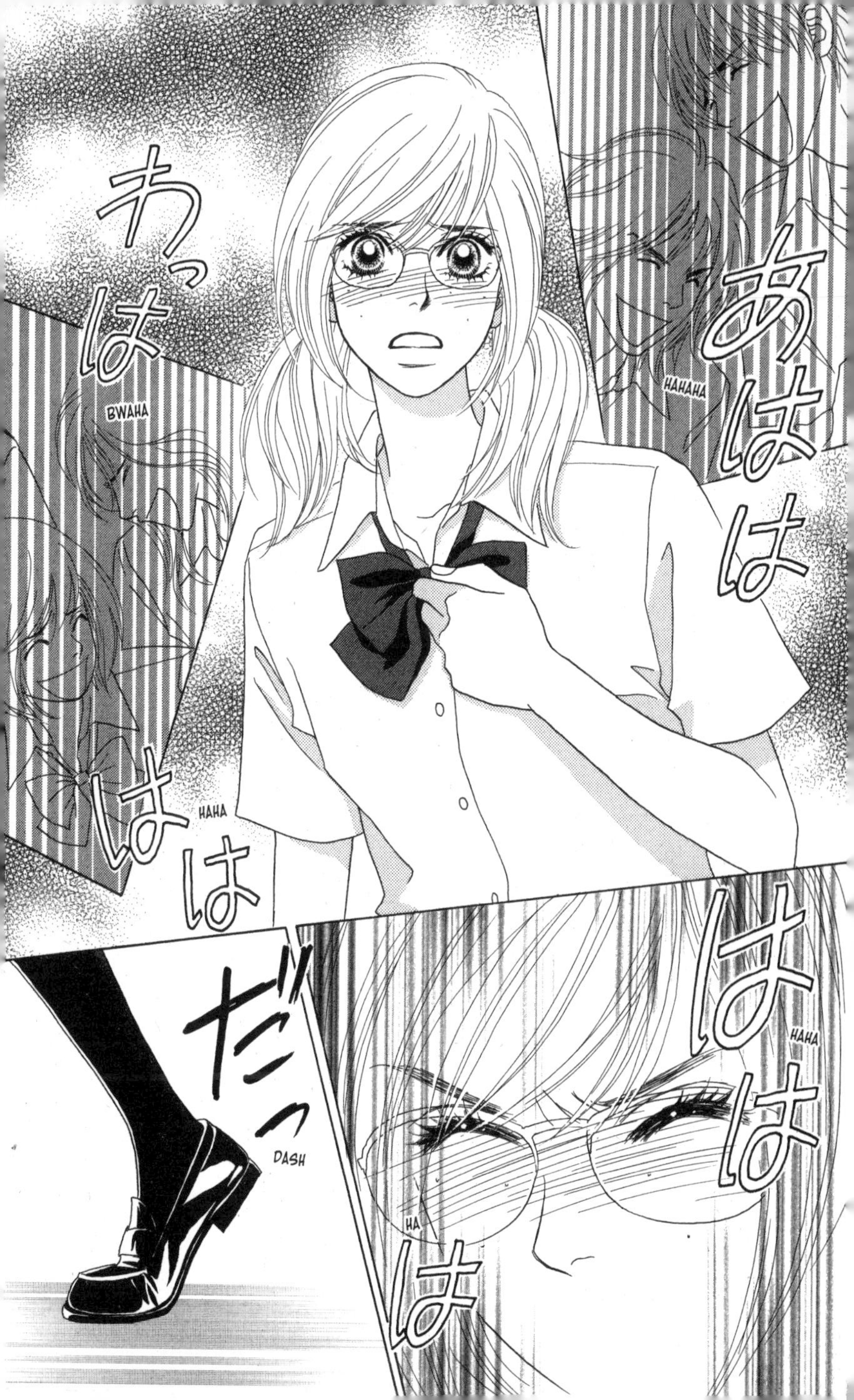

あはは
HAHAHA
わっはは
BWAHA
は
HAHA
はは
HAHA
は
HA
だっ
DASH

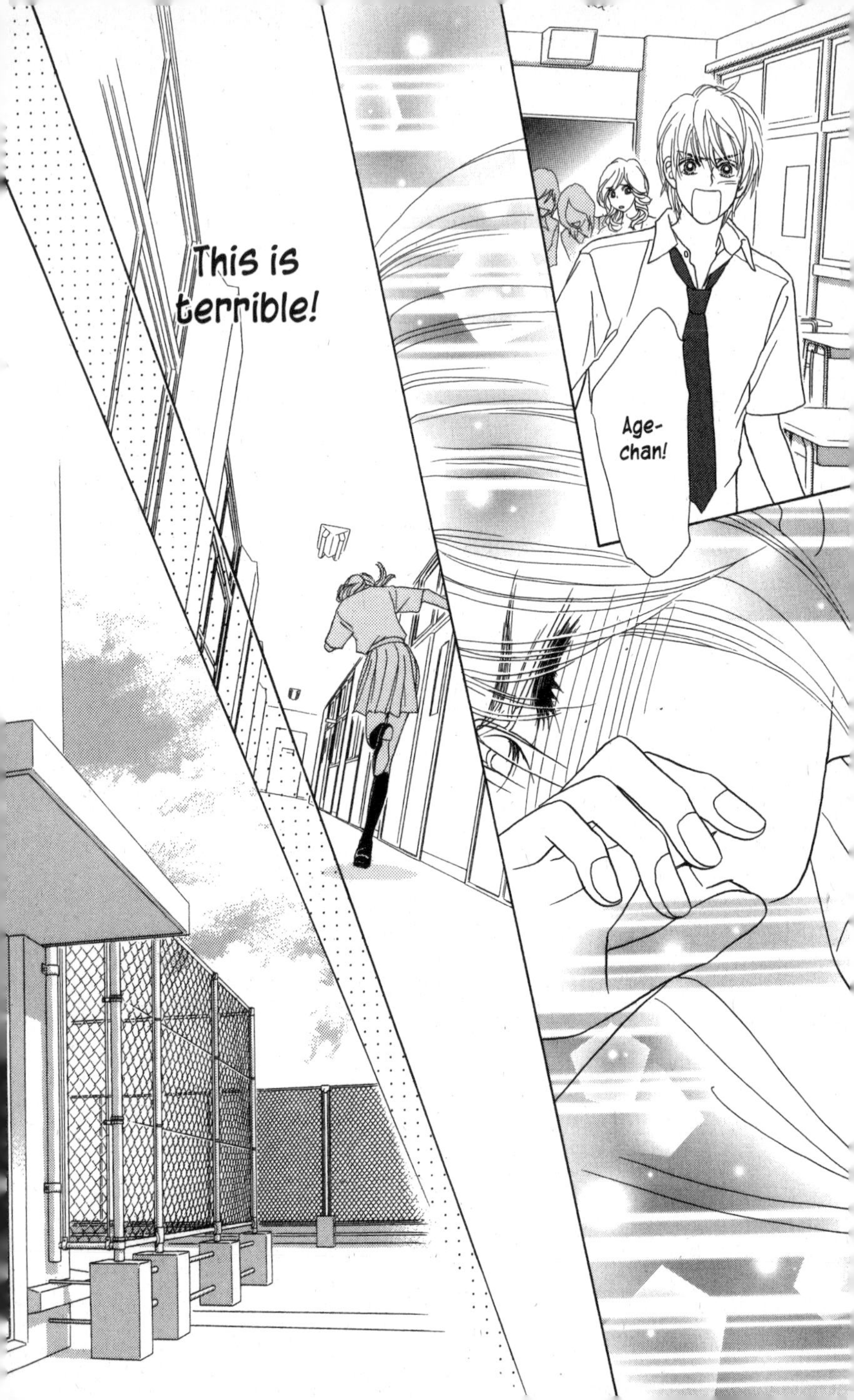
Age-chan!
This is terrible!

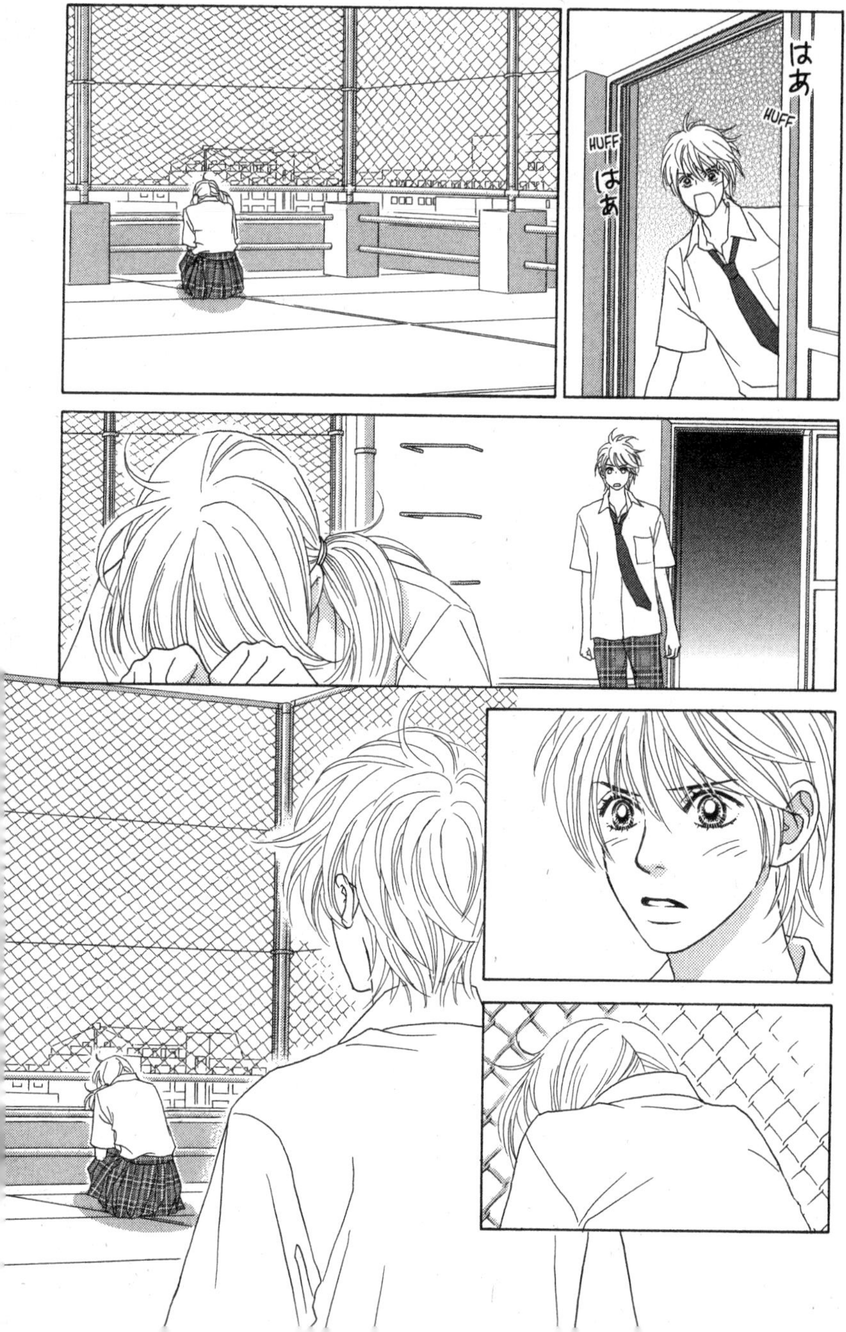
はあ
HUFF
HUFF
はあ

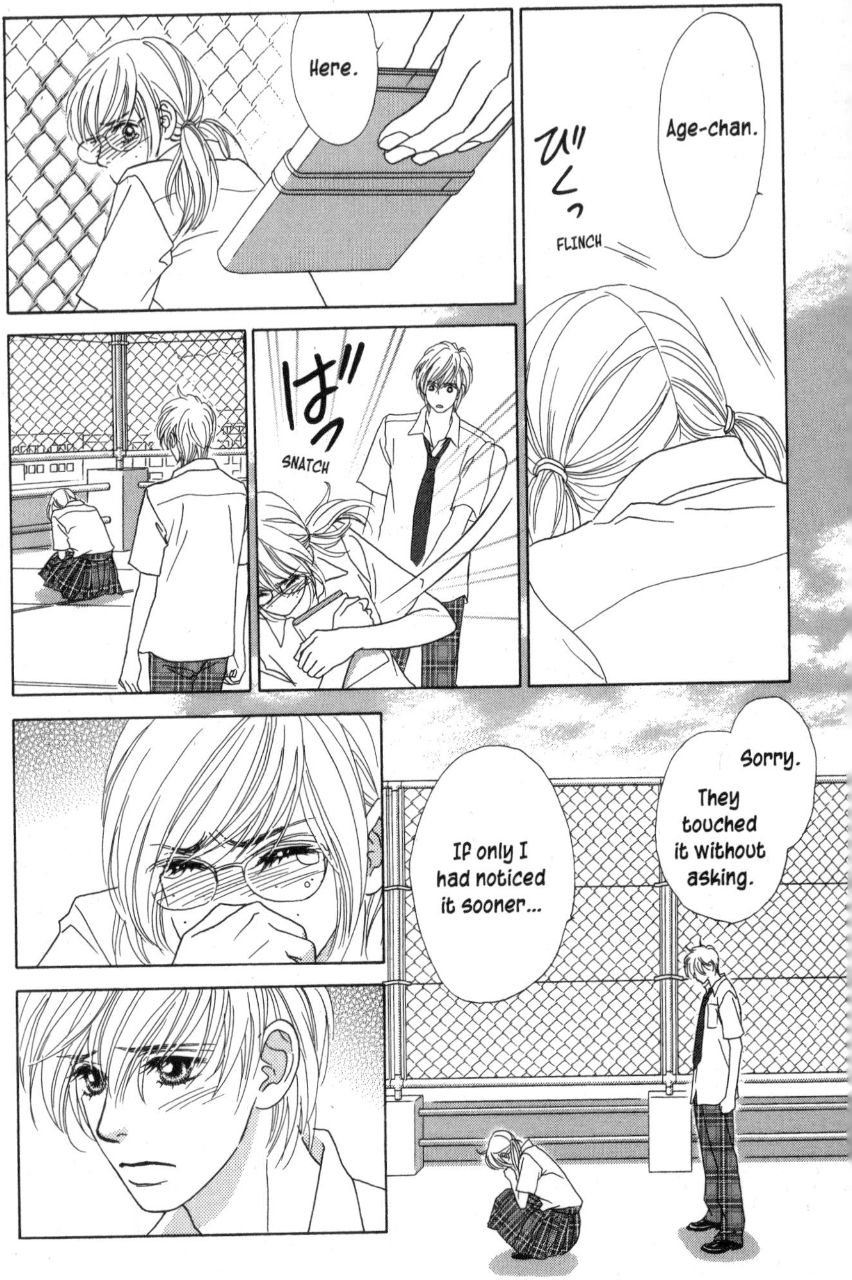
Age-chan.
びくっ
FLINCH
Here.
ばっ
SNATCH
Sorry.
They touched it without asking.
If only I had noticed it sooner...

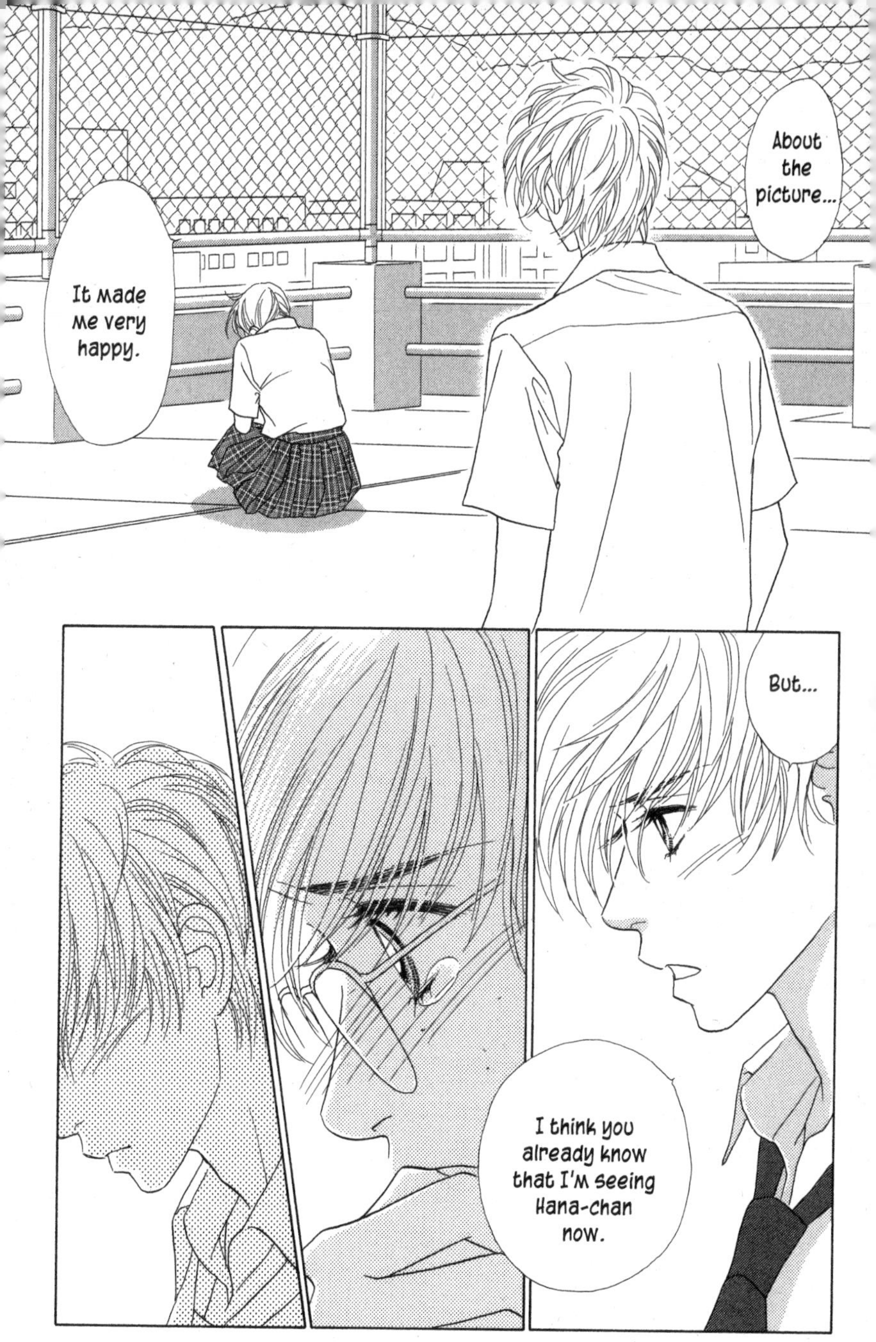
About the picture...
It made me very happy.
But...
I think you already know that I'm seeing Hana-chan now.

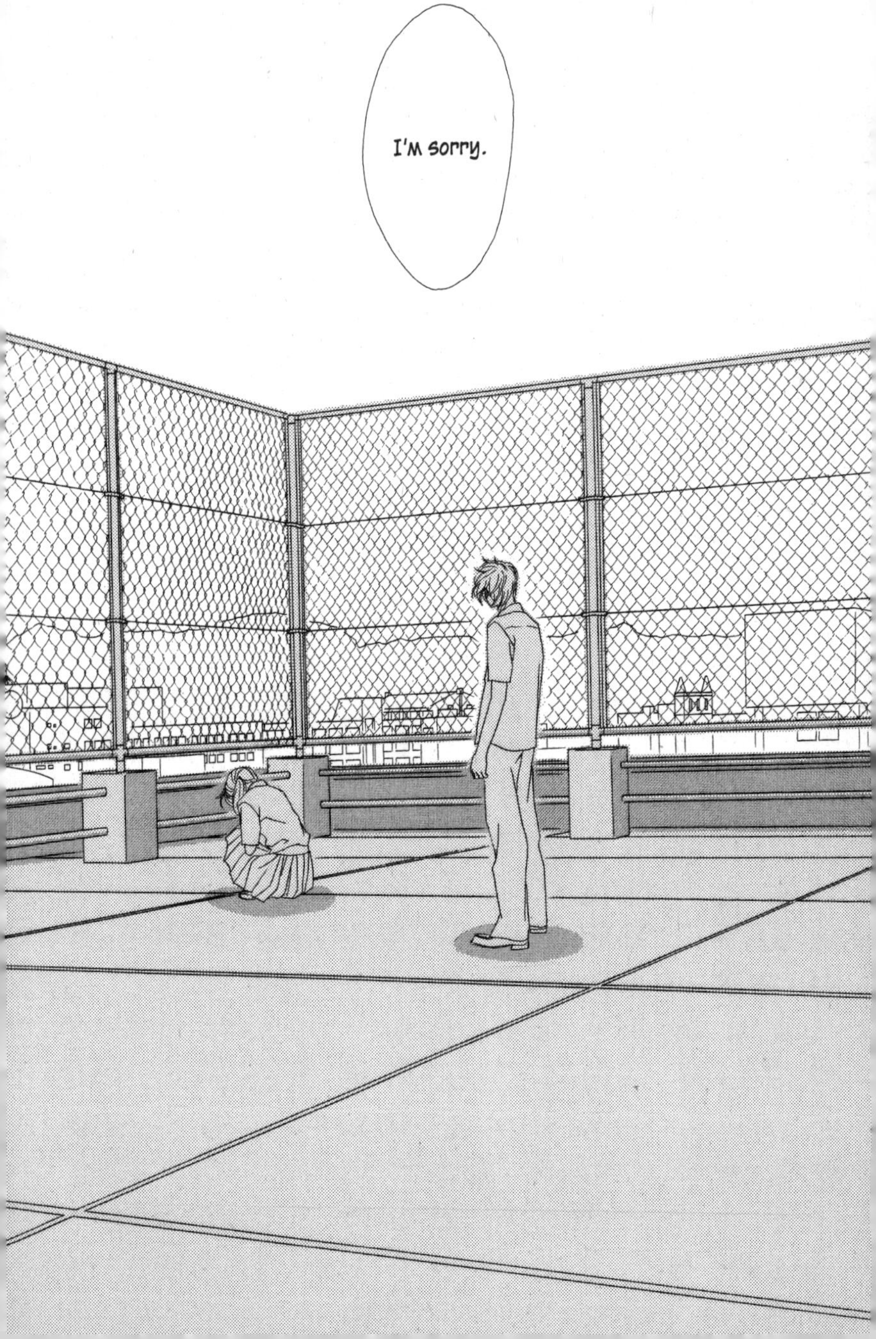
I'm sorry.

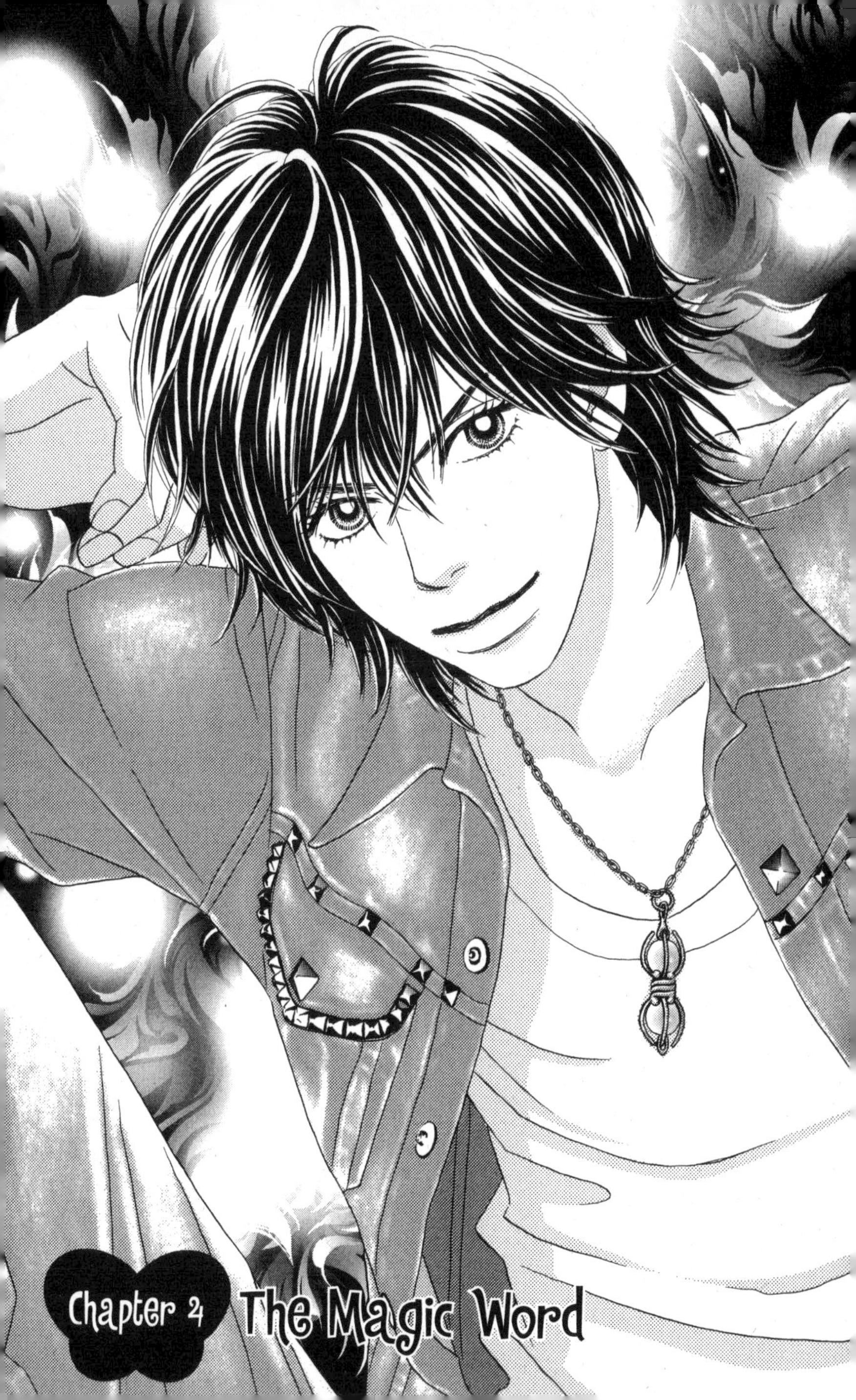

Chapter 4 The Magic Word

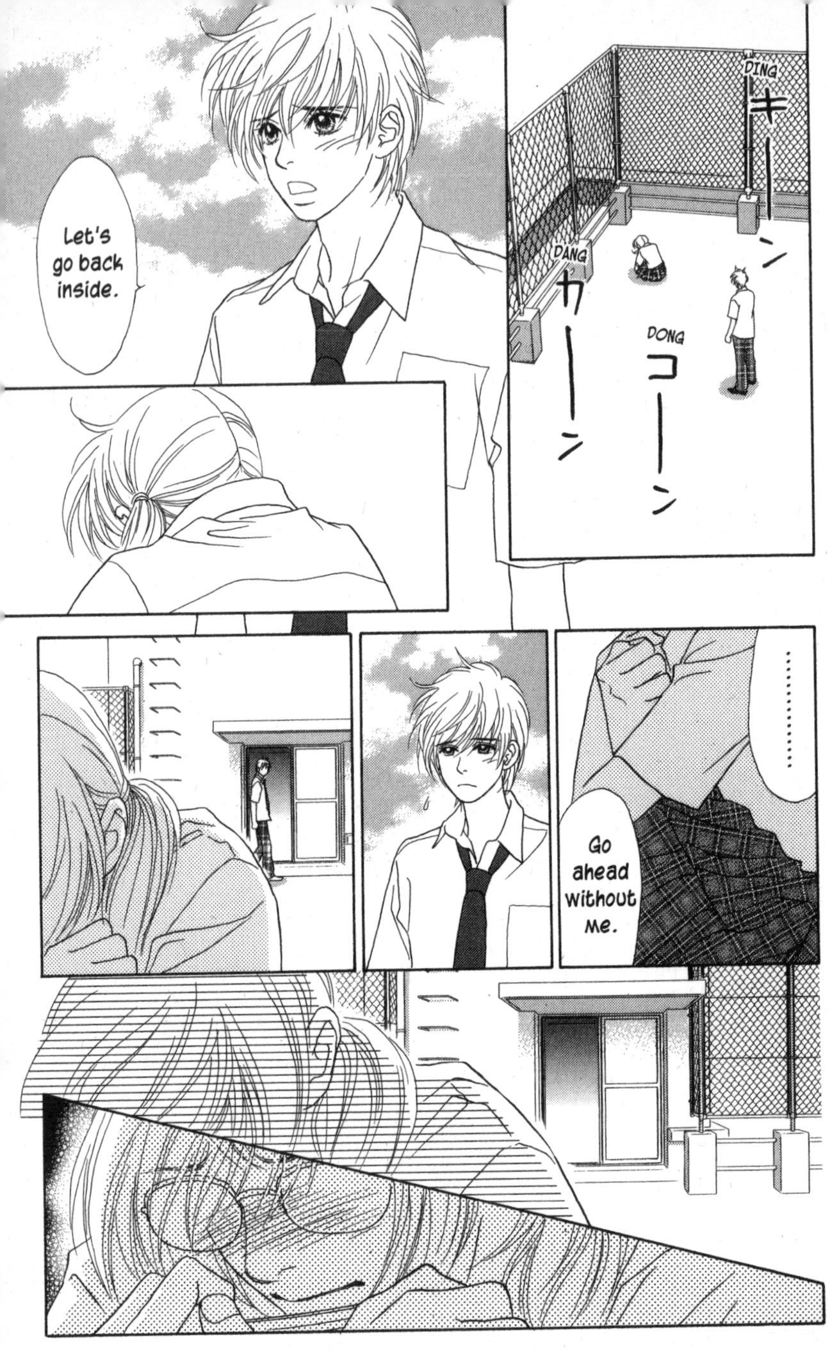
DING
キーン
DANG
カーン
DONG
コーン
Let's go back inside.
......
Go ahead without me.

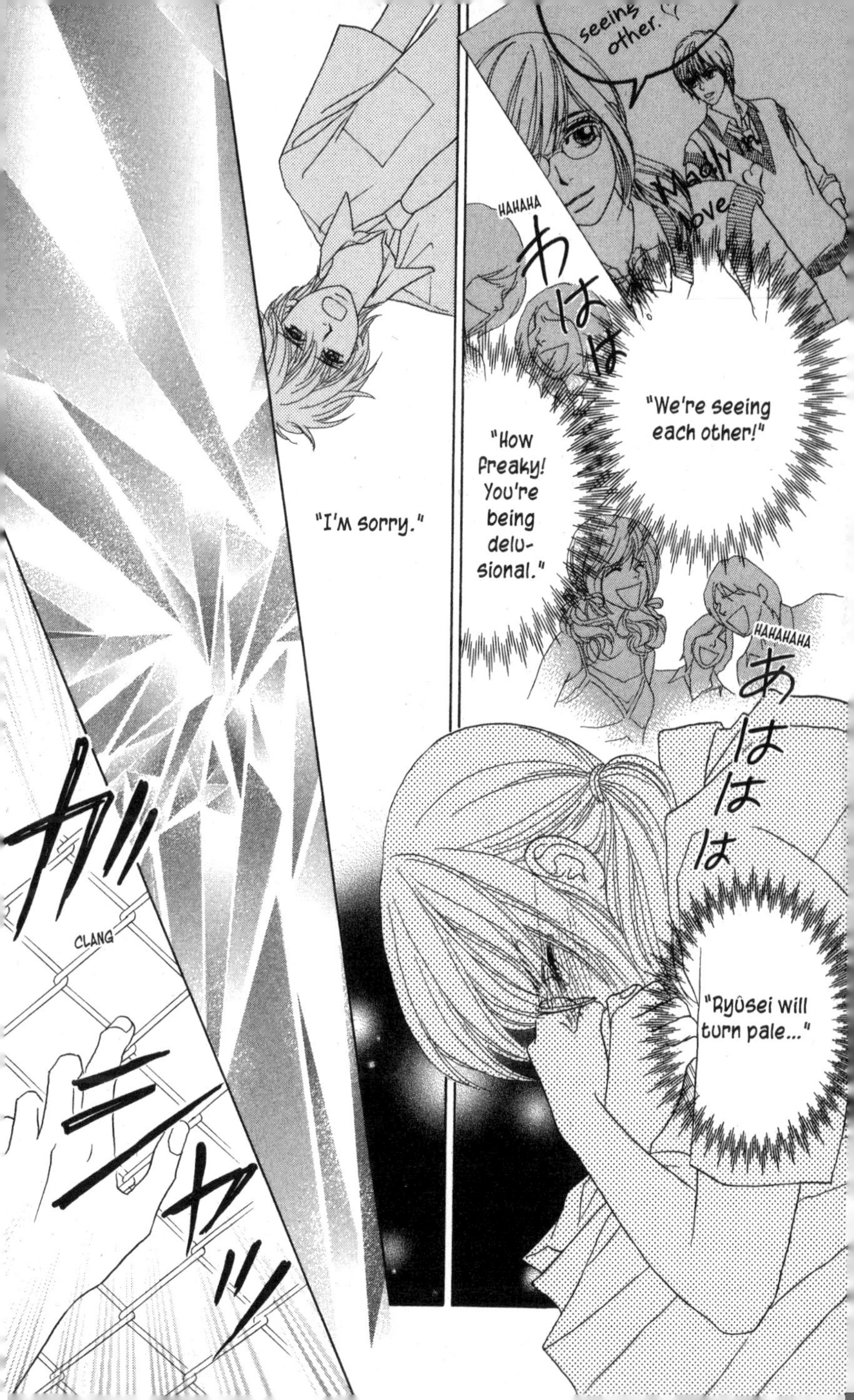

seeing other.
Madly in love.
HAHAHA
わはは
"We're seeing each other!"
"How freaky! You're being delusional."
HAHAHAHA
あははは
"Ryûsei will turn pale..."
"I'm sorry."
CLANG

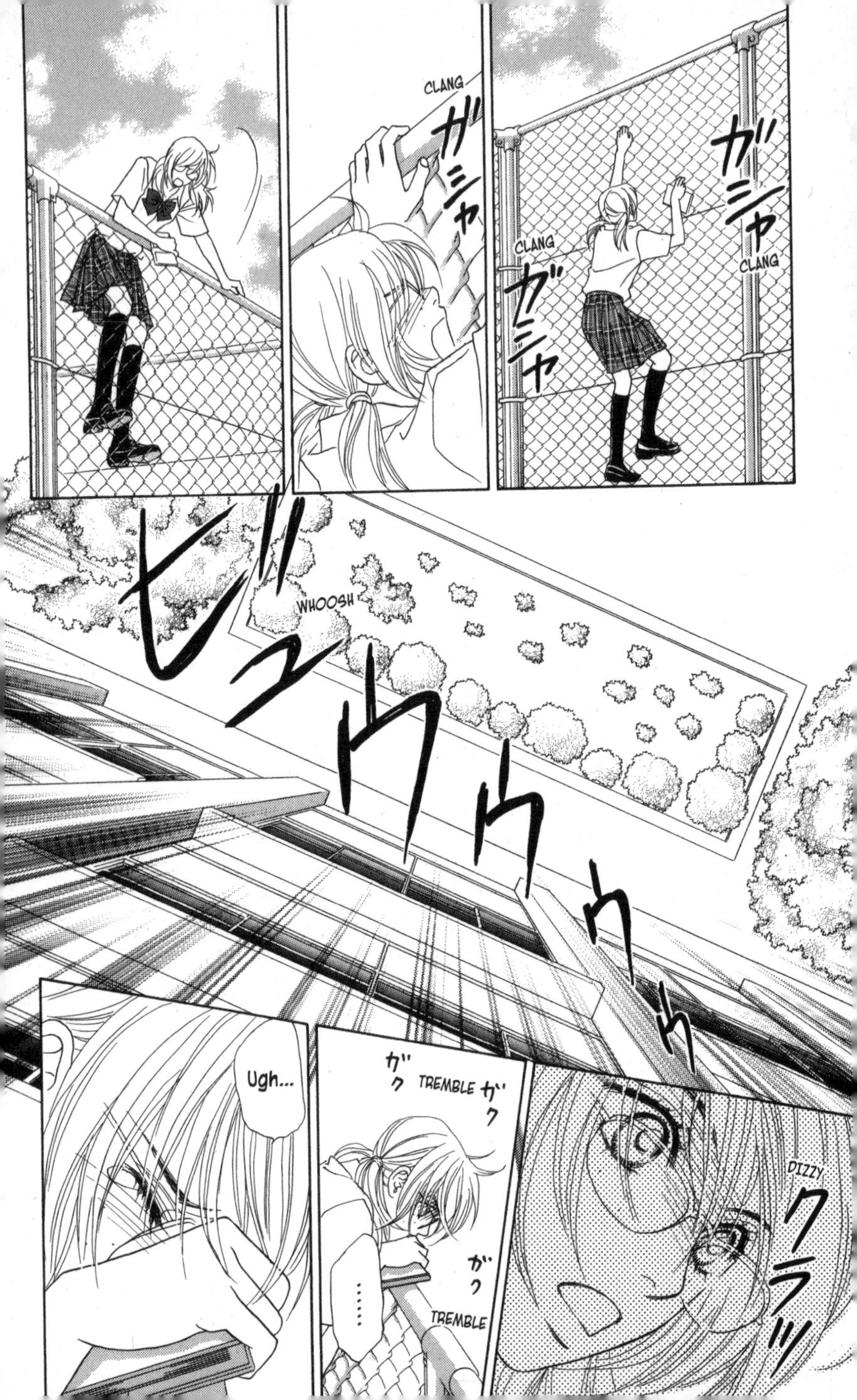
ガシャ
CLANG
ガシャ
CLANG
CLANG
ガシャ
ビュウウゥゥ
WHOOSH
DIZZY
クラッ
ガク
TREMBLE
ガク
......
がく
TREMBLE
Ugh...

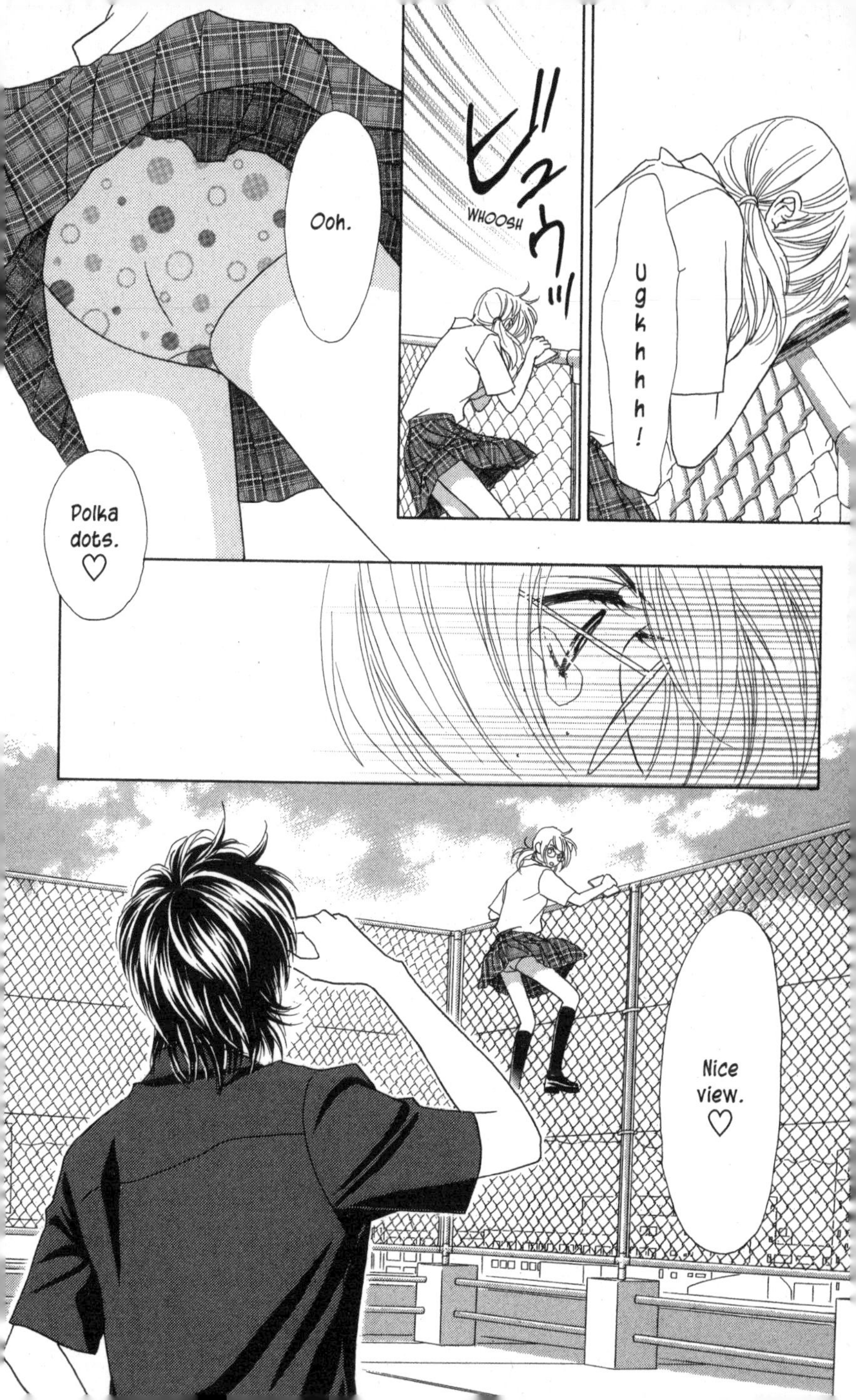
Ugkhhhh!
ビュウッ
WHOOSH
Ooh.
Polka dots. ♡
Nice view. ♡

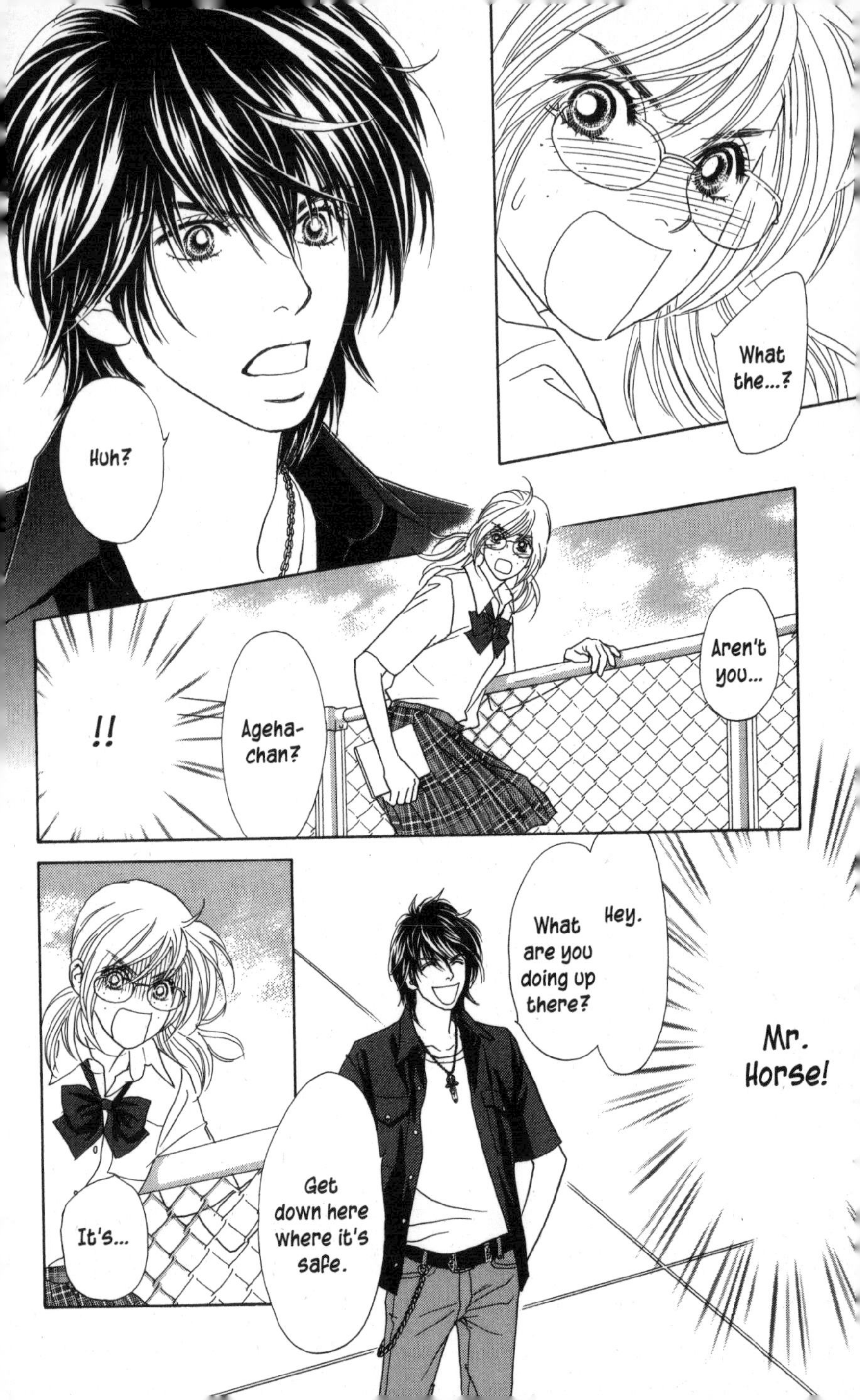
What the...?
Huh?
Aren't you...
Ageha-chan?
!!
Mr. Horse!
Hey.
What are you doing up there?
Get down here where it's safe.
It's...

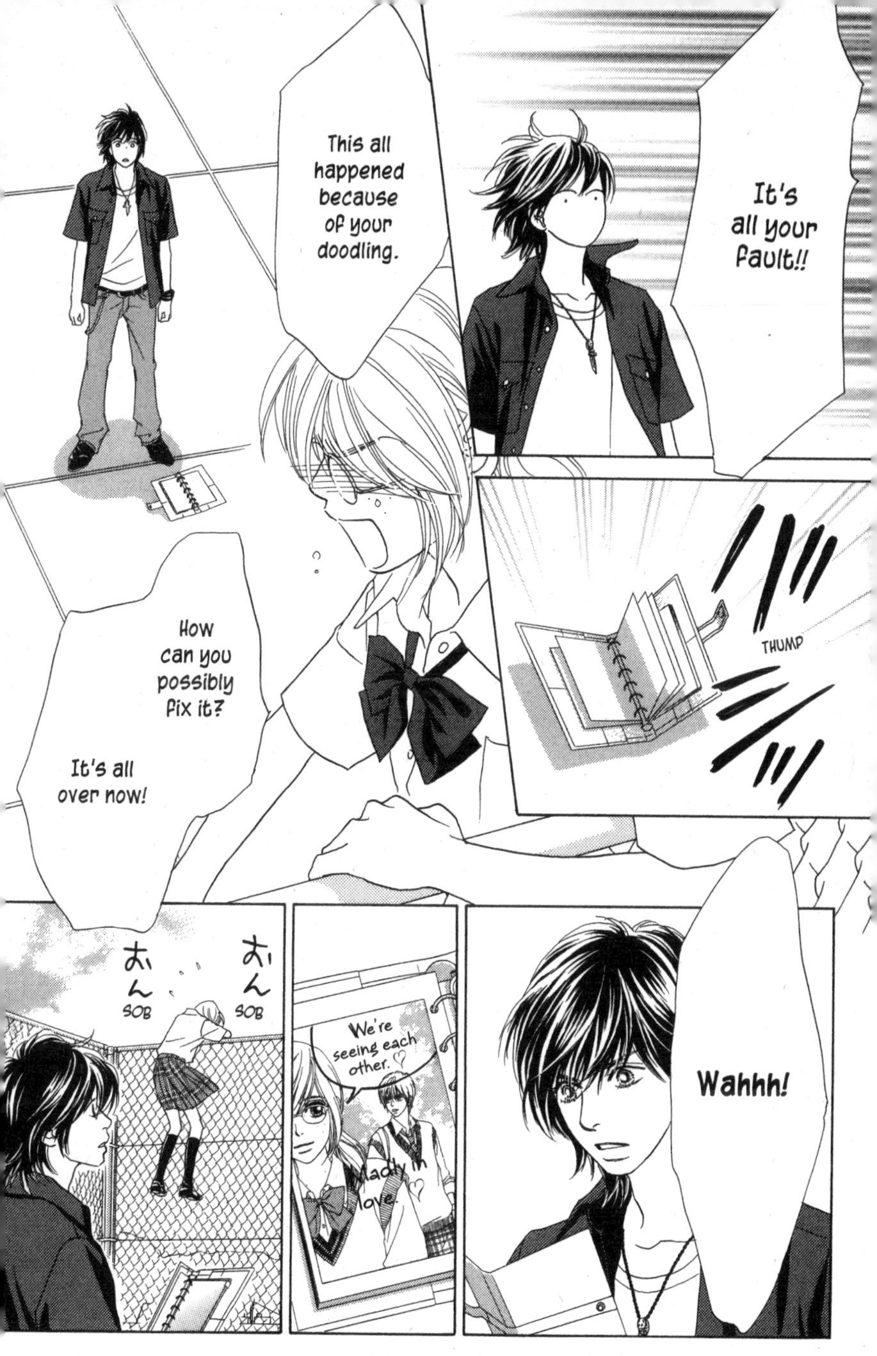
It's all your fault!!
This all happened because of your doodling.
THUMP
How can you possibly fix it?
It's all over now!
Wahhh!
We're seeing each other. ♡
Madly in love. ♡
おん SOB
おん SOB

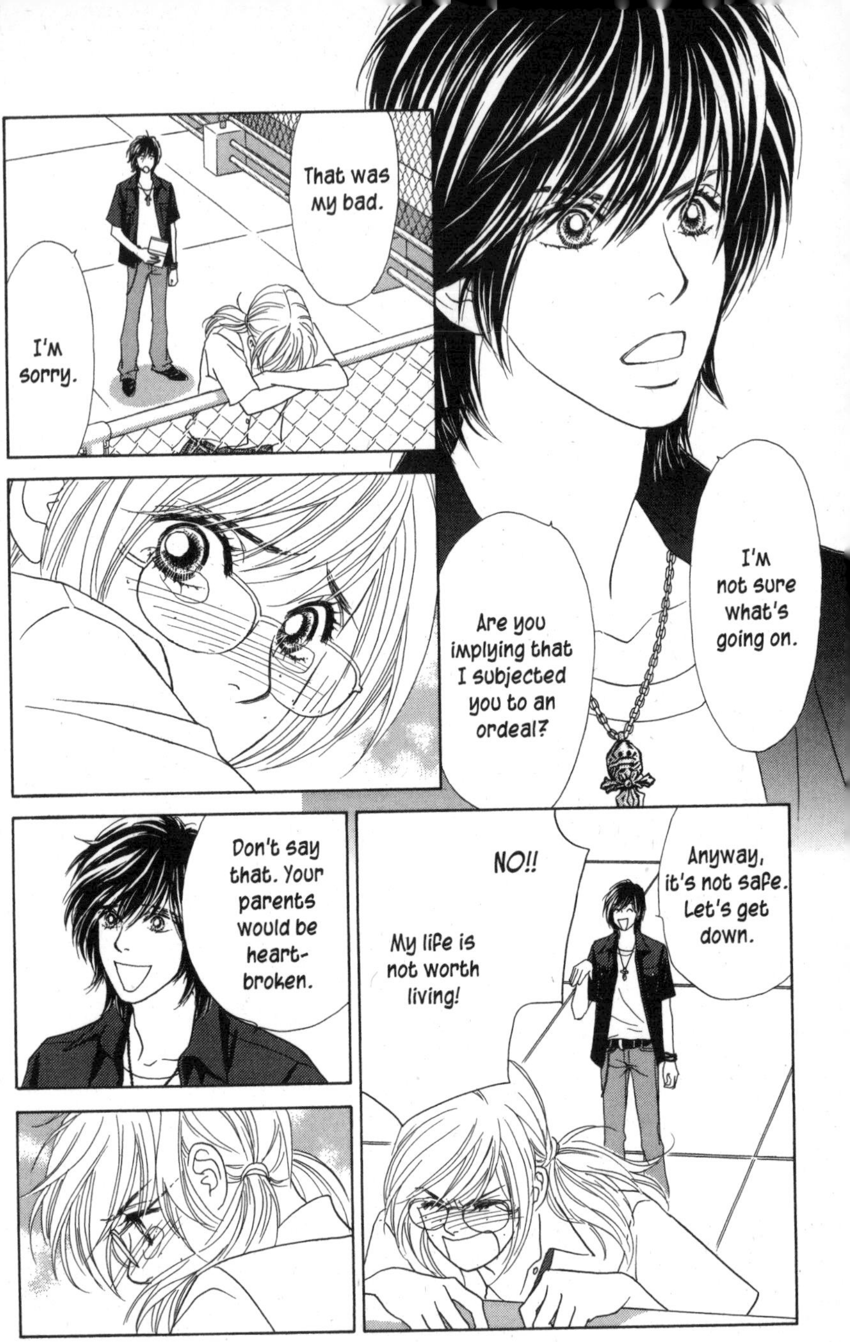
I'm not sure what's going on.
Are you implying that I subjected you to an ordeal?
That was my bad.
I'm sorry.
Anyway, it's not safe. Let's get down.
NO!!
My life is not worth living!
Don't say that. Your parents would be heart-broken.

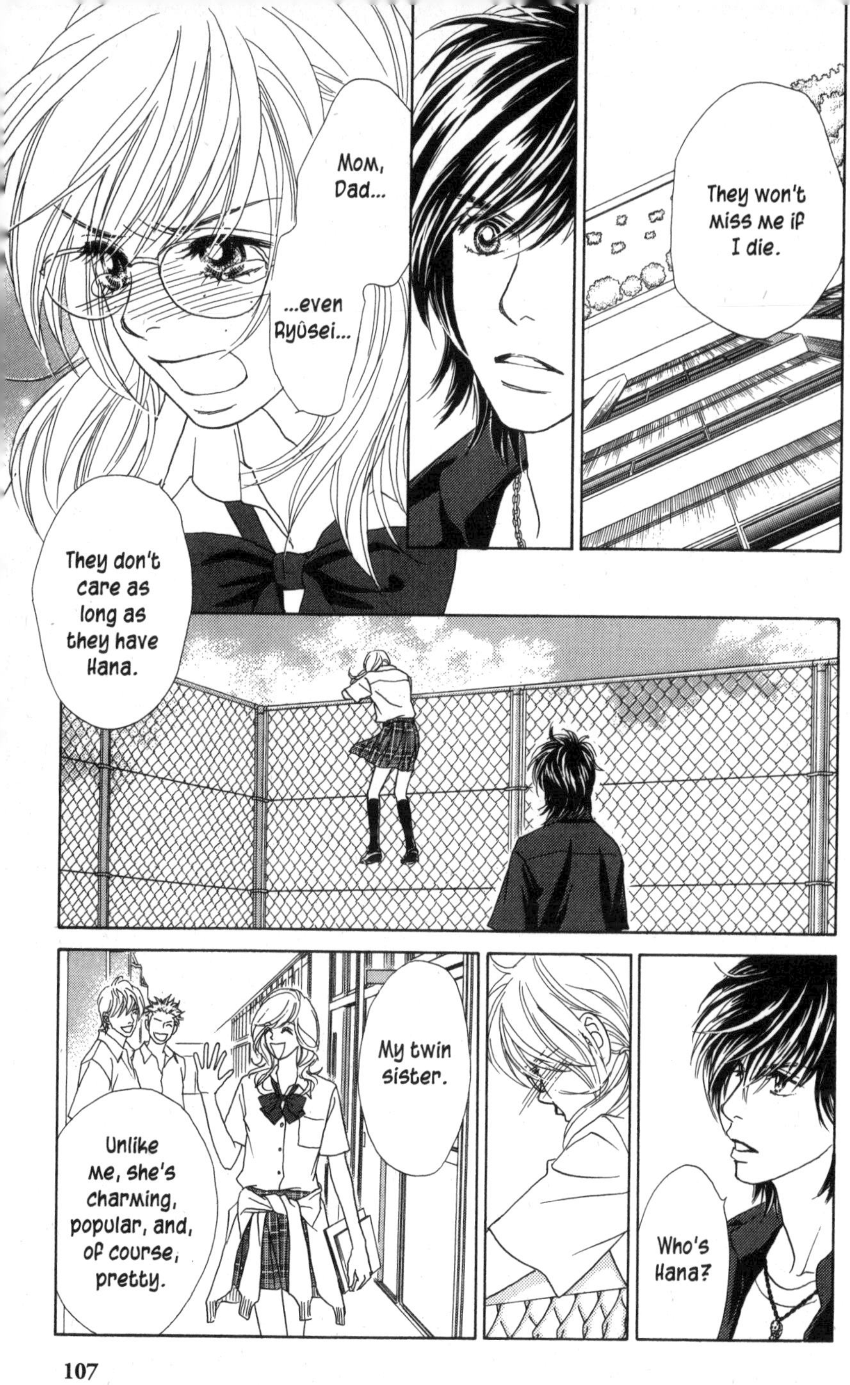
They won't miss me if I die.
Mom, Dad...
...even Ryûsei...
They don't care as long as they have Hana.
Who's Hana?
My twin sister.
Unlike me, she's charming, popular, and, of course, pretty.

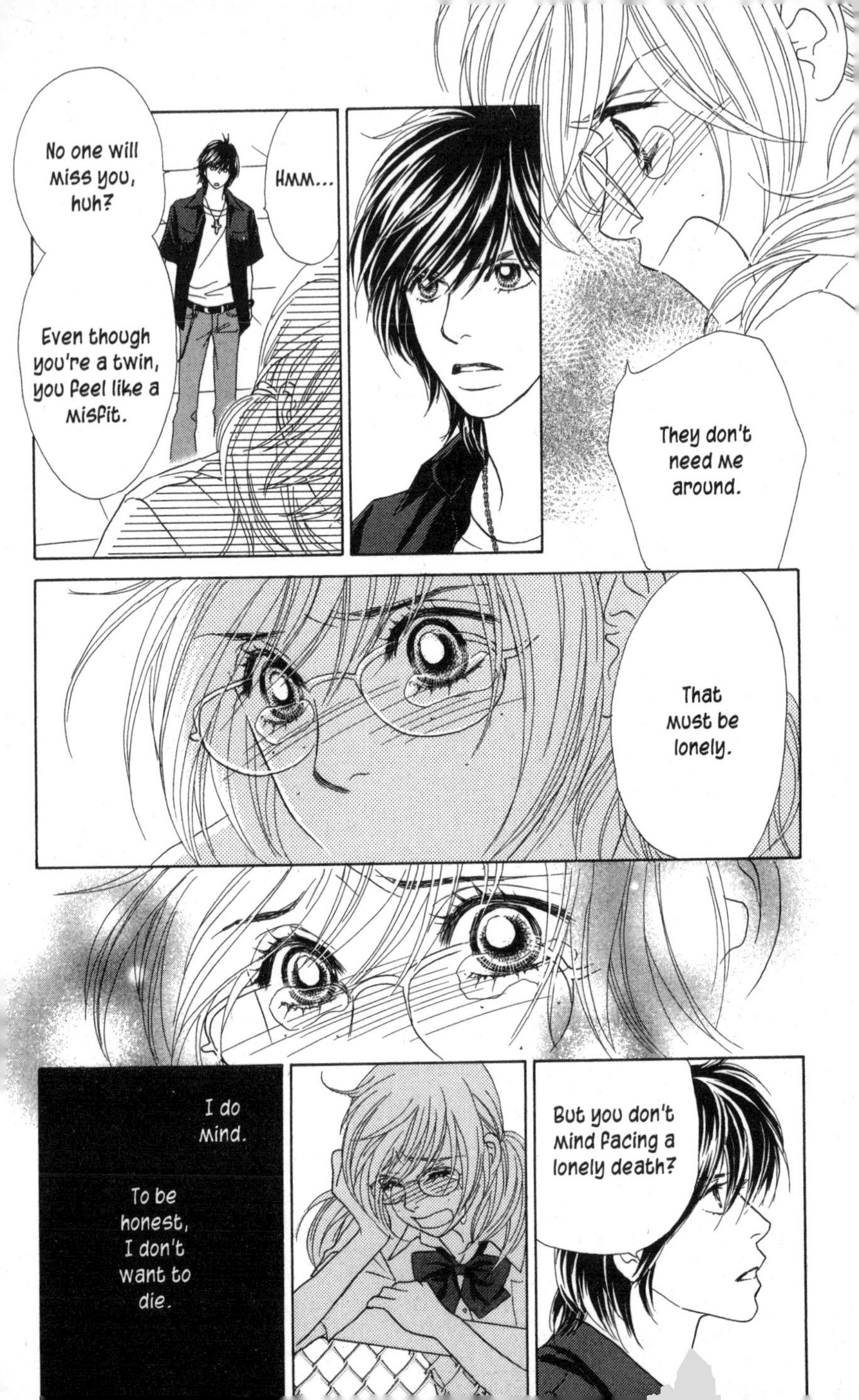
They don't need me around.
Hmm...
No one will miss you, huh?
Even though you're a twin, you feel like a misfit.
That must be lonely.
But you don't mind facing a lonely death?
I do mind.
To be honest, I don't want to die.

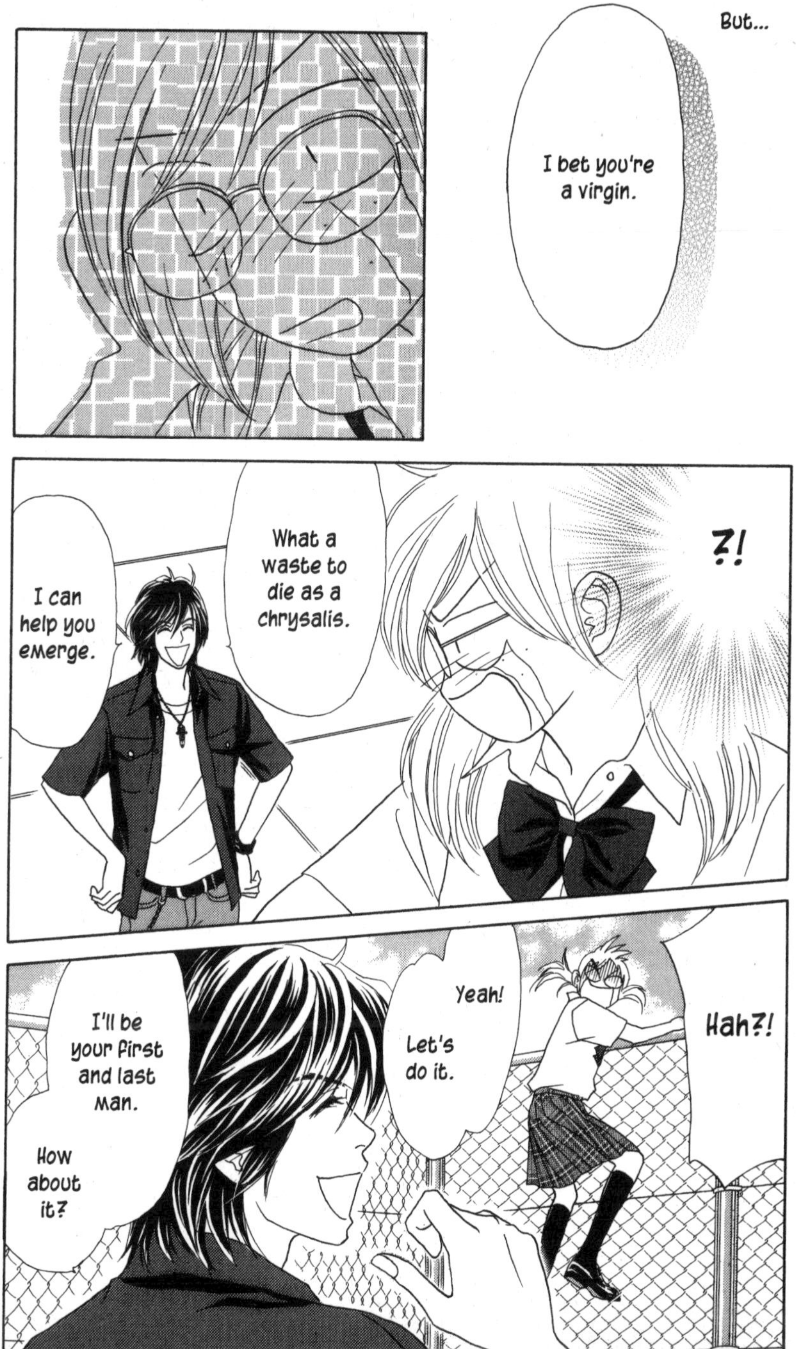
But...
I bet you're a virgin.
?!
What a waste to die as a chrysalis.
I can help you emerge.
Hah?!
Yeah!
Let's do it.
I'll be your first and last man.
How about it?

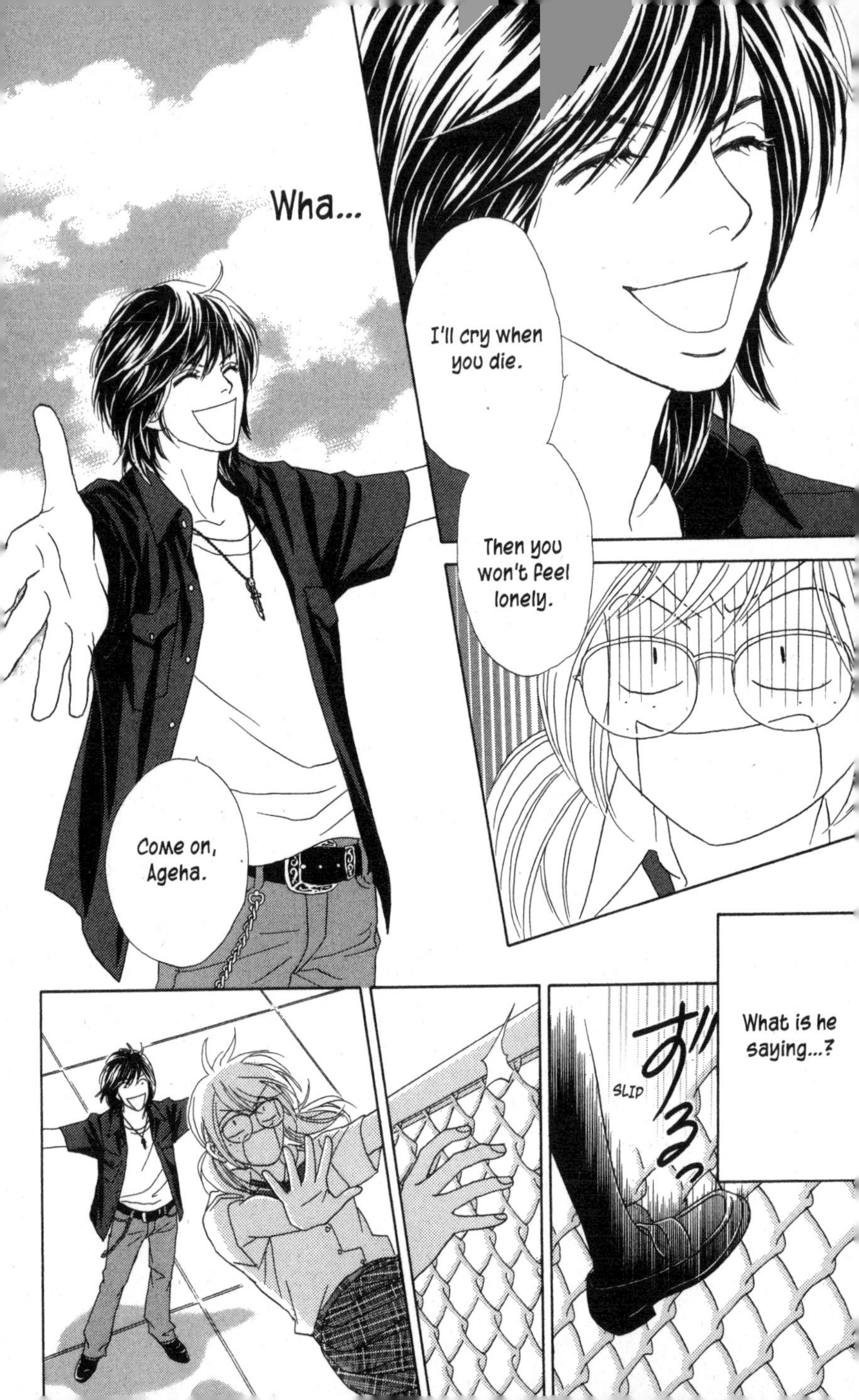

I'll cry when you die.
Then you won't feel lonely.
Wha...
Come on, Ageha.
What is he saying...?
ずるっ
SLIP

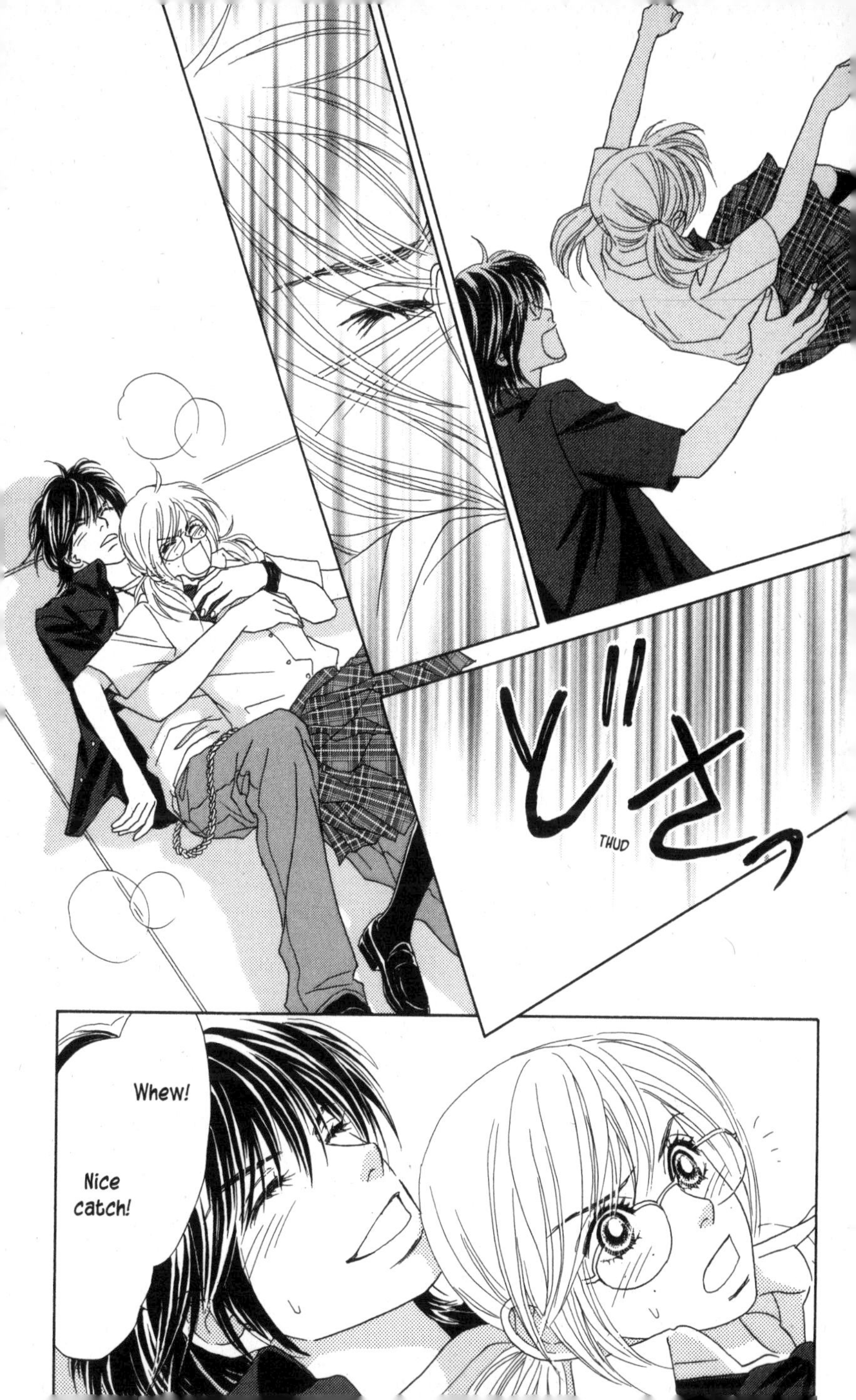
どさっ
THUD
Whew!
Nice catch!

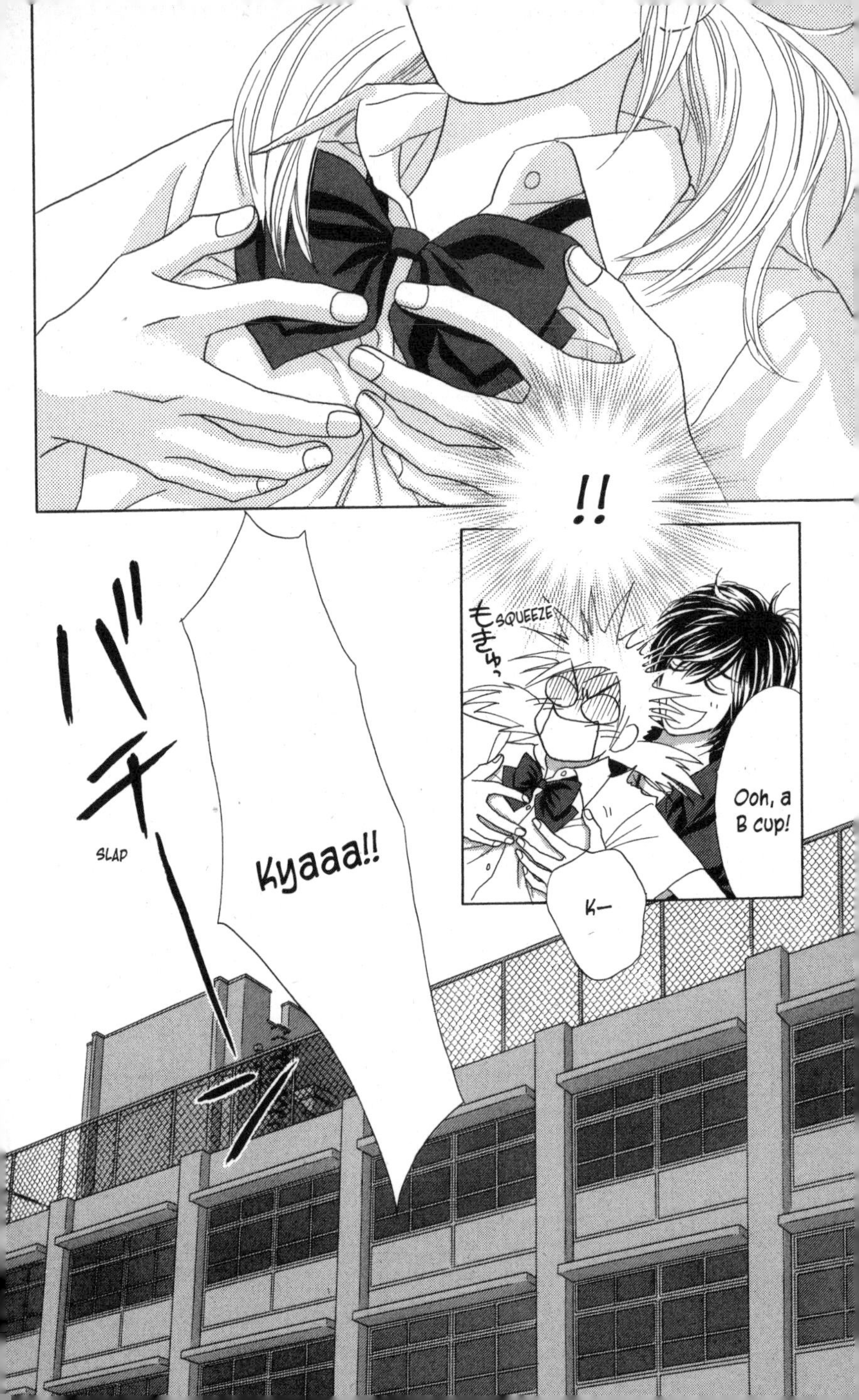
!!
もぎゅ
SQUEEZE
Ooh, a B cup!
K–
Kyaaa!!
バチーン
SLAP

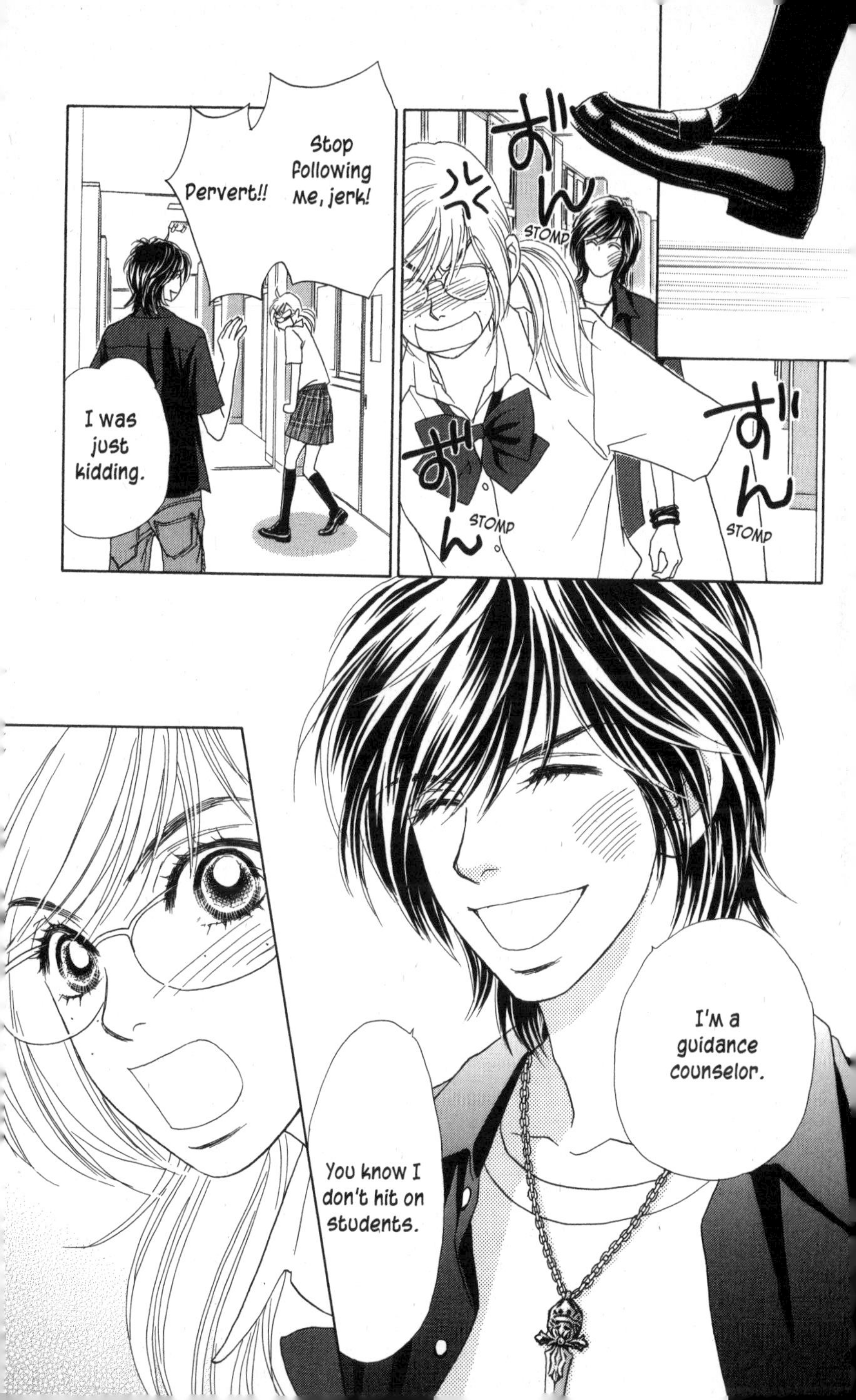
ずん
STOMP
ずん
STOMP
ずん
STOMP
Stop following me, jerk!
Pervert!!
I was just kidding.
I'm a guidance counselor.
You know I don't hit on students.

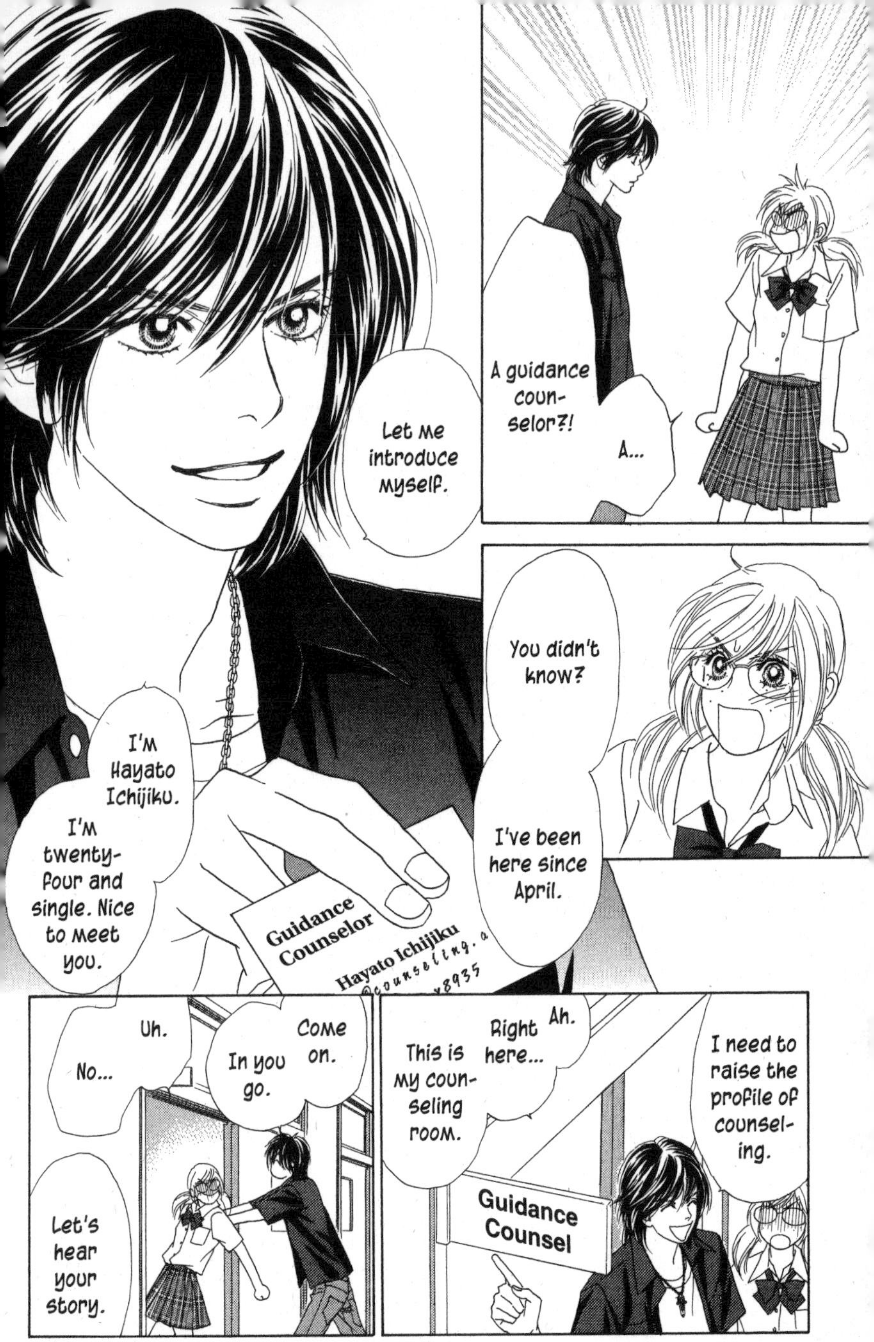
A...
A guidance coun-selor?!
You didn't know?
I've been here since April.
Let me introduce myself.
I'm Hayato Ichijiku.
I'm twenty-four and single. Nice to meet you.
Guidance Counselor
Hayato Ichijiku
I need to raise the profile of counsel-ing.
Ah.
Right here...
This is my coun-seling room.
Guidance Counsel
Come on.
In you go.
Uh.
No...
Let's hear your story.

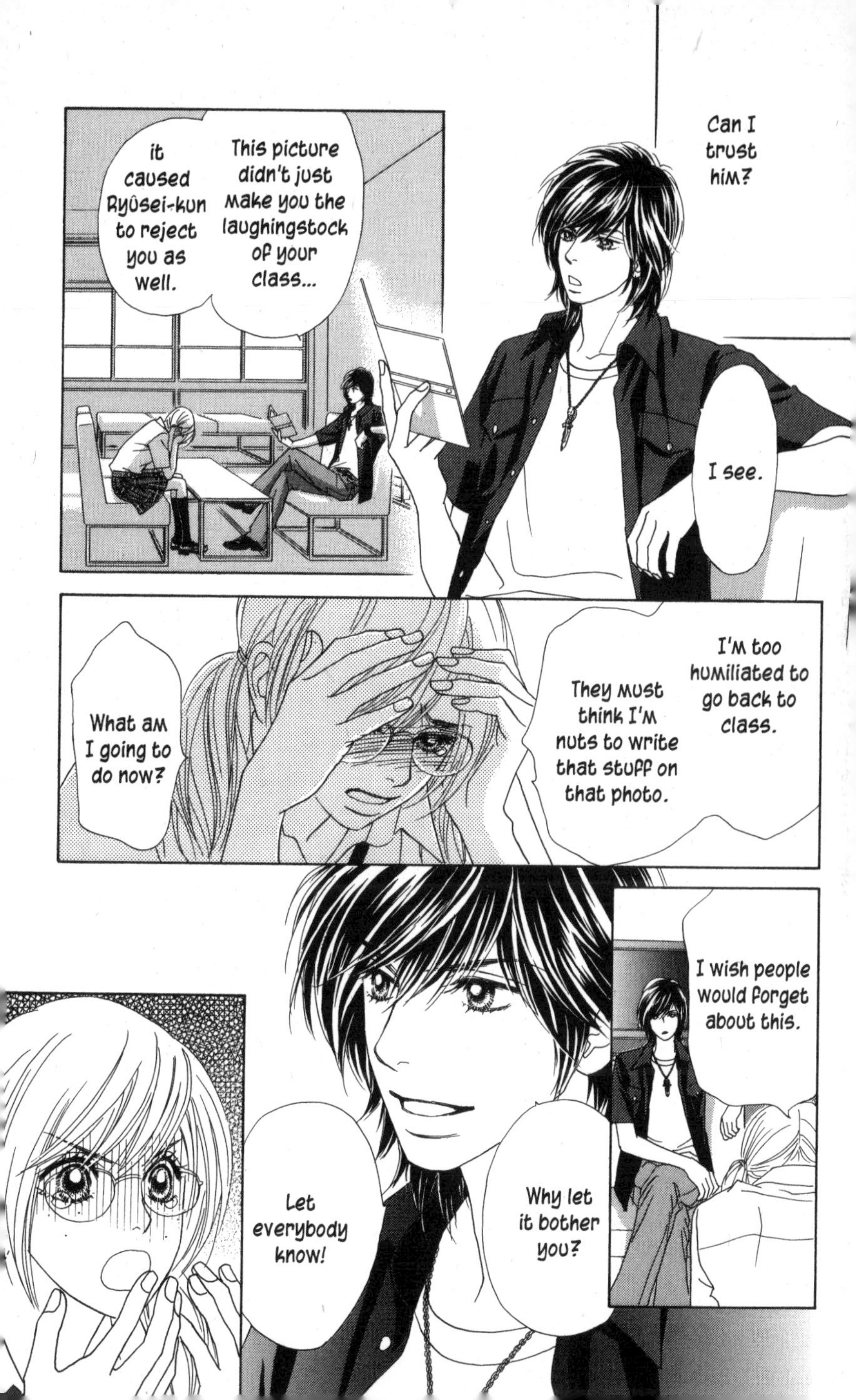
Can I trust him?
I see.
This picture didn't just make you the laughingstock of your class...
it caused Ryûsei-kun to reject you as well.
I'm too humiliated to go back to class.
They must think I'm nuts to write that stuff on that photo.
What am I going to do now?
I wish people would forget about this.
Why let it bother you?
Let everybody know!

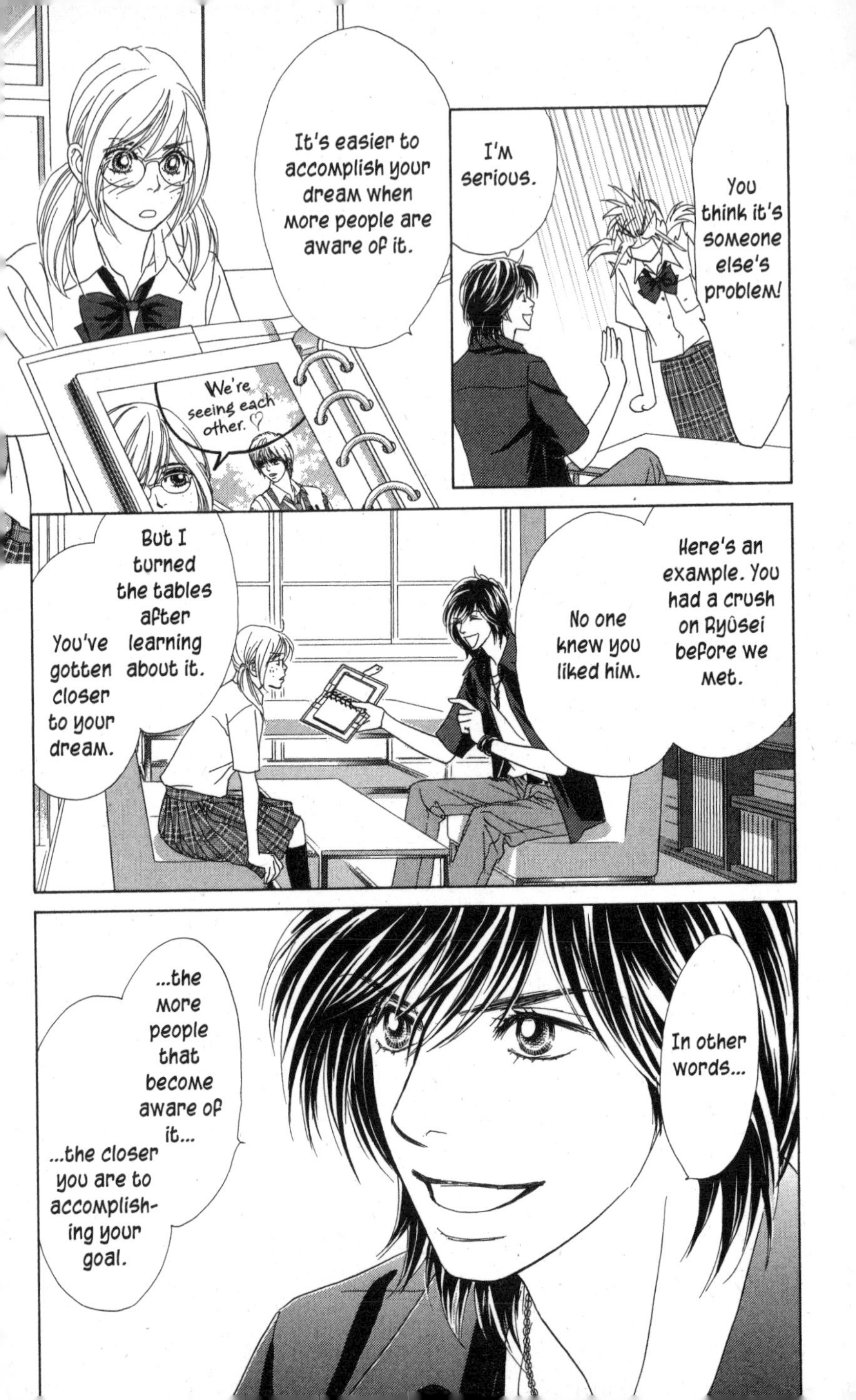
You think it's someone else's problem!
I'm serious.
It's easier to accomplish your dream when more people are aware of it.
We're seeing each other. ♡
Here's an example. You had a crush on Ryûsei before we met.
No one knew you liked him.
But I turned the tables after learning about it.
You've gotten closer to your dream.
In other words...
...the more people that become aware of it...
...the closer you are to accomplishing your goal.

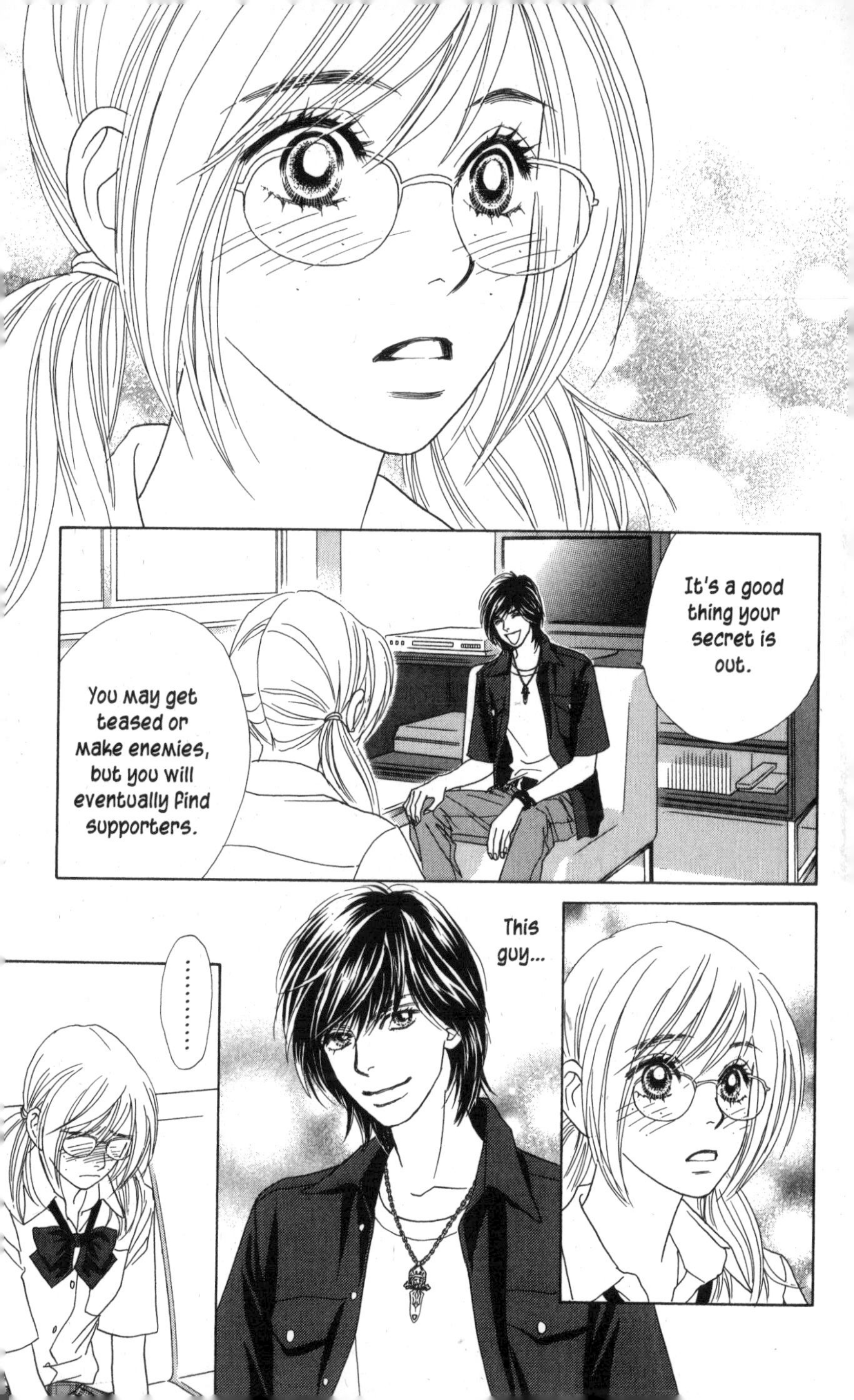
It's a good thing your secret is out.
You may get teased or make enemies, but you will eventually find supporters.
This guy...
....

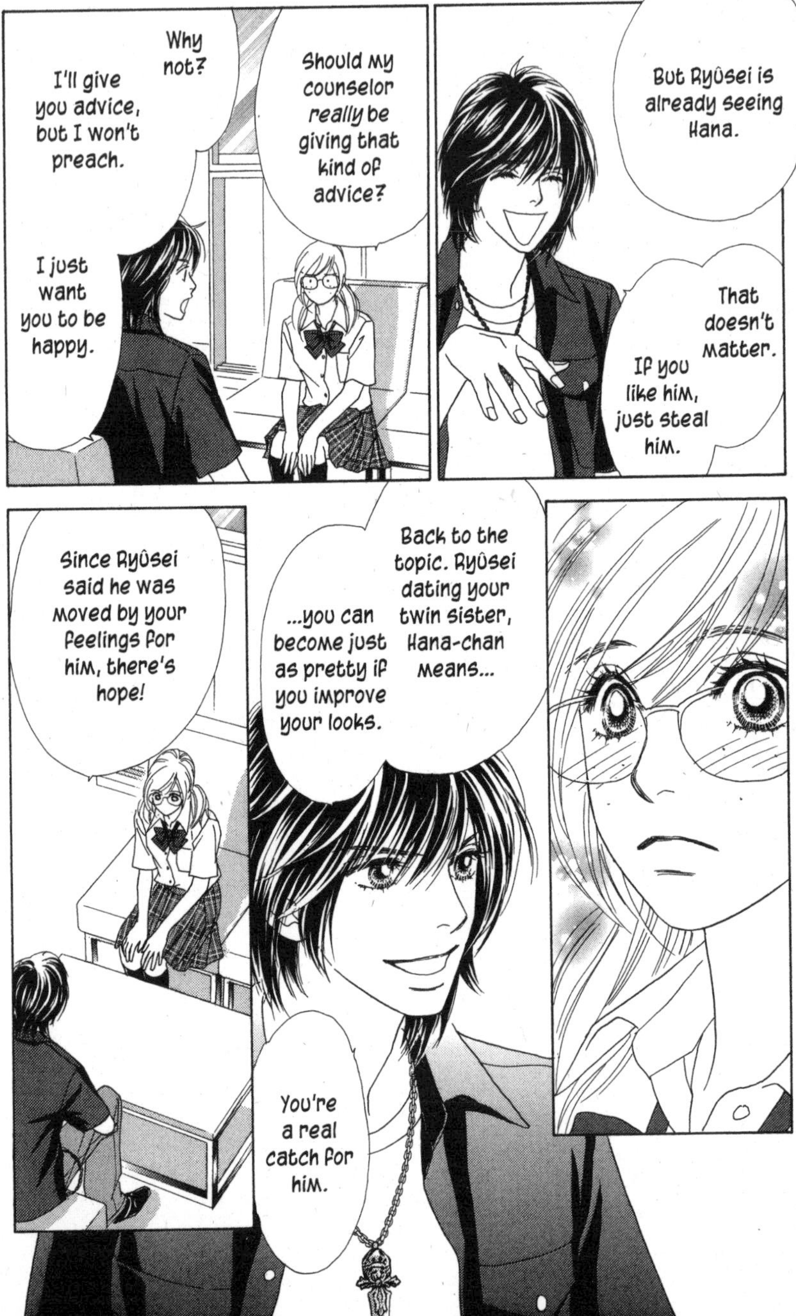
But Ryûsei is already seeing Hana.
That doesn't matter.
If you like him, just steal him.
Should my counselor *really* be giving that kind of advice?
Why not?
I'll give you advice, but I won't preach.
I just want you to be happy.
Back to the topic. Ryûsei dating your twin sister, Hana-chan means...
...you can become just as pretty if you improve your looks.
You're a real catch for him.
Since Ryûsei said he was moved by your feelings for him, there's hope!

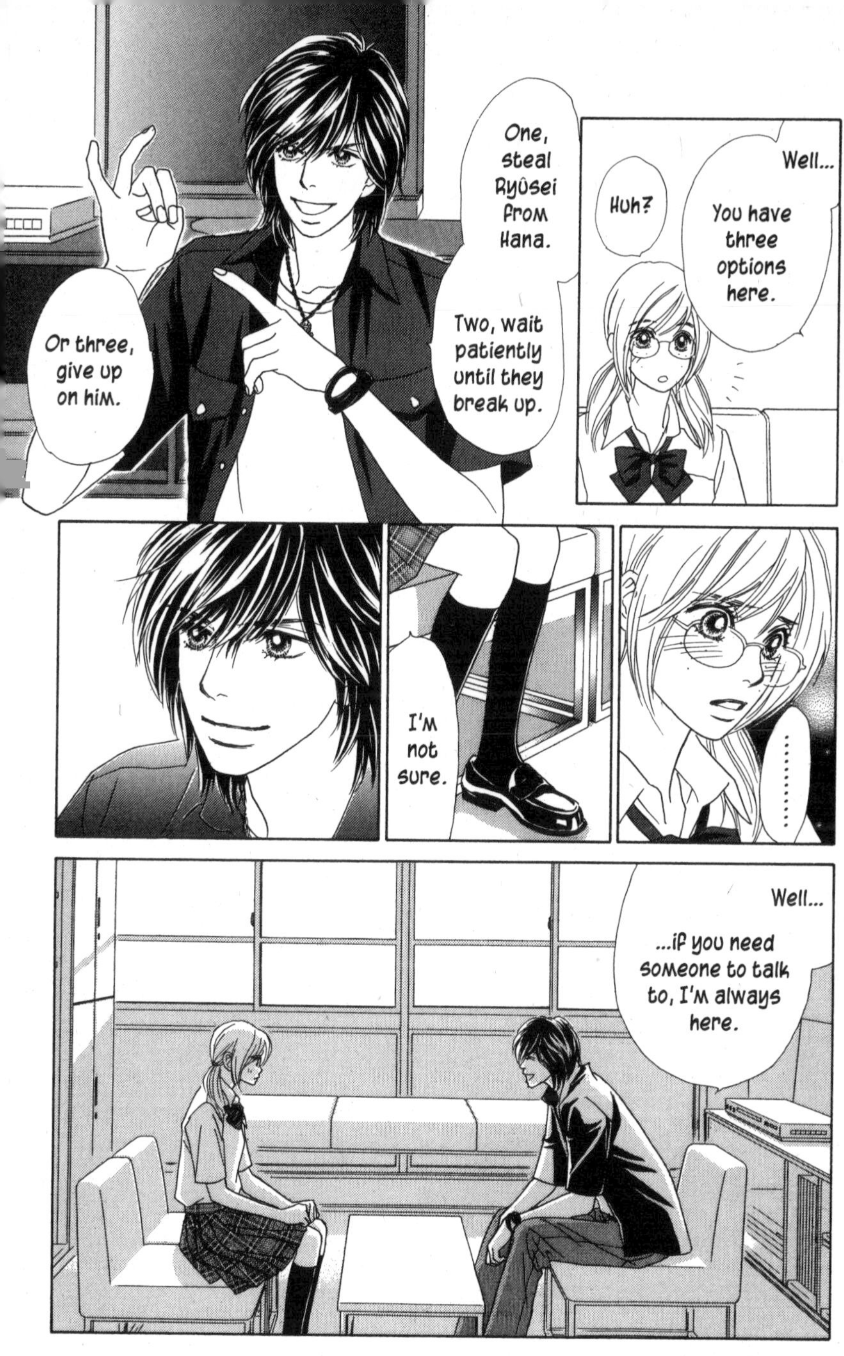
Well...
You have three options here.
Huh?
One, steal Ryûsei from Hana.
Two, wait patiently until they break up.
Or three, give up on him.
......
I'm not sure.
Well...
...if you need someone to talk to, I'm always here.

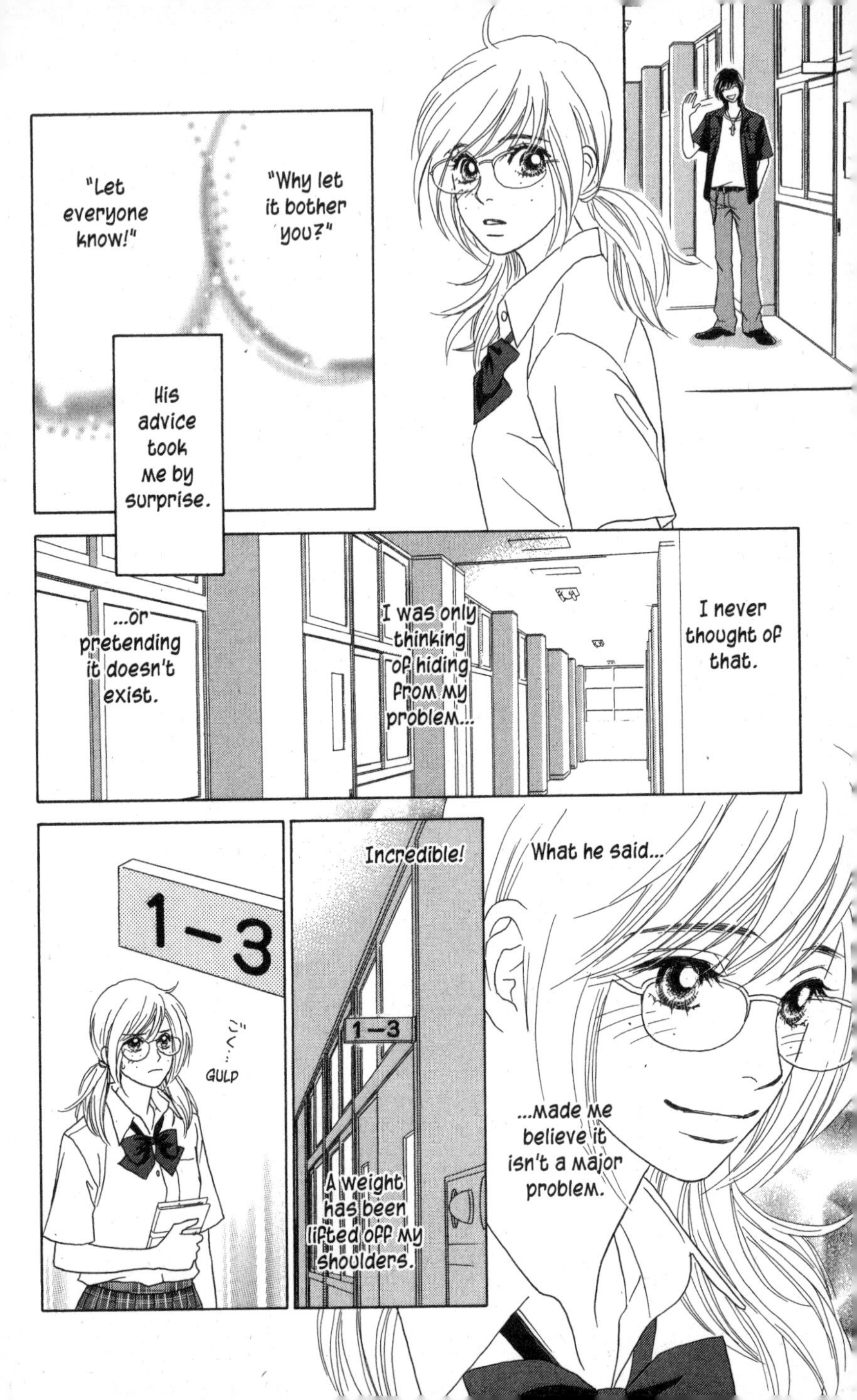
"Why let it bother you?"
"Let everyone know!"
His advice took me by surprise.
I never thought of that.
I was only thinking of hiding from my problem...
...or pretending it doesn't exist.
What he said...
...made me believe it isn't a major problem.
Incredible!
1-3
A weight has been lifted off my shoulders.
1-3
ごく…
GULP

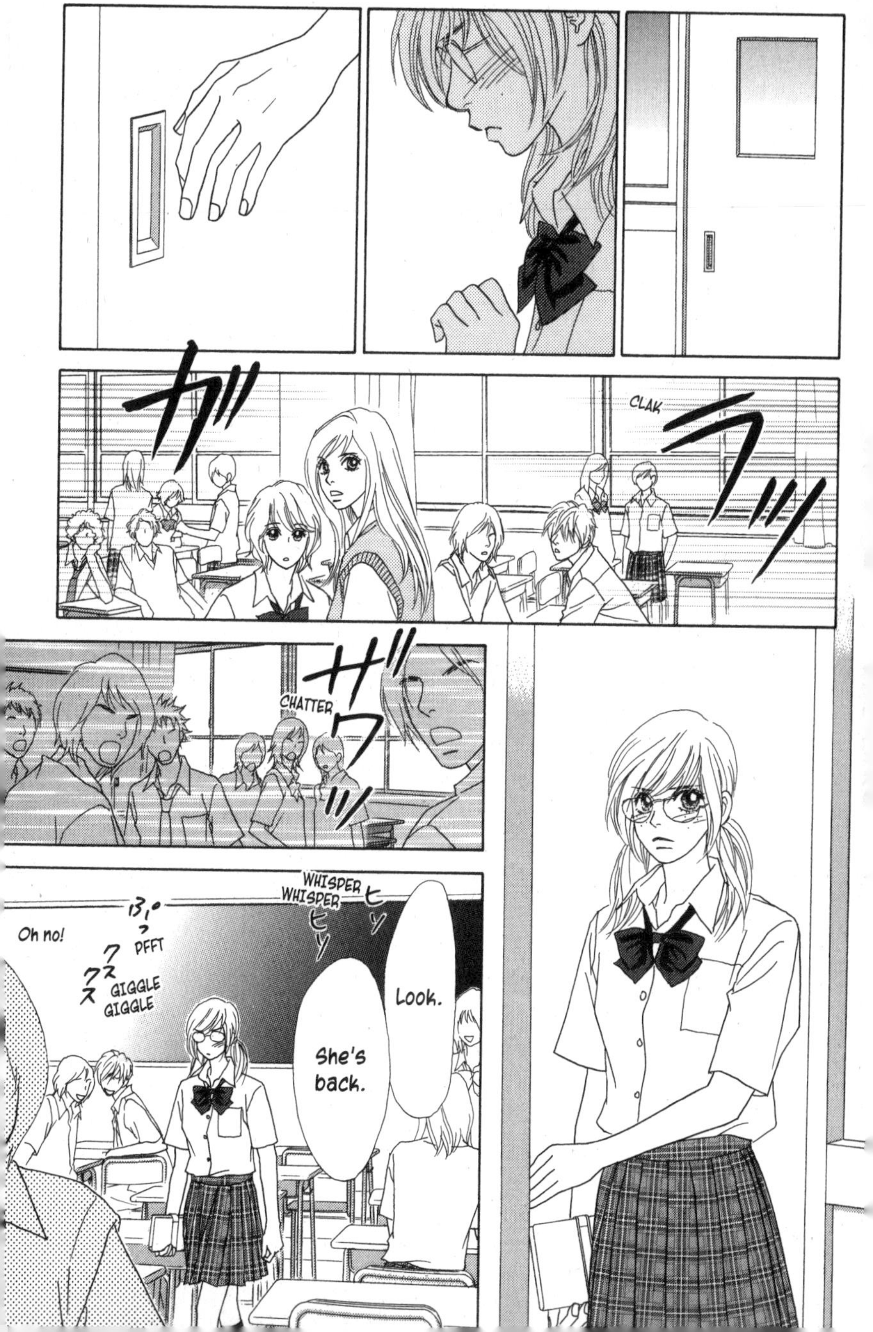

CLAK
ガラッ
CHATTER
ザワッ
Look.
She's back.
ヒソ ヒソ
WHISPER WHISPER
ぷっ
PFFT
クス クス
GIGGLE GIGGLE
Oh no!

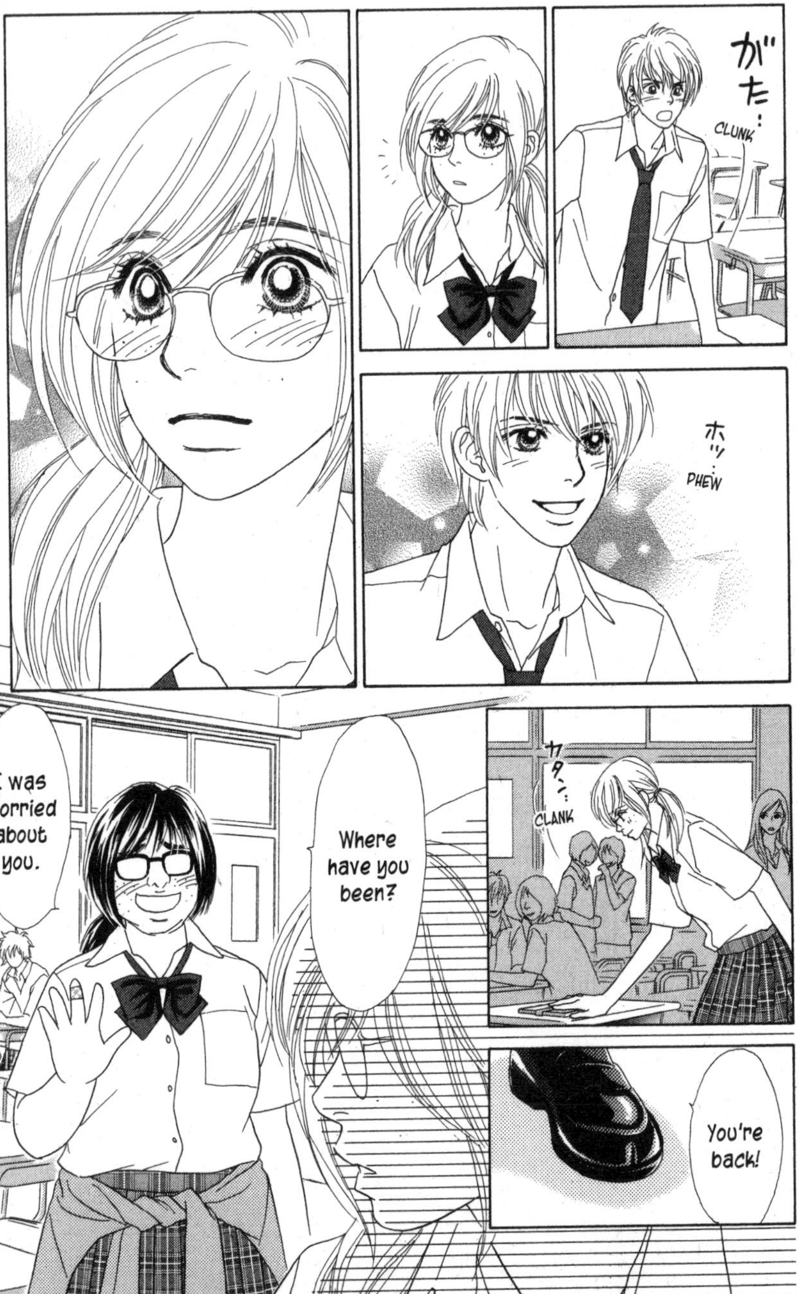
がた…
CLUNK
ホッ…
PHEW
カタ…
CLANK
You're back!
Where have you been?
I was worried about you.

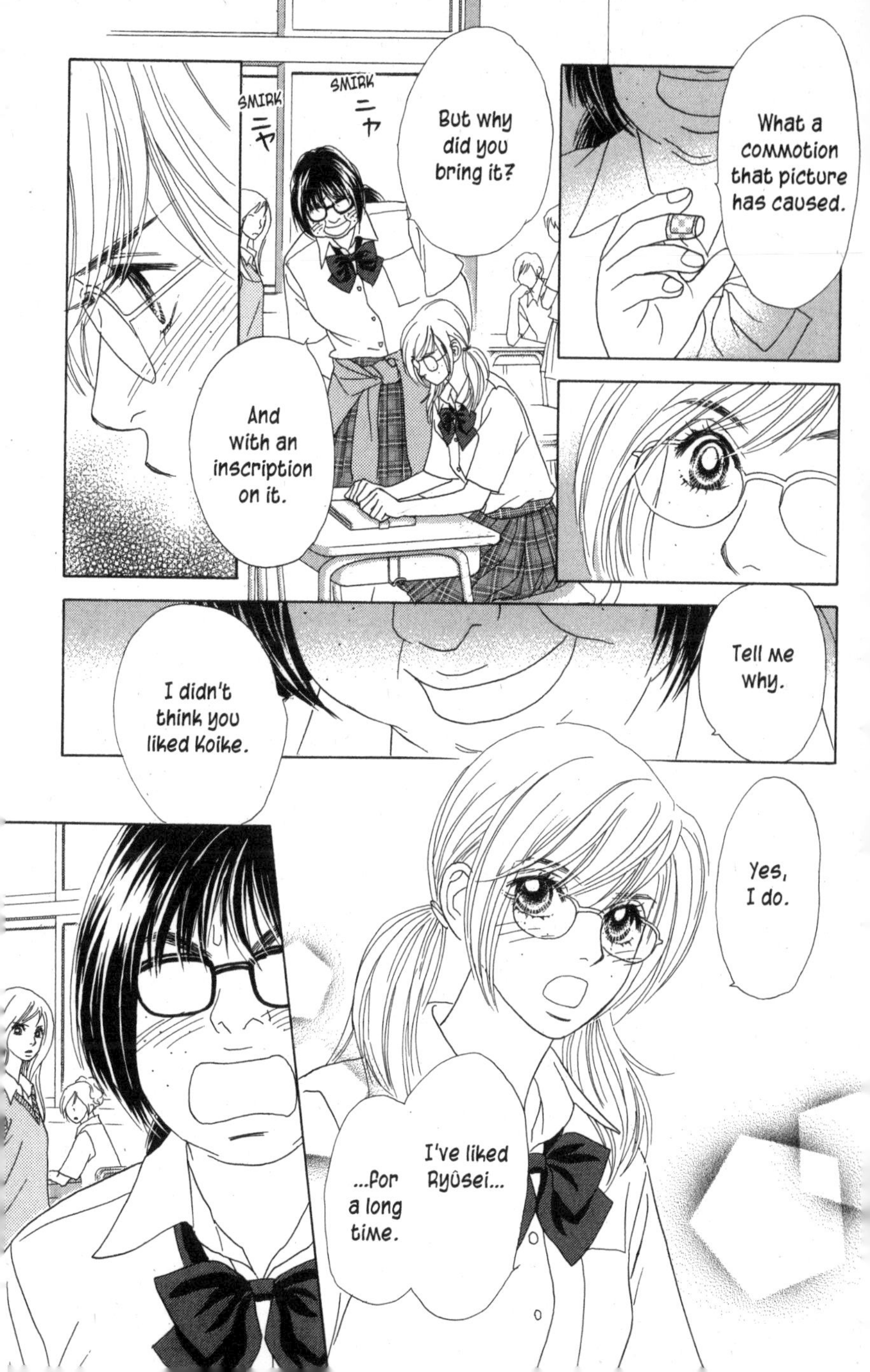
What a commotion that picture has caused.
But why did you bring it?
SMIRK ニヤ
SMIRK ニヤ
And with an inscription on it.
Tell me why.
I didn't think you liked Koike.
Yes, I do.
I've liked Ryûsei...
...for a long time.

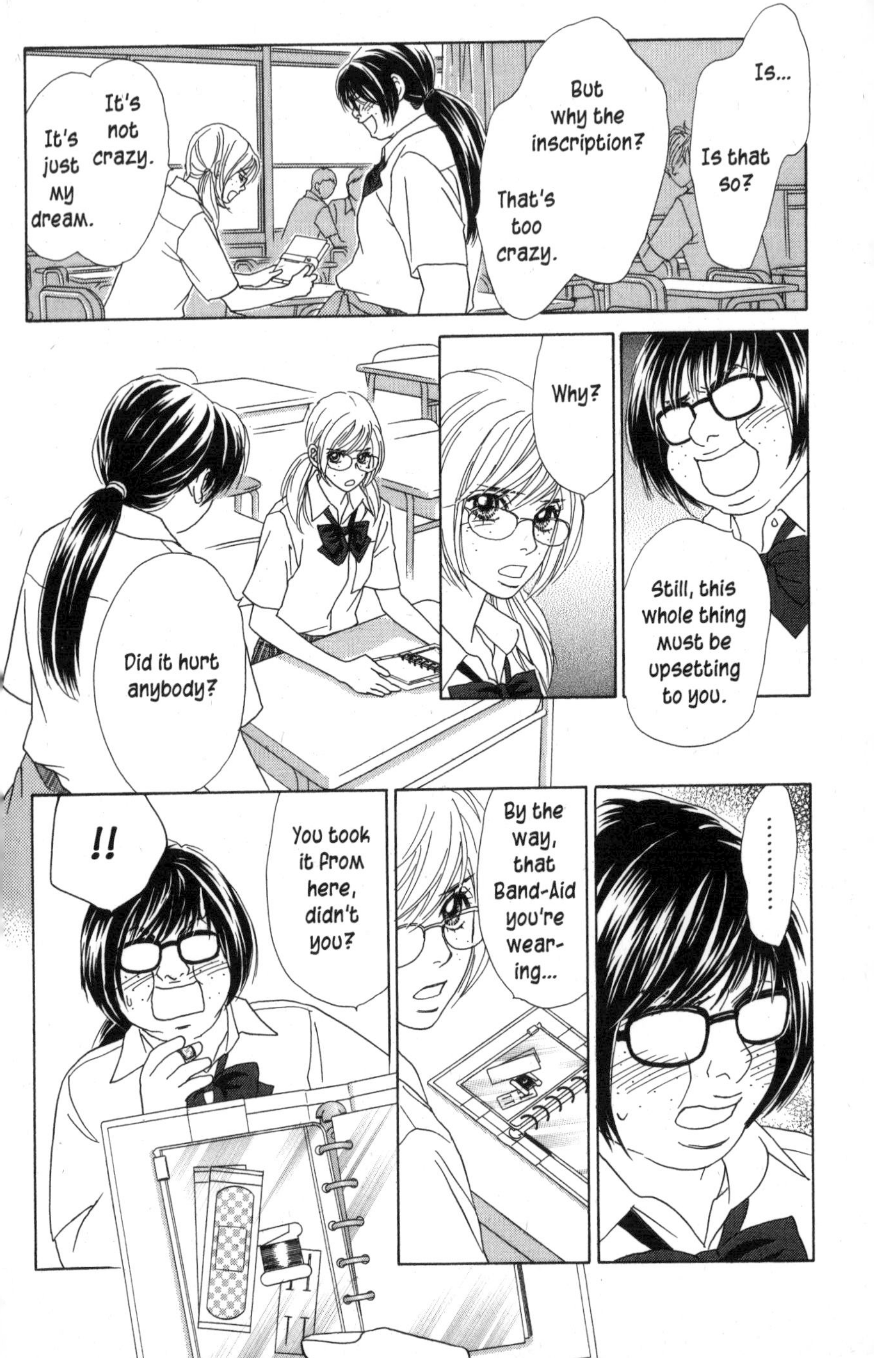
Is...
Is that so?
But why the inscription?
That's too crazy.
It's not crazy.
It's just my dream.
Still, this whole thing must be upsetting to you.
Why?
Did it hurt anybody?
....
By the way, that Band-Aid you're wear-ing...
You took it from here, didn't you?
!!

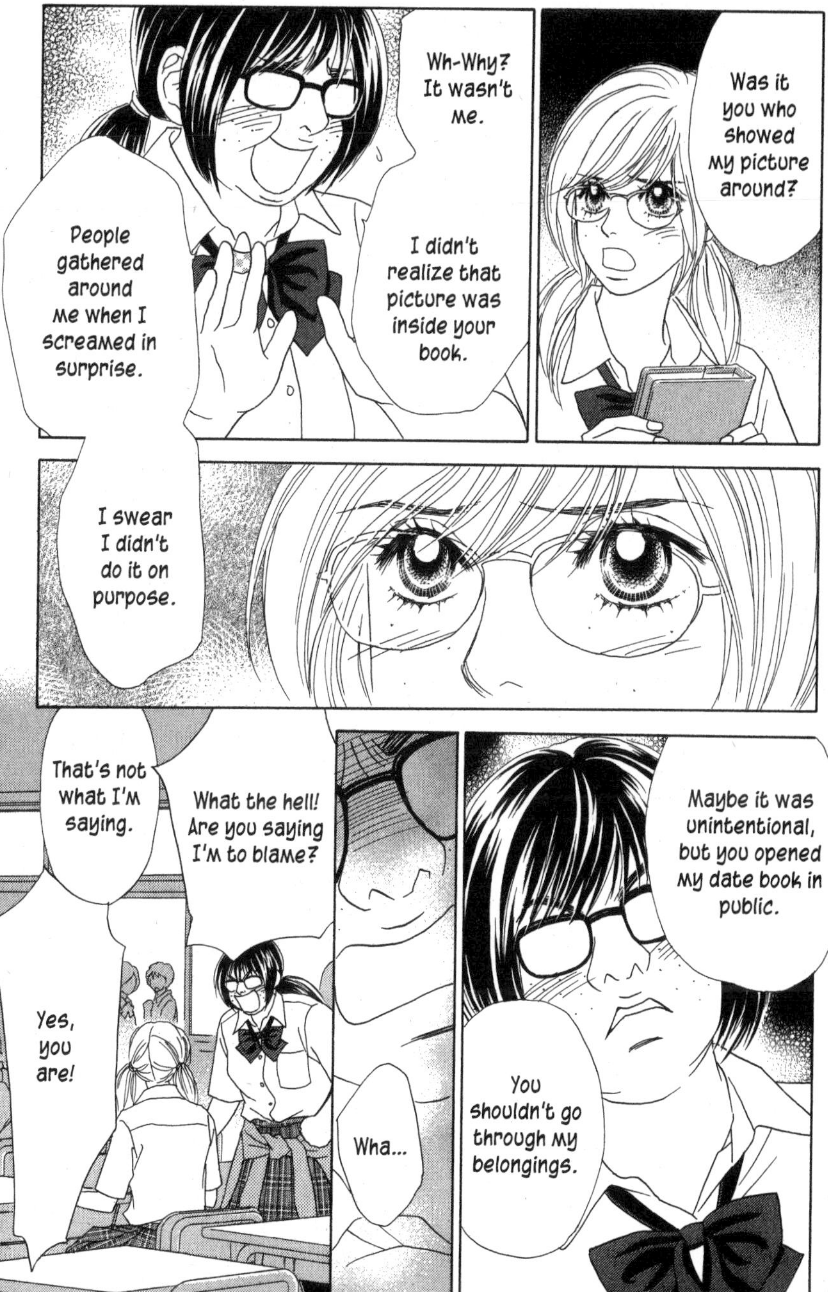
Was it you who showed my picture around?
Wh-Why? It wasn't me.
I didn't realize that picture was inside your book.
People gathered around me when I screamed in surprise.
I swear I didn't do it on purpose.
Maybe it was unintentional, but you opened my date book in public.
You shouldn't go through my belongings.
Wha...
What the hell! Are you saying I'm to blame?
That's not what I'm saying.
Yes, you are!

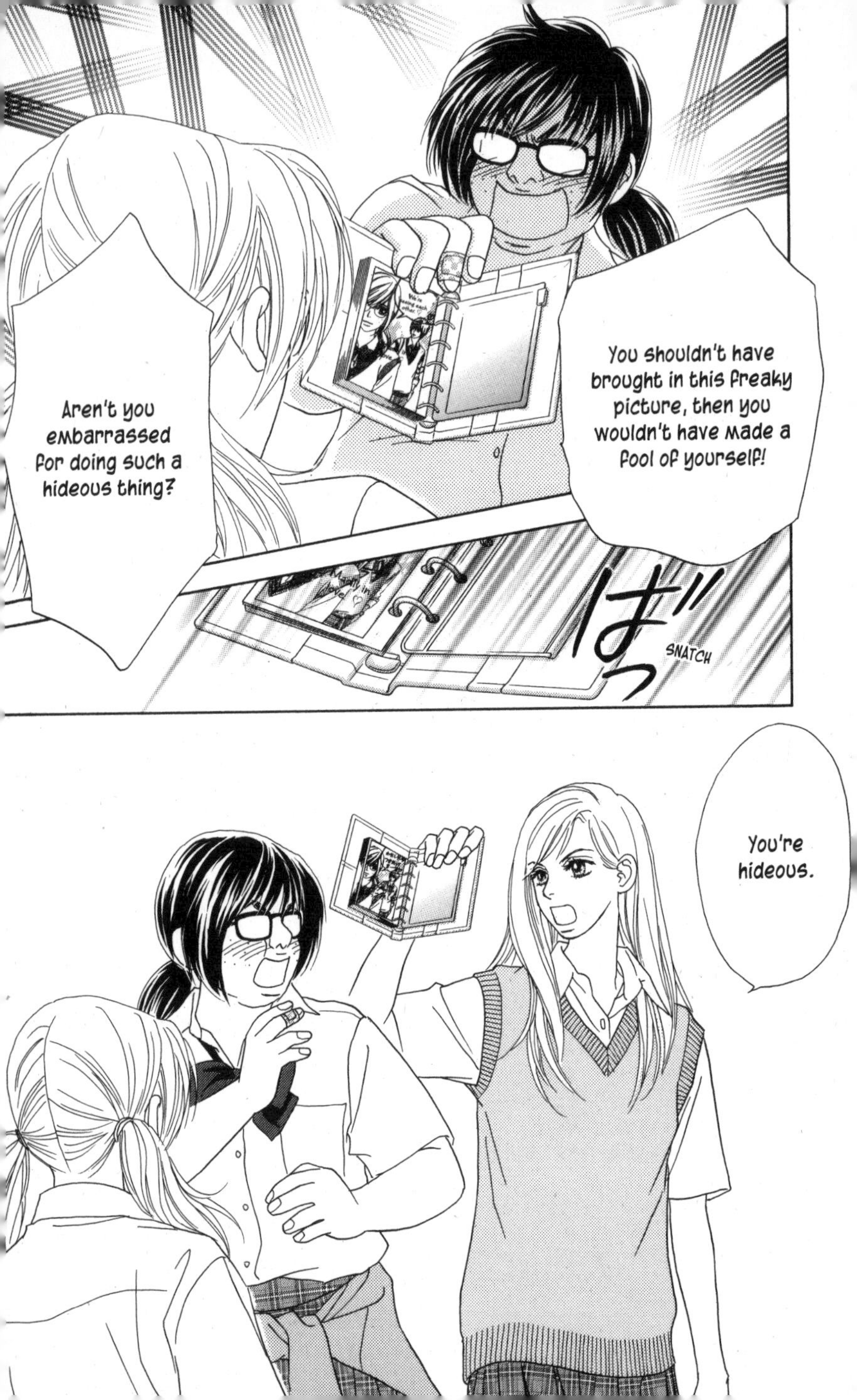
You shouldn't have brought in this freaky picture, then you wouldn't have made a fool of yourself!
Aren't you embarrassed for doing such a hideous thing?
SNATCH
You're hideous.

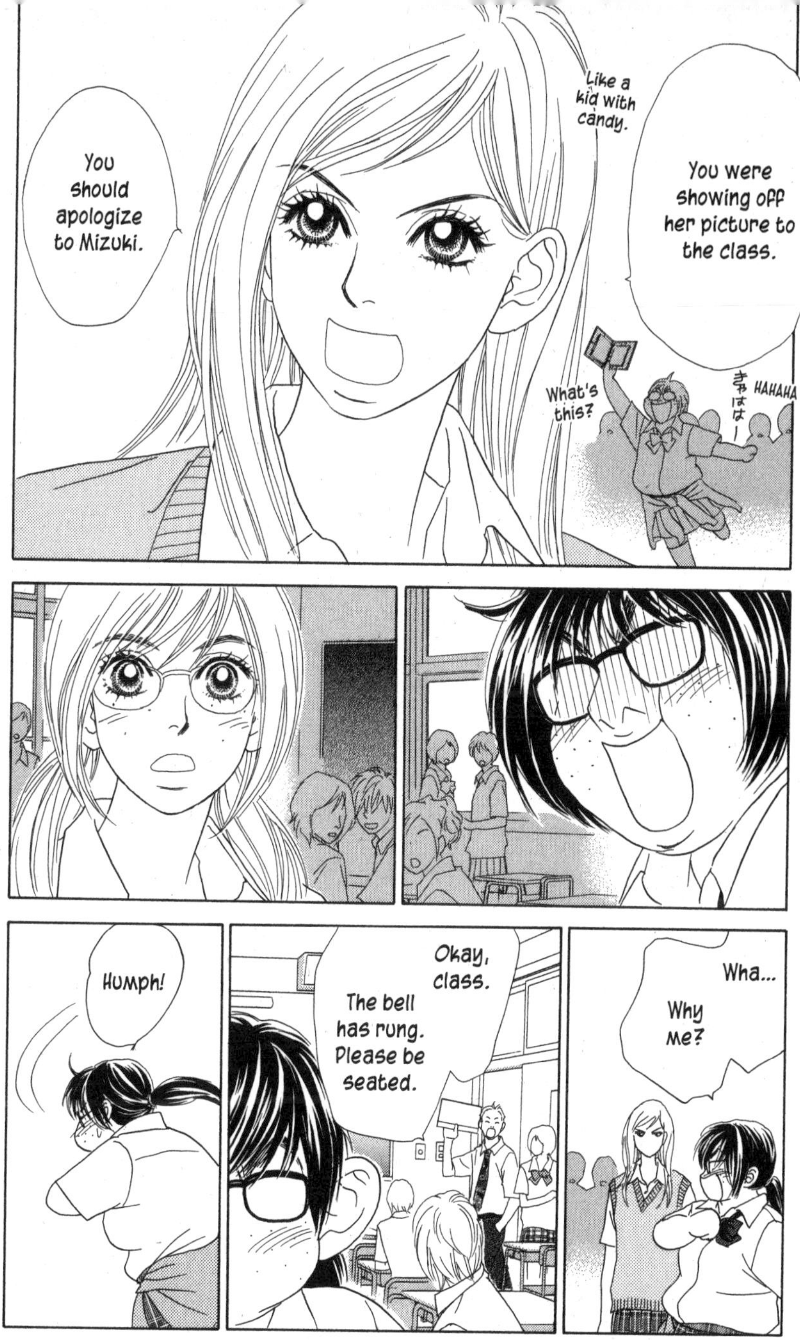
You were showing off her picture to the class.
Like a kid with candy.
きゃはは—
HAHAHA
What's this?
You should apologize to Mizuki.
Wha...
Why me?
Okay, class.
The bell has rung. Please be seated.
Humph!

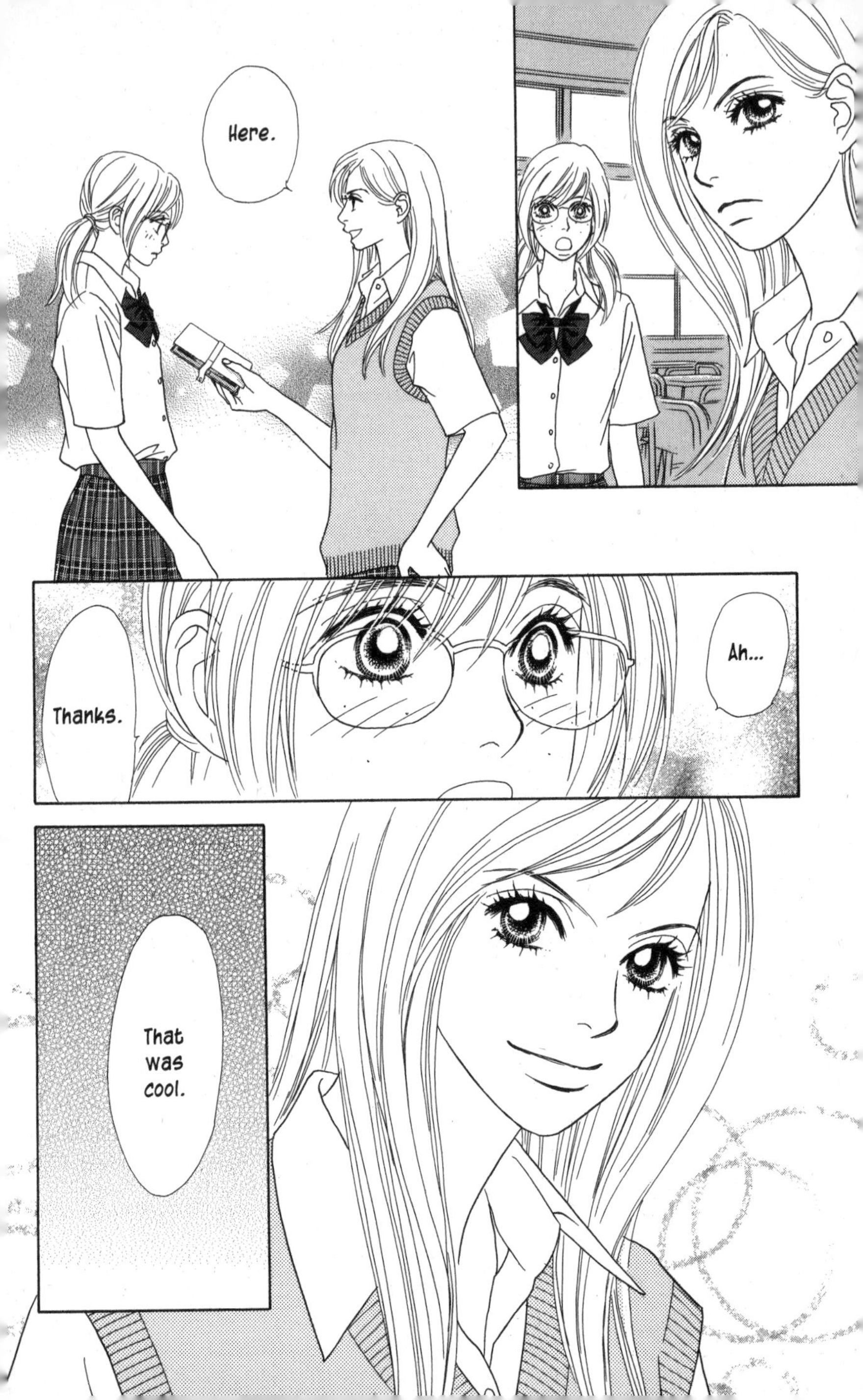
Here.
Ah...
Thanks.
That was cool.

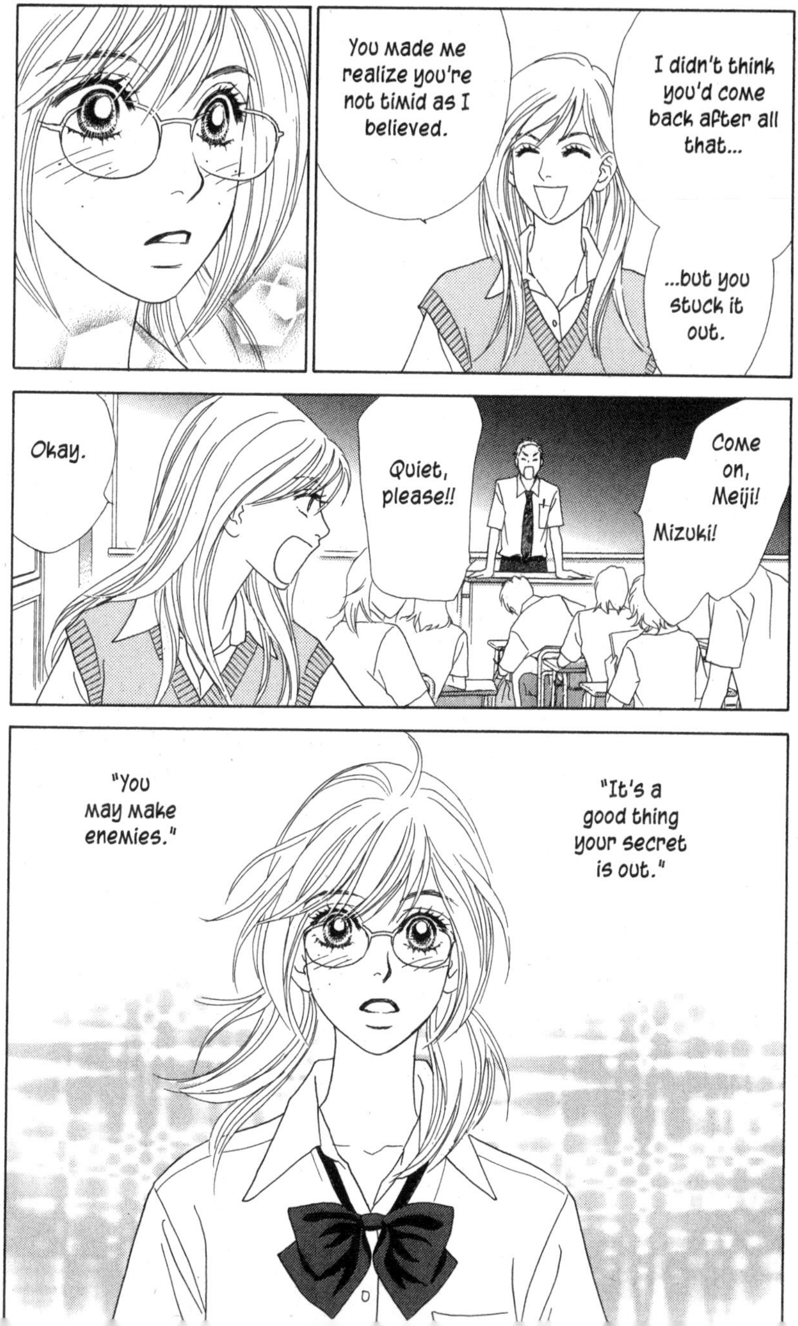
I didn't think you'd come back after all that...
...but you stuck it out.
You made me realize you're not timid as I believed.
Come on, Meiji!
Mizuki!
Quiet, please!!
Okay.
"It's a good thing your secret is out."
"You may make enemies."

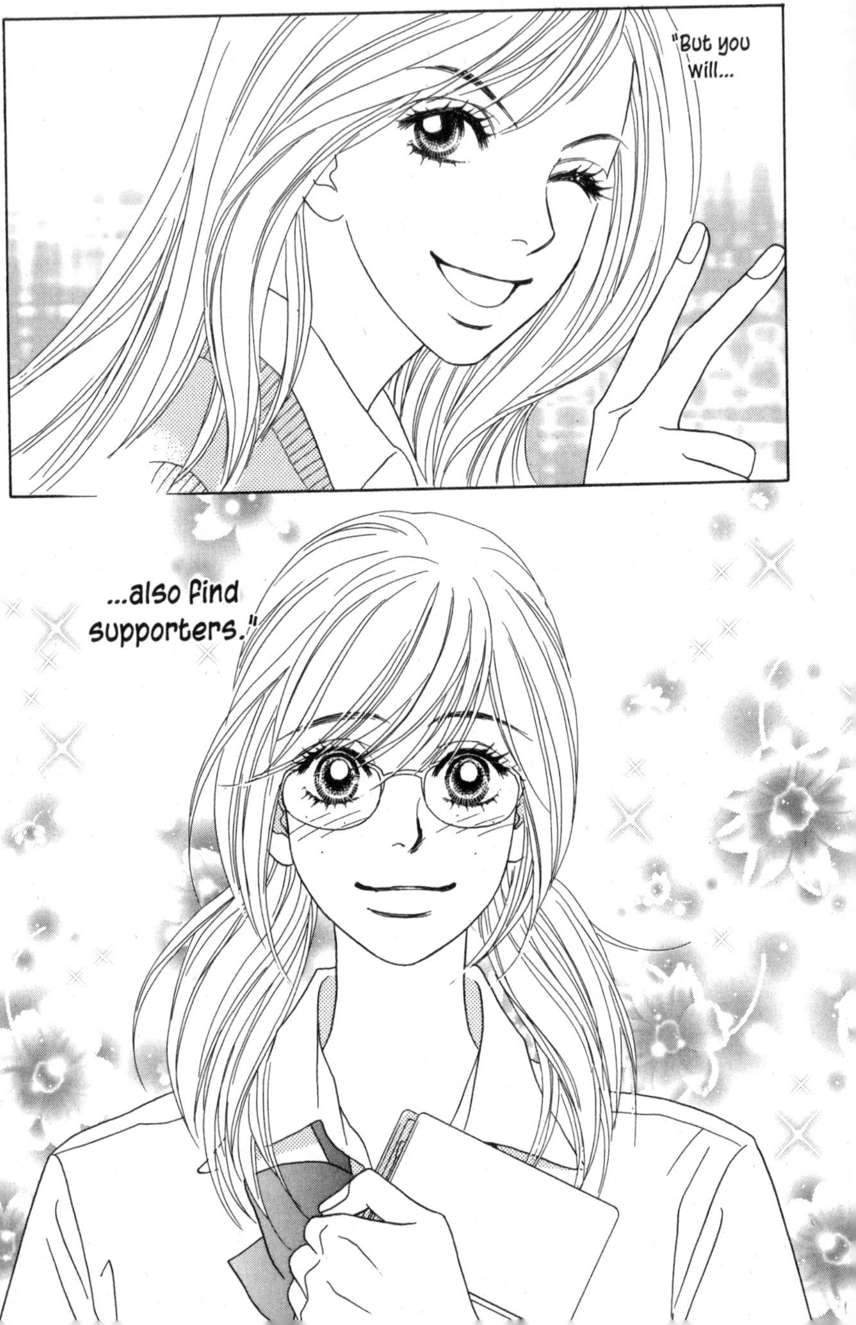
"But you will...
...also find supporters."

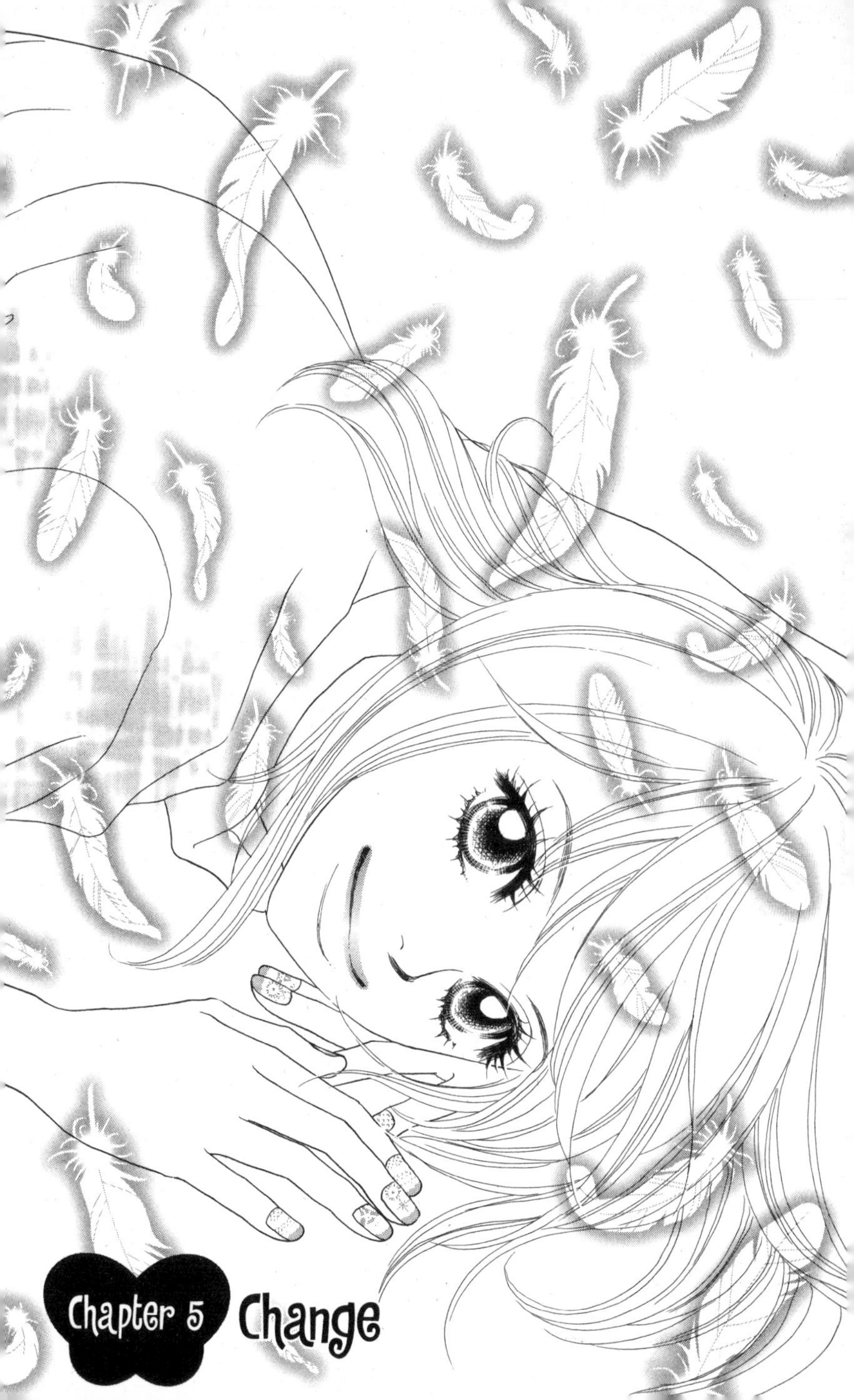
Chapter 5
Change

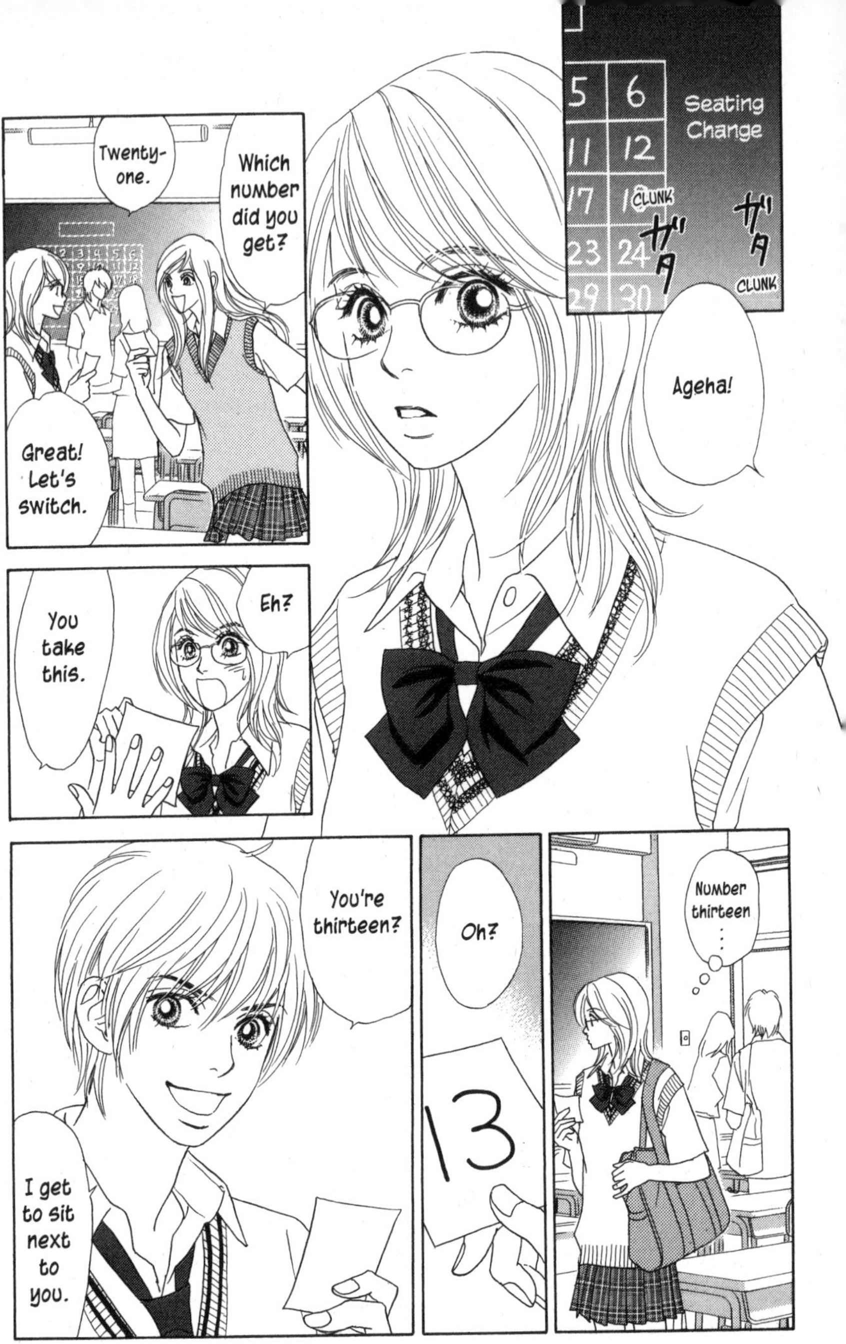
Seating Change
CLUNK
ガタ
ガタ
CLUNK
Ageha!
Which number did you get?
Twenty-one.
Great! Let's switch.
Eh?
You take this.
Number thirteen . . .
Oh?
13
You're thirteen?
I get to sit next to you.

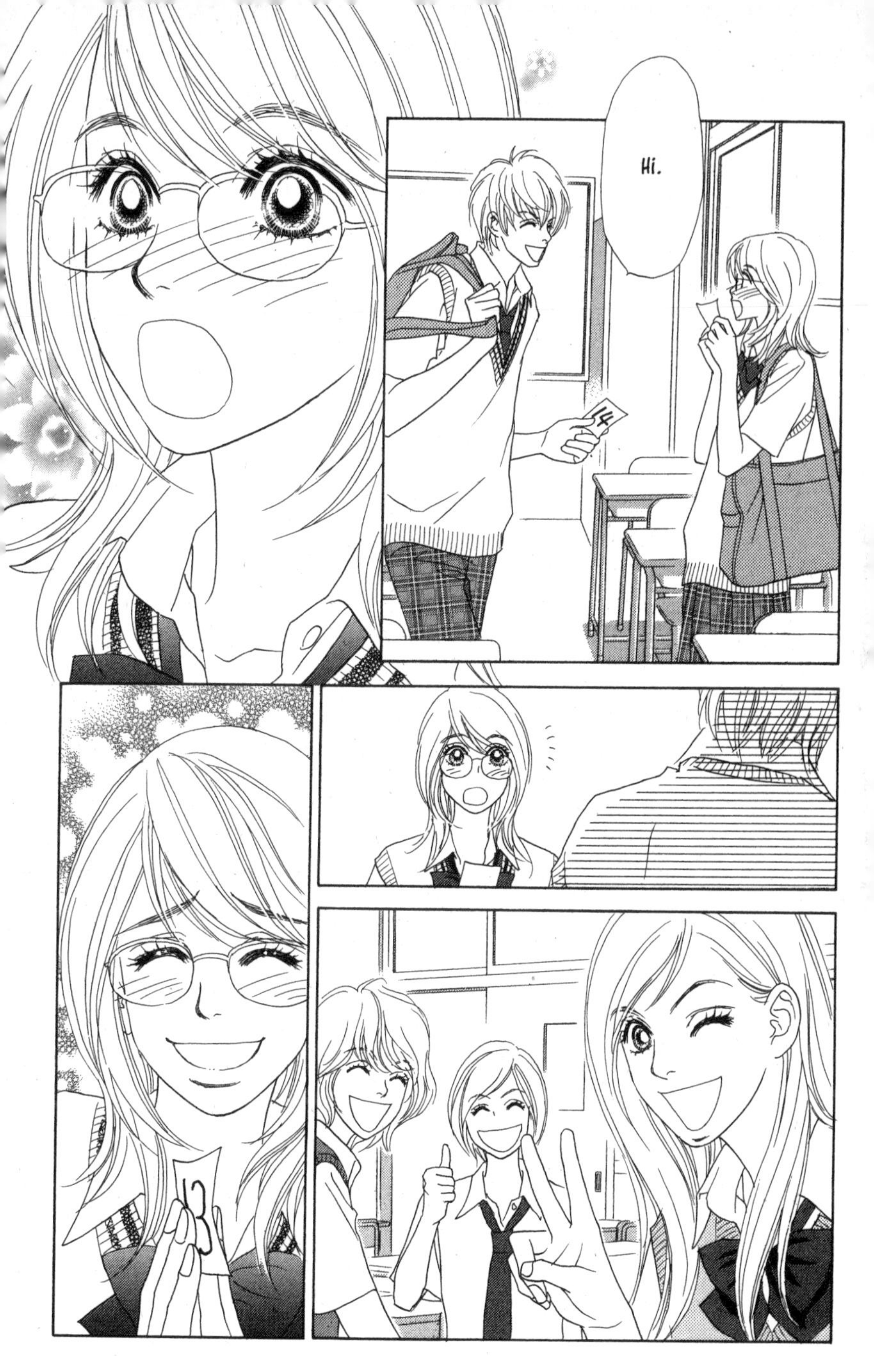
Hi.

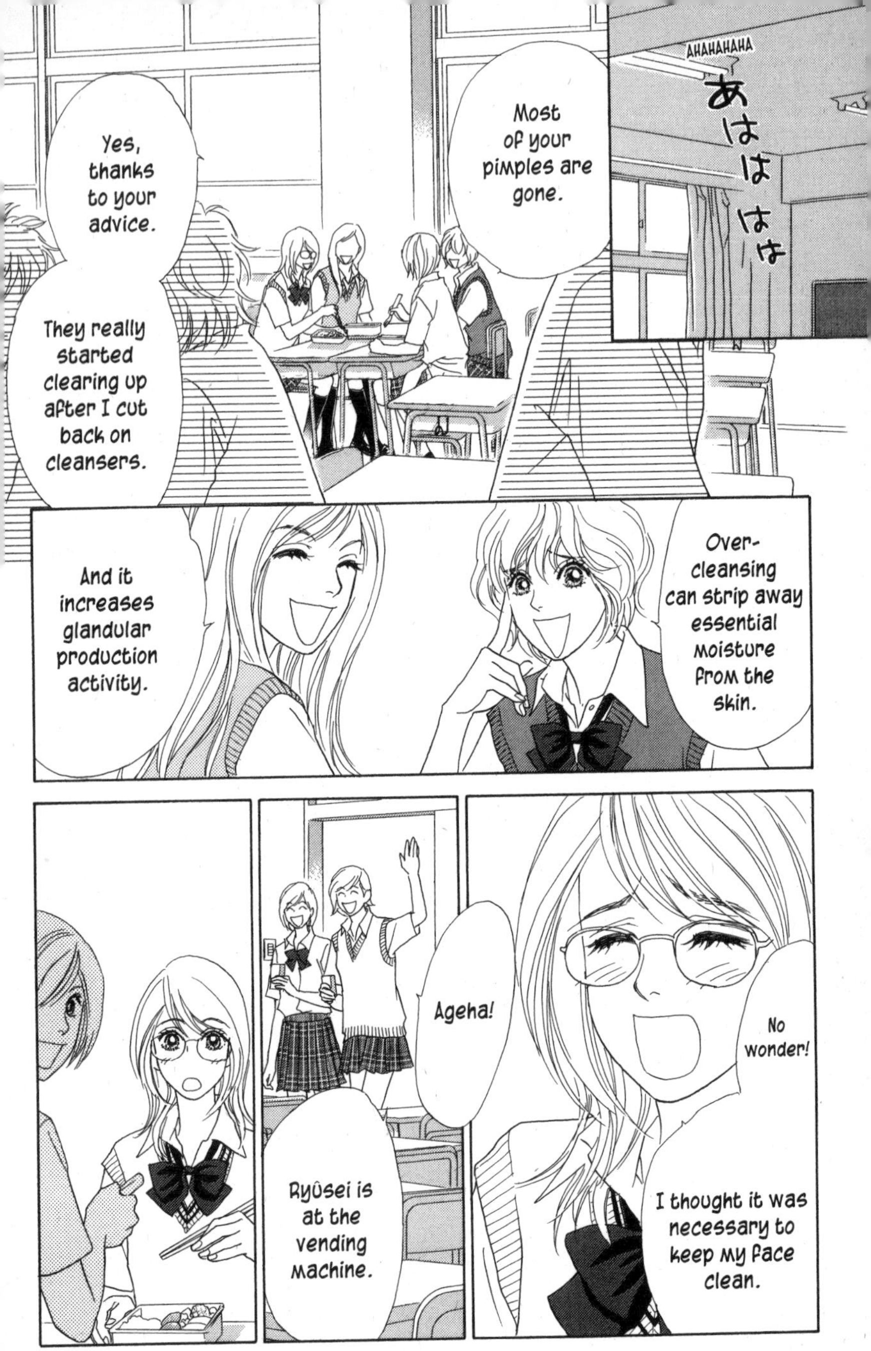
AHAHAHAHA
あははは
Most of your pimples are gone.
Yes, thanks to your advice.
They really started clearing up after I cut back on cleansers.
Over-cleansing can strip away essential moisture from the skin.
And it increases glandular production activity.
No wonder!
I thought it was necessary to keep my face clean.
Ageha!
Ryûsei is at the vending machine.

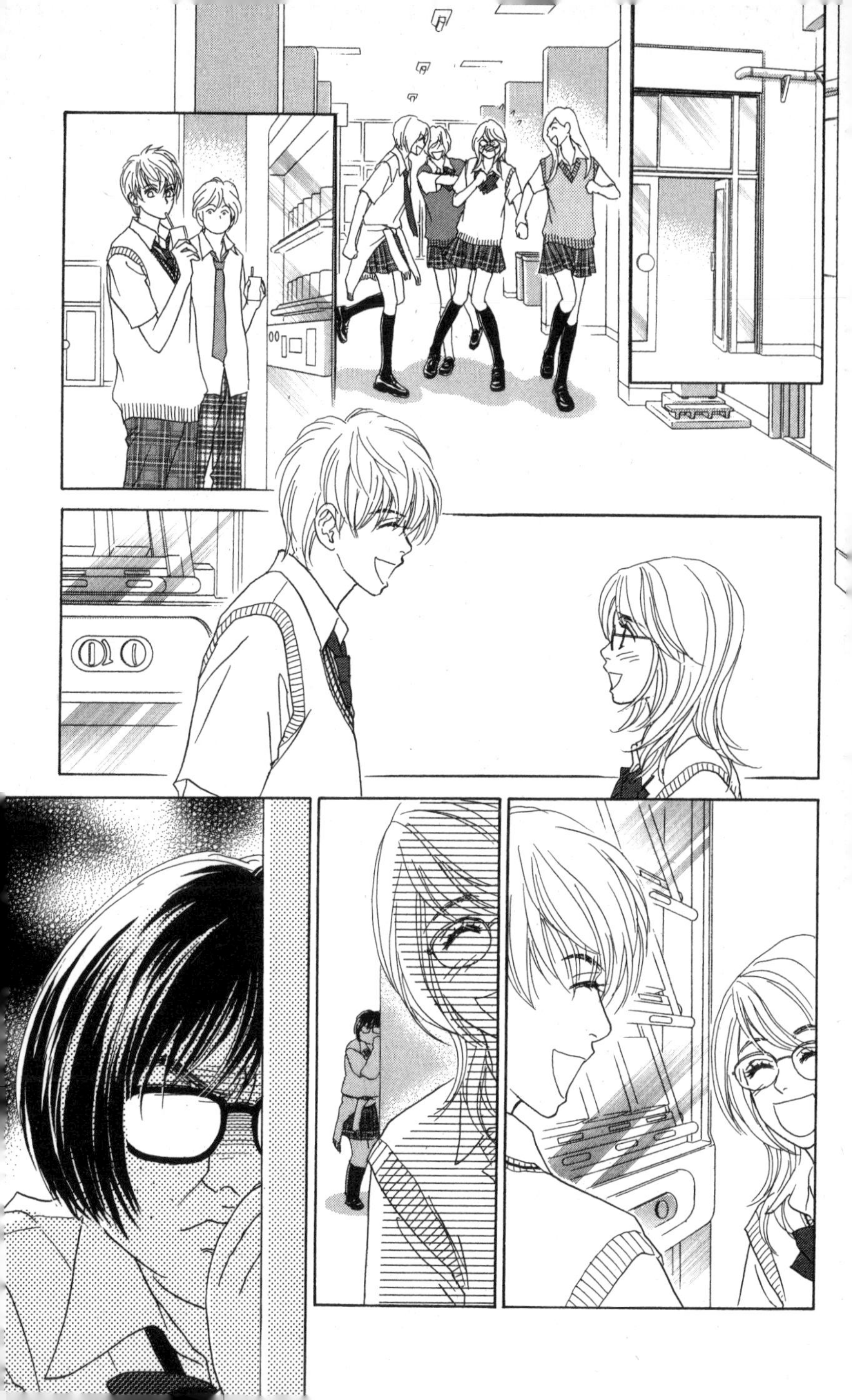

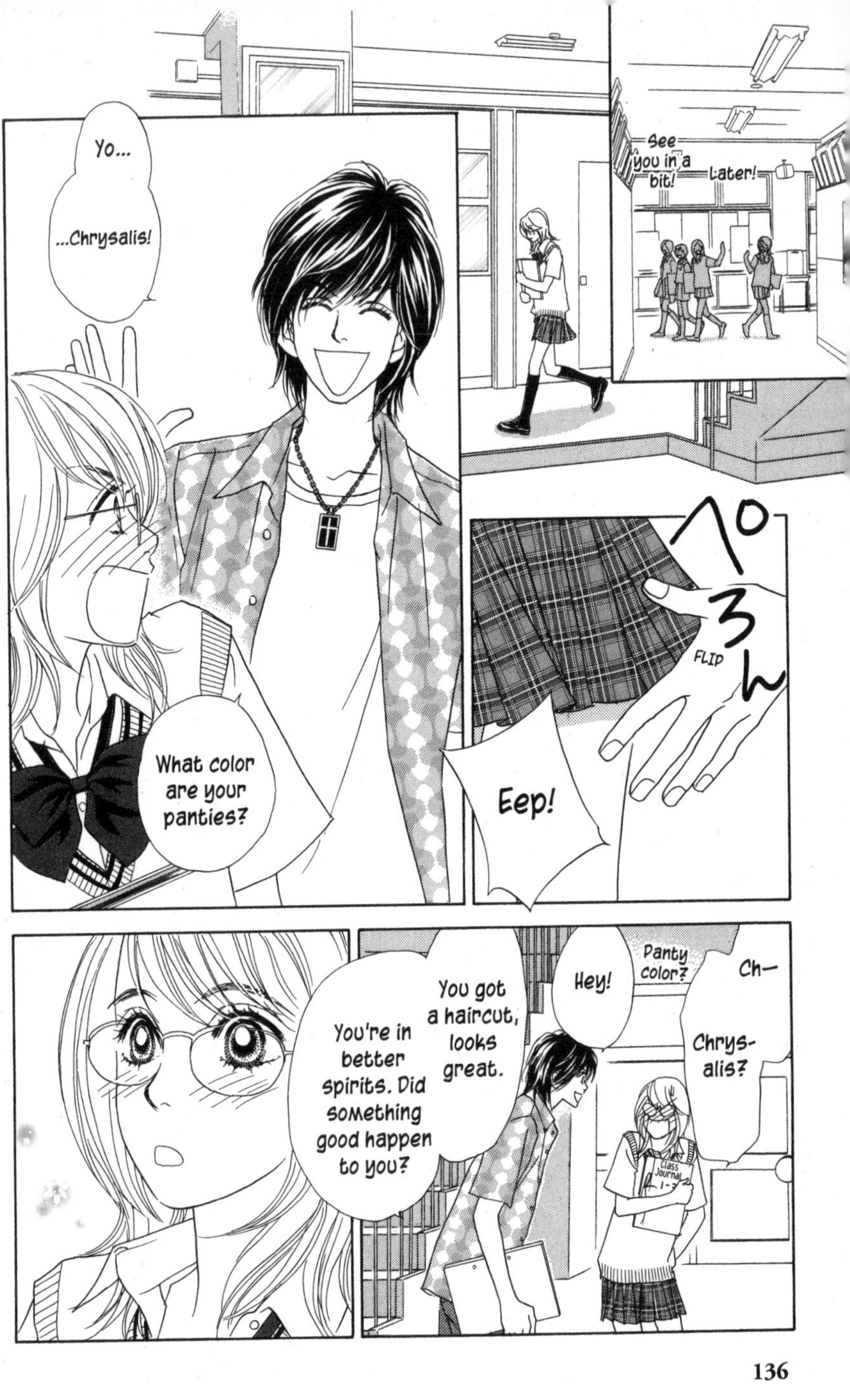
See you in a bit!
Later!
Eep!
FLIP
Yo...
...Chrysalis!
What color are your panties?
Ch—
Chrysalis?
Panty color?
Hey!
You got a haircut, looks great.
Class Journal
You're in better spirits. Did something good happen to you?

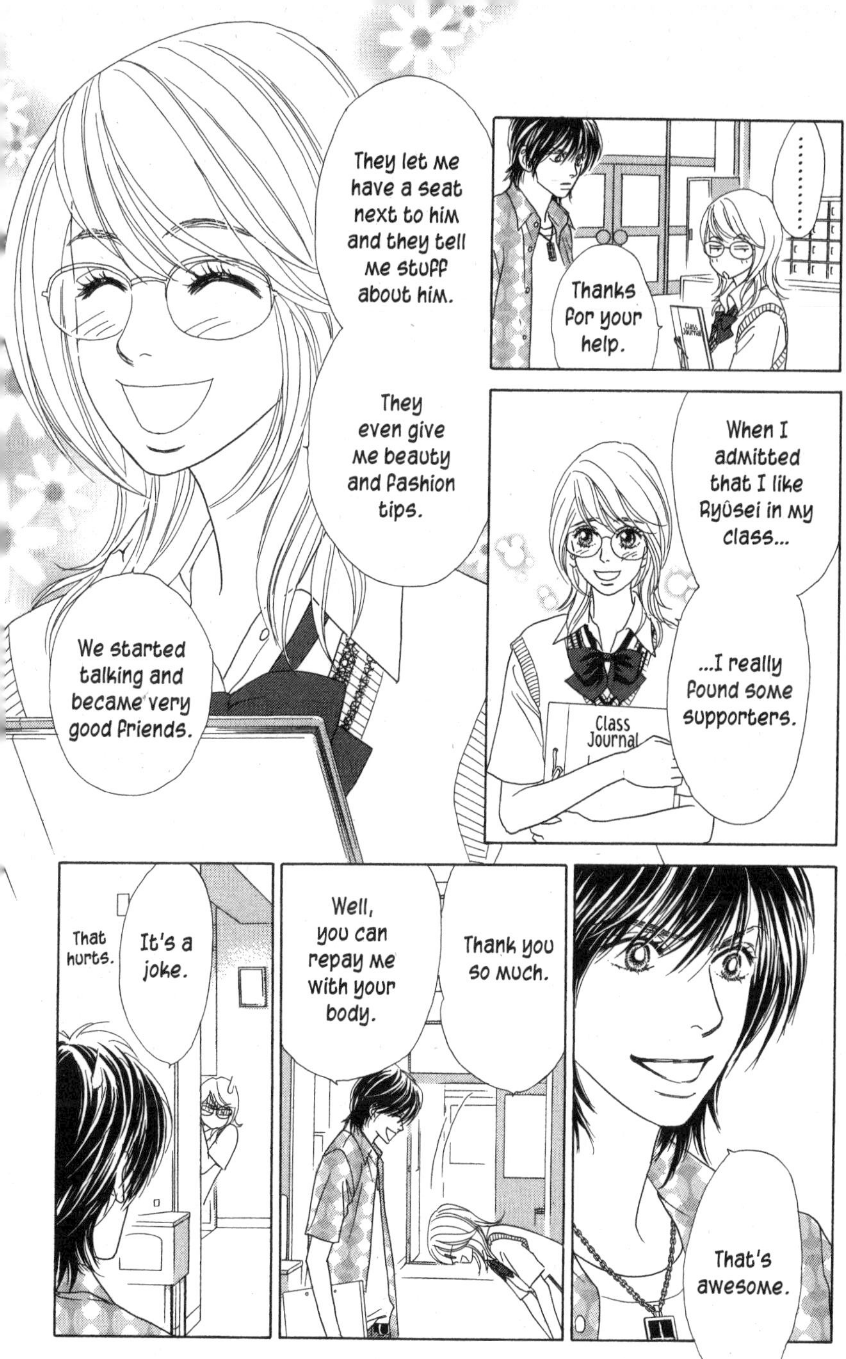
......
Thanks for your help.
Class Journal
When I admitted that I like Ryûsei in my class...
...I really found some supporters.
Class Journal
They let me have a seat next to him and they tell me stuff about him.
They even give me beauty and fashion tips.
We started talking and became very good friends.
That's awesome.
Thank you so much.
Well, you can repay me with your body.
It's a joke.
That hurts.

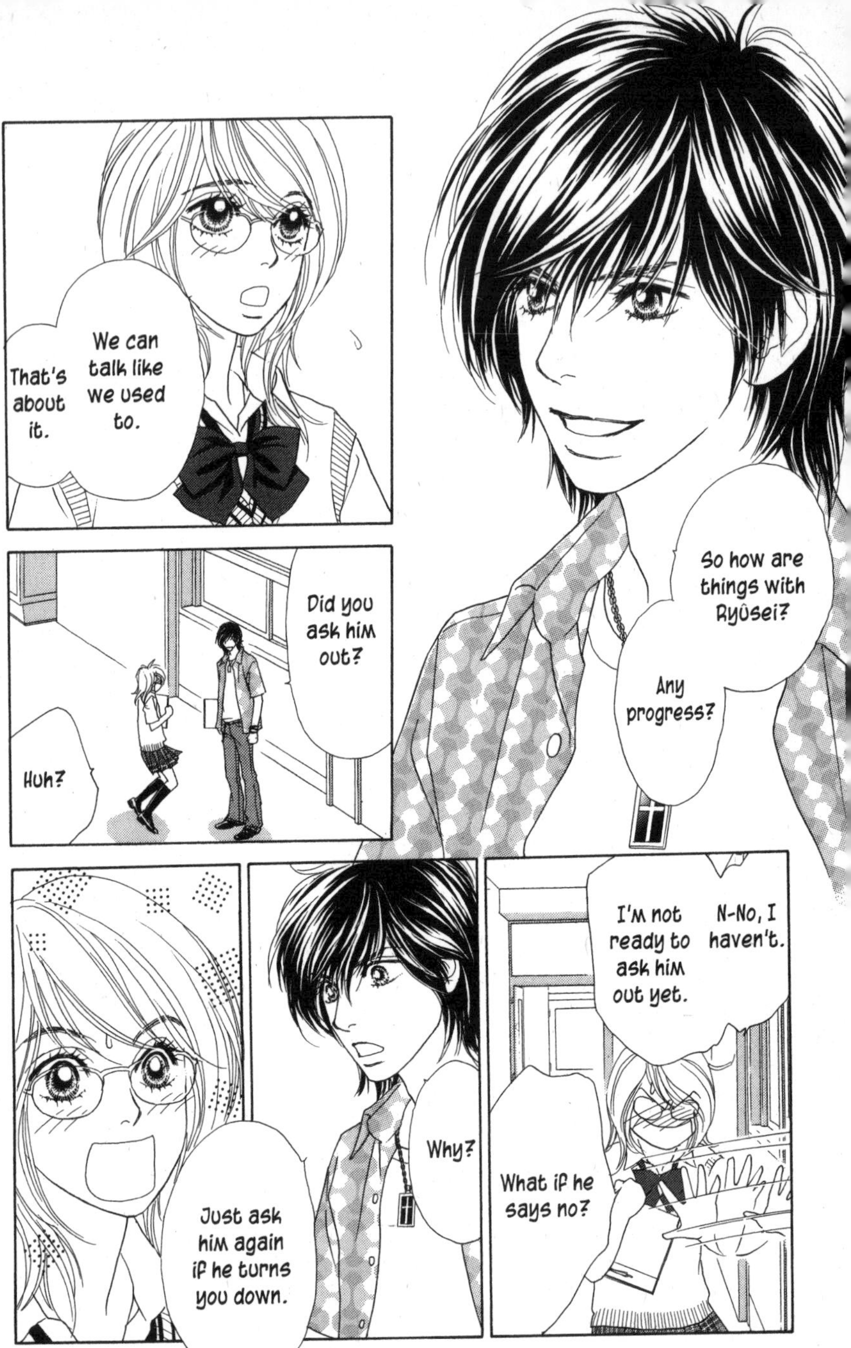
So how are things with Ryûsei?
Any progress?
We can talk like we used to.
That's about it.
Did you ask him out?
Huh?
N-No, I haven't.
I'm not ready to ask him out yet.
What if he says no?
Why?
Just ask him again if he turns you down.

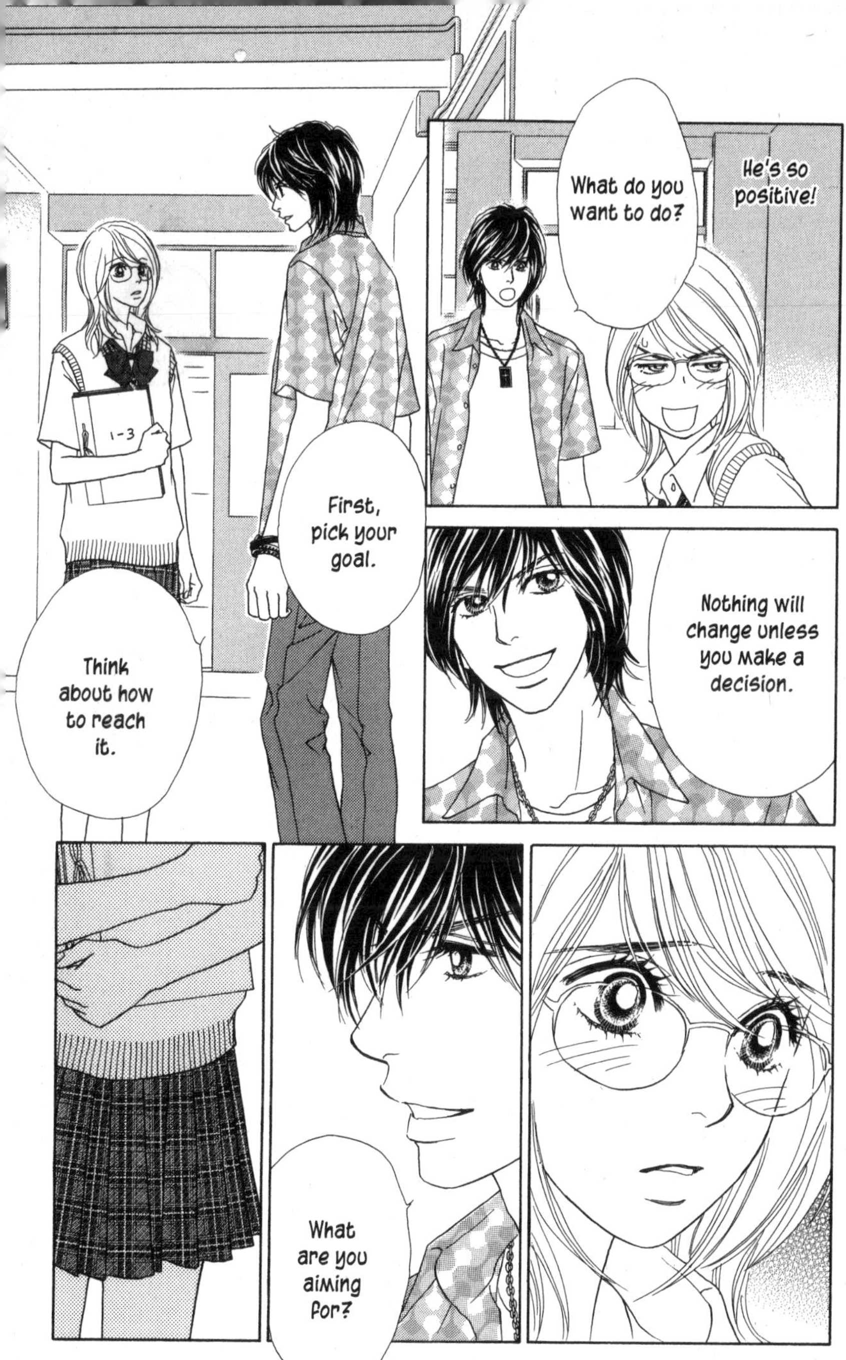
He's so positive!
What do you want to do?
Nothing will change unless you make a decision.
First, pick your goal.
Think about how to reach it.
1-3
What are you aiming for?

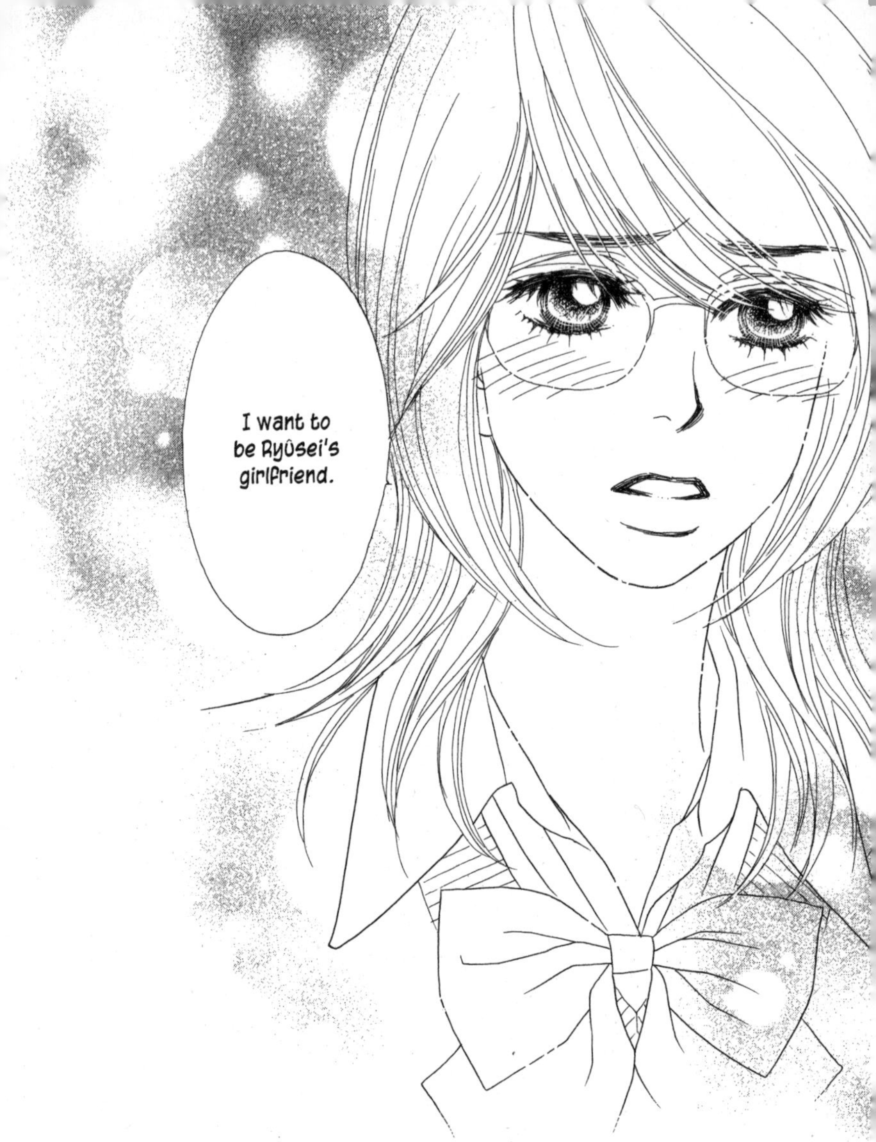
I want to be Ryûsei's girlfriend.

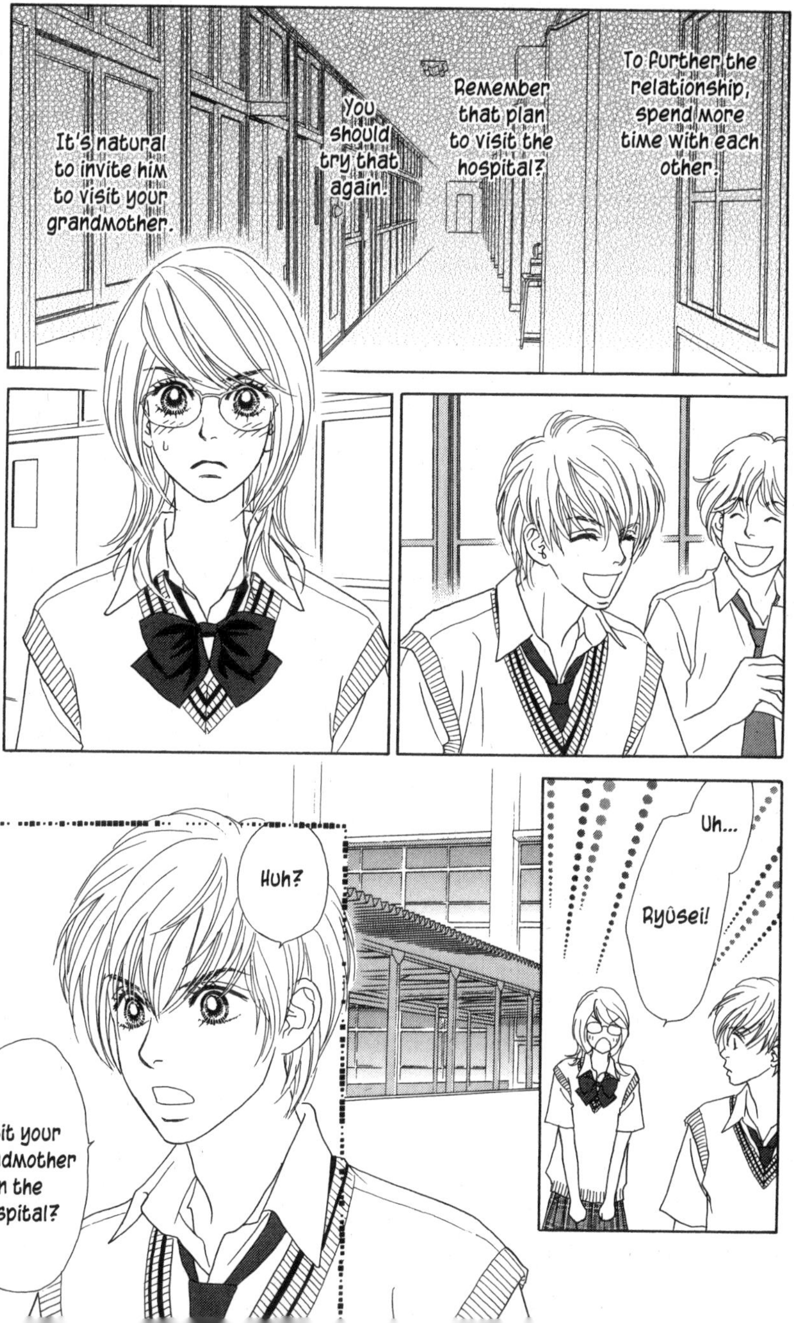
To further the relationship, spend more time with each other.
Remember that plan to visit the hospital?
You should try that again.
It's natural to invite him to visit your grandmother.
Uh...
Ryûsei!
Huh?
Visit your grandmother in the hospital?

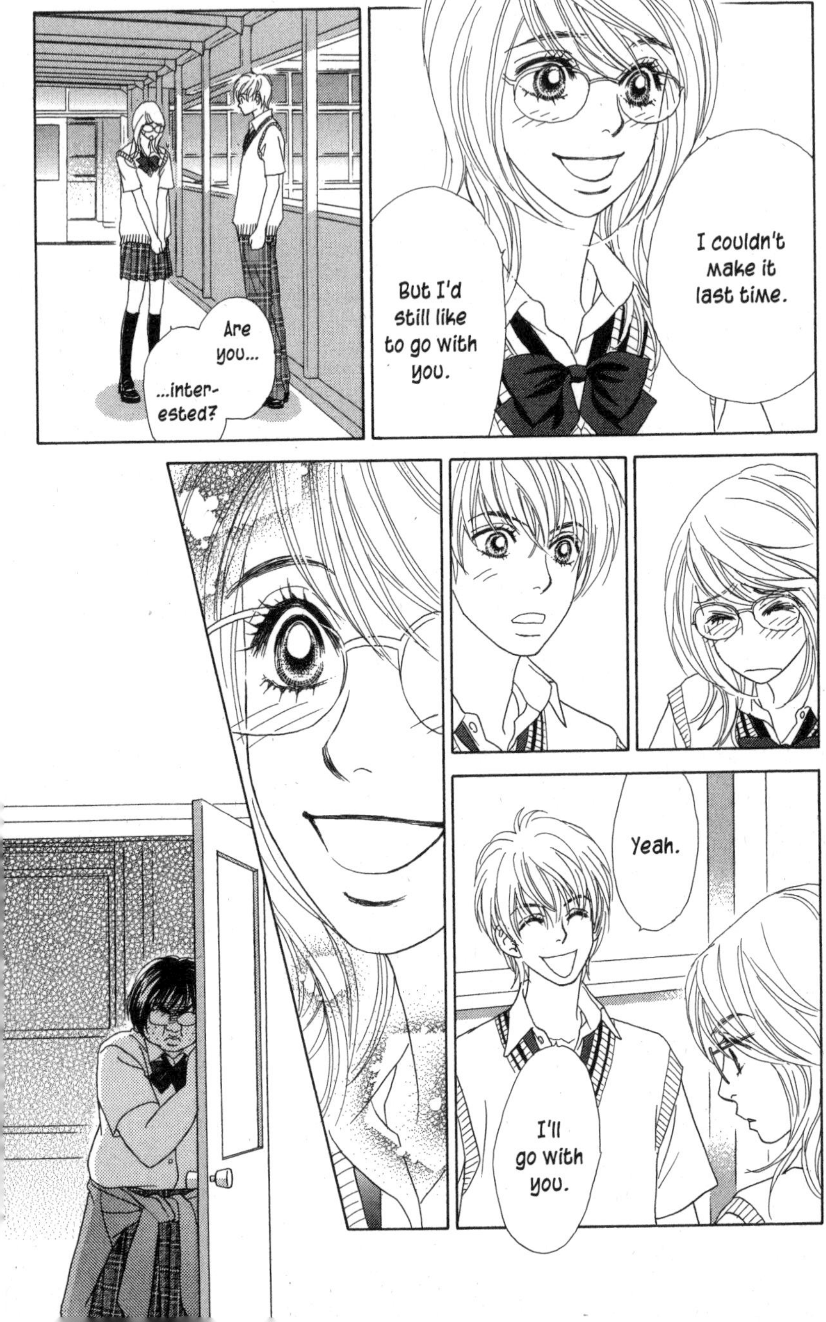
I couldn't make it last time.
But I'd still like to go with you.
Are you...
...interested?
Yeah.
I'll go with you.

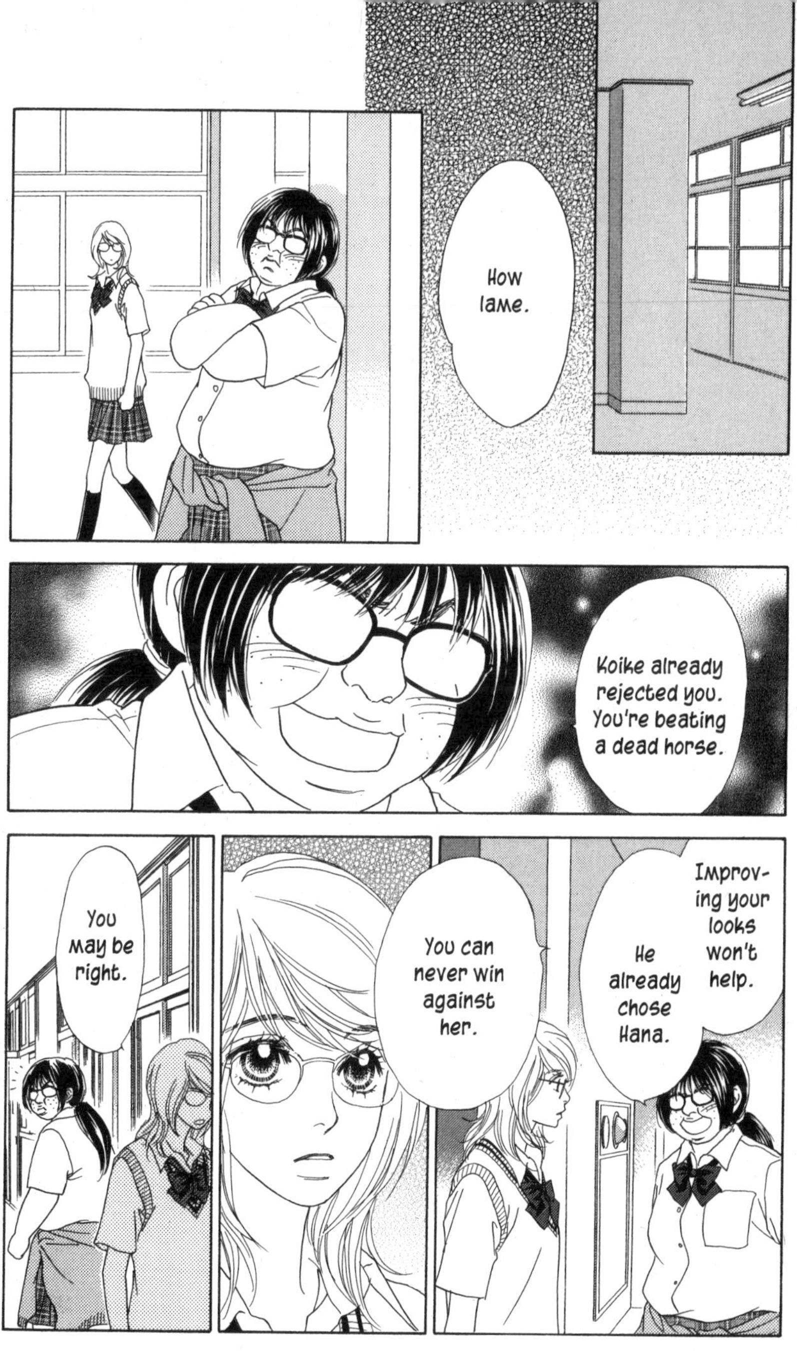
How lame.
Koike already rejected you. You're beating a dead horse.
Improving your looks won't help.
He already chose Hana.
You can never win against her.
You may be right.

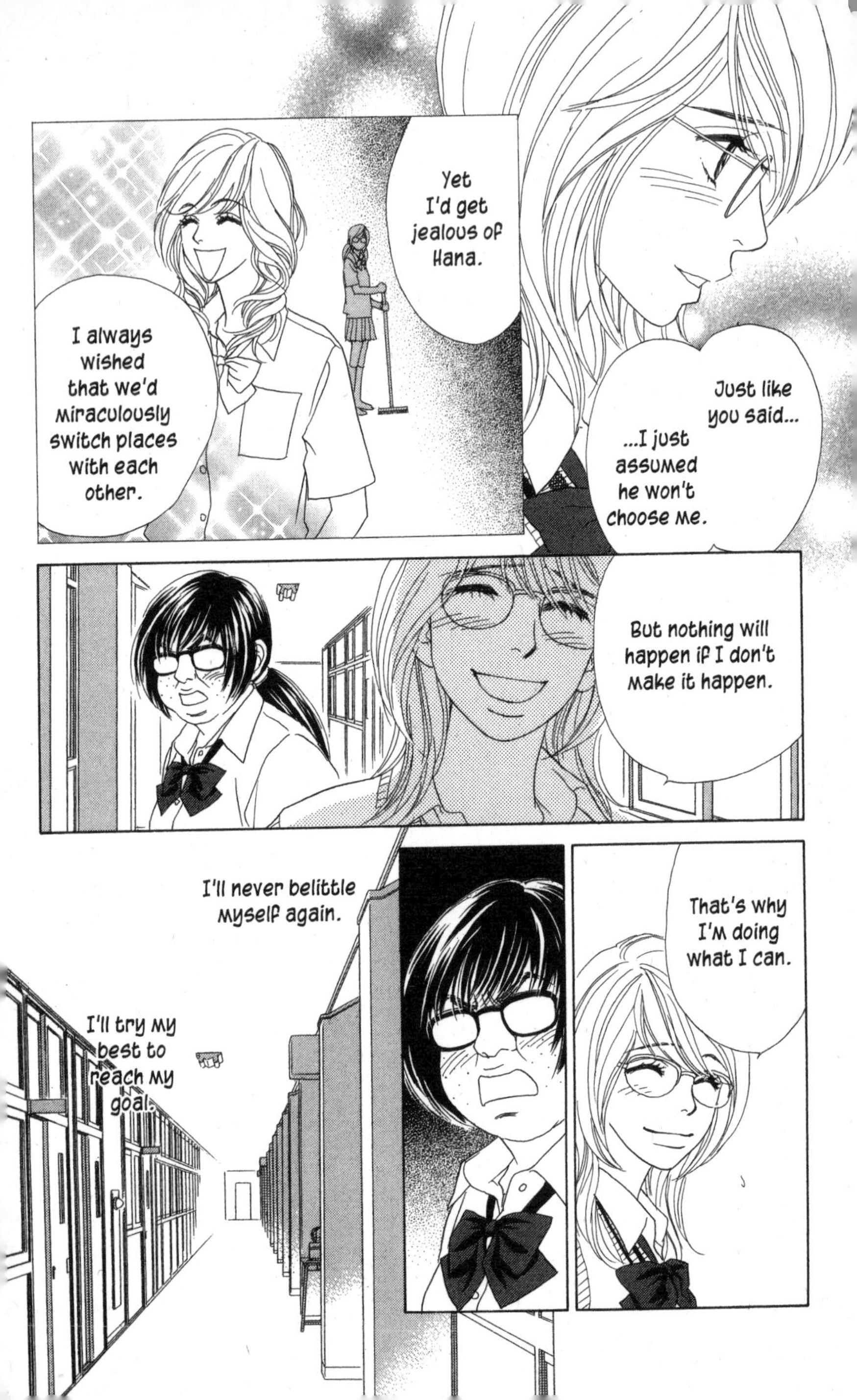

Just like you said...
...I just assumed he won't choose me.
Yet I'd get jealous of Hana.
I always wished that we'd miraculously switch places with each other.
But nothing will happen if I don't make it happen.
That's why I'm doing what I can.
I'll never belittle myself again.
I'll try my best to reach my goal.

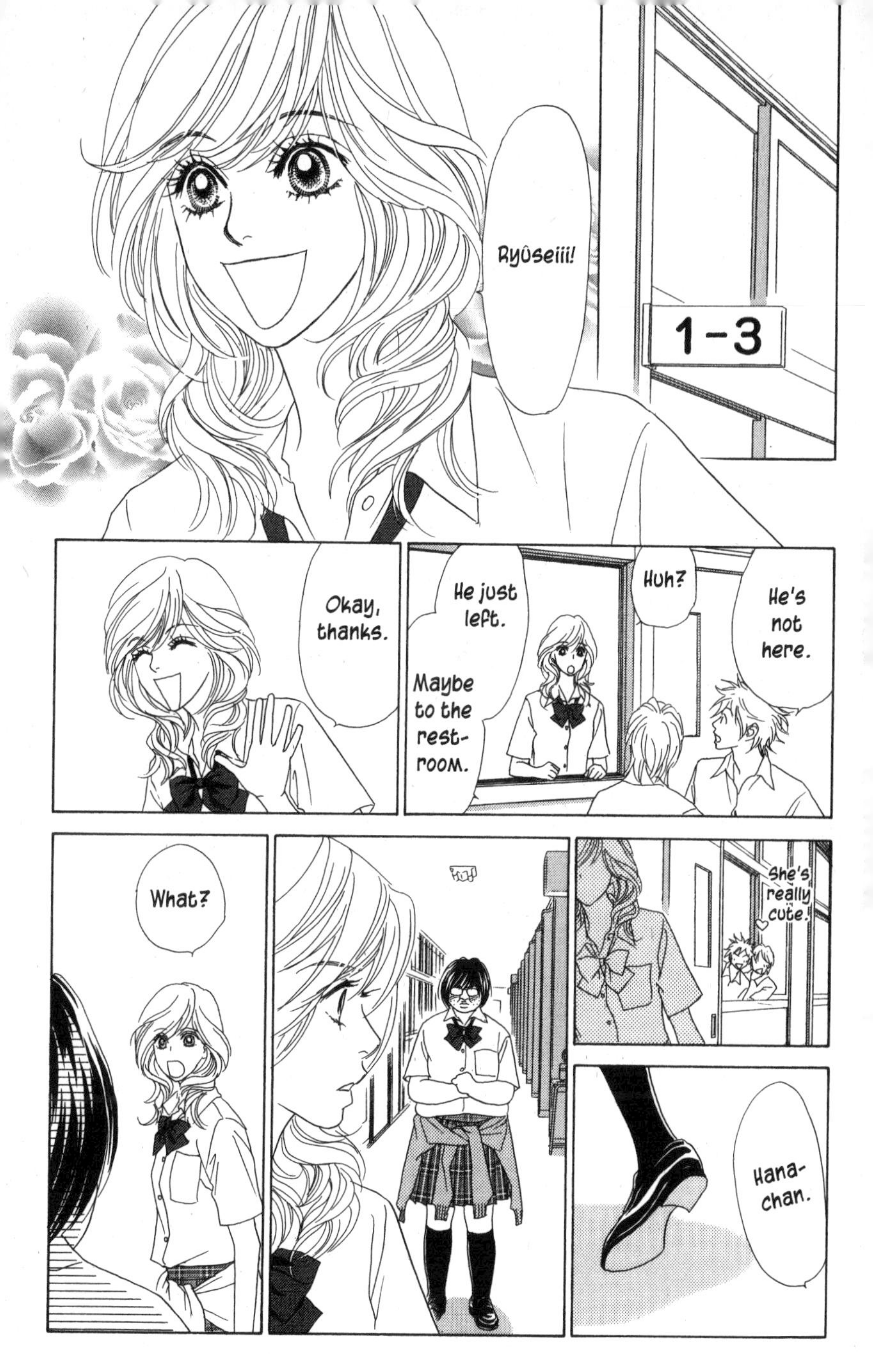
Ryûseiii!
1-3
He's not here.
Huh?
He just left.
Maybe to the rest-room.
Okay, thanks.
She's really cute!
Hana-chan.
What?

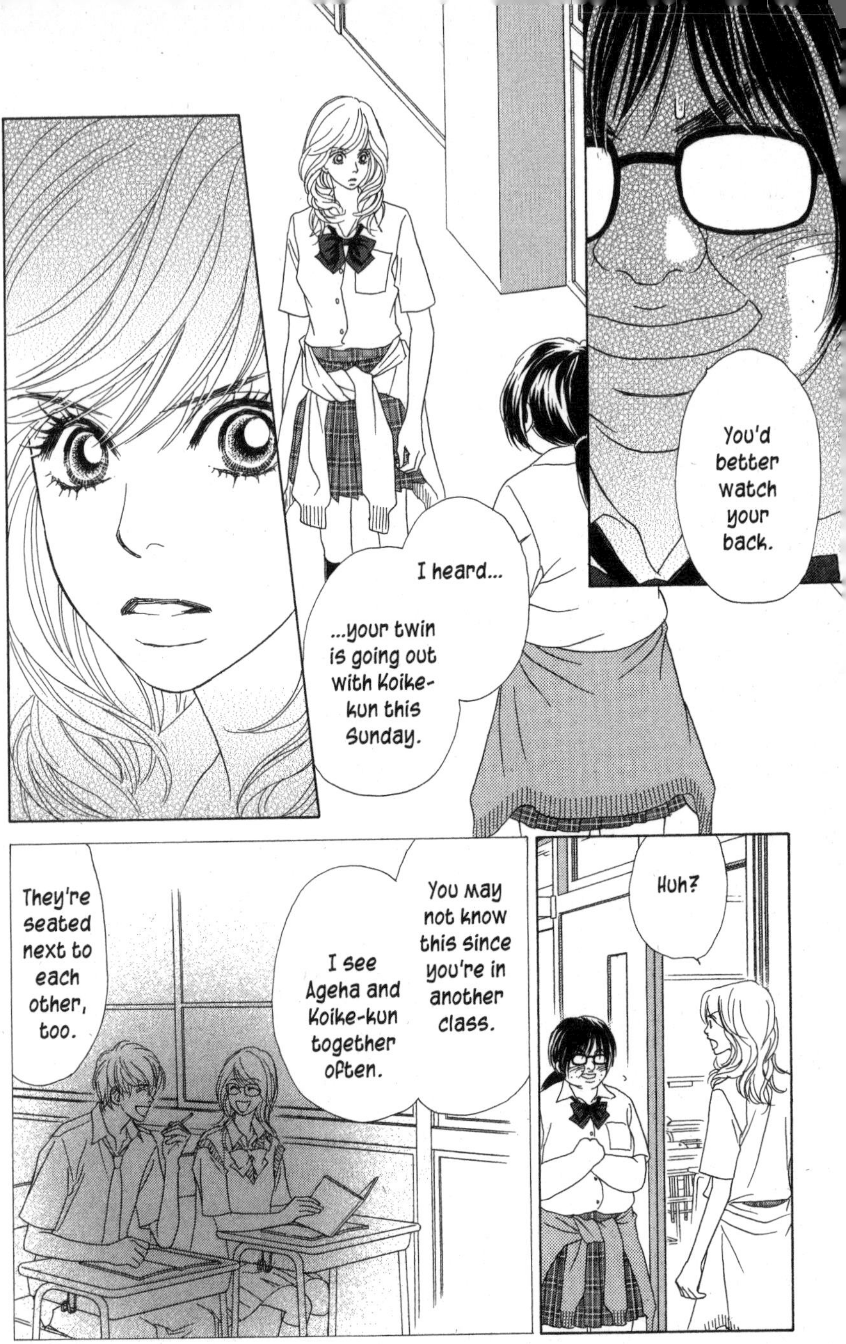
You'd better watch your back.
I heard...
...your twin is going out with Koike-kun this Sunday.
Huh?
You may not know this since you're in another class.
I see Ageha and Koike-kun together often.
They're seated next to each other, too.

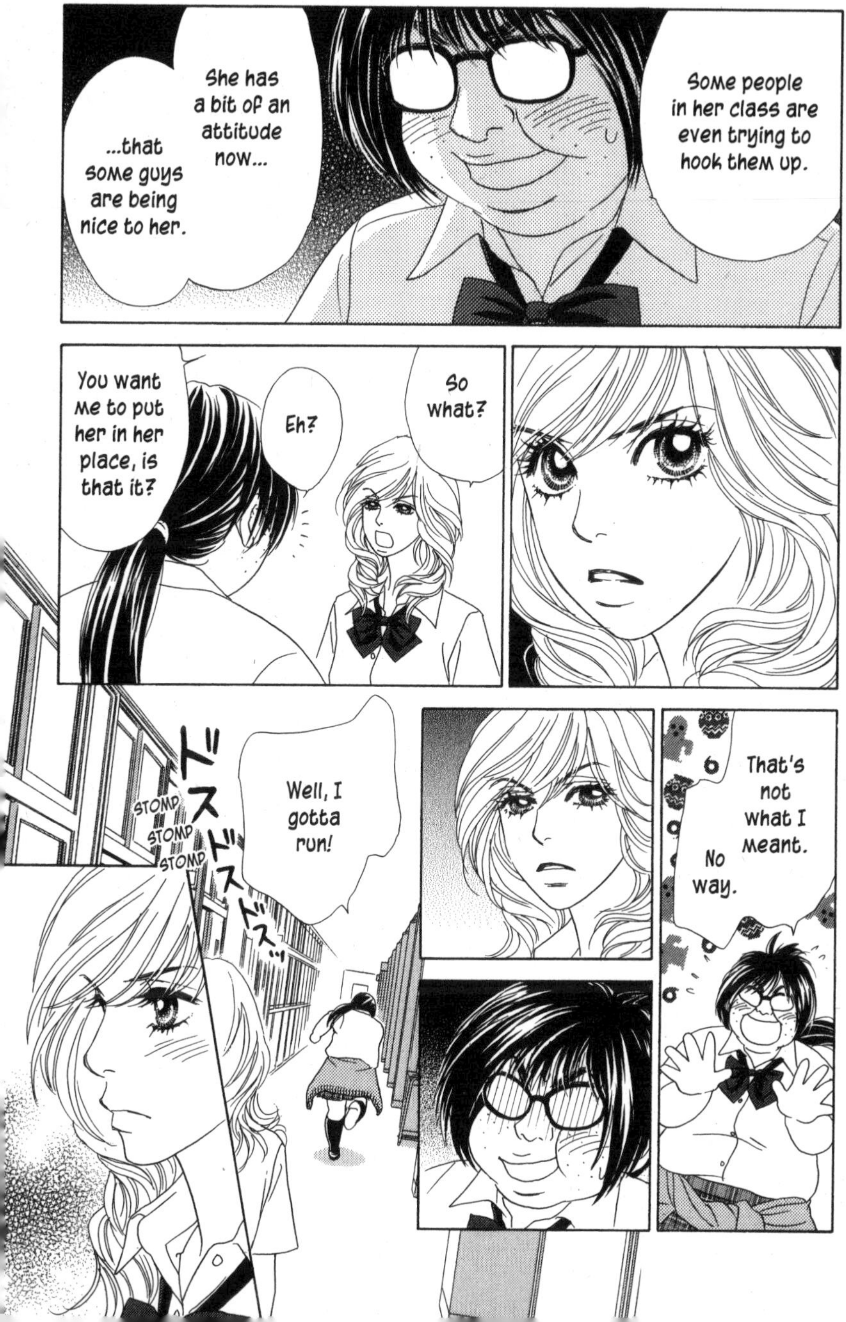

Some people in her class are even trying to hook them up.
She has a bit of an attitude now...
...that some guys are being nice to her.
So what?
Eh?
You want me to put her in her place, is that it?
That's not what I meant.
No way.
Well, I gotta run!
ドスドスドス...
STOMP STOMP STOMP

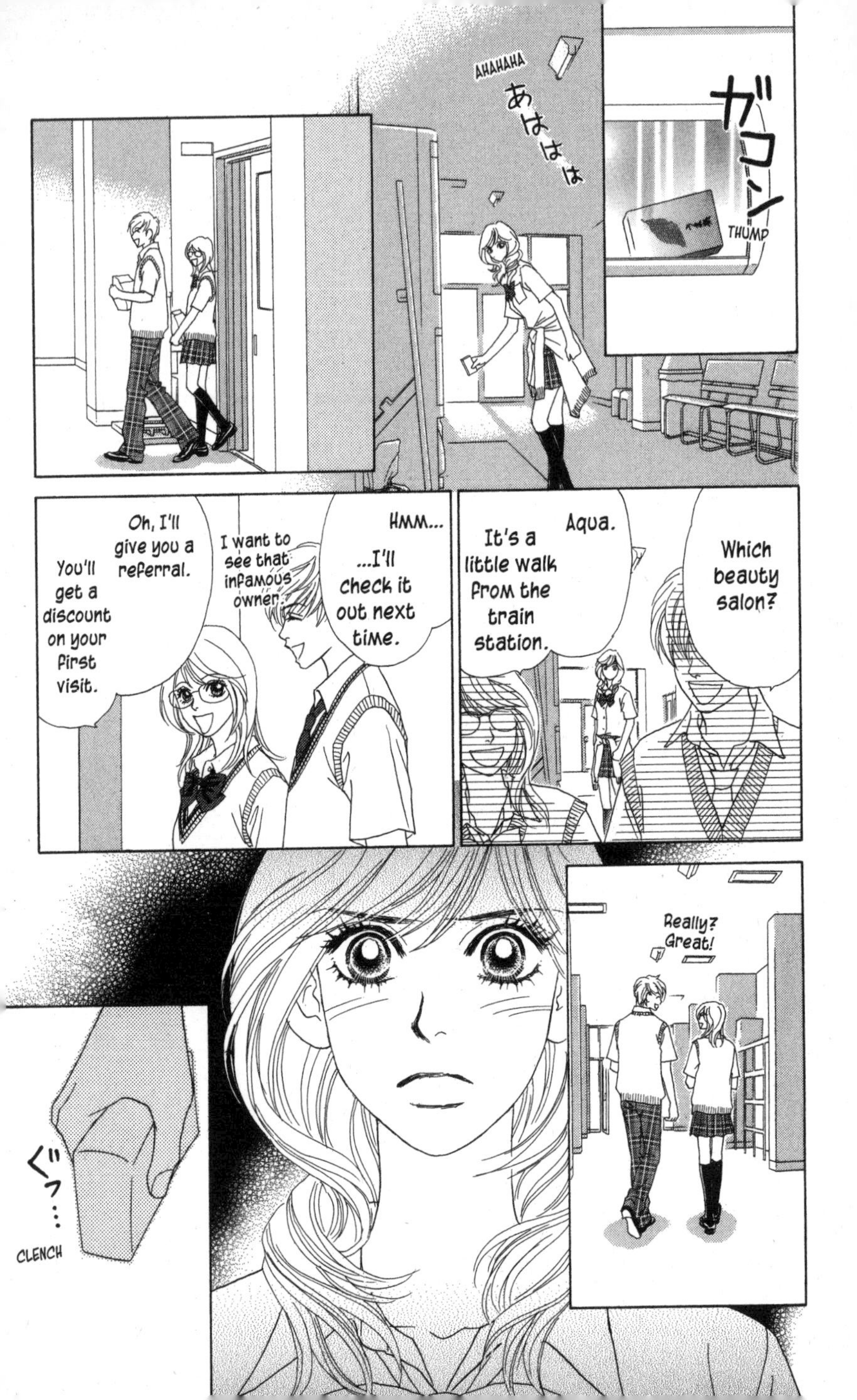
ガコン
THUMP
あははは
AHAHAHA
Which beauty salon?
Aqua.
It's a little walk from the train station.
HMM...
...I'll check it out next time.
I want to see that infamous owner.
Oh, I'll give you a referral.
You'll get a discount on your first visit.
Really? Great!
ぐっ…
CLENCH

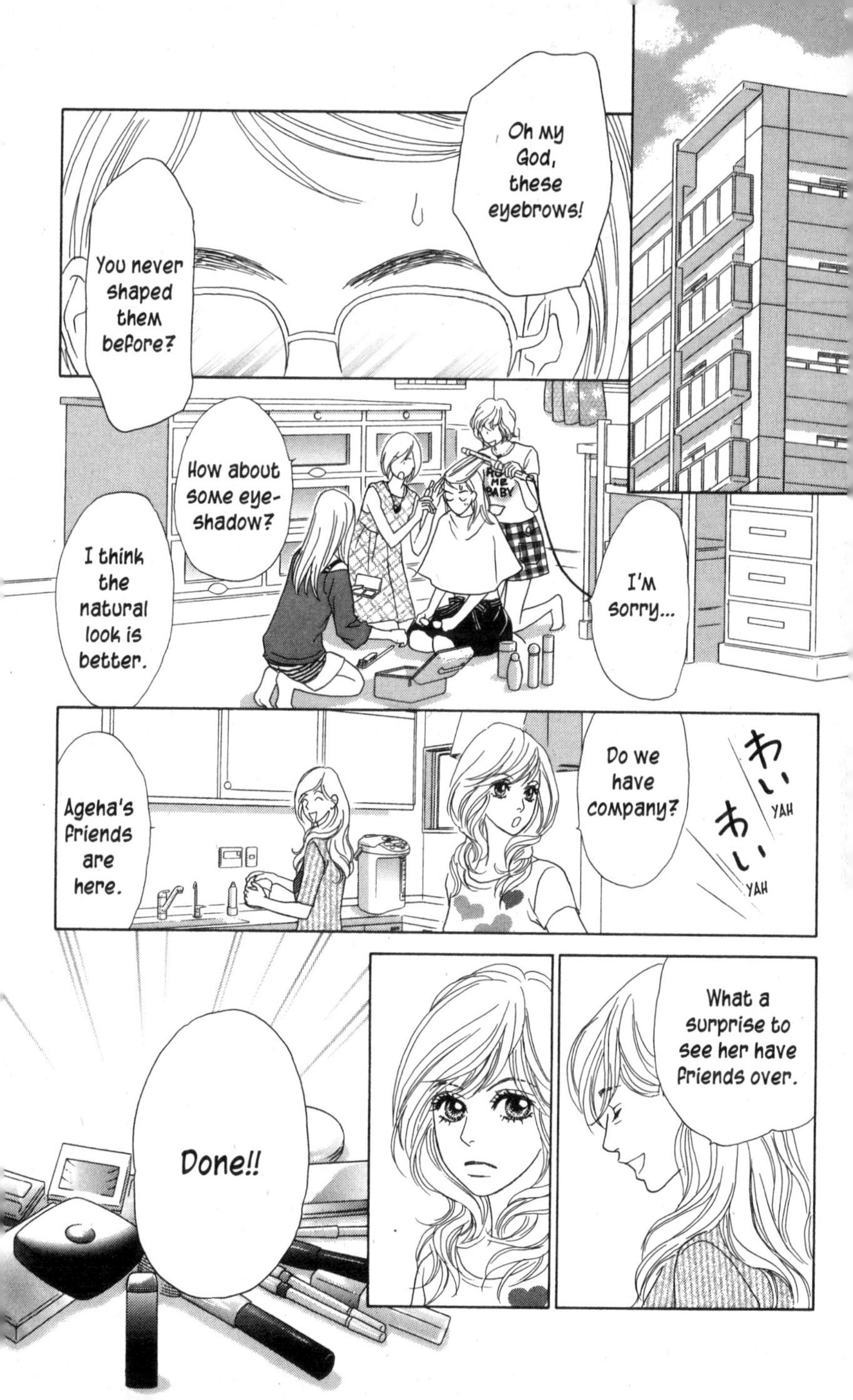
Oh my God, these eyebrows!
You never shaped them before?
I'm sorry...
How about some eye-shadow?
I think the natural look is better.
わい
YAH
わい
YAH
Do we have company?
Ageha's friends are here.
What a surprise to see her have friends over.
Done!!

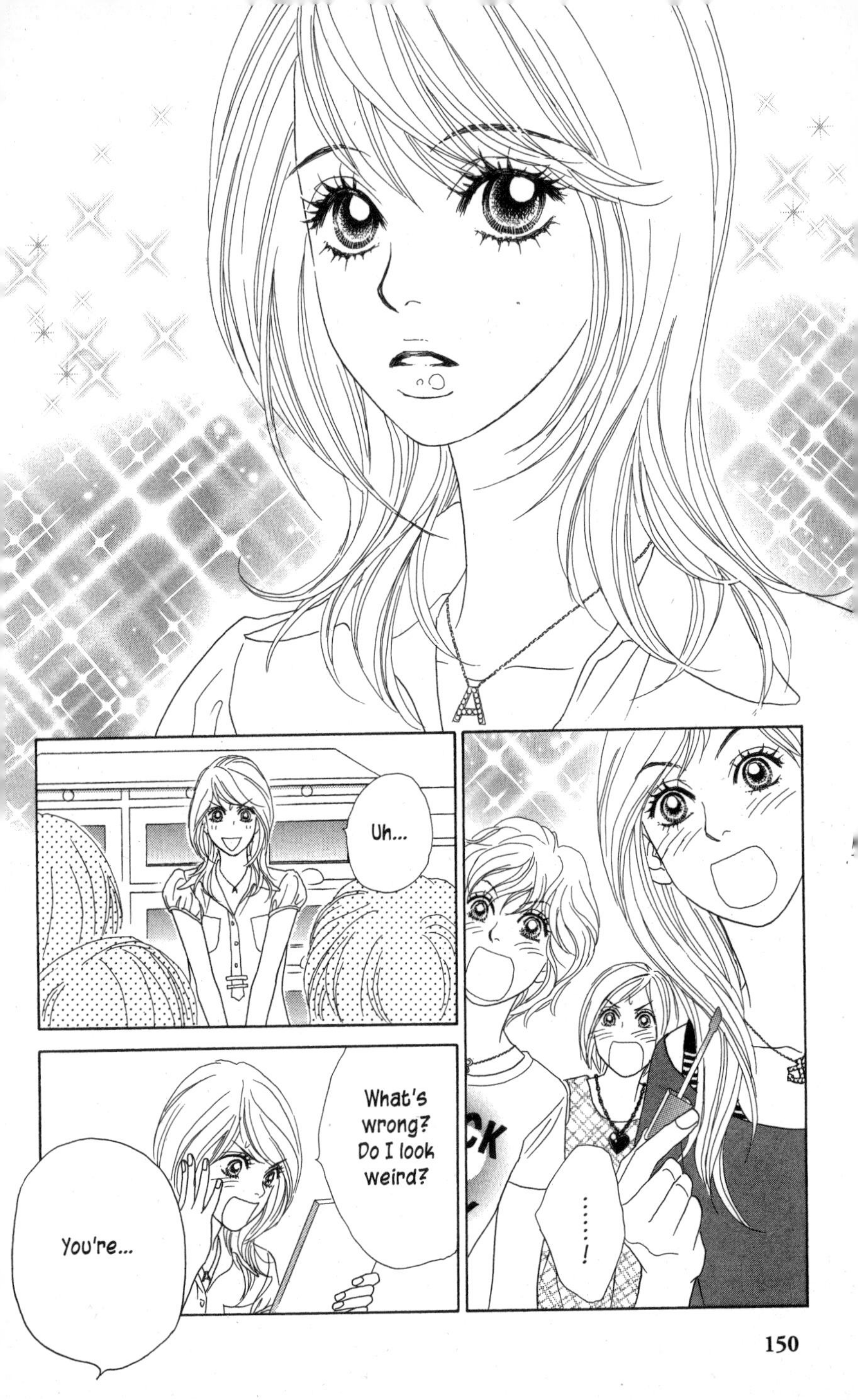
......!
Uh...
What's wrong? Do I look weird?
You're...

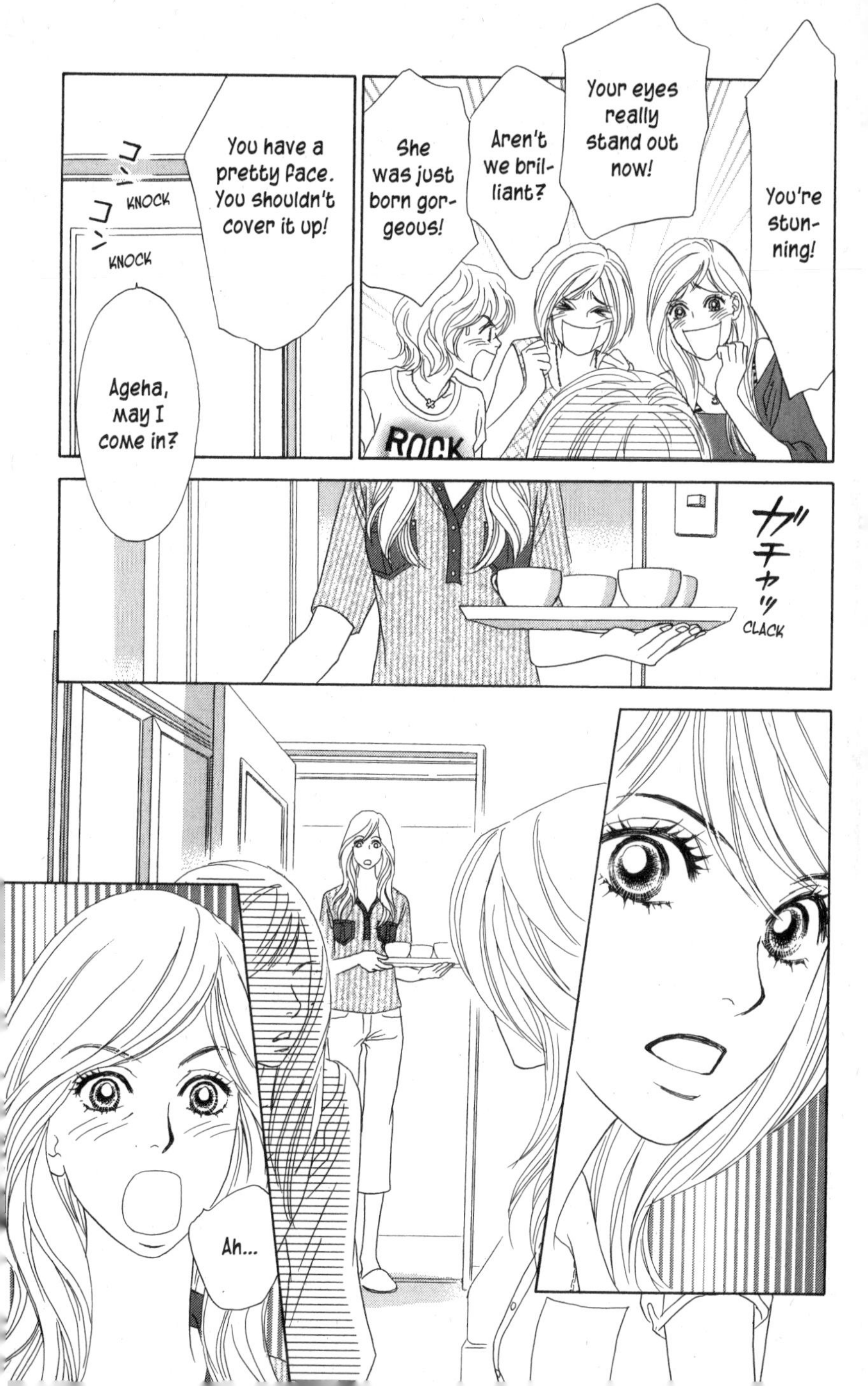
You're stunning!
Your eyes really stand out now!
Aren't we brilliant?
She was just born gorgeous!
ROCK
You have a pretty face. You shouldn't cover it up!
コン KNOCK
コン KNOCK
Ageha, may I come in?
ガチャッ CLACK
Ah...

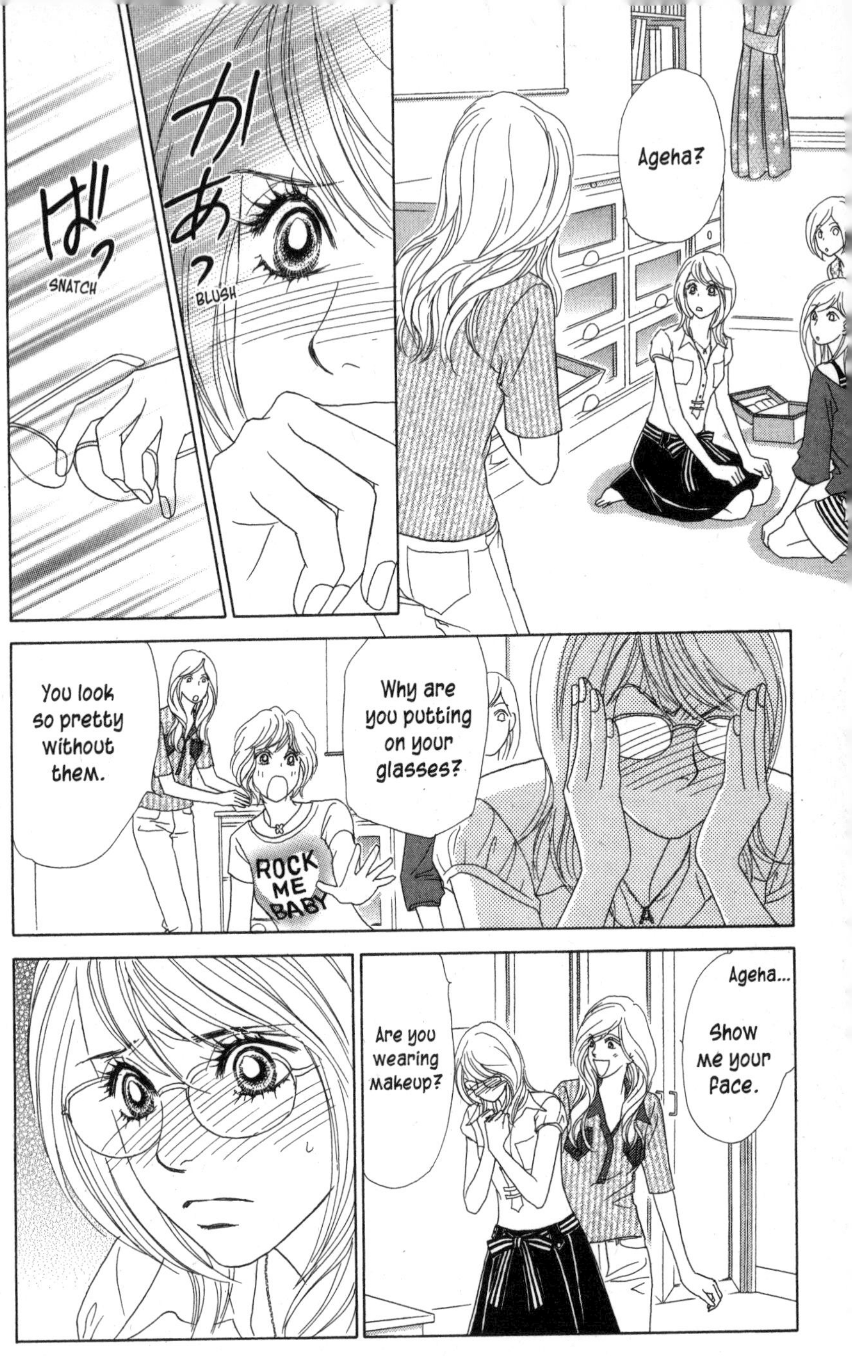
Ageha?
かぁっ
BLUSH
ぱっ
SNATCH
Why are you putting on your glasses?
You look so pretty without them.
Ageha...
Show me your face.
Are you wearing makeup?

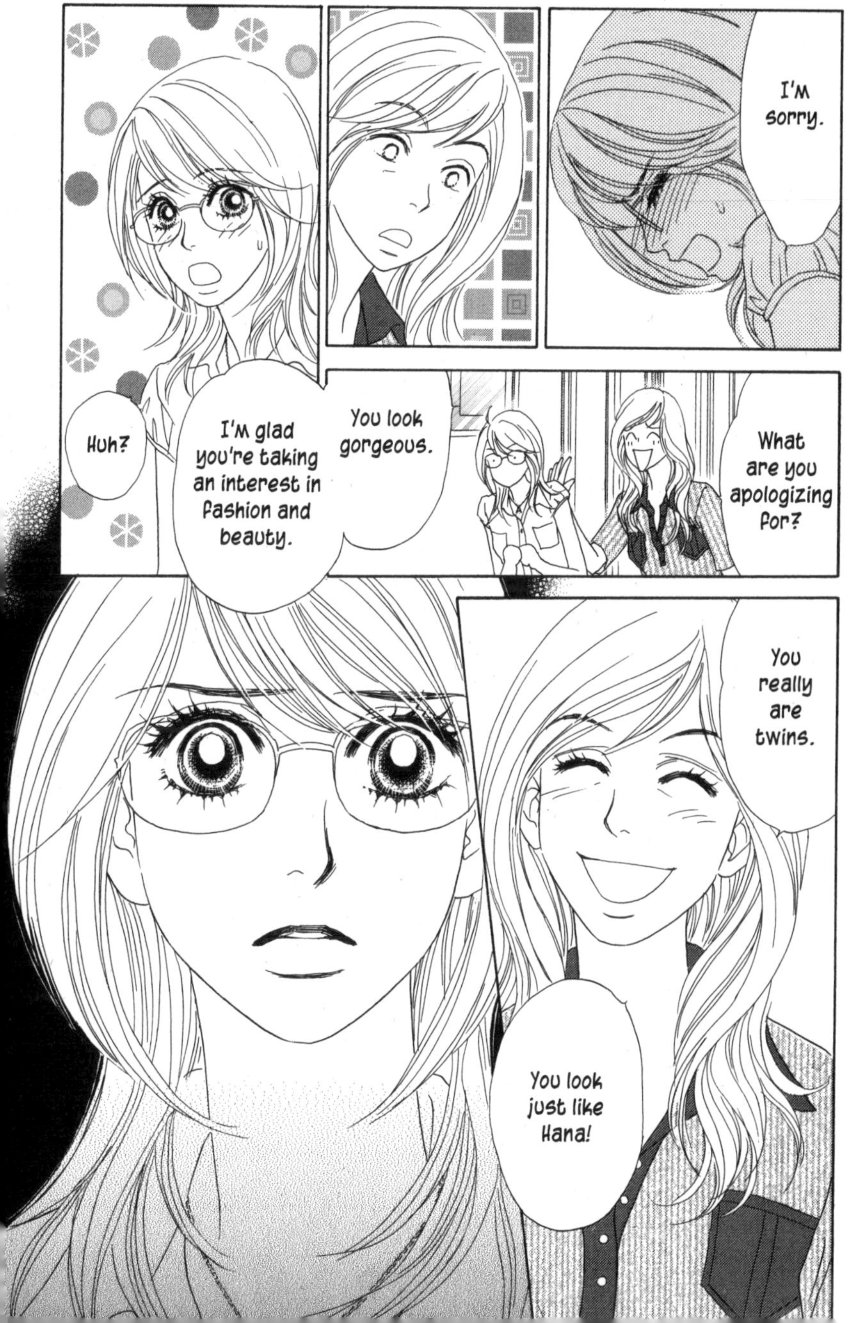

I'm sorry.
What are you apologizing for?
You look gorgeous.
I'm glad you're taking an interest in fashion and beauty.
Huh?
You really are twins.
You look just like Hana!

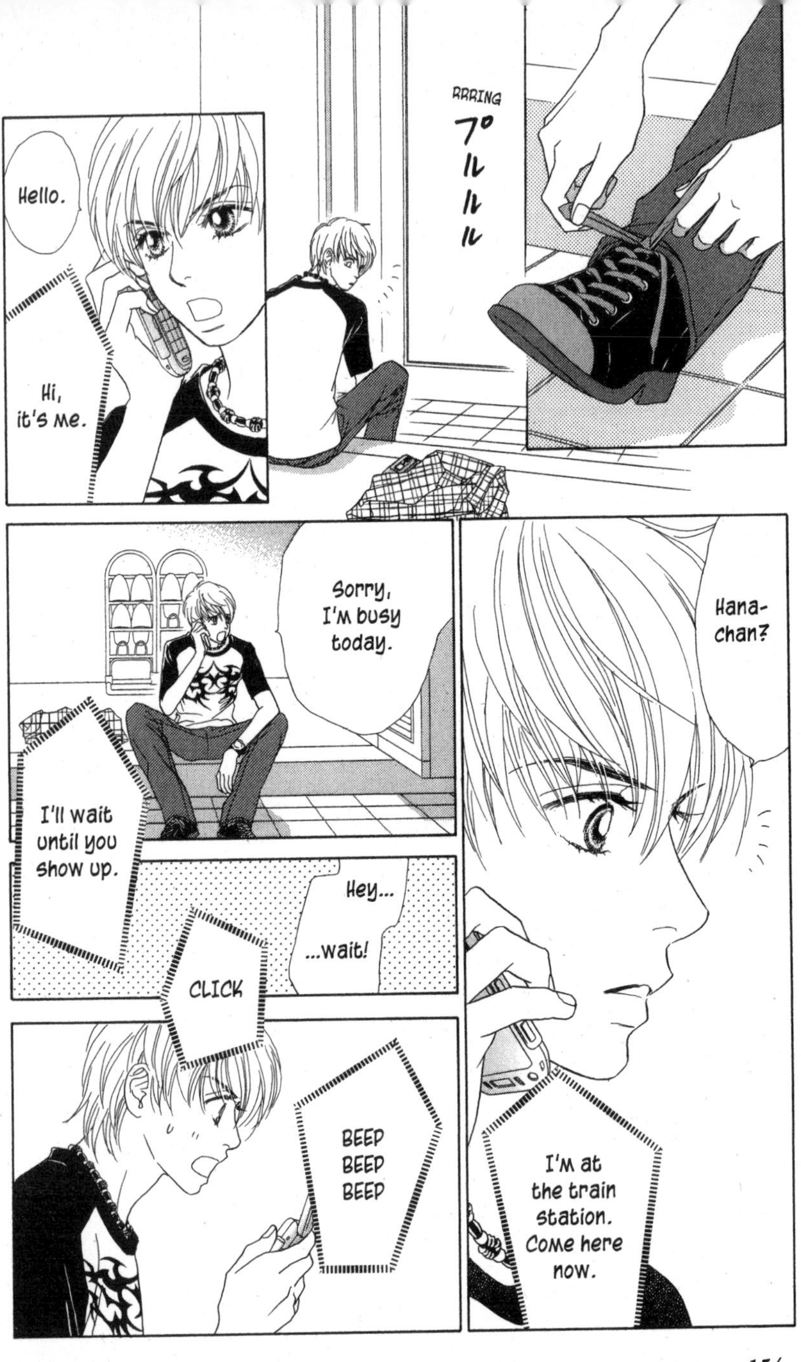
RRRING
プルルル
Hello.
Hi, it's me.
Hana-chan?
I'm at the train station. Come here now.
Sorry, I'm busy today.
I'll wait until you show up.
Hey...
...wait!
CLICK
BEEP BEEP BEEP

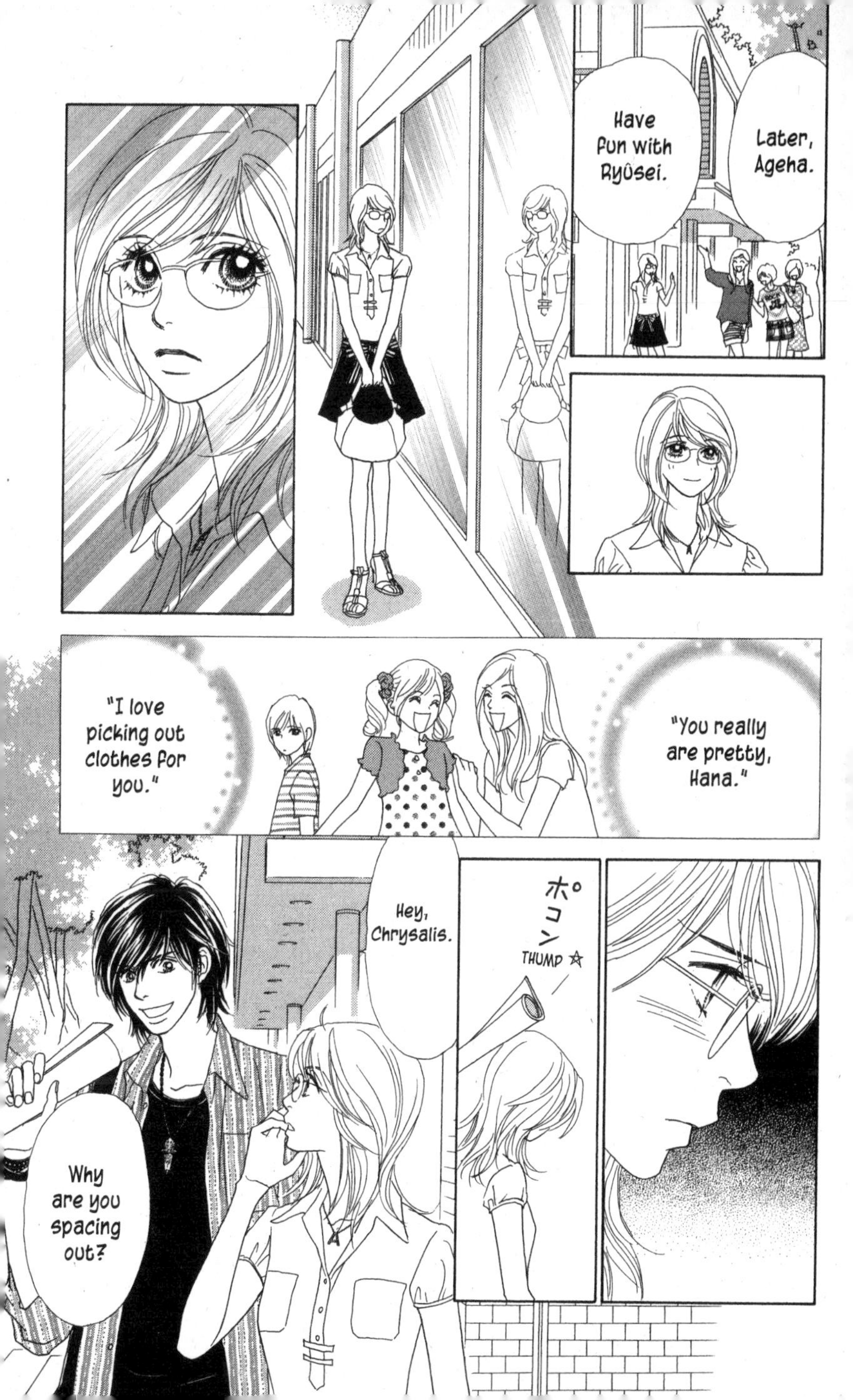
Later, Ageha.
Have fun with Ryûsei.
"You really are pretty, Hana."
"I love picking out clothes for you."
ポコン
THUMP ☆
Hey, Chrysalis.
Why are you spacing out?

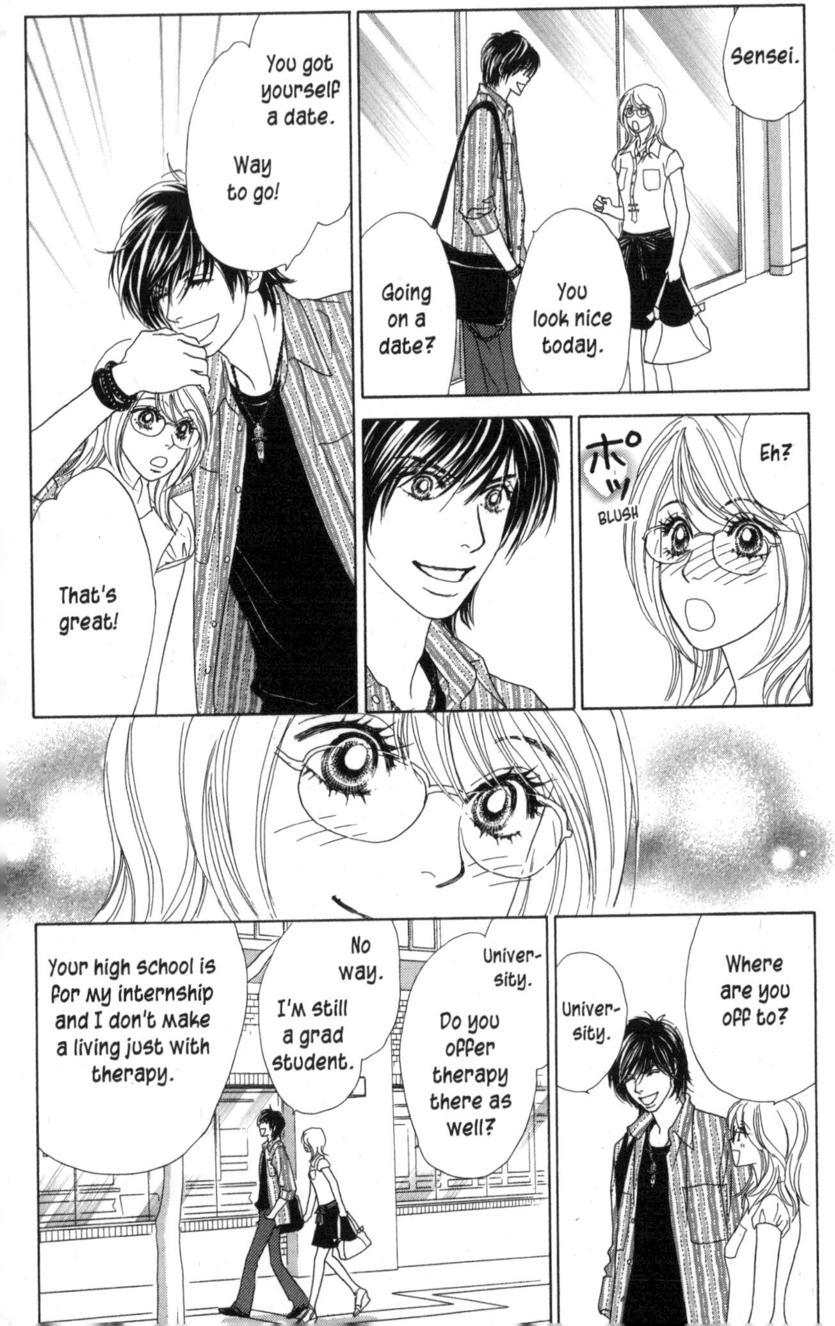
Sensei.
You look nice today.
Going on a date?
Eh?
ポッ
BLUSH
You got yourself a date.
Way to go!
That's great!
Where are you off to?
Univer-sity.
Univer-sity.
Do you offer therapy there as well?
No way.
I'm still a grad student.
Your high school is for my internship and I don't make a living just with therapy.

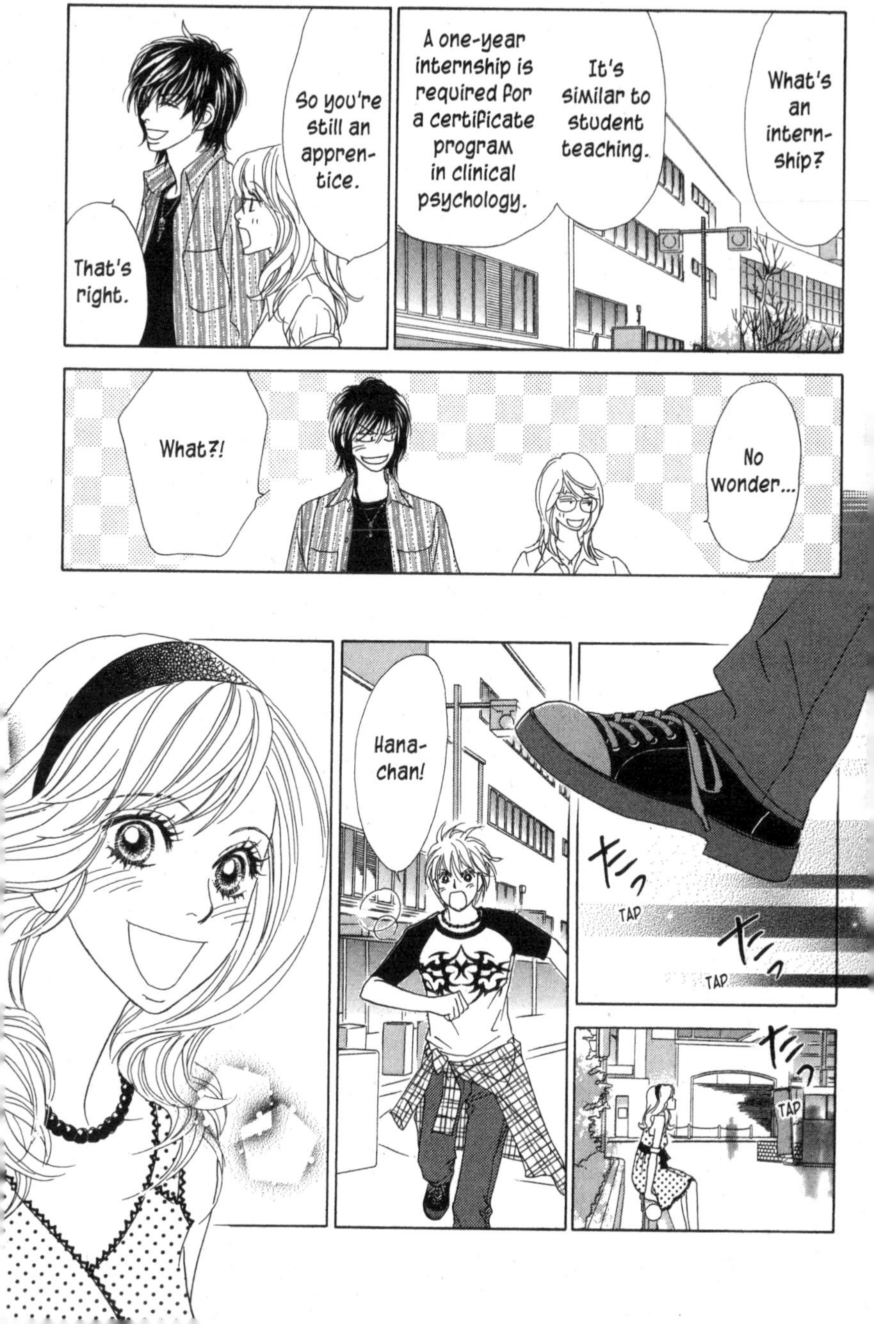
What's an internship?
It's similar to student teaching.
A one-year internship is required for a certificate program in clinical psychology.
So you're still an apprentice.
That's right.
No wonder...
What?!
TAP
TAP
TAP
Hana-chan!

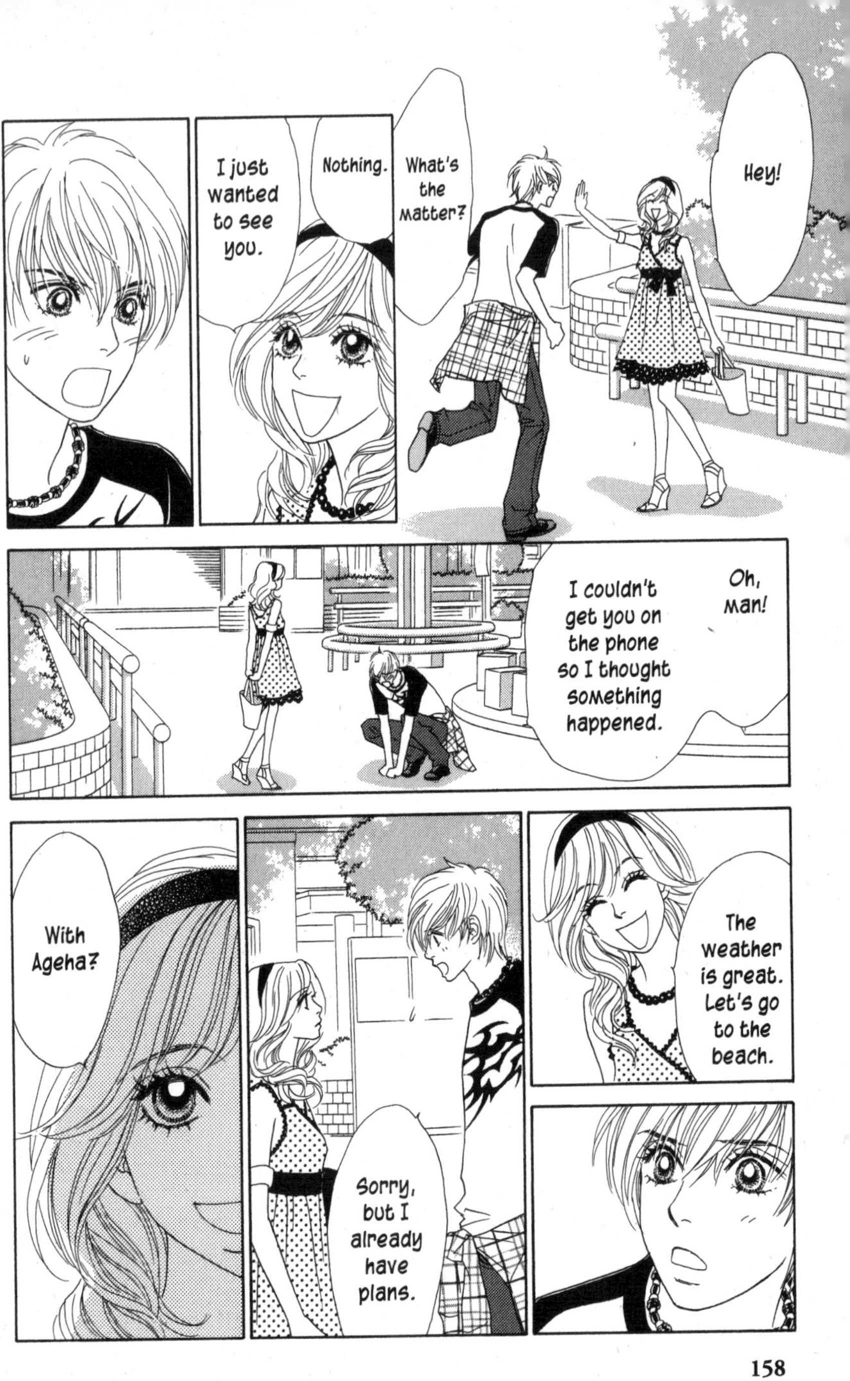
Hey!
What's the matter?
Nothing.
I just wanted to see you.
Oh, man!
I couldn't get you on the phone so I thought something happened.
The weather is great. Let's go to the beach.
Sorry, but I already have plans.
With Ageha?

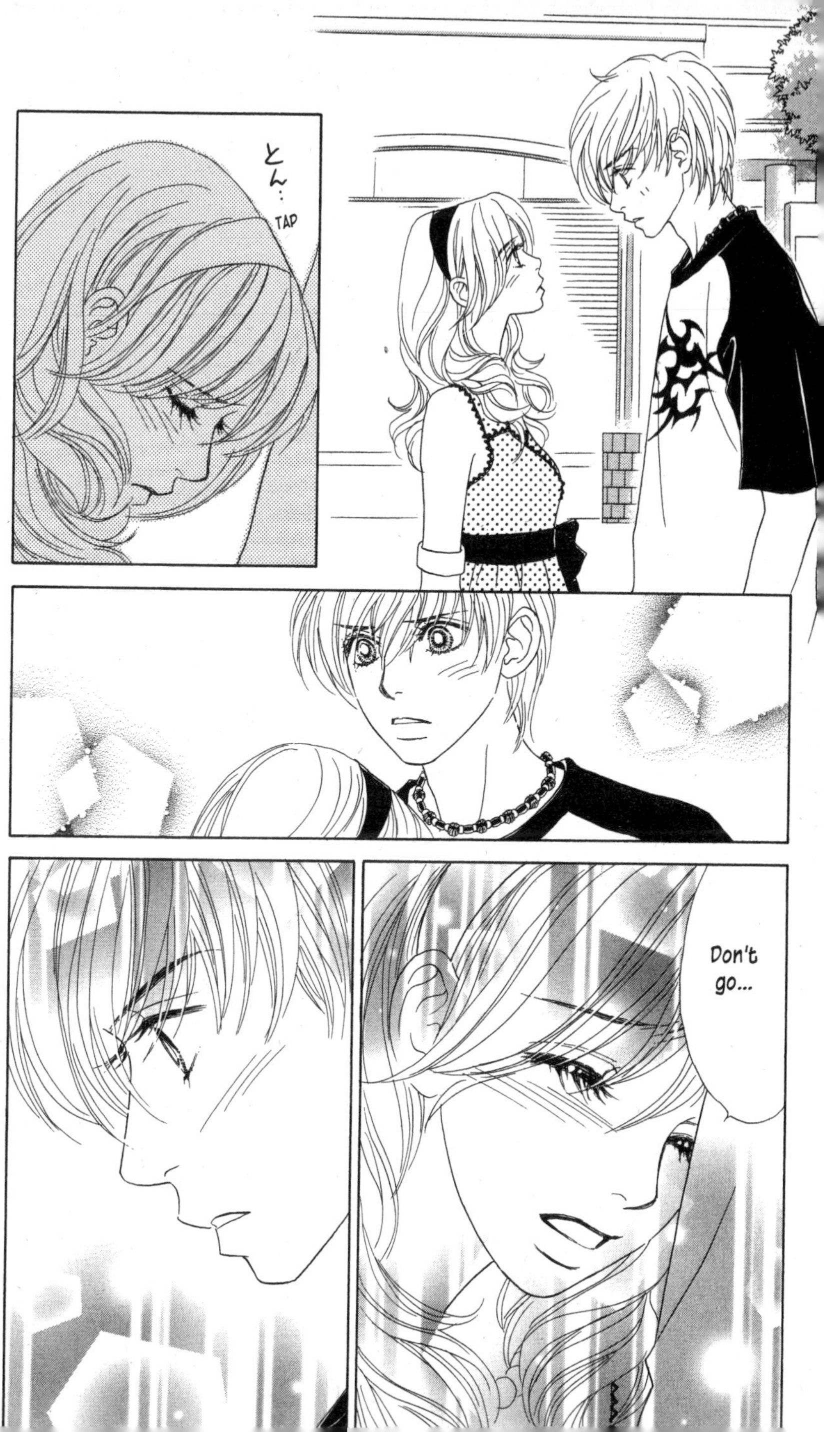

とん…
TAP
Don't go...

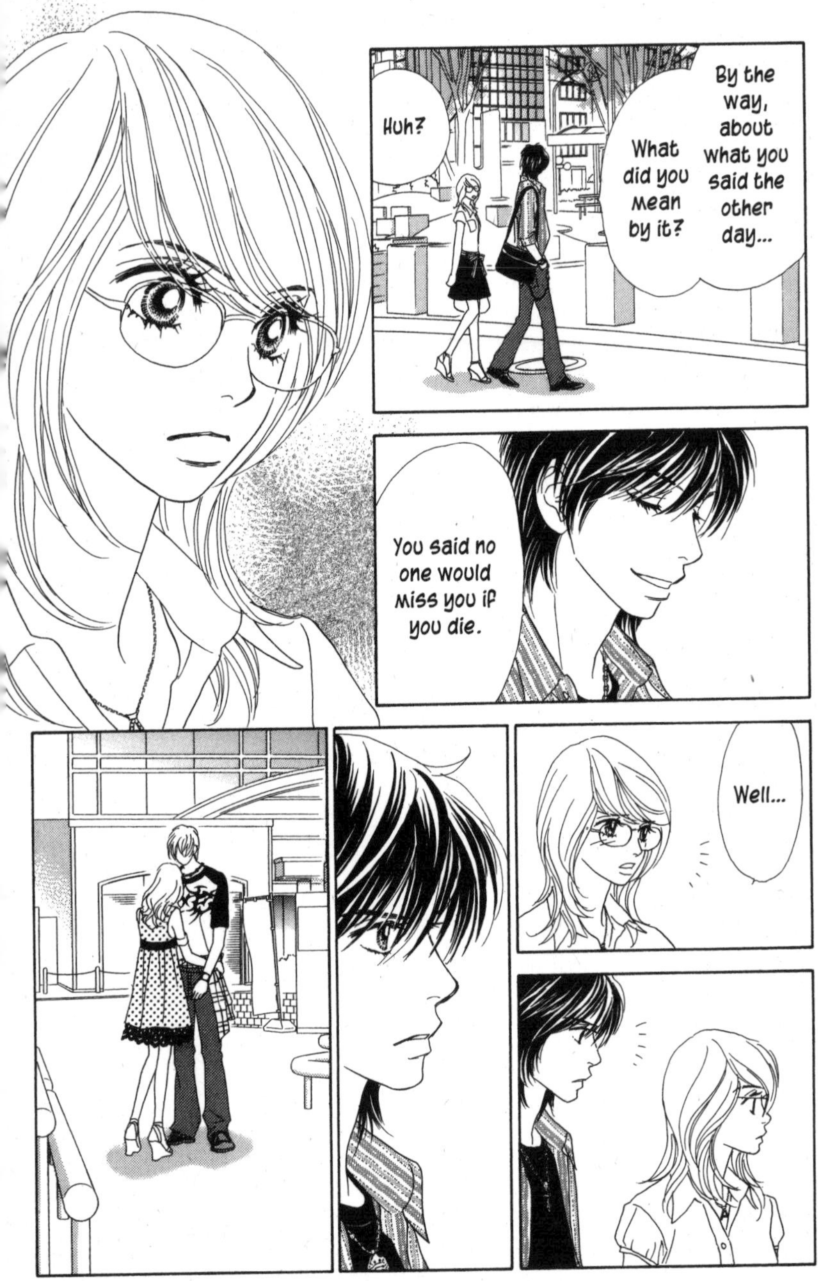
By the way, about what you said the other day...
What did you mean by it?
Huh?
You said no one would miss you if you die.
Well...

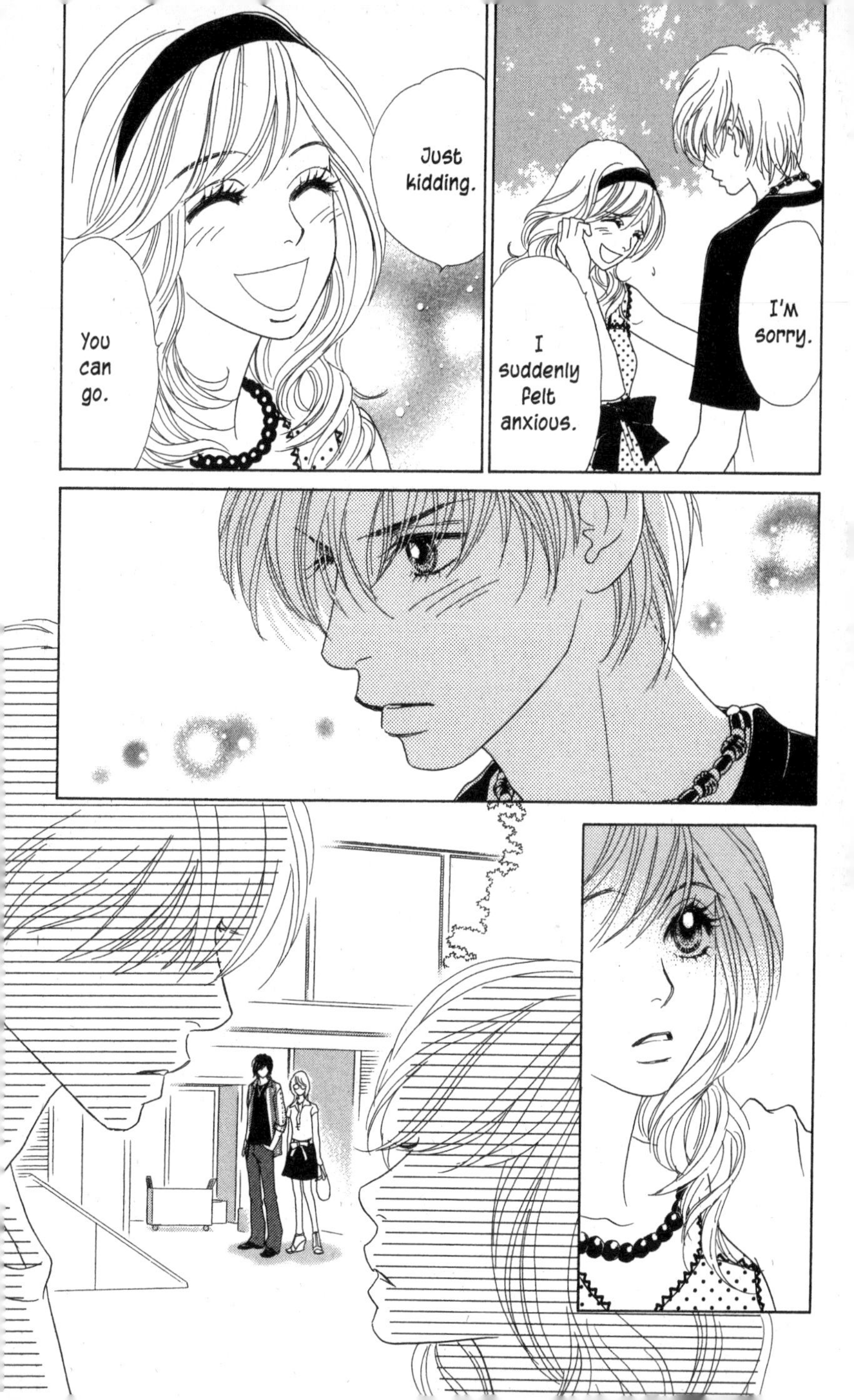
I'M sorry.
I suddenly felt anxious.
Just kidding.
You can go.

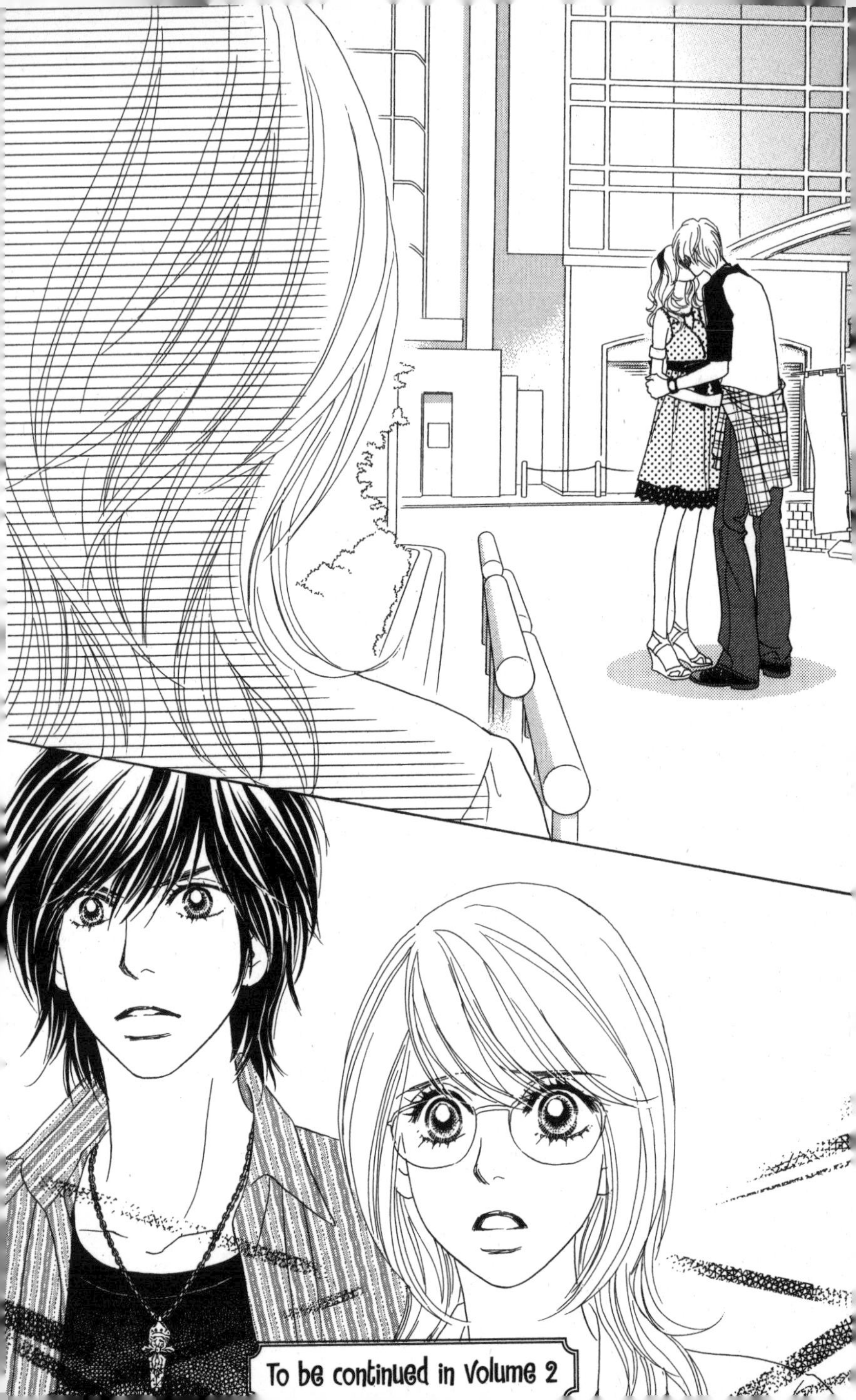
To be continued in Volume 2

Staff

Aiko   Amemori
Tomomi   Kasue
Satsuki   Furukawa
Akiko   Kawashima
Ayumi   Yoshida

Editor
Toshiyuki   Tanaka

November 11, 2006

Miwa   Ueda

SPECIAL THANKS

I would like to take this opportunity to thank the people who were involved in creating *Papillon*.

Kenichi Nakahara-san, Therapist

Widely active in Tokyo and Osaka, Kenichi-san is a therapist specializing in relationship issues such as love, marriage, and infidelity. He appeared on the TV program *TV Champion Bankon Shôshika Kaiketsu?! Special! Dame Dokushin Otoko Motesase Ô Senshuken* on TV Tokyo in February 2006.

Since Kenichi-san and I already knew each other, I jumped at the chance to interview him for this manga. I thank him for explaining the difference between a counselor and a clinical psychologist. ♡ When I saw him, my story and character sketches were vague and I had nothing more than a rough concept for the story: I wanted to do something about a guidance counselor helping to change an ordinary girl. Yet he was able to give me complete psychological profiles of Ageha and Hana based only on my brief descriptions. Afterward, I felt like I understood the characters' backgrounds and feelings much better. It was a fascinating experience.

Even though the manga departs from the particulars of our discussion, hearing his psychological analysis of Ageha and Hana was still beneficial. His interview was interesting, and his analytical abilities were so very sharp that we kept getting sidetracked by him giving me personal advice (laugh) and we lost track of time. ♡ ♡

If you have love problems, or just an interest in therapy, visit Kenichi-san's blog listed below.

http://blog.livedoor.jp/cs_co8823/

Martin-sensei

Well-known as a writer for his top selling e-newsletter *Martin-sensei no Renai Kyôshitsu* ("Martin-sensei's Relationship Class"), Martin-sensei is a popular relationship counselor, with more than 30,000 clients. Martin-sensei's relationship theory is absolutely persuasive. As a regular reader of the free and premium editions of his e-newsletters, I consulted him in my research for this manga.

Judging from his picture, I thought he was really handsome, and I had the vague idea that the picture was an unusually good one after hearing that he picked it out of many from his e-newsletter. However, to my dismay, I discovered that he's just as handsome in person! My conversation with him was so interesting that our three hours went surprisingly fast.

Kyû-chan advising Ageha to "tell the world about her dream" was Martin-sensei's idea. Like Ageha, I was only seeking a way to escape this dilemma of how to resolve her problem, and his advice made perfect sense when I heard it. It's an innovative idea that only Martin-sensei could have come up with! I have the greatest admiration for his positive attitude.

In addition to his e-newsletter, I recommend Martin-sensei's books to anyone interested. They're definitely full of advice you can use. I have every book listed below. ♡

URL to Martin-sensei's website: http://www.martin.ne.jp/

Publication List:

- *Martin-sensei no Renai Kyôshitsu*
- *Himitsu no Renai Rule*
- *Kare wo Ichigeki Hissatsu ♡ Happy H no Susume*
- *Gyakuten no Renai Rule*
- *Otoko no Hitotte, Onna ga Donna Koto Shite Kureru to Ureshiino? Motto Himitsu no Renai Rule*
- *Himitsu no Renai Jissen Manual*
- *Nazeka Moteru Himitsu no Rule*
- *Ganbari ga Mukuwareru Renaijutsu*

...And more.

Thank you to everyone for your advice and support.

About the Creator

Miwa Ueda was born on September 29, in Hyogo, Japan.
Her original series, *Peach Girl*, won the Kodansha Shojo Manga
of the Year Award in 1999. *Papillon* is her latest creation.

Translation Notes

Japanese is a tricky language for most Westerners, and translation is often more art than science. For your edification and reading pleasure, here are notes on some of the places where we could have gone in a different direction with our translation of the work, or where a Japanese cultural reference is used.

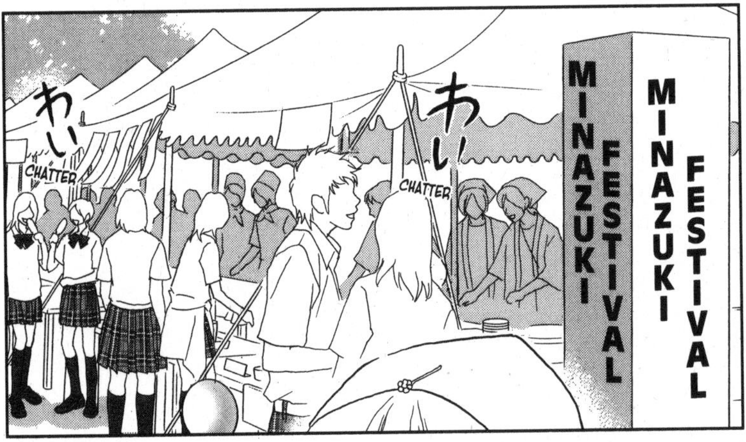
MINAZUKI FESTIVAL
MINAZUKI FESTIVAL
わい
CHATTER
わい
CHATTER

School Festival, page 7

Every high school in Japan holds a School Festival once a year. These events are open to the public and usually offer exhibitions, food booths, and performances.

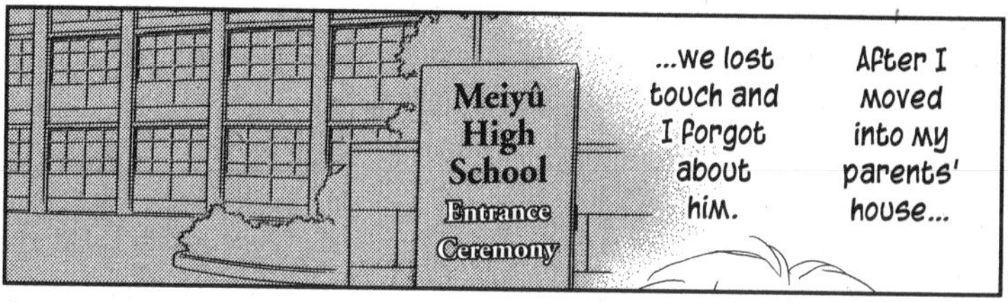
After I moved into my parents' house...
...we lost touch and I forgot about him.
Meiyû High School
Entrance Ceremony

Entrance Ceremony, page 17

The "entrance ceremony" is held in April—the beginning of the Japanese school year—to welcome incoming freshmen.

Kyû-chan, page 19

Ichijiku's nickname comes from a Japanese character in his last name, which can also be read as *kyû*.

Butterfly and flower, page 24

The full Japanese title of this series is *Papillon: Chô to Hana*. Ageha and Hana's names contain the Japanese characters *chô* and *hana*, which mean "butterfly" and "flower" respectively. *Papillon* is a French word for "butterfly," which is why there are numerous references to the chrysalis and the butterfly throughout this story.

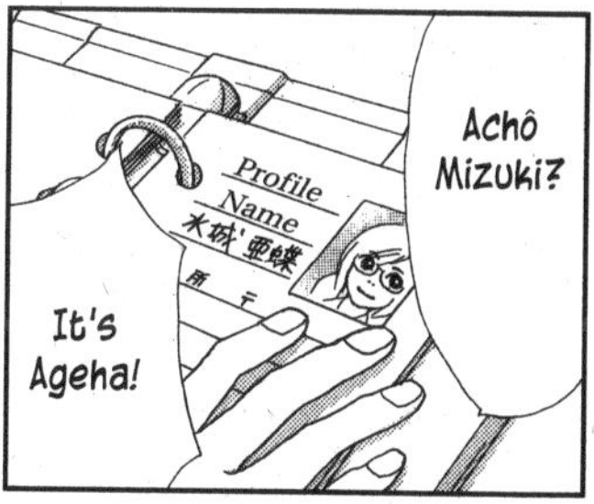
Achô Mizuki?
It's Ageha!
Profile
Name

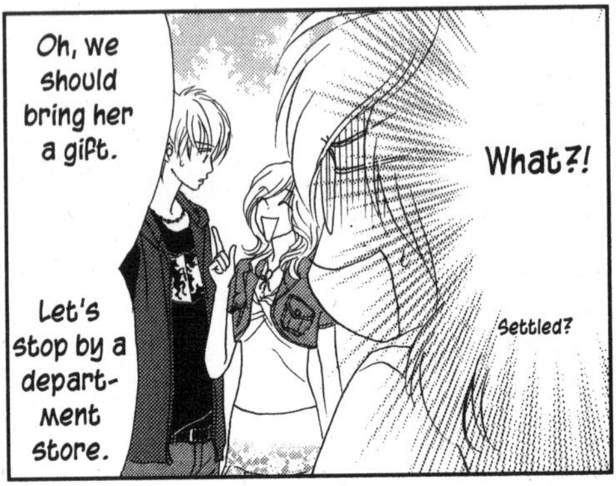
What?!
Settled?
Oh, we should bring her a gift.
Let's stop by a department store.

Department store, page 48

Department stores in Japan have food departments that are generally located on the ground floor.

***Kinako*, page 50**

Kinako is toasted soybean flour that's mixed with sugar and used for coating *mochi*, or glutinous rice cake.

***Warabi mochi*, page 50**

Unlike the typical *mochi* made from glutinous rice, *warabi mochi* is a Japanese confection made from *warabi*, or bracken flour, and dusted with *kinako*.

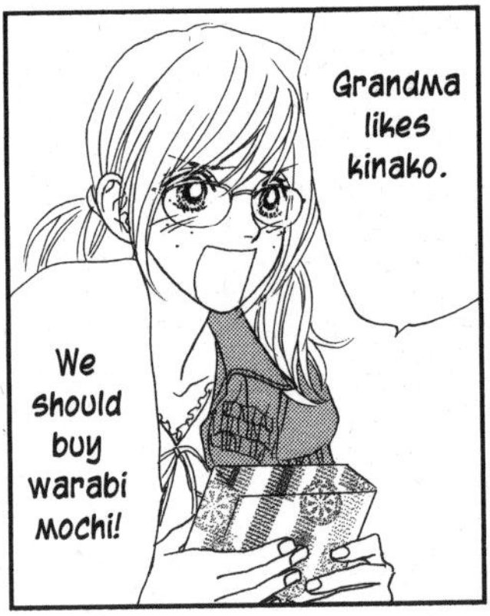
Grandma likes kinako.
We should buy warabi mochi!

Watery Nose, page 54

Hana's last name, Mizuki, contains a Japanese character for "water" and her first name, Hana, can mean "nose," though the word for "nose" is written with a different character. Hana's classmates combined these words to come up with the cruel nickname *Mizuppana*, which literally means "watery nose" or "runny nose."

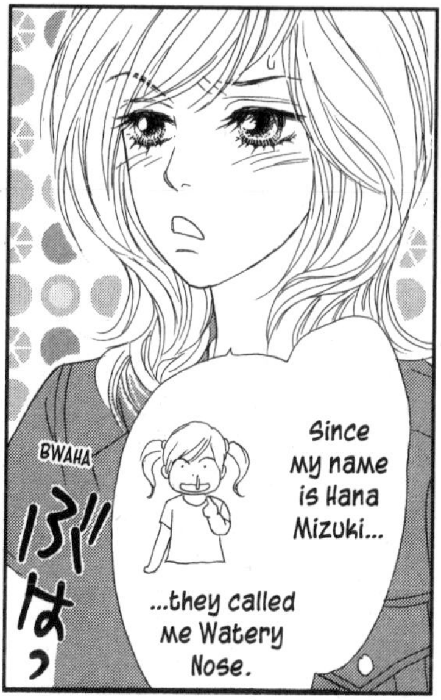
Since my name is Hana Mizuki...
...they called me Watery Nose.
BWAHA
ぶはっ

High school, page 57

Japanese high school consists of a total of three years and covers our grades ten through twelve.

Class journal, page 137

Every day or week, a student is chosen as the "class leader," and is therefore responsible for a number of organzational tasks, such as keeping the class journal.

When I admitted that I like Ryôsei in my class...

...I really found some supporters.

Class Journal

TV Champion Bankon Shôshika Kaiketsu?! Special! Dame Dokushin Otoko Motesase Ô Senshuken, page 167

This is a show whose title is literally translated as *TV Champion: Late Marriages with Fewer Children Issue?! Special! Help the Unpopular Single Men Tournament*. It was a special reality program shown on TV Tokyo, in which three contestants were paired with Japan's most ineligible bachelors and competed in transforming them into major hunks.

Preview of *Papillon*, Volume 2

We're pleased to present you a preview from volume 2. Please check our website (www.delreymanga.com) to see when this volume will be available in English. For now you'll have to make do with Japanese!

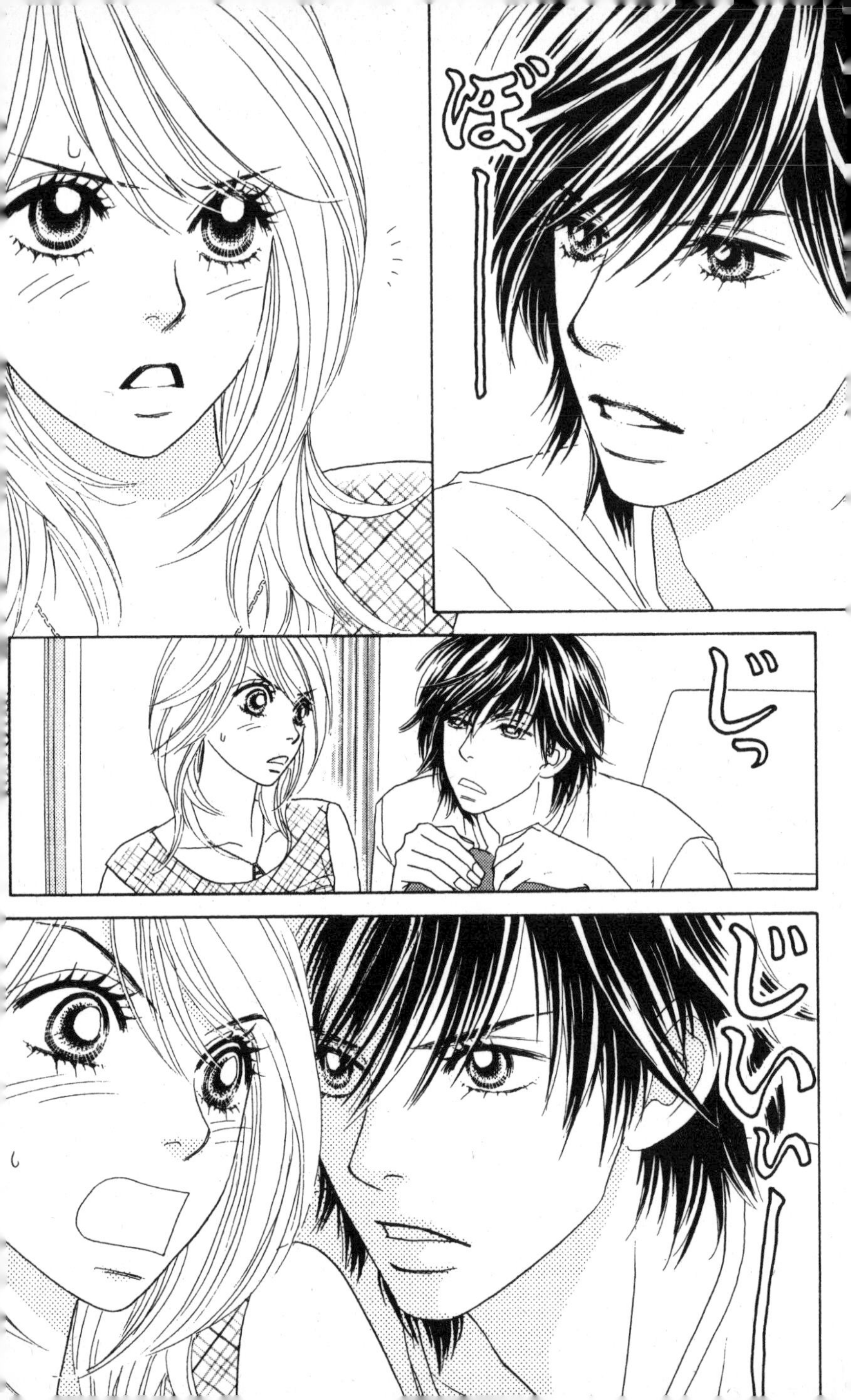
ぼー
じっ
じぃぃー

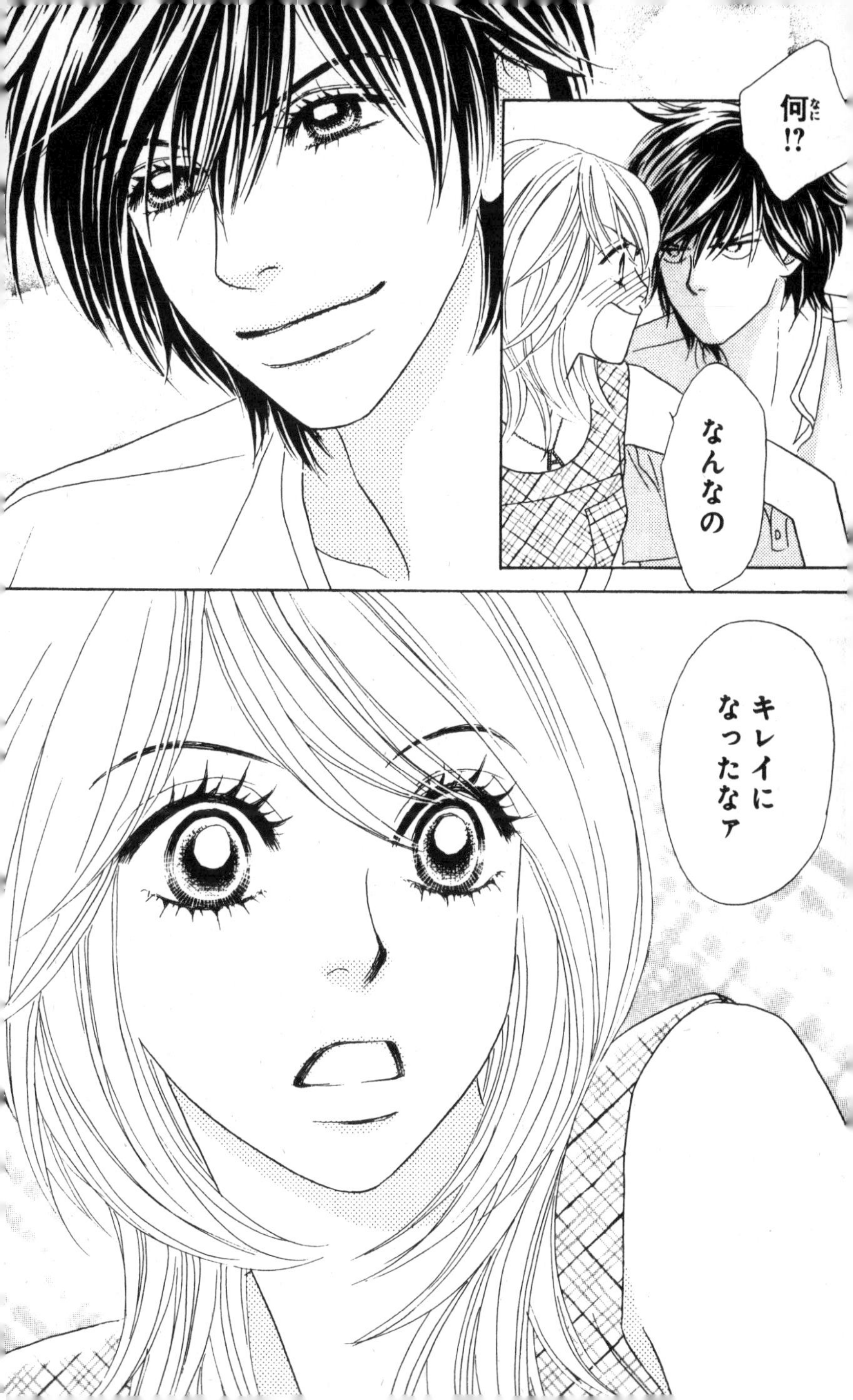
何!?
なんなの
キレイになったなァ

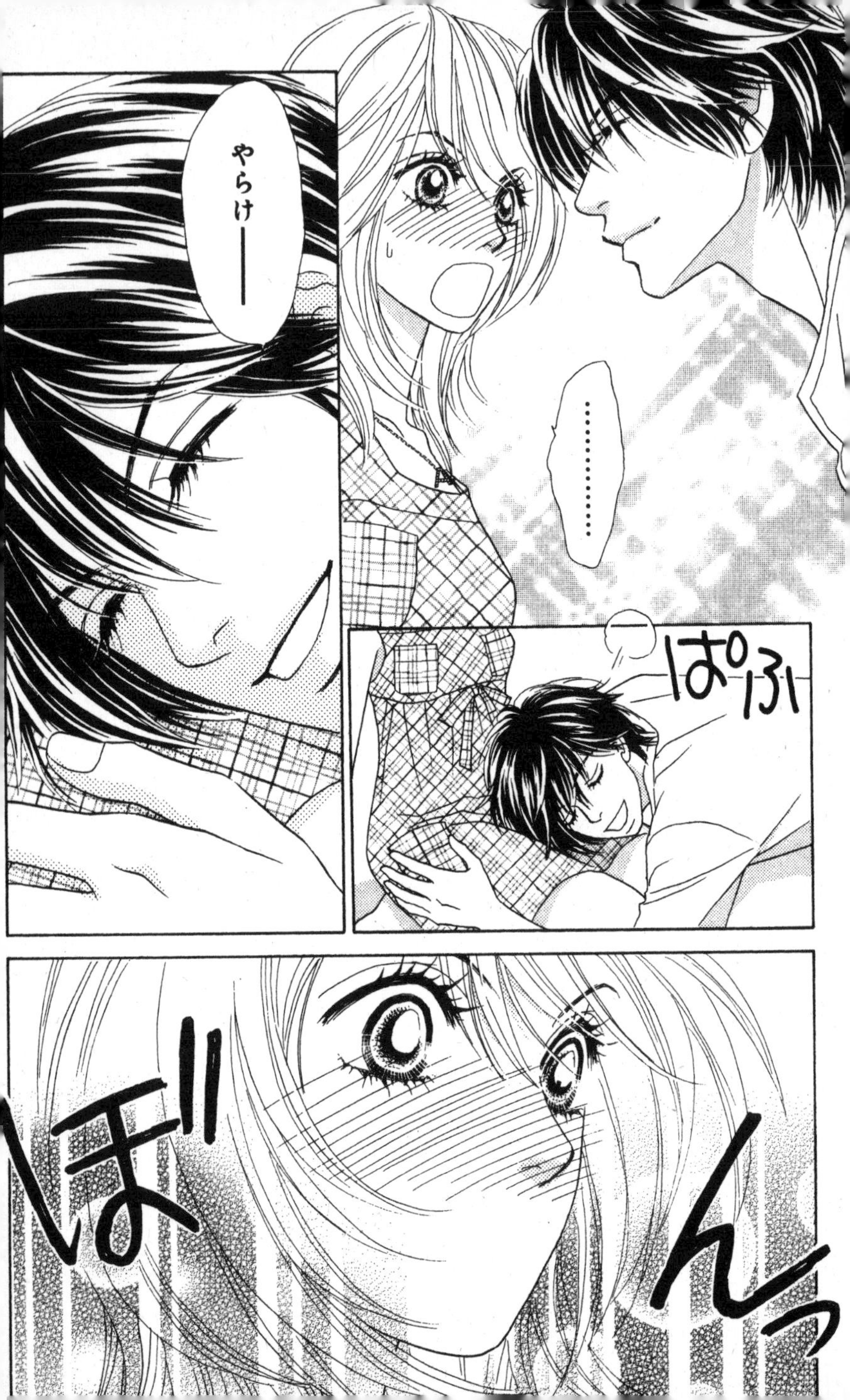
……
ー
ぱふ
やらけ——
ぼんっ

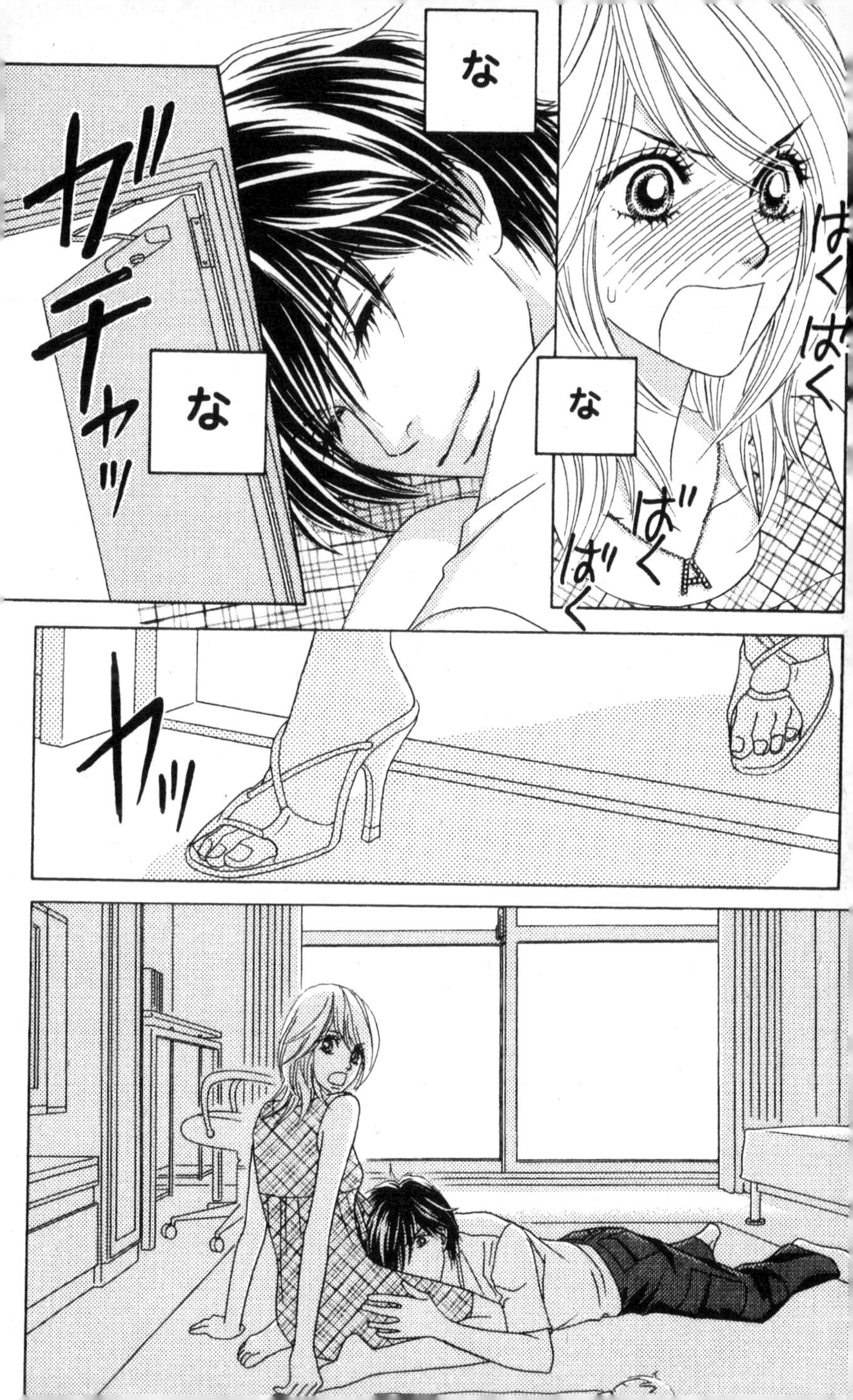

はくはく
な
ばくばく
な
な
ガチャッ
ヤッ

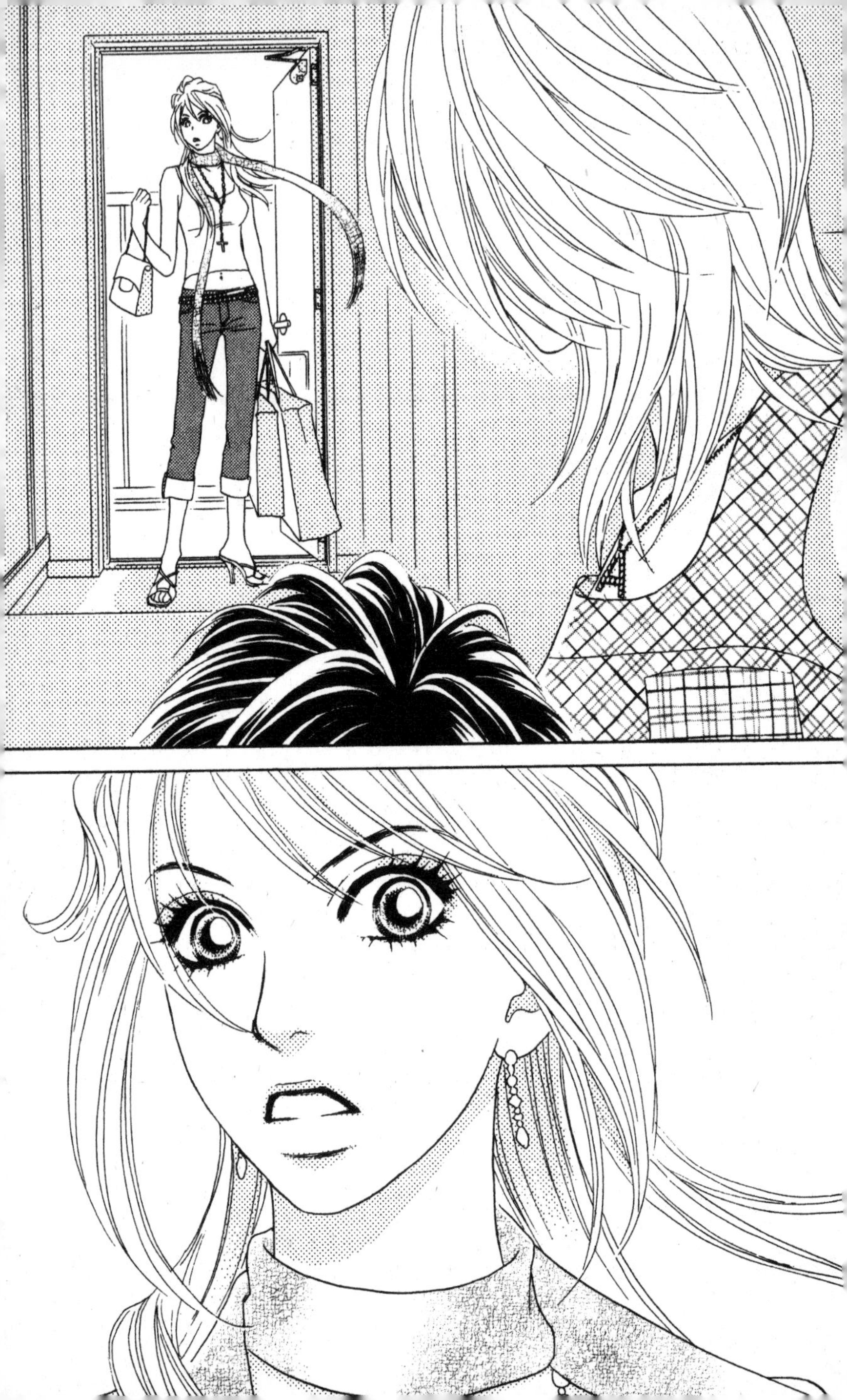

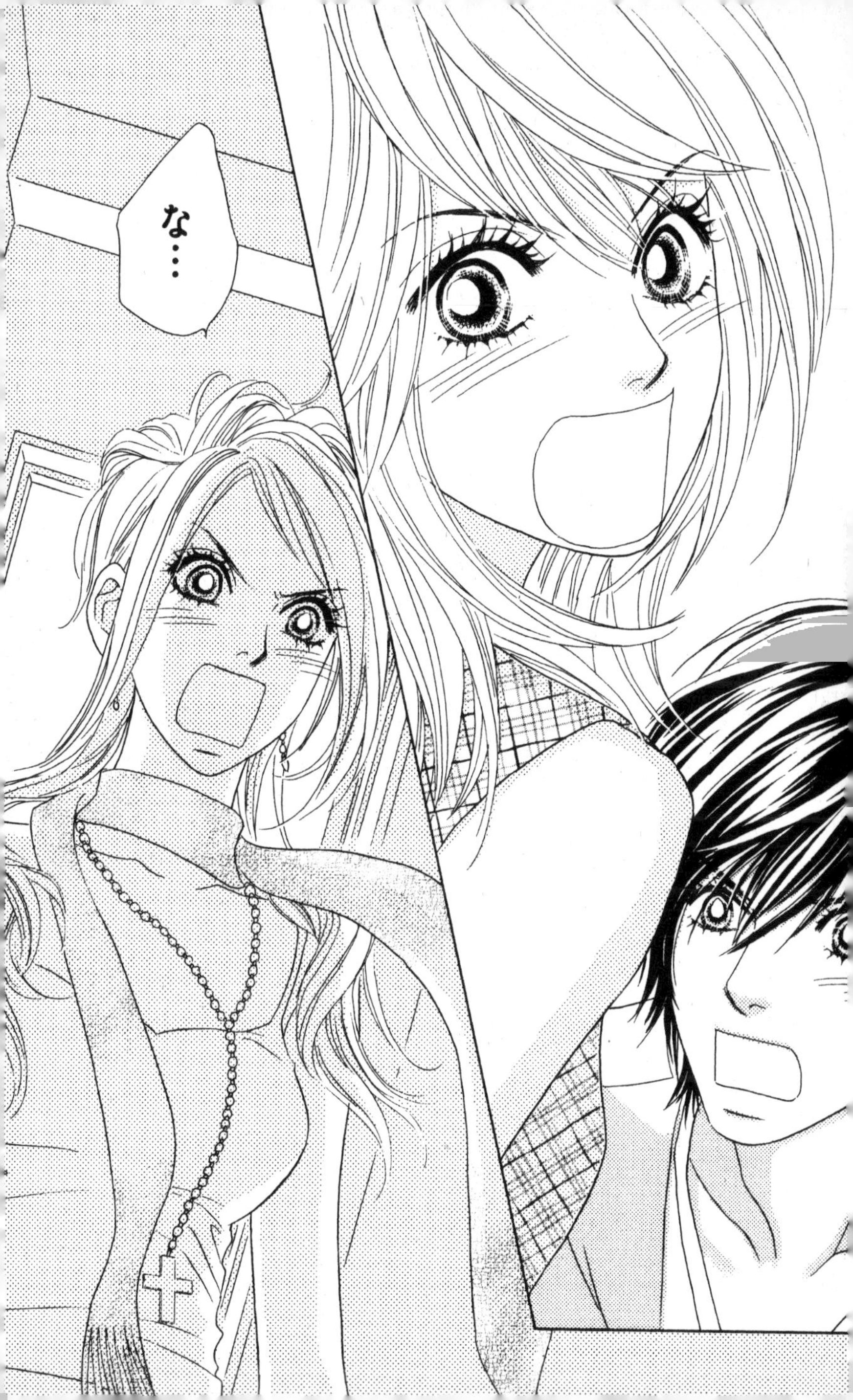
な…

MY HEAVENLY HOCKEY CLUB

BY AI MORINAGA

WHERE THE BOYS ARE!

Hana Suzuki loves only two things in life: eating and sleeping. So when handsome classmate Izumi Oda asks Hana—his major crush—to join the school hockey club, convincing her proves to be a difficult task. True, the Grand Hockey Club is full of boys—and all the boys are super-cute—but, given a choice, Hana prefers a sizzling steak to a hot date. Then Izumi mentions the field trips to fancy resorts. Now Hana can't wait for the first away game, with its promise of delicious food and luxurious linens. Of course there's the getting up early, working hard, and playing well with others. How will Hana survive?

Special extras in each volume! Read them all!

KITCHEN PRINCESS

STORY BY MIYUKI KOBAYASHI
MANGA BY NATSUMI ANDO
CREATOR OF ZODIAC P.I.

HUNGRY HEART

Najika is a great cook and likes to make meals for the people she loves. But something is missing from her life. When she was a child, she met a boy who touched her heart—and now Najika is determined to find him. The only clue she has is a silver spoon that leads her to the prestigious Seika Academy.

Attending Seika will be a challenge. Every kid at the school has a special talent, and the girls in Najika's class think she doesn't deserve to be there. But Sora and Daichi, two popular brothers who barely speak to each other, recognize Najika's cooking for what it is—magical. Could one of the boys be Najika's mysterious prince?

Special extras in each volume! Read them all!

Kamichama Karin Chu

BY KOGE-DONBO

A GODDESS IN LOVE!

Karin is your lovable girl next door—if the girl next door also happens to be a goddess! Karin has a magic ring that gives her the power to do anything she'd like. Though what she'd like most is to live happily ever after with Kazune, the boy of her dreams. Magic brought Kazune to her, but it also has a way of complicating things. It's not easy to be a goddess and a girl in love!

- Sequel series to the fan-favorite *Kamichama Karin*

Kamichama
Karin Chu 1
Koge-Donbo

Special extras in each volume! Read them all!

VISIT WWW.DELREYMANGA.COM TO:
- Read sample pages
- View release date calendars for upcoming volumes
- Sign up for Del Rey's free manga e-newsletter
- Find out the latest about new Del Rey Manga series

RATING T AGES 13+

DEL REY MANGA デルレイ
The Otaku's Choice™

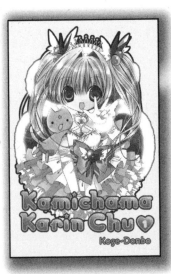

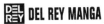

Yozakura Quartet

BY SUZUHITO YASUDA

A DIFFERENT SET OF SUPERTEENS!

Hime is a superheroine. Ao can read minds. Kotoha can conjure up anything with the right word. And Akina . . . well, he's just a regular guy, surrounded by three girls with superpowers! Together, they are the Hizumi Everyday Life Consultation Office, dedicated to protect the town of Sakurashin. And with demon dogs and supernatural threats around every corner, there's plenty to keep them busy!

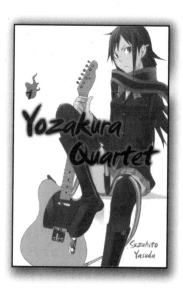

Special extras in each volume! Read them all!